LAUGHTER
IS THE BEST MEDICINE

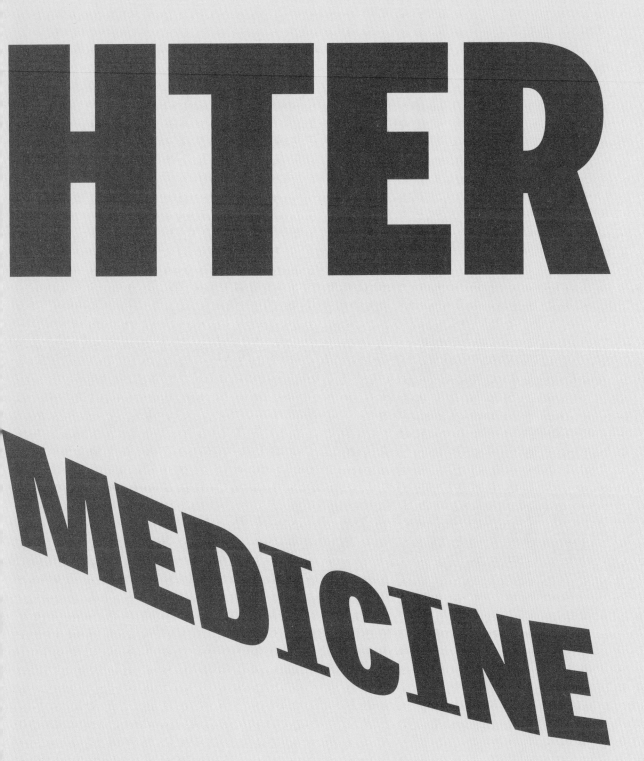

HTER

MEDICINE

Published by The Reader's Digest Association Limited
London • New York • Sydney • Montreal

CONTENTS

Laughter is a great form of communication. Catch the eye of a stranger, and share a smile at something that amuses both of you, and you have an immediate bond.

Laughter's always been around, passed on at parties or in pubs, at work or in playgrounds. What was the first joke? Certainly the Ancient Egyptians knew a version of this one:

A man meets an identical twin and asks, 'Now was it you or your brother who died?'

And here's one that has been repeatedly buffed up since at least the 15th century:

DOCTOR: You're coughing more easily this morning.
PATIENT: I should be. I've been practising all night.

But although jokes are everywhere, it can be hard to find something to laugh at the moment you need it. You haven't got time to riffle through magazines, search your bookshelves or trawl through a DVD for a moment of comic genius. What you need is something that gets all that great stuff together in one volume. How fortunate then that *Laughter is the Best Medicine* now exists to fill that void with an enormous dollop of the best humour – and no duds.

Victoria Wood, Ronnie Barker, P.G. Wodehouse, French and Saunders,

The contents include not just jokes, but literary extracts, snappy quotations, magic moments from favourite TV and radio shows, and hundreds of the world's funniest cartoons. This is a book to dip into at leisure – every page is certain to contain something that will bring a smile to the sourest face. And, though not primarily a reference book, it can be of practical value too, particularly for people facing the second most terrifying experience of life (death being the first) – making a speech in public. There's nothing that relaxes an audience so much or gets it more on the speaker's side than a good joke. So, to help you find the right funny for the right occasion, the jokes, plus all the sketches and cartoons, are arranged in themed sections, as well as catalogued in the funniest index ever made. So, if you're in need of a witticism about 'Love and Sex' – say, for that daunting best man's toast to the bridesmaids – you know exactly where to look.

> Are you married? No, I've always been round-shouldered.

Or if you've got to give of yourself after the Golf Club Dinner, just turn to 'Games and Sports'.

> 'Damn,' said the golfer, as he sliced yet another ball into the rough. 'I'm not playing my usual game today.'
> 'Oh,' asked his caddy, 'and what game is that?'

In fact, whoever you're talking to, don't worry – you'll find something here that you can shoehorn into your speech or presentation.

> How do you kill a circus?
> Go for the juggler.

There's more than enough laughter in these pages for everyone – thousands of magic moments, from classic rib-ticklers such as *The Diary of a Nobody* and *Steptoe and Son* to recent hilarity from *The Office* and *Absolutely Fabulous*. And it's brought to you by over two hundred funny people – the comedy greats such as Tommy Cooper and Spike Milligan, new kids on the block such as Ricky Gervais and Harry Hill, and many often overlooked maestros of mirth. And, if you want to find out more about many of these laughter makers, there's a handy section of potted biographies at the back of the book.

You also owe it yourself to read this book as a responsible human being. Amid all the stringent diets, exercise regimes and other recommendations of health and fitness gurus, how good it is to know that there's one conditioning programme that you can positively enjoy. Scientific research bears witness to the therapeutic effects of laughing. It can help in healing and pain reduction; it gives a cardiovascular and respiratory workout; it can steady blood pressure. When you laugh, your immune system is more active, your digestion improves and stress levels decrease.

Knowing all that, you can now dip in and out of this book not only with genuine glee but also with a level of self-righteousness. **You're not wasting time – you're reading for your health. After all, as the title says, *Laughter is the Best Medicine*.**

SIMON BRETT

Jerry Seinfeld

'Damn,' Rowan Atkinson, Edward Lear, Monty Python, W.C. Fields,

r Cook, Tony Hancock, Steve Coogan,

Bundles of joy

Arriving home one evening, a man finds his pregnant wife in labour, so he phones the hospital. **'My wife is having contractions and they're only two minutes apart**, tell me what I should do!' he says frantically. 'Is this her first child?' asks the doctor. 'No, you fool,' the man shouts, 'this is her husband!'

I always wondered why babies spend so much time sucking their thumbs. Then I tasted baby food.

ROBERT ORBEN

My Dad knew I was going to be a comedian. When I was a baby he said, 'Is this a joke?'

KEN DODD

RUPERT FAWCETT

My, haven't they grown?

Why, a four-year-old child could **understand this report**. Run out and find me a four-year-old child. I can't **make head or tail** out of it.

GROUCHO MARX in the film *DUCK SOUP*

Little Johnny had been a very naughty boy so his father was surprised when his wife suggested they buy him a bicycle.

'Do you think it will improve his behaviour?' the father asked.

'No,' his wife replied grimly. 'But it'll spread it over a wider area.'

'I hope the children aren't bothering you.'
MARTIN HONEYSETT

A little girl was in church with her mother and she **started feeling sick.** Her mother asked her if she had time to get outside, and told her to be sick in the bushes by the church gate.

The little girl rushed out and was back within seconds.

'Surely you **didn't have time to get as far as the bushes?**' asked her mother.

'No,' said the child. 'But right by the church door there was a box saying "For The Sick", so I used that.'

Two aunts were watching their four-year-old niece watching television.
One said to the other, 'What a pity that she isn't very **P - R - E - T - T - Y**.'
The little girl turned round and said, 'It doesn't matter, so long as I'm **C - L - E - V - E - R**.'

PRODIGY: A child who plays the piano when he ought to be asleep in bed.

BEACHCOMBER

A father asked his little daughter what she'd like for Christmas. She said what she wanted more than anything else was a baby brother.
The timing was perfect, and on Christmas Eve her mother came back from hospital with a baby boy.

The following year, the father again asked his daughter what she'd like for Christmas.
'Well,' she replied, 'if it's not too uncomfortable for Mummy, I'd like a pony.'

'Mummy! Mummy! Daddy's batteries have run out!'
MICHAEL HEATH

BOYISH:
**Adjective
applied
to girls.**
BEACHCOMBER

At the age of four
I was left an orphan.
I ask you - what could
I do with an orphan?

Children aren't
happy with
nothing to ignore,
**And that's what
parents were
created for.**
OGDEN NASH from 'ENGLAND EXPECTS'

RUPERT FAWCETT

THE AGES OF MAN
School daze

Two little girls were in the primary school playground. 'I like our new teacher,' says one. 'Yes, so do I. I wonder how old she is.' 'Well, I know how we can find out.' 'How?' 'Look inside her knickers.' 'How will that help?' 'Well, inside mine it says "Five to Six Years".'

Proud of his new lodgings, a student was showing his mother his room. 'It's quite cosy,' she observed, 'but what's all that mess on the walls?' 'Part of the deal,' the son replied. 'A hundred pounds a week with meals thrown in.'

'We'd all like to be strip club proprietors, Milcroft.'
HECTOR BREEZE

'Old Smithers hasn't changed much has he?'
MARTIN HONEYSETT

FATHER: Now listen, son, from now on you must do your own homework. I'm not going to do any more for you – it's not right.
SON: I know, but have a shot at it just the same.

A boy came back from his first day at school. 'So what did you learn?' asked his mother. 'Not enough. They want me to come back tomorrow.'

Working on a homework problem, a young boy asked his father to help him find the lowest common denominator. 'Gosh,' said his father, 'haven't they found that yet? They were looking for it when I was a lad.'

English teacher to pupil who is not paying attention:...

WHO'D BE A TEACHER!

Paul Pennyfeather, sent down from Oxford, is, to his surprise, made a master at Llanabba Castle school in Wales. It's his first lesson and things aren't going well...

The ten boys stopped talking and sat perfectly still, staring at him. He felt himself getting hot and red under their scrutiny.

'I suppose the first thing I ought to do is to get your names clear. What is your name?' he asked, turning to the first boy.

'Tangent, sir.'

'And yours?'

'Tangent, sir,' said the next boy. Paul's heart sank.

'But you can't both be called Tangent.'

'No, sir, *I'm* Tangent. He's just trying to be funny.'

'I like that. *Me* trying to be funny! Please, sir, I'm Tangent, sir really I am.'

'If it comes to that,' said Clutterbuck from the back of the room, 'there is only one Tangent here, and that is me. Anyone else can jolly well go to blazes.'

Paul felt desperate.

'Well, is there anyone who isn't Tangent?'

Four or five voices instantly arose.

'I'm not, sir; I'm not Tangent. I wouldn't be called Tangent, not on the end of a bargepole.'

In a few seconds the room had become divided into two parties: those who were Tangent and those who were not. Blows were already being exchanged, when the door opened and Grimes came in. There was a slight hush.

'I thought you might want this,' he said, handing Paul a walking stick. 'And if you take my advice, you'll set them something to do.'

He went out; and Paul, firmly grasping the walking stick, faced his form.

'Listen,' he said, 'I don't care a damn what any of you are called, but if there's another word from anyone I shall keep you all in this afternoon.'

'You can't keep me in,' said Clutterbuck; 'I'm going for a walk with Captain Grimes.'

'Then I shall very nearly kill you with this stick. Meanwhile you will all write an essay on "Self-indulgence". There will be a prize of half a crown for the longest essay, irrespective of any possible merit.'

From then onwards all was silence until break. Paul, still holding the stick, gazed despondently out of the window. Now and then there rose from below the shrill voices of the servants scolding each other in Welsh. By the time the bell rang Clutterbuck had covered sixteen pages, and was awarded the half-crown.

EVELYN WAUGH *DECLINE AND FALL* (1928)

..... 'Edward, give me two pronouns.' Edward: 'Who, me?'

JIM,

who ran away from his nurse, and was eaten by a lion.

There was a Boy whose name was Jim;
His Friends were very good to him.
They gave him Tea, and Cakes, and Jam,
And slices of delicious Ham,
And Chocolate with pink inside,
And little Tricycles to ride,

And read him Stories through and through,
And even took him to the Zoo –
But there it was the dreadful Fate
Befell him, which I now relate.

You know – at least you *ought* to know,
For I have often told you so –
That Children never are allowed
To leave their Nurses in a Crowd;
Now this was Jim's especial Foible,
He ran away when he was able,
And on this inauspicious day
He slipped his hand and ran away!
He hadn't gone a yard when –

BANG!
With open Jaws, a Lion sprang,
And hungrily began to eat
The Boy: beginning at his feet

Now, just imagine how it feels
When first your toes and then your heels,
And then by gradual degrees,
Your shins and ankles, calves and knees,
Are slowly eaten, bit by bit.

No wonder Jim detested it!
No wonder that he shouted 'Hi!'
The Honest Keeper heard his cry,

Though very fat

he almost ran
To help the little gentleman.
'Ponto!' he ordered as he came
(For Ponto was the Lion's name),
'Ponto!' he cried,

with angry Frown.
'Let go Sir! Down, Sir! Put it down!'

The Lion made a sudden Stop,
He let the Dainty Morsel drop,
And slunk reluctant to his Cage,
Snarling with Disappointed Rage
But when he bent him over Jim,
The Honest Keeper's

Eyes were dim.
The Lion having reached his Head,
The Miserable Boy was Dead!

When Nurse informed his Parents, they
Were more Concerned than I can say: –
His Mother, as She dried her eyes,
Said, 'Well – it gives me no surprise,
He would not do as he was told!'
His Father, who was self-controlled,
Bade all the children round attend
To James' miserable end,
And always keep a-hold of Nurse
For fear of finding something worse.

HILAIRE BELLOC illustrated by BTB
CAUTIONARY TALES FOR CHILDREN (1907)

THE AGES OF MAN

Act your age, not your shoe size

Jogging through the town, a young woman saw a wizened old man smiling at her from his drive. 'You look so happy!' she said to him. 'What's your secret for a long, satisfying life?' 'I smoke three packs of cigarettes a day,' he smiled. 'And I drink a case of whisky every week, eat nothing but fatty foods and never exercise.' 'That's amazing,' the woman marvelled. 'How old are you?' 'Thirty-two,' he answered.

'How old are you?'
'Thirty.'
'Thirty, eh?'
'How about you? How old are you?'
'Well, by your method of counting, I don't think I've been born yet.'

I THINK THIRTY'S A NICE AGE FOR A WOMAN.

Especially if she happens to be forty.

One should never trust a woman who tells one her real age. A woman who would tell one that would tell one anything.

OSCAR WILDE

Alex PEATTIE + TAYLOR

THIS IS ALL VERY SUDDEN, CLIVE.

I'VE PUT IT OFF FOR TOO LONG, BRIDGET.

I'M 28 NOW,...NO LONGER IN THE FIRST FLUSH OF YOUTH... IT'S TIME TO FACE UP TO MY RESPONSIBILITIES... GIVE ME YOUR ANSWER, BRIDGET.

CLIVE, THE ANSWER IS: NO.

CAN YOU REALLY MEAN THAT?

GIVE ME YOUR HAND,... PLEASE...

OH, IF YOU INSIST.

THERE... YOU HAVE MY WORD OF HONOUR ON IT... YOU DO NOT HAVE A BALD PATCH.

BRIDGET, YOU'VE MADE ME THE HAPPIEST MAN IN THE WORLD...

CHARLES PEATTIE AND RUSSELL TAYLOR

RUPERT FAWCETT

THE OFFICE — THIRTY, AND RISING

Brent is talking to Tim.

BRENT: Happy birthday, by the way. Which one is it?

TIM: It's thirty.

BRENT: The big three-o. That's the worst one, innit? Oh, I know what you're thinking. 'My youth's over.' I remember when I was thirty, like you, I was going, 'Ooh, I'm in a rubbish job. My life's rubbish. Nothing good ever happens to me. When will it change?'

But, you know ...

Points at himself as if to say 'Look at me now'.

BRENT: ... things do change ... And it could be worse – there's a neighbour of mine. Kelvin, he's thirty-two, and he still lives with his parents.

TIM: I live with my parents.

BRENT: *(Backtracking)* Cherish 'em. Really. Because you'll miss them when they're not around, both of them. Both of mine are dead, so ...

TIM: Oh ...

BRENT: Well, my dad isn't dead, he's in a home. So as good as ... shot to bits ... he was, erm ... oh God. I was called out the other night, 3 a.m., by the nurses. He was convinced there was a Japanese sniper on the roof of Debenhams.

GARETH: Does that look into his room?

BRENT: The back of the roof looks directly into his room, yeah.

GARETH: Good spot. That's a good spot. That's where I'd be if I had to take someone out ... that lived there.

BRENT: And I had to go up to the room with him and go, 'Look, Dad, there's no Japanese sniper.'

GARETH: So who was it who was up there?

BRENT: No one was there. It was his imagination, he was just ... there was no one there.

GARETH: Lucky. That's lucky. 'Cos if there was a sniper up there you wouldn't see him. He'd be like, 'Oh, oh, no one there.' Ph-tow!

Gareth graphically mimes being shot in the back of the head, brains and blood splattering everywhere.

BRENT: Anyway, he is a vegetable now and that's something we've all got to look forward to. So ... happy birthday. *(Pats Tim on the back.)*

See you later.

RICKY GERVAIS AND STEPHEN MERCHANT

Stuck in the middle

A woman bought a whole range of anti-ageing cosmetics and spent a whole afternoon in the bedroom applying creams and potions to various parts of her body. Then she went downstairs and said to her husband, 'Tell me honestly, darling – how old do I look?'

He replied, 'From your skin – 17; from your hair – 20; from your figure – 22.'

'Ooh, you flatterer,' she gushed.

'Wait a minute,' he said. 'I haven't added them up yet.'

Middle age is when you've met so many people that every new person you meet reminds you of someone else.

OGDEN NASH from 'LET'S NOT CLIMB THE WASHINGTON MONUMENT TONIGHT'

FIRST WOMAN: How do you keep your youth? **SECOND WOMAN:** I lock him in the wardrobe.

'Good, life is passing the Smith-Watsons by as well.'
NICK BAKER

When my wife got to forty, I wanted to change her for two twenties.

Middle age is when, whenever you go on holiday, you pack a sweater.

DENIS NORDEN

THE GOOD OLD DAYS

the ages of man

It is sundowner time at a tropical paradise. Four north-countrymen, in late middle age and tuxedos, sit contemplating the sunset.

A waiter pours some claret for one of them to taste.

JOSHUA: Very passable. Not bad at all.

(The waiter pours the wine for the rest of them, and departs.)

OBADIAH: Can't beat a good glass of Château de Chasselas, eh, Josiah?

JOSIAH: Aye, you're right there, Obadiah.

EZEKIEL: Who'd have thought ... forty years ago ... that we'd be sitting here, drinking Château de Chasselas?

JOSHUA: Aye. In those days we were glad to have the price of a cup of tea.

OBADIAH: Aye, a cup of *cold* tea ...

EZEKIEL: Without milk or sugar ...

JOSIAH: *Or* tea ...

JOSHUA: Aye, and a cracked cup at that.

EZEKIEL: We never had a cup. We used to drink out of a rolled-up newspaper.

OBADIAH: Best we could manage was to chew a piece of damp cloth.

JOSIAH: But y'know ... we were happier in those days, although we were poor.

JOSHUA: *Because* we were poor ... My old dad used to say, 'Money doesn't bring you happiness, son.'

EZEKIEL: He was right. I was happier then and I had *nothing*. We used to live in a tiny old tumbledown house with great holes in the roof.

OBADIAH: A house! You were lucky to have a house. We used to live in one room, twenty-six of us, no furniture, and half the floor was missing. We were all huddled in one corner, for fear of falling.

JOSIAH: You were lucky to have a room. We used to live in the corridor.

JOSHUA: Ooooh, I used to *dream* of living in a corridor. That would have been a palace to us. We lived in an old water tank in the rubbish tip. We were woken up every morning by having a load of rotting fish dumped on us. House, huh!

EZEKIEL: Well, when I said *house* ... it was only a hole in the ground covered by a couple of foot of torn canvas, but it was a house to us.

OBADIAH: We were evicted from our hole in the ground. We had to go and live in the lake.

JOSIAH: Eee! You were lucky to have a lake. There were over 150 of us living in a small shoebox in the middle of the road.

JOSHUA: A *cardboard* box?

JOSIAH: Yes.

JOSHUA: You were lucky. We lived for three months in a rolled-up newspaper in a septic tank. We used to get up at six, clean the newspaper, eat a crust of stale bread, work fourteen hours at the mill, day in, day out, for sixpence a week, come home, and Dad would thrash us to sleep with his belt.

OBADIAH: Luxury! We used to get out of the lake at three, clean it, eat a handful of hot gravel, work twenty hours at t'mill for twopence a month, come home, and Dad would beat us about the head and neck with a broken bottle, *if* we were *lucky*.

(*A pause*)

JOSIAH: Aye, well, we had it *tough*. I had to get out of the shoebox at midnight, lick the road clean, eat a couple of bits of cold gravel, work twenty-three hours a day at the mill for a penny every four years and when we got home Dad would slice us in half with a bread knife.

(*A longer pause*)

EZEKIEL: Right ... I had to get up in the morning at ten o'clock at night, half an hour before I went to bed, eat a lump of poison, work twenty-nine hours a day at t'mill and pay boss to let us work, come home, and each night Dad used to kill us and dance about on our graves, singing.

(*A very long pause*)

JOSHUA: Aye, and you try and tell the young people of today that, and they won't believe you.

JOHN CLEESE, MARTY FELDMAN, GRAHAM CHAPMAN AND TIM BROOKE-TAYLOR,
AT LAST THE 1948 SHOW

THE AGES OF MAN

You're not getting any younger

Retirement at sixty-five is **ridiculous.**
When I was sixty-five I **still had
pimples**.

GEORGE BURNS

I'm sixty-five
and I guess that puts
me in with the geriatrics,
but if there were fifteen
months in every year, I'd
only be forty-eight.

JAMES THURBER

I refuse to admit **that I am
more than fifty-two, even if
that does** make my sons
illegitimate.

NANCY ASTOR

ROBERT THOMPSON

If you resolve to
give up **smoking,
drinking and
loving, you don't
actually live
longer;** it just
seems longer.

CLEMENT FREUD

Just because there's snow on the roof...

KENNELS AND CATTERY

'Perhaps one of these years your Mum might like to come with us.'
MARK LEWIS

A septuagenarian millionaire had just married a 20-year-old woman. 'You crafty old thing,' said his friend. 'How did you manage to get such a lovely young wife?' 'Easy,' replied the millionaire. 'I told her I was 95.'

I'm sixty-one today,
A year beyond the barrier,
And what was once a Magic Flute
Is now a Water Carrier.
ANON

OLD MOTHER HUBBARD WENT TO THE CUPBOARD...

NOW WHAT DID I COME HERE FOR?

GEOFF THOMPSON

'I've forgotten, Martha – tell me again what it was you used to see in me.'
BERNARD COOKSON

.it doesn't mean the boiler has gone out.

An old bag is folding clothes.

I can remember when pants were pants. You wore them for twenty years, then you cut them down for pan scrubs. Or quilts. We used to make lovely quilts out of Celanese bloomers. Every gusset a memory.

Not bras. They won't lie flat. We didn't wear bras till after the war, round here. We stayed in and polished the lino.

I didn't see an Oxo cube till I was twenty-five. That's when I got my glasses. And we weren't having hysterectomies every two minutes either, like the girls these days. If something went wrong down below, you kept your gob shut and turned up the wireless.

We never got woken with a teasmade. We were knocked up every morning by a man with a six-foot pole. It wasn't all fun. We'd no showers. We used to club together and send the dirtiest one to the Slipper Baths. We might have been mucky but we had clean slippers.

And it was all clogs. Clogs on cobbles – you could hardly hear yourself coughing up blood. Clogs – when times were hard we had them for every meal, with condensed milk, if we were lucky.

    And no one had cars. If you wanted to get run over, you'd to catch a bus to the main road. And of course, corner shop was the only one with gas, so you'd to go cap in hand if you wanted to gas yourself.

For years we had to make our own rugs. We used to stitch mice on to pieces of sacking. We weren't always making jokes either. I once passed a remark about parsnips and couldn't sit down for a week.

Oh, but I shall never forget the Coronation. 1953. We all crammed into the one front room and stared at this tiny grey picture. Somebody had cut it out of the paper – nobody got television till the year after.

I think we were more neighbourly. If anyone was ill in bed, the whole street would let themselves in and ransack the parlour.

And we didn't do all this keep-fit. We got our exercise lowering coffins out of upstairs windows. In fact, if people were very heavy we used to ask them to die downstairs.

It wasn't all gloom. My brother went to Spain, which was very unusual in those days. Mind you, that was the Civil War, and he got shot for trying to paddle.

We couldn't afford holidays.
Sometimes us kids would take some dry bread and a bottle of water and sit in the TB clinic, but that was about it.

We had community spirit
round here, right to the end. The day they demolished our street it was like the war all over again – dead bodies, hands sticking out of the rubble. The council should have let us know.

That's me done,
best be off. Got a bit of cellular blanket for my supper, don't want it to spoil. Ta-ra ...

VICTORIA WOOD

Growing old disgracefully

You know you're getting old when the candles cost more than the cake.

BOB HOPE

Life is like a roll of toilet paper – the closer it gets to the end, the faster it goes.

ANON

I'm at an age where my back goes out more than I do.

PHYLLIS DILLER

I don't mind dying. I just don't want to be there when it happens.

WOODY ALLEN

An old man went to a fancy dress party stark naked. He was awarded First Prize for his prune costume. He was furious – he'd gone as the Dead Sea Scrolls.

A medicine man was selling his magical potion to a crowd in an American small town. 'Look at me,' he cried. I'm fit as a fiddle and I'm three hundred years old.' One of the locals asked the medicine man's assistant, 'Is he really three hundred years old?' 'I don't know' said the assistant. 'I've only worked for him for a hundred years.'

'The fact is, my dear fellow – and you may as well admit it – we're not so young as we were forty years ago.'
PONT

POSY SIMMONDS

It's a funny old world **– a man's lucky if he gets** out of it alive.

W.C. FIELDS in the film *YOU'RE TELLING ME!*

First you forget names, then you forget faces. Next you forget to pull your zipper up and finally, you forget to pull it down.

GEORGE BURNS

In an old people's home, an 87-year-old woman walked into the recreation room, holding her clenched fist in the air, and announced, 'Anyone who can guess what I've got in my hand can have sex with me tonight.'
One uninterested old codger called out, 'An elephant.'
The old woman said, 'Near enough.'

THE TWO RONNIES – HOTEL LOUNGERS

A General and an Admiral sitting in a hotel lounge; a tea-time trio is playing. They sit, in uniform, in two easy chairs; they are very old. A pretty waitress in a short skirt delivers tea to the Admiral. The General ogles her legs. She goes.

ADMIRAL (Ronnie Barker): Thank you, Dulcie.

GENERAL (Ronnie Corbett): Nice legs.

ADMIRAL: Yes, very good tone, as well.

GENERAL: What?

ADMIRAL: The piano.

GENERAL: No, the waitress. Nice legs.

ADMIRAL: A trim craft. Fond of women are you?

GENERAL: I used to be.

ADMIRAL: Gone off 'em, have you?

GENERAL: Not at all. Just as keen as ever.

ADMIRAL: It's just opportunity, really, isn't it?

GENERAL: Yes. Lately I never seem to get the chance to show my prowess.

ADMIRAL: How long is it?

GENERAL: What?

ADMIRAL: How long is it? – since you had, since you made, since you were, er … since you did, er … the … er … made love. To a woman, I mean.

GENERAL: I don't see that's any of your business.

ADMIRAL: No, no. I'm sorry.

GENERAL: Since *you* did, I bet a pound.

ADMIRAL: What?

GENERAL: When did *you* last make love?

ADMIRAL: If you must know, it was round about 1945.

GENERAL: 1945? Ha! Well that's a damn long time ago!

ADMIRAL: Not really. *(Looks at watch)* It's only 22.30 now.

RONNIE BARKER

Deathly prose – famous last words

If I could drop dead right now,
I'd be the happiest man alive.
SAM GOLDWYN

Die! That's the last thing I shall do!
LORD PALMERSTON

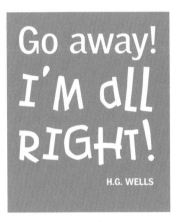

Go away!
I'M all
RIGHT!

H.G. WELLS

Codeine ... bourbon.
TALLULAH BANKHEAD

'Good Lord Fenton, I had no idea you had died.'
MICHAEL HEATH

I should never have switched
from Scotch to Martinis.
HUMPHREY BOGART

How were the receipts today at
Madison Square Garden?
P.T. BARNUM

'He was okay with the sex and drugs. It was
the rock'n'roll that finished him.'
TONY HUSBAND

I've never felt better.
DOUGLAS FAIRBANKS, SR

THE ROYLE FAMILY – CAN'T TAKE IT WITH YOU

Living room. Early evening. The TV is off. We hear Nana sobbing and Barbara gently comforting her.

NANA: Oh Barbara, you know, I'd always thought I'd be the first to go you know.

MAM: Oh Mam, come on now. Come on. Shh, it'll be all right. Shh.

Pause. Crying. Jim walks in and sits in his chair. He looks at the sofa and puts the TV on straight away.

NANA: Weren't that lovely Barbara, them volvulent. What was in 'em? It was a sort of a mushroomy thing, weren't it?

MAM: Mushrooms Mam.

NANA: Was it?

MAM: Yeah.

NANA: I thought it was. Hey, can I have them when I go, Barbara?

Jim crosses his fingers and looks heavenwards.

MAM: Oh, I thought you wanted melon boats like we had at Denise's wedding?

NANA: Well yes I do, I do, but can I have them as well do you think?

MAM: Yeah, course you can.

NANA: Ohhh d'you know I, I just feel like I'm all on me own now without Elsie next door, God rest her soul. I used to let myself in to her place with a key you know and p'haps just wipe her mouth with a cloth or summit. Well it was contact wasn't it?

MAM: Yeah.

Nana's thoughts have turned to Elsie's belongings. Denise and Cheryl have returned from the precinct.

NANA: I wonder what will

happen to Elsie's telly now. Her telly was two inches bigger than mine, you know.

MAM: Oooh.

NANA: And the reds were redder.

JIM: Bloody hell. She hasn't got more bottles of Guinness perishing away has she?

DENISE: Nana, did Elsie have a copy of the *Radio Times*? A recent one?

NANA: I don't know love. I'll er, I'll have a look but er, I don't like to root you know.

MAM: Mam, I really liked that set of pans that Elsie had.

NANA: Ohhh I know. Non stick.

MAM: Oh were they?

NANA: Aye. Shall I bring them back here?

MAM: Oh yeah.

NANA: Oh yeah. Marion will be awash with pans so it will help her when she's sorting out …
(To Cheryl) She's very high up in North West Water you know.

DAD: Did Elsie say you could have all them things, Norma?

NANA: Well she got very confused in the end, but I don't think she'd mind. It's not the place to ask in a hospice is it?

CAROLINE AHERNE AND CRAIG CASH

Epitaph – the last laugh

Under the sod, under the trees
Lies the body of Jonathan Pease
He is not here
But only his pod:
He shelled out his peas
And went to God.

NANTUCKET, MASSACHUSETTS

On a Fat Woman

'All flesh is grass'
The Scriptures they do say,
And grass when dead
Is turned into hay.
Now when the reapers her away do take,
Moi what a wopping haystack she will make.

JERSEY, CHANNEL ISLANDS

Though shot and shell around flew fast
On Balaclava's plain,
Unscathed he passed to fall at last,
Run over by a train.

MARTHAM, NORFOLK

ANYTHING FOR A CHANGE.

KNOXVILLE, TENNESSEE

THE BODY

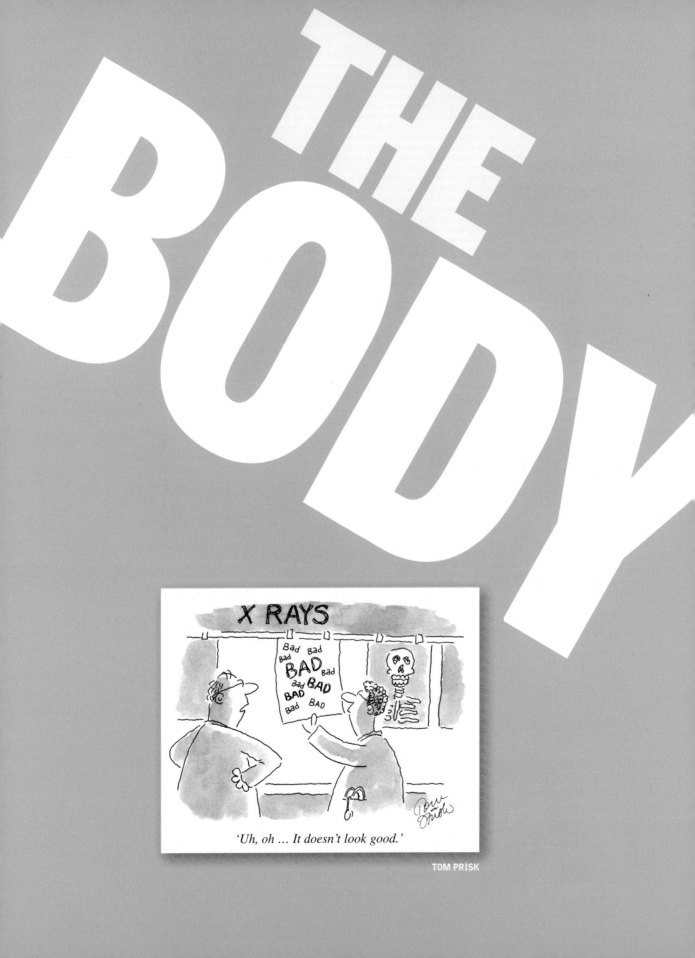

'Uh, oh … It doesn't look good.'

TOM PRISK

Hell's teeth!

So I went to the dentist. He said, 'Say Aaah.' I said 'Why?' He said, 'My dog's died.'

TOMMY COOPER

T. PARKES

I'm always amazed to hear of air-crash victims so badly mutilated that they have to be identified by their dental records. What I can't understand is, if they don't know who you are, how do they know who your dentist is?

PAUL MERTON

'This tooth will be difficult to remove,' **the dentist told his patient. 'I think you should have an anaesthetic even though it will be a little more expensive.' 'OK,' agreed the patient and began feeling in his pocket for his money. 'You needn't pay me yet,' said the dentist. 'I know,' replied the patient. 'I'm just counting my money before you put me under.'**

CHIP SANSOM

Out on a limb

'Looks like housemaid's knee.'
RICHARD JOLLEY

I went to a museum – it had all the heads and arms from the statues that are in all the other museums.

STEVEN WRIGHT

While shopping one day, I fell and broke my arm. A group of people gathered round and started to discuss how best to help me, but, as a trained first-aider I knew that you should secure your arm to your side and I begged someone to go into the nearby shop and buy me a long scarf. The crowd stopped their debate and a man bent down and told me gently, 'Don't worry dear, you can finish your shopping later.'

'Bloomin' foot's gone dead again.'
ROBERT THOMPSON

I'D GIVE MY RIGHT HAND

TEST YOUR STRENGTH! SEPARATE THE TROLLEYS AND WIN A PRIZE.

MARK WOOD

It's been a rough day. I got up this morning, put on a shirt and a button fell off. I picked up my briefcase and the handle came off. I'm afraid to go to the bathroom.
RODNEY DANGERFIELD

A man with two left feet goes to a shoe shop and asks: 'You don't happen to have any flip-flips, do you?'

Fred went to see his doctor. 'What seems to be the trouble?' asked the GP. 'When I touch my leg it hurts,' explained Fred. 'And when I touch my arm and my head it's really painful too.' 'I see,' said the doctor. 'I think you have a broken finger.'

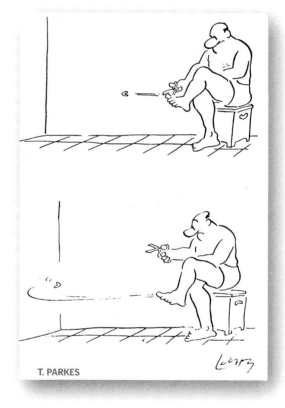

T. PARKES

TO BE AMBIDEXTROUS.

ANON

Fuzzy faces

Elizabeth

Although this memorable Queen was a man, she was constantly addressed by her courtiers by various affectionate female nicknames, such as Auroraborealis, Ruritania, Black Beauty (or Bête Noire), and Brown Bess. She also very graciously walked on Sir Walter Raleigh's overcoat whenever he dropped it in the mud and was, in fact, in every respect a good and romantic queen.

Wave of Beards

One of the most romantic aspects of the Elizabethan age was the wave of beards which suddenly swept across History and settled upon all the great men of the period. The most memorable of these beards was the cause of the outstanding event of the reign, which occurred in the following way.

A wave of beards

The Great Armadillo

The Spaniards complained that Captain F. Drake, the memorable bowlsman, had singed the King of Spain's beard (or Spanish Mane, as it was called) one day when it was in Cadiz Harbour.

Drake replied that he was in his hammock at the time and a thousand miles away. The King of Spain, however, insisted that the beard had been spoilt and sent the Great Spanish Armadillo to ravish the shores of England.

The crisis was boldly faced in England, especially by Big Bess herself, who instantly put on an enormous quantity of clothing and rode to and fro on a white horse at Tilbury – a courageous act which was warmly applauded by the English sailors.

In this striking and romantic manner the English were once more victorious.

W.C. SELLAR AND R.J. YEATMAN

1066 AND ALL THAT (1930)

Spanish Mane

GLEN BAXTER

IT SEEMED TO AMUSE HIM, SO
I COMPLIED WITH HIS ODD REQUEST...

"TAKE A TIP FROM ME, YOUNG FELLER—
ALWAYS CARRY A SPARE GOATEE...."

There was an Old Man with a beard,

who said, "It is just as I feared!—
Two owls and a Hen,

four Larks and a Wren,

Have all built their nest in my beard!'

EDWARD LEAR

A case of hypochondria

THREE INVALIDS IN A BOAT

There were four of us – George, and William Samuel Harris, and myself, and Montmorency. We were sitting in my room, smoking, and talking about how bad we were – bad from a medical point of view I mean, of course.

We were all feeling seedy, and we were getting quite nervous about it. Harris said he felt such extraordinary fits of giddiness come over him at times, that he hardly knew what he was doing; and then George said that *he* had fits of giddiness too, and hardly knew what *he* was doing. With me, it was my liver that was out of order. I knew it was my liver that was out of order, because I had just been reading a patent liver-pill circular, in which were detailed various symptoms by which a man could tell when his liver was out of order. I had them all.

It is a most extraordinary thing, but I never read a patent medicine advertisement without being impelled to the conclusion that I am suffering from the particular disease therein dealt with, in its most virulent form. The diagnosis seems in every case to correspond exactly with all the sensations that I have ever felt.

I remember going to the British Museum one day to read up the treatment for some slight ailment of which I had a touch – hay fever, I fancy it was. I got down the book, and read all I came to read; and then, in an unthinking moment, I idly turned the leaves, and began to indolently study diseases, generally. I forget which was the first distemper I plunged into – some fearful, devastating scourge, I know – and, before I had glanced half down the list of 'premonitory symptoms', it was borne in upon me that I had fairly got it.

I sat for a while frozen with horror; and then in the listlessness of despair, I again turned over the pages. I came to typhoid fever – read the symptoms – discovered that I had typhoid fever, must have had it for months without knowing it – wondered what else I had got; turned up St Vitus's Dance – found, as I expected, that I had that too – began to get interested in my case, and determined to sift it to the bottom, and so started alphabetically – read up ague, and learnt that I was sickening for it, and that the acute stage would commence in about another fortnight. Bright's disease, I was relieved to find, I had only in a modified form, and, so far as that was concerned, I might live for years. Cholera I had, with severe complications; and diphtheria I seemed to have been born with. I plodded conscientiously through the twenty-six letters, and the only malady I could conclude I had not got was housemaid's knee.

I felt rather hurt about this at first; it seemed somehow to be a sort of slight. Why hadn't I got housemaid's knee? Why this invidious reservation? After a while, however, less grasping feelings prevailed. I reflected that I had every other known malady in the pharmacology, and I grew less selfish, and determined to do without housemaid's knee. Gout, in its most malignant stage, it would appear, had seized me without my being aware of it; and zymosis I had evidently been suffering with from boyhood. There were no more diseases after zymosis, so I concluded there was nothing else the matter with me.

I sat and pondered. I thought what an interesting case I must be from a medical point of view, what an acquisition I should be to a class! Students would have no need to walk the hospitals, if they had me. I was a hospital in myself. All they need do would be to walk round me, and, after that, take their diploma.

Then I wondered how long I had to live. I tried to examine myself. I felt my pulse. I could not at first feel any pulse at all. Then, all of a sudden, it seemed to start off. I pulled out my watch and timed it. I made it a hundred and forty-seven to the minute. I tried to feel my heart. I could not feel my heart. It had stopped beating. I have since been induced to come to the opinion that it must have been there all the time, and must have been beating, but I cannot account for it. I patted myself all over my front, from what I call my waist up to my head, and I went a bit round each side, and a little way up the back. But I could not feel or hear anything. I tried to look at my tongue. I stuck it out as far as ever it would go, and I shut one eye, and tried to examine it with the other. I could only see the tip, and the only thing that I could gain from that was to feel more certain than before that I had scarlet fever.

I walked into that reading-room a happy healthy man. I crawled out a decrepit wreck.

I went to my medical man. He is an old chum of mine, and feels my pulse, and looks at my tongue, and talks about the weather, all for nothing, when I fancy I'm ill; so I thought I would do him a good turn by going to him now. 'What a doctor wants', I said, 'is practice. He shall have me. He will get more practice out of me than out of seventeen hundred of your ordinary, commonplace patients, with only one or two diseases each.' So I went straight up and saw him, and he said:

'Well, what's the matter with you?'

I said: 'I will not take up your time, dear boy, with telling you what is the matter with me. Life is brief, and you might pass away before I had finished. But I will tell you what is *not* the matter with me. I have not got housemaid's knee. Why I have not got housemaid's knee, I cannot tell you; but the fact remains that I have not got it. Everything else, however, I *have* got.'

And I told him how I came to discover it all.

Then he opened me and looked down me, and clutched hold of my wrist, and then he hit me over the chest when I wasn't expecting it – a cowardly thing to do, I call it – and immediately afterwards butted me with the side of his head. After that, he sat down and wrote out a prescription, and folded it up and gave it me, and I put it in my pocket and went out.

I did not open it. I took it to the nearest chemist's, and handed it in. The man read it, and then handed it back.

He said he didn't keep it.

I said: 'You are a chemist?'

He said: 'I am a chemist. If I was a co-operative stores and family hotel combined, I might be able to oblige you. Being only a chemist hampers me.'

I read the prescription. It ran:

1 lb beefsteak, with
1 pt bitter beer
every 6 hours.
1 ten-mile walk every morning.
1 bed at 11 sharp every night.

And don't stuff up your head with things you don't understand.

I followed the directions, with the happy result – speaking for myself – that my life was preserved, and is still going on.

JEROME K. JEROME *THREE MEN IN A BOAT* (1889)

DOCTOR: … Now this won't hurt. You'll just feel a slight prick on the end of your thumb.

(Tony winces in readiness, eyes screwed shut. The doctor jabs the needle in.)

TONY: *(Gets up as doctor smears the drop of blood from the needle on to a slide.)* Well, I'll bid you good day, thank you very much, whenever you want any more, don't hesitate to get in touch with me.

DOCTOR: Where are you going?

TONY: To have my tea and biscuits.

DOCTOR: I thought you came here to give some of your blood!

TONY: You've just had it.

DOCTOR: This is just a smear.

TONY: It may be just a smear to you, mate, but it's life and death to some poor wretch.

DOCTOR: No, no, no. I've just taken a small sample to test.

TONY: A sample? How much do you want then?

DOCTOR: Well, a pint, of course.

TONY: A pint? Have you gone raving mad? Oh, you must be joking.

DOCTOR: A pint is a perfectly normal quantity to take.

TONY: You don't seriously expect me to believe that? I came in here in all good faith to help my country. I don't mind giving a reasonable amount, but a pint – why, that's very nearly an armful. I don't mind that much *(Holds out his finger)*. But not up to here, mate, I'm sorry *(Indicates just below his shoulder)*. I'm not walking around with an empty arm for anybody. I mean, a joke's a joke.

DOCTOR: Mr Hancock, obviously you don't know very much about the workings of the human body. You won't have an empty arm, or an empty anything. The blood is circulating all the time. A normal healthy individual can give a pint of blood without any ill effects whatsoever. You do have eight pints of blood, you know.

TONY: Look, chum, everybody to his own trade, I'll grant you, but if I've got eight pints, obviously I need eight pints, and not seven, as I will have by the time you've finished with me. No, I'm sorry, I've

been misinformed, I've made a mistake. I'll do something else, I'll be a traffic warden …

DOCTOR: Well, of course, I can't force you to donate your blood, but it's a great shame – you're AB Negative.

TONY: Is that bad?

DOCTOR: No, no, you're Rhesus-positive.

TONY: Rhesus? They're monkeys, aren't they? How dare you! What are you implying? I didn't come here to be insulted by a legalised vampire.

DOCTOR: Mr Hancock, that is your blood group. AB Negative. It is one of the rarest blood groups there is.

TONY: *(Pleased)* Really?

DOCTOR: Yes, it is. Very rare indeed.

TONY: Yes, well, of course, this does throw a different complexion on the matter. I mean, if I am one of the few sources, one doesn't like to hog it all, so to speak. I'm not un-Christian. Very rare, eh?

DOCTOR: I assure you there will be no ill effects, you'll make up the deficiency in no time at all.

TONY: Oh well, in that case, I'll do it. I mean, we AB Negatives must stick together. A minority group like us, we could be persecuted.

DOCTOR: Thank you very much, Mr Hancock, I'm most grateful. If you would go over to the bed and lie down, it won't take very long. Afterwards you rest for half an hour and then you're free to go.

(Tony lies down on the bed. The nurse wheels the blood-taking equipment apparatus over. Tony watches apprehensively.)

DOCTOR: Roll up your sleeve.

(Tony does so. The doctor starts preparing the apparatus. He dabs Tony's arm with cotton wool.)

TONY: As a matter of interest, what group are you?

DOCTOR: Group A.

TONY: *(Disparagingly)* Huh.

DOCTOR: Now this won't hurt … relax …

(Tony tenses himself, relaxes at the command, then winces as the needle goes in, his face screwed up. He has a look down at his arm and then turns his head away, feeling weak. He faints.)

RAY GALTON AND ALAN SIMPSON, *HANCOCK'S HALF HOUR*

Piling on the agony

POEM ABOUT LOSING MY GLASSES

the place is unfamiliar
my face is bare
I've mislaid my glasses
I've looked in my glasses case
but they're not there
and I need my glasses
to find my glasses
but I'll be alright
I've got a spare pair
Somewhere

JOHN HEGLEY

Janet went to a chemist to buy some Viagra tablets. 'Tell your husband to swallow them quickly,' advised the pharmacist, 'or he'll get a stiff neck.'

In a chemist's shop a woman asked the chemist if he had anything for hiccups. He immediately slapped her face. 'I bet that's cured your hiccups,' he said. 'No,' replied the woman. 'My sister outside in the car has them.'

As his sight was failing, a Czech man decided to go and have his eyes tested. The optician showed him a wall chart that displayed the letters **C V K P N W X S C Z Y**, and asked the man if he could read it. 'Can I read it?' the man replied. 'I know him.'

ADRIAN RAESIDE

THE BODY
Nurse!

ROUND THE HORNE — NEED A SECOND OPINION?

KENNETH (HORNE): Now, many of you have written in with medical problems, in particular 'Lefty' of Potters Bar, and all I can say to him is, don't worry. It's quite common for one to be longer than the other. I suggest you consult an earlobe specialist. However, in view of these letters, we've persuaded Nurse Florence MacGanderpoke to come along and give us the benefit of her advice.

BETTY (MARSDEN): *(Scots)* Thank you. First, I'd like to talk to you about old wives' tales. These can now be successfully operated on and any old wife who has one shouldn't worry too much. One listener has written to say that his stomach hangs out over his bathing trunks. Well, if I were him I would diet. Preferably the same colour as his trunks.

Some of you have asked me how to remove unsightly moles from the lower limbs. I myself find that a sharp blow with a rolled-up newspaper soon has them scurrying for their burrows. And finally, a piece of advice on how to avoid Macwhirter's disease. Keep away from Macwhirter.

KENNETH: Thank you, nurse. Next week she'll be giving you advice on your moulting toupee, and if you accept the advice, be it on your own head.

BARRY TOOK AND MARTY FELDMAN

Get your head straight

JORODO

A couple of friends meet in the street and ask each other how they are. **'I've been feeling a little strange lately,'** said one. 'In fact I thought I was a German shepherd for a while.' 'But you're all right now?' asked the other. 'Oh, I'm fine,' said the first, 'feel my nose.'

A psychiatrist received a postcard from one of his patients who had gone away on holiday. 'Having a lovely time,' it read. 'Why?'

A psychiatrist congratulated his patient on the progress he had made. 'You call this progress?' **shrieked the patient. 'Six months ago I was Napoleon and now I'm nobody.'**

MIKE BALDWIN

Doctor, doctor

'I'm suffering from terrible constipation,' said the patient to his doctor. 'What have you been eating?' asked the GP. 'Snooker balls,' replied the patient. 'I had two reds for breakfast, three blues for lunch and ten browns, a pink and a black for dinner.' 'I think I know what the problem is,' replied the doctor. 'You're not eating enough greens.'

My doctor is wonderful. Once, in 1955, when I couldn't afford an operation, he touched up the X-rays.

JOEY BISHOP

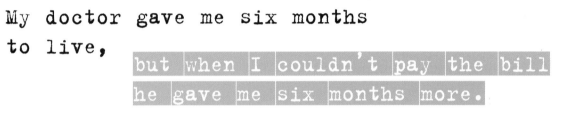

My doctor gave me six months to live, but when I couldn't pay the bill he gave me six months more.

WALTER MATTHAU

RICHARD JOLLEY

PATIENT: Have you got anything to keep my hair in? DOCTOR: How about a shoebox?

'The ringing in your ears – I think I can help.'
LEO CULLUM

**A man went to the doctor's with a carrot in his right ear, a cucumber in his left ear, and a banana stuck up his nose. 'What do you think's wrong with me?' he asked.
'Simple,' replied the doctor. 'You're not eating properly.'**

A man with a green shoot sprouting from his face went to the doctor. Puzzled, the physician gave him some medicine, but the next week the patient returned with a fully grown tree coming out of his head. The GP, completely baffled, increased the strength of the prescription and sent him away. When the man called back the following week his whole head was covered by a field, trees, a lake and people picnicking. 'Now I know what the problem is,' said the doctor. 'You've got a beauty spot.'

I went to my doctor and asked for something for persistent wind. He gave me a kite.

LES DAWSON

the body

MORECAMBE AND WISE – OH DOCTOR!

ERNIE: Ah, come in! You're coughing more easily this morning.

ERIC: I should be – I've been practising all night.

ERNIE: But aren't you taking the medicine I gave you?

ERIC: No. I tasted it and I decided to keep coughing.

ERNIE: But haven't you followed my advice for getting rid of a cold – to drink frozen orange juice after a hot bath?

ERIC: Yes, but I haven't finished drinking the hot bath yet.

ERNIE: Well, I've got a cold too, so cheer up, I've got the same complaint as you.

ERIC: True, but you are lucky in one respect.

ERNIE: What's that?

ERIC: You don't have the same doctor.

ERNIE: Well, I can't tell what's wrong with you. I think it's drink.

ERIC: OK – I'll come back when you're sober.

ERNIE: Maybe you'd better give me a specimen.

ERIC: OK.

ERNIE: If you could just fill that bottle over there.

ERIC: From here?

ERNIE: Can you remember if your eyes have been checked before?

ERIC: No, they've always been blue.

ERNIE: Why do you wear those glasses?

ERIC: I've got spots before my eyes.

ERNIE: And do the glasses help?

ERIC: Yes – the spots are much bigger now.

FRED METCALF

Doctor, doctor, I keep thinking I'm a pair of curtains.
Well, pull yourself together.

Doctor, doctor, I've got a cricket ball in my ear.
How's that?
Oh, don't *you* start.

Doctor, doctor, I keep thinking I'm a bridge.

What's come over you?

Three lorries, two cars and a motorbike.

'You've got high-ho-high-ho-high-ho blood pressure.'
N. BENNETT

Doctor, doctor, I can't pronounce my Fs, Ts or Hs.
Well, you can't say fairer than that.

Doctor, doctor, I keep thinking I'm a pack of cards.
I'll deal with you later.

Doctor, doctor, I think I'm shrinking.

Well, you'll just have to be a little patient.

It's an emergency

One morning a man is woken by a knock at the door. He gets up and goes downstairs to open the door and is met by a six-foot-six-inch spider which immediately head-butts him, runs inside, tramples all over the man, kicks him in the back, boots his ribs and stamps all over him. Next thing the householder remembers is waking up in hospital. Turning to the doctor he says, 'I feel terrible. What's wrong with me?' The doctor tells him, 'I'm afraid there's a vicious bug going about.'

'When will he be able to sit up and take criticism?'

CHON DAY

A FAMILY MAN
A family man from Siberia
As a father was very inferior,
But one operation
Revised the situation
And now he's a Mother Superior.

SPIKE MILLIGAN

A minor operation—one performed on someone else.

ANON

I had an operation, and the surgeon left a sponge in me.
Is it painful?
No, but, gosh, I get thirsty.

'Your husband's cholesterol level is just fine. It's his chlorophyll level that's got all the doctors worried.'

TIM HAGGERTY

Uplifting stories

While on the operating table following a heart attack, a middle-aged woman had a near-death experience. She asked God if this was the end. He told her she still had 29 years to live. After recovering, the woman decided to make the most of the long life that lay ahead and had extensive facial surgery, liposuction, a tummy tuck and breast implants. The time came to leave hospital. She was waiting outside for a taxi when lightning struck and killed her outright. On meeting God for the second time, she angrily demanded, 'Why did you say I had another 29 years to live? What happened?' 'Sorry,' God replied, 'I didn't recognise you.'

She got
her good looks
from her father –
he's a plastic
surgeon.

GROUCHO MARX

Do you know how you can tell whether a woman's had her face lifted?
Every time she crosses her legs, her mouth snaps open.

JOAN RIVERS

THE WONDERBRA

I bought myself a Wonderbra
For fourteen ninety-nine,
It looked so good on the model girl's chest,
And I hoped it would on mine,
I took it from the packaging
And when I tried it on,
The Wonderbra restored to me
All I believed had gone.

*Singing ... let's all salute the Wonderbra,
The Wonderbra, the Wonderbra,
Let's all salute the Wonderbra,
For fourteen ninety-nine.*

It gave me such a figure,
I can't believe it's mine,
I showed it to my husband
And it made his eyeballs shine,
And when I served the breakfast,
The kids cried out, 'Hooray!
Here comes our darling mother,
with her bosom on a tray!'

I didn't really need one,
My present bra, it's true,
Had only been in constant use
Since nineteen eighty-two,
But the silhouette I dreamed about,
Is mine, is mine at last,
And builders on the scaffolding,
Drop off as I walk past.

*Singing ... let's all salute the Wonderbra,
The Wonderbra, the Wonderbra,
Let's all salute the Wonderbra
For fourteen ninety-nine!*

PAM AYRES

More uplift ...

I don't know what all this fuss is about weight. My wife lost two stone swimming last year. I don't know how. I tied them round her neck tight enough.

LES DAWSON

I have everything now that I had twenty years ago – except now it's all lower.

GYPSY ROSE LEE

EDWARD MCLACHLAN

Albert comes running out into the hall and picks up letters, looks at them.

ALBERT: The West London Chest Clinic. Oh my gawd. *(He goes into the room.)* Harold. The West London Chest Clinic.

HAROLD: Oh, that's probably the results of our X-rays.
Albert is frightened. He hands them to Harold as though they are diseased.

HAROLD: A.E.L. Steptoe. That's you, *(He hands one of the letters to Albert. Albert recoils.)*

ALBERT: I don't want it.

HAROLD: Open it.
(Albert takes the letter. He is frightened to open it.)

ALBERT: Open yours first.

HAROLD: Oh Gawd! All right then.
(He opens his letter and reads it.)
'Dear Sir, we are happy to inform you that your recent chest X-ray is completely clear and shows no abnormalities.' There you are. Nothing to worry about. Go on, open it.

ALBERT: *(Opens his letter. Reads it.)* Oh no. Oh my Gawd. *(He clutches Harold and vase disintegrates.)*

HAROLD: What?

ALBERT: *(Reading letter)* 'Dear sir, your recent chest x-ray was unsatisfactory due to a technical fault. An appointment has been made for you at the West London Hospital for a further X-ray.' *(Albert sinks into chair.)* I've got it. I'm dangerously ill. It's all your fault. You and your bleeding X-rays. I was all right till then.

HAROLD: Don't be ridiculous. X-rays can't give you T.B. Anyway, it doesn't say you've got it. It just says unsatisfactory due to a technical fault.

ALBERT: They always say that. So as not to frighten you. I'm dying.
(He suddenly looks very ill. He starts coughing lightly.) I'm not long for this world. I can feel it. I can feel the life draining out of me.

HAROLD: Now look Dad, you mustn't panic. You've got to be rational. Let's assume the worst. You've got T.B. *(Albert groans.)*

HAROLD: There's nothing to worry about. It's not like it used to be. Not like it was in your days. With all these new drugs you'll be cured in no time at all.

ALBERT: No I won't. I've had it. I probably won't last the week out.

HAROLD: Now you mustn't talk like that, Dad. A couple of months in a sanatorium and you'll be as right as rain.

CONTINUED OVERLEAF

ALBERT: Don't let them take me away, Harold. I want to die in my own bed. Promise me you won't let them take me away.

HAROLD: Oh shut up. Nobody's going to take you away. I've never been that lucky. When have you got go go to the hospital? *(Albert looks at his letter, which is still clasped in his hand.)*

ALBERT: It says tomorrow after ... wait a minute.

HAROLD: What?

ALBERT: This ain't mine. It's yours.

HAROLD: Pardon?

ALBERT: H.A.K. Steptoe. That's you. *(He grins in delight.)* They've put them in the wrong envelopes.

HAROLD: Don't be ridiculous. They wouldn't make a mistake like that.
(He looks at his letter.) A.E.L. Steptoe. Oh my Gawd. *(Sinks into chair, shattered.)*

Albert leaps up a changed man.

ALBERT: I'm all right. There's nothing wrong with me.

Albert changes letters with Harold. Harold reads his, frightened out of his life.

ALBERT: I told you. Fit as a fiddle. Where's my fags? *(Looks at Harold.)* What's the matter with you?

HAROLD: T.B. I've got T.B. Consumption. *(He clasps his chest.)*

ALBERT: It don't say you've got it. It just says the X-ray was unsatisfactory due to a technical fault.

HAROLD: They always say that. They never tell you the truth. I'm ill. I've had it.

ALBERT: You haven't had it. Young lad like you.

HAROLD: *(Coughs delicately. Holds his chest.)* I've got a cough. Dad, I've got a cough.

ALBERT: Call that a cough? *(He coughs violently.)* … **That's** a cough.

HAROLD: *(Breathes in and out through his mouth.)* Hear that? Listen. *(He breathes in and out.)* My lungs must be like lace curtains.
… Dad, I can't breathe properly.
I'm out of breath. Now I come to think of it, I haven't been feeling well lately. I've been so tired all the time.

ALBERT: That's too much of the other.

HAROLD: No it's not. It's your fault. You never looked after me when I was a kid. I never had any decent food. Rotten damp house. What chance did I have? It's lowered my resistance. It's your fault.

ALBERT: You had the best food money could buy.

HAROLD: What money? You never had any money. You spent it in the pub … with me standing out in the rain all evening. With a bottle of lemonade and an arrowroot biscuit. That's why I've got it.

ALBERT: You haven't got it.

HAROLD: Yes I have. I've lost a lot of weight lately.

ALBERT: Of course you have, you've been on a diet. Trying to get into them velvet trousers you bought.

HAROLD: No, it's more than that. It's been falling off me. I'm wasting away. That's a symptom. And lack of energy.

ALBERT: You've had that ever since you were born.

(Harold grabs hold of Albert.)

HAROLD: Dad, Dad, I'm frightened.

ALBERT: Don't you come too close to me. It's catching.

HAROLD: Dad … I'm your son. Your own flesh and blood.

ALBERT: There's no point in us both having it. It's going to be hard enough running the business on my own, while you're away. I don't know how I'm going to manage. I'll be here on my own. What's going to happen to me, that's what I want to know. I'll have to go on the assistance. As if I haven't got enough to put up with. What a terrible thing to happen to me at my time of life.

HAROLD: What about me, it's me that's ill.

ALBERT: That's your fault. You should have looked after yourself. I've done nothing, but it's me that's going to be left all alone. Well, I hope you're satisfied.

HAROLD: I wouldn't have believed it. There's me, gasping my life away and all you can think of is yourself. I don't think there's another living soul in this whole world who could be as callous as you. I'll never forget this. I'll take the memory of this day to my dying grave. *(He gets up slowly.)*

ALBERT: Where are you going?

HAROLD: I'm going to my grave – i.e. my bed.

ALBERT: You've only just got up.

HAROLD: I'm very tired. I must try and get as much rest as I can. I've got to conserve my energy for the battle that lies ahead. I'll see you tomorrow … God willing. *(He slowly walks to the door and goes out.)*

(Albert is worried.)

RAY GALTON AND ALAN SIMPSON

FOOD, BOOZE & SMOKES

BERNARD SCHOENBAUM

Food, glorious food

IT WAS A DEVICE FOR TURNING SCHOOL MEALS BACK INTO FOOD

GLEN BAXTER

A man goes into a butcher's shop. The butcher points to some beef hanging above them and says, 'I bet you £50 that you can't touch that meat.' 'No thanks,' replies the man. 'The steaks are too high.'

A wife wanted snails for dinner and sent her husband to get some. After buying them he stopped off at a bar for a quick drink. Staggering home four hours later, he tripped outside his house and dropped the snails everywhere. His wife heard the commotion and came to see what had happened. 'You've been gone four hours!' she shouted. 'Come on you lot,' said her husband to the snails. 'We're nearly there.'

Two cannibals were eating a clown. One said to the other: 'Does this taste funny to you?'

ANON

"SHE'S TRYING TO MAKE BEING A VEGETARIAN EXCITING."

STEVE BEST

Q: What do you get if you cross a door knocker with a courgette?
A: Rat-a-tat-a-touille.

food, booze & smokes

TV AM set – large sofa. Jennifer is the interviewer, Dawn the perennial 'expert'. They never know quite which camera is on.

JENNIFER (SAUNDERS): Welcome back. On the sofa with me today is our resident Health Expert, Dawn French. I'm going to be asking her what's good for our health and what's bad. Dawn, hello.

DAWN (FRENCH): Hello.

JENNIFER: So, tell us, Dawn, what is good for our health and what is bad?

DAWN: Things that are generally good for our health are: breathing, walking and reacting to sudden light by blinking.

THE SWEETBREAD

That sweetbread gazing up at me
Is not what it purports to be.
Says Webster in one paragraph,
It is the pancreas of a calf.
Since it is neither sweet nor bread,
I think I'll take a bun instead.

OGDEN NASH

BREAD THAT
MUST BE

Custard, n. A detestable substance produced by a malevolent conspiracy of the hen, the cow and the cook.

AMBROSE BIERCE,

THE DEVIL'S DICTIONARY (1911)

JENNIFER: And what's bad for our health?

DAWN: Bad for our health? Well, heart attacks, comas and gangrene. All of these things are bad for our health.

JENNIFER: Can I just say to viewers, we're not trying to make a point here. We're not trying to say anything this morning. That's very interesting, we've been literally flooded with letters asking us what we can and can't eat.

Dawn picks up basket of fruit from side of her.

DAWN: Well, of course, the easy guideline to what we can eat is anything that's edible, for instance Smarties are edible.

JENNIFER: Well, that's all very well, but many people are puzzled about what *not* to eat.

DAWN: You'd be surprised at the things that are bad to eat, metal, concrete, wood, don't eat trousers and please, please don't eat instant noodles.

JENNIFER: I see, we're surrounded by things we can't eat. Obviously it's very difficult for some of our viewers to make the right decisions with regards to food when faced with *so* much choice. What can they do?

DAWN: My tip is take advice about this from experts. When you're in a food shop, take food from the shelf, hold it up to the assistant and simply ask, 'Excuse me, is this edible?'

JENNIFER: Well, I hope that's clarified this murky area and let's all look forward to a happier and healthier life as a result of our little chat here.

DAWN: Do you want to know anything about organic food?

JENNIFER: No, that's a bit complicated and political for our viewers. OK, lovely, this is rather nice. *(Touching the food hamper)*

DAWN: The thing is, a lot of our viewers would simply throw the fruit out of this basket and try to eat the basket.

JENNIFER: Is it an epidemic?

DAWN: Not at the moment.

DAWN FRENCH AND JENNIFER SAUNDERS

SLICED WITH

AN AXE

is bread that is too nourishing.

FRAN LEBOWITZ

THE KIPPER
For half a century, man and nipper,
I've **doted** on a tasty kipper,
But since I am no **Jack the Ripper**
I wish the kipper had a zipper.
OGDEN NASH

HENRY KING,

Who chewed bits of String, and was early cut off in Dreadful Agonies.

The Chief Defect of Henry King
Was chewing little bits of String.

At last he swallowed some which tied
Itself in ugly Knots inside.

Physicians of the Utmost Fame
Were called at once: but when they came
They answered as they took their Fees,

'There is no Cure for this Disease.
Henry will very soon be dead.'

His Parents stood about his Bed
Lamenting his Untimely Death,
When Henry, with his Latest Breath.
Cried, 'Oh, my Friends, be warned by me,
That Breakfast, Dinner, Lunch, and Tea
Are all the Human Frame requires ...'
With that, the Wretched Child expires.

HILAIRE BELLOC illustrated by **BTB**

CAUTIONARY TALES FOR CHILDREN (1907)

DAD'S ARMY –
CHIPS FOR THE HOME GUARD

Interior. Side office. Day. Mainwaring crosses to the desk and picks up the phone.

MAINWARING: Captain Mainwaring.

COLONEL: G.H.Q. here, everything all right, Mainwaring?

MAINWARING: Yes, sir, I've got the prisoners safe and sound, they're all ready for you to pick them up.

COLONEL: I'm afraid the escort won't be able to get over there until tomorrow morning.

MAINWARING: Do you mean to say that we've got to look after them all night?

COLONEL: Sorry, can't do anything about it. Just give them a blanket each and bed them down. And give them something to eat, of course.

MAINWARING: But we've only got our own sandwiches, Colonel.

COLONEL: Well send out for some fish and chips.

MAINWARING: Send out for ...

COLONEL: I'll see that you get the money back. Be over about eight in the morning. Cheerio.

MAINWARING: *(Hanging up)* Fish and chips! *(He quickly strides to the door and opens it.)*

Interior. Church hall. Day.

MAINWARING: Wilson, Jones.

WILSON: Yes, sir.

MAINWARING: The escort can't get over until the morning, they've got to be here all night.

JONES: In that case, I really think we ought to cut their trouser buttons off, sir. *(Drags out his bayonet.)* Let me do it, let me do it, sir.

MAINWARING: Put that away, Jones. I shall have a word with the prisoners, Wilson.

WILSON: But you don't speak German.

CONTINUED OVERLEAF

MAINWARING: Oh, they'll know by the tone of my voice who's in charge, believe me, Wilson, they recognise authority. *(Mainwaring crosses to the prisoners, followed by Wilson and Jones.)* Right now, pay attention. *(The prisoners all come smartly to attention.)*

WILSON: They're awfully well disciplined, sir.

MAINWARING: Nothing of the sort, it's a slavish, blind obedience, not like the cheerful, light-hearted discipline that you get with our Jolly Jack Tars. I tell you, they're a nation of unthinking automatons, led by a lunatic who looks like Charlie Chaplin.

CAPTAIN: How dare you compare our glorious leader with that non-Aryan clown? *(He takes out a notebook and pencil and writes.)* I am making a note of your insults, captain. Your name will go on the list, and when we win the war, you will be brought to account.

MAINWARING: You can put down what you like, you're not going to win this war.

CAPTAIN: Oh yes we are.

MAINWARING: Oh no you're not.

CAPTAIN: Oh yes we are.

PIKE: *(Sings)* Whistle while you work, Hitler is a twerp, He's half barmy, So's his army. *(The captain crosses to the ladder, the words die on Pike's lips.)* Whistle ...

CAPTAIN: Your name will also go on the list. What is it?

Mainwaring crosses over, followed by Wilson.

MAINWARING: Don't tell him, Pike.

CAPTAIN: Pike, thank you.

MAINWARING: *(Boiling)* Now, look here, I've had just about enough. Tell your men from me that they're going to be here all night, and they'd better behave themselves. Now, get on with it.

The captain shrugs his shoulders.

PIKE: *(To Wilson)* Uncle Arthur, I don't think it's fair that my name should be on the list, I was only joking.

WILSON: You should be more careful, Frank. You know that the Germans haven't got a sense of humour.

PIKE: But you've said much worse things about Hitler. He's said much worse things.

WILSON: Quiet, Frank, he'll hear you.

PIKE: Do you think if you talked to him nicely, he'll take my name off the list? *(During this, the captain is speaking to the prisoners in German.)*

MAINWARING: Have you told them what I said?

CAPTAIN: Yes.

MAINWARING: Walker!

WALKER: Yes, Captain Mainwaring?

MAINWARING: Is the fish and chip shop still open?

WALKER: I think so, why?

MAINWARING: (*Handing him a ten-shilling note*) Go and get some for the prisoners. Jones, Wilson a conference. (*He walks over to Wilson and Jones.*)

WALKER: (*To captain*) Right, eight cod and chips.

CAPTAIN: I want plaice.

WALKER: Right, seven cod, one plaice. Who wants vinegar?

CAPTAIN: (*In German*) Who wants vinegar?

Four hold up their hands.

WALKER: Right, four vinegar. Salt?

CAPTAIN: (*In German*) Who wants salt?

Three hold up hands.

WALKER: That's three salt. How many without salt and vinegar?

CAPTAIN: (*In German*) How many without salt and vinegar?

More hands.

WALKER: Two without. Now, let's see if I've got this right.

MAINWARING: What do you think you're doing, Walker?

WALKER: I was just taking the order.

CAPTAIN: And I don't want nasty, soggy chips.

Mainwaring reacts.

CAPTAIN: I want mine crisp and light brown.

MAINWARING: How dare you? Now, listen to me, I've had just about enough. You'll have what you're given, and if I say you'll eat soggy chips, you'll eat soggy chips.

JIMMY PERRY AND
DAVID CROFT

Waiter, do you have frogs' legs?

I went to a restaurant that serves 'breakfast at any time'. So I ordered French toast during the Renaissance.

STEVEN WRIGHT

'Waiter,' said the customer, 'there's a hair in this honey.' 'Ah,' replied the waiter, 'it must be from the comb.'

Having worked in a new restaurant for a week, a chef from India was fired. Apparently, he kept favouring curry.

Visiting a restaurant, a couple decided to order steak. As the waitress put their plates on the table they noticed the strange way she was holding them. 'You've got your thumbs on our steaks!' complained the wife. 'Well, you don't want me to drop them again, do you?' the waitress replied.

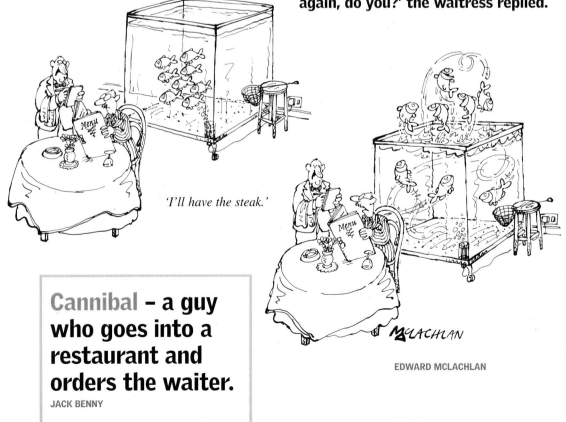

'I'll have the steak.'

EDWARD MCLACHLAN

Cannibal – a guy who goes into a restaurant and orders the waiter.

JACK BENNY

For what we are about to receive, may we be truly able to afford it..

MEL CALMAN

The hotel guest summoned the waiter over to order breakfast: 'I'd like two boiled eggs, one of them viscous, the other so over-cooked it blunts the teeth. Also, I'd like a portion of grilled bacon that has gone cold and soggy, burnt toast that cracks into smithereens as soon as you show a knife to it, butter straight from the freezer so it's impossible to spread and a pot of coffee with the consistency of lukewarm creosote, please.' 'That's a complicated order, sir,' said the bewildered waiter. 'I'm afraid it might be difficult to arrange at such short notice.' The guest remained unmoved: 'I don't understand – that's what I had yesterday.'

One day a man's overcoat was stolen in a restaurant. 'Did you see the person who took my coat?' the man asked a passing waiter. 'Yes, sir,' he replied. 'What did he look like?' 'Ridiculous,' said the waiter. 'The sleeves were far too short.'

A customer is ordering food in an Indian restaurant: 'Waiter, what's this chicken tarka?' Waiter: 'Sir, it's the same as chicken tikka, but a little 'otter.'

'Monsieur, may I suggest...'
CHARLES BARSOTTI

'Waiter, waiter, there's a fly in my soup.'
'No, sir, actually that's the chef. The last customer was a witch doctor.'

'Forget the crêpe suzette, Minchin ... I'll have the rice pudding.'
HOLTE

'Tell Luigi to be a little more careful with the pepper.'
EDWARD MCLACHLAN

THE DUMB WAITER!

ERNIE: Ah, good evening, I've been looking forward to patronising this restaurant.

ERIC: Good evening, sir – and now we are looking forward to patronising you.

ERNIE: Tell me – do you serve crabs?

ERIC: We serve anyone, sir. Take a seat.

ERNIE: Thank you, boy. I'm so hungry I could eat a horse.

ERIC: You've certainly come to the right place, sir.

ERNIE: Have you any wild duck?

ERIC: No, sir – but we've got a tame one we could aggravate for you.

ERNIE: Er, no thanks. Have you got pig's trotters?

ERIC: No, sir – flat feet.

FRED METCALF

'*I'm sorry, but your restaurant has failed on a number of health and safety issues.*'
NAF

'Waiter, waiter, what's this fly doing in my soup?'
'Looks like the breast-stroke, sir.'

Sunday evening; the dining room. Basil approaches the Heaths' table – Mr and Mrs and their eleven-year-old son, Ronald.

BASIL: Good evening. Is everything to your satisfaction?

MR HEATH: Yes thank –

MRS HEATH: *(Interrupting)* Well … *(She turns expectantly to their son)*

RONALD: I don't like the chips.

BASIL: Sorry?

RONALD: The chips are awful.

BASIL: *(Smiling balefully)* Oh dear. What's er … what's *wrong* with them, then?

RONALD: They're the wrong shape and they're just awful.

MRS HEATH: I'm afraid he gets everything cooked the way he likes it at home.

BASIL: Oh, does he, does he?

RONALD: Yes I do, and it's better than this pig's garbage.

MRS HEATH: *(Slightly amused)* Now, Ronald.

RONALD: These eggs look like you just laid them.

MRS HEATH: *(Ineffectually)* Ronald …

MR HEATH: *(To Ronald, friendlily)* Now look here, old chap …

MRS HEATH: Shut up!! Leave him alone! *(To Basil)* He's very clever, rather highly strung.

BASIL: Yes, yes, he should be.

RONALD: Haven't you got any *proper* chips?

BASIL: Well, these are proper French Fried Potatoes. You see, the chef is Continental.

RONALD: Couldn't you get an English one?

MRS HEATH: *(To Ronald)* Why don't you eat just one or two, dear?

RONALD: They're the wrong shape.

BASIL: Oh dear – what shape do you usually have? Mickey Mouse shape? Smarties shape? Amphibious landing craft shape? Poke in the eye shape?

RONALD: … God, you're *dumb*.

MRS HEATH: Oh, now …

BASIL: *(Controlling himself)* Is there something we can get you instead, *Sonny*?

RONALD: I'd like some bread and salad cream.

BASIL: … To *eat*? Well … *(Pointing)* there's the bread, and there's the mayonnaise.

RONALD: I said salad cream, stupid.

BASIL: We don't have any salad cream. The chef made *this (Indicating the mayonnaise)* freshly this morning.

RONALD: What a dump!

MR HEATH: *(Offering Ronald the mayonnaise)* This is very good.

MRS HEATH: *(Coldly)* He likes salad cream.

RONALD: *(To Basil)* That's puke, that is.

BASIL: Well, at least it's fresh puke.

MRS HEATH: *(Shocked)* Oh dear!!

BASIL: *(Indignantly)* Well, he said it!

MRS HEATH: *(Loftily)* May I ask why you don't have proper salad cream. I mean, most restaurants …

BASIL: Well, the chef only buys it on special occasions, you know, gourmet nights and so on, but … when he's got a bottle – ah! – he's a genius with it. He can unscrew the cap like Robert Carrier. It's a treat to watch him. *(He mimes)* And then ... right on the plate! None on the walls! Magic! He's a wizard with a tin-opener, too. He got a Pulitzer Prize for that. He can have the stuff in the saucepan before you can say haute cuisine. You name it, he'll heat it up and scrape it off the pan for you. Mind you, skill like that isn't picked up overnight. Still, I'll tell him to get some salad cream, you never know when Henry Kissinger is going to drop in, do you. *(Mrs Heath is silenced; Basil smiles charmingly, looks at his watch and in so doing neatly elbows Ronald in the head)* Sorry, sorry! *(He moves off)*

MR HEATH: Nice man.

JOHN CLEESE AND CONNIE BOOTH

THE LAY OF THE LONE FISH-BALL

A wretched man walked up and down
To buy his dinner in the town.
At last he found a wretched place
And entered it with modest grace,
Took off his coat, took off his hat,
And wiped his feet upon the mat,
Took out his purse to count his pence,
And found he had but two half cents.
The bill of fare, he scanned it through
To see what two half-cents would do.
The only item of them all
For two half-cents was one fish-ball.
So to the waiter he did call
And gently whispered: 'One fish-ball.'
The waiter bellowed down the hall:
'The gentleman here wants one fish-ball.'
The diners looked both one and all
To see who wanted one fish-ball.
The wretched man, all ill at ease,
Said: 'A little bread, sir, if you please.'
The waiter bellowed down the hall:
'We don't serve bread with one fish-ball.'
The wretched man, he felt so small,
He quickly left the dining hall.
The wretched man, he went outside
And shot himself until he died.
This is the moral of it all,
Don't ask for bread with one fish-ball.

GEORGE MARTIN LANE

FOOD, BOOZE & SMOKES

Water ...

DON'T DRINK THE WATER

We found ourselves short of water at Hambledon lock; so we took our jar and went up to the lock-keeper's house to beg for some.

George was our spokesman. He put on a winning smile, and said:

'Oh, please could you spare us a little water?'

'Certainly,' replied the old gentleman; 'take as much as you want, and leave the rest.'

'Thank you so much,' murmured George, looking about him. 'Where – where do you keep it?'

'It's always in the same place, my boy,' was the stolid reply: 'just behind you.'

'I don't see it,' said George, turning round.

'Why, bless us, where's your eyes?' was the man's comment, as he twisted George round and pointed up and down the stream. 'There's enough of it to see, ain't there?'

'Oh!' exclaimed George, grasping the idea; 'but we can't drink the river, you know!'

'No; but you can drink some of it,' replied the old fellow. 'It's what I've drunk for the last fifteen years.'

George told him that his appearance, after the course, did not seem a sufficiently good advertisement for the brand; and that he would prefer it out of a pump.

We got some from a cottage a little higher up. I dare say that was only river water, if we had known. But we did not know, so it was all right. What the eye does not see, the stomach does not get upset over.

We tried river water once, later on in the season, but it was not a success. We

... and wine

'God! They're bringing a bottle of red again and they know damn well it's going to be fish!'

CHIC JACOB

LOSS

The day he moved out was terrible

That evening she went through hell.

His absence wasn't a problem

But the corkscrew

had gone as well.

WENDY COPE

were coming down-stream, and had pulled up to have tea in a backwater near Windsor. Our jar was empty, and it was a case of going without our tea or taking water from the river. Harris was for chancing it. He said it must be all right if we boiled the water. He said that the various germs of poison present in the water would be killed by the boiling. So we filled our kettle with Thames backwater, and boiled it; and very careful we were to see that it did boil.

We had made the tea, and were just settling down comfortably to drink it, when George, with his cup half-way to his lips, paused and exclaimed:

'What's that?'

'What's what?' asked Harris and I.

'Why that!' said George, looking westward.

Harris and I followed his gaze, and saw, coming down towards us on the sluggish current, a dog. It was one of the quietest and peacefullest dogs I have ever seen. I never met a dog who seemed more contented – more easy in its mind. It was floating dreamily on its back, with its four legs stuck up straight into the air. It was what I should call a full-bodied dog, with a well-developed chest. On he came, serene, dignified, and calm, until he was abreast of our boat, and there, among the rushes, he eased up, and settled down cosily for the evening.

George said he didn't want any tea, and emptied his cup into the water, Harris did not feel thirsty, either, and followed suit. I had drunk half mine, but I wished I had not.

I asked George if he thought I was likely to have typhoid.

He said: Oh no; he thought I had a very good chance indeed of escaping it. Anyhow, I should know in about a fortnight whether I had or had not.

JEROME K. JEROME, *THREE MEN IN A BOAT* **(1889)**

If people were wine   RONALD SEARLE

Elegant, but lacking backbone   *Overripeness coupled with some tartness*

A man walks into a bar ...

There was only one customer in the local pub so the barman phoned his wife and told her he'd be home early. But just then another man came in. 'Where are you from?' asked the first customer. 'Five miles west of town,' answered the newcomer. 'I live five miles west of town, too. Let's drink to that.' As they drained their glasses, the first man learned that his drinking companion's age was 43. 'I'm 43, too.' 'We'd better drink to that as well.' It then turned out that both were born in the same hospital, and another round was ordered. Calling his wife, the barman said, 'Forget it, dear – the Farquharson twins are at it again.'

A man walked into a pub and ordered six whiskies. Lining them up on the bar, he downed the first glass, then the third and finally the fifth. 'Excuse me,' said the barman as the man turned to leave. 'But you've left three of the whiskies you ordered untouched.' 'Yes,' said the man. 'My doctor said it was OK to take the odd drink.'

A man enters a pub by doing a double forward somersault followed by a backward somersault with a half twist, and then lands on a stool with an elegant jump. 'Good afternoon!' says the surprised barman. 'Are you some sort of magician?'

The man explains that he's an acrobat with the circus and would like a beer. While the barman is pouring the drink, a new customer comes in. This one does a triple forward somersault followed by a backward somersault with a full twist, and gracefully lands with his feet in the sink. 'Let me guess,' says the barman. 'You're also with the circus?' 'No,' the man corrects him. 'But I'd like to point out that your doormat is loose.'

PETER WALDNER

A man walked into a bar with a lump of tarmac under his arm. 'What would you like?' asked the barman. 'A pint of beer and one for the road,' replied the man.

EDWARD MCLACHLAN

A man walks into a bar, orders a drink and sits down. A few minutes later, he hears someone shouting abuse at him. 'You look terrible in those jeans,' says the voice, 'get down to the gym and lose some weight!' The man turns round to find that the abuse is coming from the cigarette machine. He tries to ignore it, but the insults continue and the man finally goes up to the bar to complain. 'I'm really sorry,' says the barman. 'That machine has been out of order for ages.'

'If it's Bo Peep, don't tell her we're here.'
S. HAKIS

food, booze & smokes

Last orders, please ...

REG SMYTHE, *ANDY CAPP*

'Fill 'er up.'
PETER ARNO

One evening in the pub a barman offered **a free round** to anyone who could order a drink he hadn't heard of. Everyone began requesting the most outlandish beverages, from Singapore slings and Manhattans to pina coladas. But each time the barman knew exactly how to make them. **Business was now booming** and nobody was even coming close to winning the barman's wager, when somebody said: **'I'd like a Southampton, please.'** The barman had to admit defeat and invited the customer behind the bar to show him what he had in mind. 'It's really very simple,' said the customer, taking a bottle from the shelf. 'It's a large port.'

A man went into a pub, walked up the wall, across the ceiling and down the other side. **After drinking a double whisky** he did the same thing all over again and then walked out. **'That was strange,'** said a customer at the bar. 'Yes,' agreed the barman. 'He usually has a pint.'

REG SMYTHE, *ANDY CAPP*

'I took one look at the price of cotton futures this morning and decided to reinvest in the stability of beer.'

JACK ZIEGLER

A man walks into a pub **with a snake** and orders two pints of beer. The man drinks his, but the snake struggles with his glass and eventually **smashes it on the floor.** The man orders another two pints and the same thing happens. 'I'm afraid **I'm going to have to ask you to leave,'** says the barman to the snake. 'I'm so sorry,' apologizes the man. 'But he just can't hold his drink.'

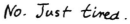

JOHN GLASHAN

A brain walks into a bar and orders a pint of lager. 'Sorry,' says the barman, 'I can't serve you.' 'Why not?' demands the brain. The barman replies, 'Because you're out of your head.'

Drunk and disorderly

You're not drunk if you can lie on the floor without holding on.
JOE E. LEWIS

Work is the curse of the drinking classes.
OSCAR WILDE

Some weasel took the cork out of my lunch.
W.C. FIELDS

For a bad hangover, take the juice of two quarts of whisky.
EDDIE CONDON

(After a few drinks)
He climbed into the bed as it came round the second time.
P.G. WODEHOUSE

An alcoholic is someone you don't like who drinks as much as you do.
DYLAN THOMAS

'It is a pleasant accompaniment to fish, shellfish, and the lighter meats, but its delicate flavour is perhaps even more appreciated at the end of the meal with melon or dessert.'
PETER ARNO

I'M ON a WHISKY DIET
I'VE LOST THREE DaYS alReaDY.
TOMMY COOPER

Two drunks were walking down the railway tracks. **After a couple of miles,** one says, 'All these steps are killing me.' **'It's not the steps that are the problem,'** replies his friend. 'It's these low handrails.'

'Well, gentlemen ... Shall we join the ladies?'
STAN McMURTRY

THE OFFICE — DOWNING THE PINTS

Interior. Reception. Day.

BRENT: Be gentle with me today, Dawn.

DAWN: *(Exasperated)* Yeah? Why's that?

BRENT: Oh God. Had a skinful last night. I was out with Finchy.

(To camera crew) Chris Finch.

(To Dawn) Had us on a pub crawl. 'El vino did flow'...

Brent mimes drinking.

BRENT: I was bl ... blattered ... bl ... bladdered ... blotto'd ... Oh, don't ever come out with me and Finchy.

DAWN: No, I won't.

BRENT: There's guys my age, and they look fifty ... How old do you think I look?

DAWN: Thirty –

BRENT: *(Interrupting)* – Thirty, yeah .. About that. Oh, but I will have to slow down. Drinking a bit too much ...

Brent pats his belly.

BRENT: ... if every single night of the week is too much.

DAWN: *(Joking)* ... And every lunchtime.

BRENT: How many have I had this week?

DAWN: What?

BRENT: How many pints have I drunk this week? If you're counting ...

DAWN: I'm not counting.

BRENT: Aren't you? Hmm, you seem to know a lot about my drinking. Does it offend you, eh? You know, getting a little bit ... a little bit personal. Imagine if I started doing that with you. I could look at you and come out with something really witty and biting like, 'You're a bit ...'

He can't think of anything.

BRENT: ... but I don't. Because I'm a professional and professionalism is ... And that is what I want, okay? That's all. That's a shame.

He strides off, leaving Dawn speechless.

RICKY GERVAIS AND STEPHEN MERCHANT

Not sobered up ... yet

A drunk went into a pub and the manager asked him to leave. There were four entrances, and the drunk came back in through the second one. He was asked to leave again. Back he came through the third entrance and there was the manager barring the way. When he returned through the fourth door, the proprietor escorted him to the pavement. Perplexed, the drunk asked, 'Do you own all the pubs around here?'

'Don't disturb Sir Roger. He's fermenting.'
MICHAEL FFOLKES

Reflections on ice-breaking
Candy is dandy,
But liquor is quicker.
OGDEN NASH

One reason I don't drink is that I want to know when I'm having a good time.
NANCY ASTOR

I always keep a stimulant handy in case I see a snake – which I also keep handy.
W.C. FIELDS

I exercise extreme self control. I never drink anything stronger than gin before breakfast.
W.C. FIELDS

I have been commissioned to write an autobiography and I would be grateful to any of your readers who could tell me what I was doing between 1960 and 1974.
JEFFREY BERNARD

EDWARD MCLACHLAN

A psychologist once said that we knew little about the conscience except that it is soluble in alcohol.

THOMAS BLACKBURN

Charlotta
There was an old man in a trunk,
Who inquired of his wife, 'Am I drunk?'
She replied with regret,
'I'm afraid so my pet.'
And he answered, 'It's just as I thunk.'

OGDEN NASH

'Twas a woman who drove me to drink.
I never had the courtesy to thank her.

W.C. FIELDS

It was early last December,
As near as I remember,
I was walking down the street in
  tipsy pride;
No one was I disturbing
As I lay down by the curbing,
And a pig came up and lay down
  by my side.
As I lay there in the gutter
Thinking thoughts I shall not utter,
A lady passing by was heard to say:
'You can tell a man who boozes
By the company he chooses';
And the pig got up and slowly
  walked away.

ANON

Albert is coughing his lungs up. He finishes coughing, then takes a cigarette out of his cigarette machine. Puts it in his mouth. Lights it and starts coughing violently again.

Harold enters. He stands there listening to Albert's coughing.

HAROLD: Oh for gawd's sake, take that fag out of your mouth. I could hear you four streets away. I could see the house vibrating from the top of the road.

ALBERT: Dah. A man's got to have some pleasures in life. Did you bring any fags in? I've had to roll up my dog ends since this morning.

HAROLD: Honestly, the state your lungs must be in. They must look like a couple of empty coal sacks. How long have you been smoking now?

ALBERT: Let's see, I started just after I left school. So I would have been er ... eight and a half. So that means ...

HAROLD: Sixty glorious years. Have you any idea how much smoking that represents?

ALBERT: I don't know.

HAROLD: Well let's work it out. *(Takes a pencil and paper.)* A fag is about three inches long. A packet of twenty, that's five foot. How many do you smoke a day?

ALBERT: Forty.

HAROLD: Forty? That's ten foot a day you're getting through. That's the equivalent of one fag twice as long as you. Do you realise you're smoking three thousand six hundred and fifty feet of fag per year. It's horrifying.

That's nearly three quarters of a mile.

ALBERT: Who cares?

HAROLD: Three quarters of a mile each year for sixty years. *(Does a quick calculation.)* That's incredible.

Since you were eight and a half you have smoked the equivalent of a fag forty-five miles long. That's from here to Reading. Or half way up the M1 to Coventry.

ALBERT: No it's not. You don't smoke them all. You can't count the dog ends.

HAROLD: That's even worse. That means you've thrown away a dog end five miles long.

ALBERT: I enjoy smoking ... and it ain't done me any harm. *(He coughs.)*

HAROLD: You must have a lining of nicotine an inch and a half thick inside your lungs. Another year and the sides will be touching. Dad, do yourself a favour, give it up.

ALBERT: No Harold, I couldn't, I'm too old to change my ways now. When you reach my age, life without a nice cough and a drag wouldn't be worth living.

HAROLD: Look. There's a mobile mass X-ray unit down the road, I passed it on my way home. Why don't you go down and have an X-ray?

ALBERT: No. I'm not having any X-rays.

HAROLD: Why not?

ALBERT: They might find something wrong with me.

HAROLD: Well, that's the idea. Then they can do something about it.

ALBERT: No. If there's anything wrong with me I'd rather not know about it.

HAROLD: But that's ridiculous. That's burying your head in the sand. If there is anything wrong with you, it won't go away, it'll just get worse.

ALBERT: *(Worried)* There's nothing wrong with me.

HAROLD: You don't know. Not till you've had a check up.

ALBERT: There's nothing wrong with me, I tell you.

HAROLD: Then there's nothing to be frightened about having an X-ray, is there?

ALBERT: I know you. You want them to find something wrong with me.

HAROLD: What a terrible thing to say.

ALBERT: Yes you do. So I'll have to go into hospital. They'll keep me there, I'll never come out again. That's what you want, isn't it?

HAROLD: If that's what I wanted I could have had your head X-rayed and had you taken away years ago. It's for your own good. Besides, everybody should be X-rayed. I'm going to have one.

ALBERT: Why, what's wrong with you?

HAROLD: Nothing's wrong with me.

ALBERT: Then what are you having one for? Wasting the public's money. That's why the health stamps keep going up.

HAROLD: Oh dear, oh dear. Look, the whole point of preventative medicine is to stop people from being ill. And the only way you can do that is to find out if they're ill or not.

CONTINUED OVERLEAF

ALBERT: Exactly. The more people you find, the more people you're going to find ill.

HAROLD: I know that.

ALBERT: That's why the hospitals are overcrowded.

HAROLD: They won't be if they can prevent disease.

ALBERT: X-rays isn't preventing it, it's looking for it. Leave well alone. If people are ill and don't know about it, what's the point of depressing them, it'll only make them ill.

HAROLD: Yes but ... look, are you coming or not?

ALBERT: No. I haven't got T.B.

HAROLD: I didn't say you have. But you have got a nasty cough.

ALBERT: I've always had that. That's not T.B. That's my lungs. *(Coughs)*

HAROLD: You're going to have a check up. You're coming with me first thing in the morning. You're going to put some clean underwear on and you're going to have that skinny little chest X-rayed, all right?

ALBERT: I don't have to put on clean underwear, do I?

HAROLD: Well you've got to give the X-rays a chance to get through, haven't you?

ALBERT: I don't want to be X-rayed Harold. *(Starts coughing)* There's nothing wrong with me, I know there isn't. I'm as healthy as anyone.

RAY GALTON AND ALAN SIMPSON

FOOD, BOOZE & SMOKES
Going up in smoke

'Pssst! Want some grass?'
LEE FERRIDAY

'I must not smoke cigars during prayers, I must not smoke cigars during ...'
RONALD SEARLE

'We have reason to believe you are carrying certain substances of a hallucinogenic nature.'
EDWARD MCLACHLAN

I was horrified to find the other week that my second son is taking drugs. My very best ones too.
BOB MONKHOUSE

'Would you mind if you passively smoked?'
MATT

I don't have a **drug problem.** I have a police problem.
KEITH RICHARDS

A woman is an occasional pleasure but a cigar is always a smoke.
GROUCHO MARX

'Don't be daft. It's the only place in the building where he can have a smoke.'
RIANA DUNCAN

LOVE & SEX

Tunnel of Married Love

HUNTer

JIM HUNTER

The fair sex

Many many moons ago (about 6,000,000,000,000,000,000 BC), a hairy thing appeared in a tree by permission of God and Co. Limited; the thing was called Man. Later another thing turned up, this was called Woman, and that's how the trouble started.

SPIKE MILLIGAN

Women should be obscene and not heard.

GROUCHO MARX

Women are like elephants to me: nice to look at, but I wouldn't want to own one.

W.C. FIELDS

WHAT HE LOVED MOST ABOUT HER WAS HER SENSE OF HUMOUR.

STEVE BEST

I look just like the girl next door ... if you happen to live next door to an amusement park.

DOLLY PARTON

They used to photograph Shirley Temple through gauze. They should photograph me through linoleum.

TALLULAH BANKHEAD

I used to be Snow White, but I drifted.

MAE WEST

Not so fair

The quickest way to a man's heart is through his chest.

ROSEANNE

Behind every successful man is a woman, behind her is his wife.

GROUCHO MARX

A hard man is good to find.

MAE WEST

It is better to have loved a short man, than never to have loved a tall.

MILES KINGTON

A man is designed to walk three miles in the rain to phone for help when the car breaks down, and a woman is designed to say, 'You took your time' when he comes back dripping wet.

VICTORIA WOOD

On the one hand, men will never experience childbirth. On the other hand, they can open all their own jars.

JEFF GREEN

I like to wake up feeling a new man.

JEAN HARLOW

'It's a love story. Nobody's ahead.'
DEAN VIETOR

J.W. TAYLOR

Be my valentine?

Friday February 13th

It was an unlucky day for me all right!

Pandora doesn't sit next to me in Geography any more. Barry Kent does. He kept copying my work and blowing bubblegum in my ears. I told Miss Elf but she is scared of Barry Kent as well, so she didn't say anything to him.

Pandora looked luscious today, she was wearing a split skirt which showed her legs. She has got a scab on one of her knees. She was wearing Nigel's football scarf round her wrist, but Miss Elf saw it and told her to take it off. Miss Elf is not scared of Pandora. I have sent her a Valentine's Day card (Pandora, not Miss Elf).

Saturday February 14th
ST VALENTINE'S DAY

I only got one Valentine's Day card. It was in my mother's handwriting so it doesn't count. My mother had a massive card delivered, it was so big that a GPO van had to bring it to the door. She went all red when she opened the envelope and saw the card. It was dead good. There was a big satin elephant holding a bunch of plastic flowers in its trunk and a bubble coming out of its mouth saying 'Hi, Honey Bun! I ain't never gonna forget you!'. There was no name written inside, just drawings of hearts with 'Pauline' written inside them. My father's card was very small and had a bunch of purple flowers on the front. My father had written on the inside 'Let's try again'.

Here is the poem I wrote inside Pandora's card.

PANDORA!

I ADORE YA.

I IMPLORE YE

DON'T IGNORE ME.

I wrote it left-handed so that she wouldn't know it was from me.

SUE TOWNSEND, *THE SECRET DIARY OF ADRIAN MOLE AGED 13 3/4*

Why I didn't get you a valentine

because I'm into saving trees

because my declarations are not determined by the calendar

because ultimately my heart is my own

because I forgot.

JOHN HEGLEY

On Valentine's Day, one of my daughter's colleagues received a bouquet of flowers accompanied by a card that simply said 'No'. She spent the whole morning trying to figure out what her husband had meant by this message. Eventually she gave up and called him. He was adamant that he hadn't attached a message. 'When I was on the phone to the florist,' he told her, 'she asked me if I had a message and I said "No" ...'

Last week I met a Dutch girl with inflatable shoes and rang to ask her out on a date. Unfortunately, she'd popped her clogs.

LOVE & SEX
It's a date!

In a Bath Teashop
'Let us not speak, for the love we bear
   one another –
Let us hold hands and look.'
She, such a very ordinary little woman;
He, such a thumping crook;
But both, for a moment, little lower than
   the angels
In the teashop's ingle-nook.

JOHN BETJEMAN

PETER WALDNER

SOCIAL NOTE
Lady, lady, should you meet
One whose ways are all discreet,
One who murmurs that his wife
Is the lodestar of his life,
One who keeps assuring you
That he never was untrue,
Never loved another one ...
Lady, lady, better run!

DOROTHY PARKER

A very old man shuffles into a pub and sees a beautiful young woman sitting on the other side of the room **at the bar. Fancying his chances he goes over,** sits down next to her **and says, 'Do I come here often?'**

'Why, Richard Honeywell, I believe you're jealous.'
CARL ROSE

A girl phoned me the other day and said, 'Come on over. There's nobody home.' I went over. Nobody was home.
RODNEY DANGERFIELD

'We had a huge fight on our first date, too.'
DANNY SHANAHAN

Lovey-dovey

EVE: Do you love only me?

ADAM: Who else?

'*Of course we must face facts. It's going to mean waiting.*'
PONT

Some of the greatest love affairs I've known involved one actor, unassisted.

WILSON MIZNER

Love, n. A temporary insanity curable by marriage.

AMBROSE BIERCE, *THE DEVIL'S DICTIONARY* (1911)

I never loved another person the way I loved myself.

MAE WEST

A SUBALTERN'S LOVE-SONG

Miss J. Hunter Dunn, Miss J. Hunter Dunn,
Furnish'd and burnish'd by Aldershot sun,
What strenuous singles we played after tea,
We in the tournament – you against me!

Love-thirty, love-forty, oh! weakness of joy,
The speed of a swallow, the grace of a boy,
With carefullest carelessness, gaily you won,
I am weak from your loveliness, Joan Hunter Dunn.

Miss Joan Hunter Dunn, Miss Joan Hunter Dunn,
How mad I am, sad I am, glad that you won.
The warm-handled racket is back in its press,
But my shock-headed victor, she loves me no less.

Her father's euonymus shines as we walk,
And swing past the summer-house, buried in talk,
And cool the verandah that welcomes us in
To the six-o'clock news and a lime-juice and gin.

The scent of the conifers, sound of the bath,
The view from my bedroom of moss-dappled path,
As I struggle with double-end evening tie,
For we dance at the Golf Club, my victor and I.

On the floor of her bedroom lie blazer and shorts
And the cream-coloured walls are be-trophied with sports,
And westering, questioning settles the sun
On your low-leaded window, Miss Joan Hunter Dunn.

Unfortunate coincidence
By the time you swear you're his.
 Shivering and sighing,
And he vows his passion is
 Infinite, undying –
Lady, make a note of this:
 One of you is lying.

DOROTHY PARKER

If love is the answer, could you
rephrase the question?

LILY TOMLIN

LOVE – the delightful interval between meeting a beautiful girl and discovering that she looks like a haddock.

JOHN BARRYMORE

The Hillman is waiting, the light's in the hall,
The pictures of Egypt are bright on the wall,
My sweet, I am standing beside the oak stair
And there on the landing's the light on your hair.

By roads 'not adopted', by woodlanded ways,
She drove to the club in the late summer haze,
Into nine-o'clock Camberley, heavy with bells
And mushroomy, pine-woody, evergreen smells.

Miss Joan Hunter Dunn, Miss Joan Hunter Dunn,
I can hear from the car-park the dance has begun.
Oh! full Surrey twilight! importunate band!
Oh! strongly adorable tennis-girl's hand!

Around us are Rovers and Austins afar,
Above us the intimate roof of the car,
And here on my right is the girl of my choice,
With the tilt of her nose and the chime of her voice,

And the scent of her wrap, and the words never said,
And the ominous, ominous dancing ahead.
We sat in the car-park till twenty to one
And now I'm engaged to Miss Joan Hunter Dunn.

JOHN BETJEMAN

'Other women? What other women?'
DAVID HALDANE

Two Cures for Love
1. Don't see him. Don't phone or write a letter.
2. The easy way: get to know him better.
WENDY COPE

Marital bliss?

'There are still a lot of things they haven't worked out.'
ED FISHER

A husband is the bloke that sticks with you through the troubles you wouldn't have had if you hadn't married him in the first place.
ANON

Marriages don't last. **When I meet a guy,** the first question I ask myself is: 'Is this the man I want my children to spend their weekends with?'
RITA RUDNER

All the unhappy marriages come from husbands having brains. What good are brains to a man? They only unsettle him.
P.G. WODEHOUSE

The trouble with marrying your mistress is that you create a job vacancy.
JAMES GOLDSMITH

'I'd marry again if I found a man who had 15 million and would sign it over to me before the marriage and guarantee he'd be dead within a year.'
BETTE DAVIS

A man in a bar notices a woman sitting alone at a table and goes over to chat her up. After talking to her for a while he makes his move. 'Stop!' says the woman as the man tries to kiss her. 'I'm sorry, but I can't do this because I'm keeping myself pure until I meet the man I truly love.' 'Gosh,' says the man, 'that must be difficult.' 'It's not too bad,' replies the woman. 'My husband's a little upset, though.'

Polygamy, n. Too much of a good thing.

AMBROSE BIERCE, *THE DEVIL'S DICTIONARY*, 1911

Man: 'I had it all – money, a fine house, a luxury car, the love of a beautiful woman. Then pow! It was all gone.'
Friend: 'How come?'
Man: 'My wife found out.'

'Coming, dearest.'

RUSSELL BROCKBANK

CHARLES PEATTIE AND RUSSELL TAYLOR

GOLF SWINGERS

The Oldest Member tells of young love from his favourite chair on the terrace above the ninth hole.

Jane Packard and William Bates (said the Oldest Member) were not, you must understand, officially engaged. They had grown up together from childhood, and there existed between them a sort of understanding – the understanding being that, if ever William could speed himself up enough to propose, Jane would accept him, and they would settle down and live stodgily and happily ever after. For William was not one of your rapid wooers. In his affair of the heart he moved somewhat slowly and ponderously, like a motor-lorry, an object which both in physique and temperament he greatly resembled. **He was an extraordinarily large,** powerful, ox-like young man, who required plenty of time to make up his mind about any given problem. I have seen him in the club dining-room musing with a thoughtful frown for fifteen minutes on end while endeavouring to weigh the rival merits of a chump chop and a sirloin steak as a luncheon dish. A placid, leisurely man, I might almost call him lymphatic. I *will* call him lymphatic. He was lymphatic.

The first glimmering of an idea that Jane might possibly be a suitable wife for him had come to William some three years before this story opens. Having brooded on the matter tensely for six months, he then sent her a bunch of roses. In the October of the following year, nothing having occurred to alter his growing conviction that she was an attractive girl, he presented her with a two-pound box of assorted chocolates. **And from then on his progress, though not rapid, was continuous,** and there seemed little reason to doubt that, should nothing come about to weaken Jane's regard for him, another five years or so would see the matter settled.

And it did not appear likely that anything would weaken Jane's regard. They had much in common, for she was a calm, slow-moving person, too. They had a mutual devotion to golf, and played together every day; and the fact that their handicaps were practically level formed a strong bond. Most divorces, as you know, spring from the fact that the husband is too markedly superior to his wife at golf; this leading him, when she starts criticizing his relations, to say bitter and unforgivable things about her mashie-shots. **Nothing of this kind could happen with William and Jane.** They would build their life on a solid foundation of sympathy and understanding. The years would find them consoling and encouraging each other, happy married lovers. If, that is to say, William ever got round to proposing.

P.G. WODEHOUSE, *THE HEART OF A GOOF*, 1926

In the bedroom

I believe that sex is a beautiful thing between two people. Between five, it's fantastic.

WOODY ALLEN

I'm a bad lover. I once caught a peeping tom booing me.

RODNEY DANGERFIELD

On arriving home from work, an unfortunate man found his **wife in bed with the milkman**. 'What on earth are you doing?' shouted the irate husband. 'See?' sighed the woman to the man lying next to her. 'Didn't I tell you he doesn't know the first thing about sex?'

The woman hurried home from her doctor's appointment devastated by what he'd just told her. When her husband came in from work she said, 'Darling, the doctor said I have only 12 hours to live. So I've decided we should go to bed and make passionate love all night. How does that sound, dearest?' 'Well, that's fine for you,' replied her husband. 'But I've got to get up in the morning.'

RUPERT FAWCETT

Sex on the brain

Busts and bosoms have I known
Of various shapes and sizes,
From grievous disappointments
To jubilant surprises.

ANON

**Why don't women blink during foreplay?
There isn't time.**

**Women need a reason to have sex.
Men just need a place.**

BILLY CRYSTAL

HUSBAND: Fancy a quickie?
WIFE: As opposed to what?

As the male rabbit said to the female rabbit, 'This is fun ... wasn't it?'

© 2002 Benita Epstein/Dist. by Creators Syndicate, Inc. www.creators.com
4/20

'You call that sharing your feelings?'
BENITA EPSTEIN

Out golfing one weekend, a young couple watch in horror as a stray shot crashes through the window of a nearby house. Rushing up, they see a handsome man in a turban. 'We're terribly sorry!' says the husband. 'We'll pay for the damage,' says the wife. 'Not at all,' replies the man. 'I am a genie, trapped for a thousand years until your golf ball came through the window and broke the bottle that was my prison. Please allow me to grant whatever you wish.' The astonished couple ask to become scratch golfers. 'It is done!' cries the genie, snapping his fingers.

Then they ask to become millionaires. Clapping his hands, the genie announces, 'I have set up a standing order to put £100,000 into your account every month for life.' 'How can we ever thank you?' says the husband. 'There is one thing,' replies the genie. 'I have been imprisoned for a thousand years and I have forgotten what it is like to hold a woman in my arms. If you could spare your beautiful wife for a single night ...?' The husband and wife decide they can live with this.

After a night of passion, the young wife is about to rejoin her husband when the genie asks her age. 'Twenty-nine,' she replies. 'I see,' he says, 'and you still believe in this genie rubbish, do you?'

Sitting with her cat, an old woman was **polishing a dusty lamp** she had found in the attic, when a genie popped out and offered her three wishes. Thinking quickly, she said, **'I'd like to be rich. I'd like to be young and I'd like my cat to turn into a handsome prince.'** There was a puff of smoke and the woman found herself young and surrounded by riches. **The cat had gone and a gorgeous prince stood beside her,** holding out his arms. She melted into his embrace. 'Now,' he whispered, 'aren't you sorry you had me neutered?'

'Light-brown hair, cuddly, good in bed ...'
ROBERT THOMPSON

"ADMIT IT, THIS IS YOUR FIRST TIME ISN'T IT?"
STEVE BEST

Walking through his church grounds one morning, a vicar sees a group of youngsters talking on the grass. Overhearing some of their conversation, he realises they're having a competition to see who can tell the most outrageous stories about their sex lives. The vicar comments, 'When I was your age, I never thought about sex.' 'OK,' says one of the youths, 'you win.'

love & sex

Two men in a pub.

NORMAN (ERIC IDLE): Is your wife a ... goer ... eh? Know what I mean? Know what I mean? Nudge nudge. Nudge nudge. Know what I mean? Say no more ... know what I mean?

HIM (TERRY JONES): I beg your pardon?

NORMAN: Your wife ... does she, er, does she 'go' – eh? eh? eh? Know what I mean, know what I mean? Nudge nudge. Say no more.

HIM: She sometimes goes, yes.

NORMAN: I bet she does. I bet she does. I bet she does. Know what I mean? Nudge nudge.

HIM: I'm sorry, I don't quite follow you.

NORMAN: Follow me! *Follow* me! I like that. That's good. A nod's as good as a wink to a blind bat, eh? *(Elbow gesture; rubs it)*

HIM: Are you trying to sell something?

NORMAN: Selling, selling. Very good. *Very* good. *(Hand tilting quickly)* Oh, wicked. Wicked. You're wicked. Eh? Know what I mean? Know what I mean? Nudge nudge. Know what I mean? Nudge nudge. Nudge nudge. *(Leaning over to him, making eye gesture; speaks slowly)* Say ... no ... more. *(Leans back as if having imparted a great secret)*

HIM: But ...

NORMAN: *(Stops him with finger which he lays alongside nose; gives slight tap)* Your wife is she, eh ... is she a sport? Eh?

HIM: She *likes* sport, yes.

NORMAN: I bet she does. I bet she does.

HIM: She's very fond of cricket, as a matter of fact.

NORMAN: *(Leans across, looking away)* Who isn't, eh? Know what I mean? Likes games, likes games. Knew she would. Knew she would! Knew she would! She's been around, eh? Been around?

HIM: She's travelled. She's from Purley.

NORMAN: Oh ... oh. Say no more, say no more. Say no more – *Purley*, say no more. Purley, eh. Know what I mean, know what I mean? Say no more.

HIM: *(About to speak; can't think of anything to say)*

NORMAN: *(Leers, grinning)* Your wife interested in er ... *(Waggles head, leans across)* photographs, eh? Know what I mean? Photographs, 'he asked him knowingly'.

HIM: Photography.

NORMAN: Yes. Nudge nudge. Snap snap. Grin, grin, wink, wink, say no more.

HIM: Holiday snaps?

NORMAN: Could be, could be taken on holiday. Could be yes – swimming costumes. Know what I mean? Candid photography. Know what I mean, nudge nudge.

HIM: No, no we don't have a camera.

NORMAN: Oh. Still *(Slaps hands lightly twice)* Woah! Eh? Wo-oah! Eh?

HIM: Look, are you insinuating something?

NORMAN: Oh ... no ... no ... Yes.

HIM: Well?

NORMAN: Well. I mean. Er, I mean. You're a man of the world, aren't you ... I mean, er, you've er ... you've been there haven't you ... I mean you've been around ... eh?

HIM: What do you mean?

NORMAN: Well I mean like you've er ... you've done it ... I mean like, you know ... you've ... er ... you've slept ... with a lady.

HIM: Yes.

NORMAN: What's it like?

MONTY PYTHON'S FLYING CIRCUS

... still on the brain

'Can you give me something to lower my sex drive, please?' an old man asked his GP. 'But surely at your age it's all in the mind,' said the doctor. 'Yes,' agreed the patient. 'That's why I want it lower.'

Q. Why does it take one million sperm cells to fertilise one egg?
A. They won't stop to ask directions.

I admit, I have a tremendous sex drive. My boyfriend lives forty miles away.
PHYLLIS DILLER

'It says here sex is determined at conception. Maybe ours isn't determined enough.'
NICK HOBART

General Review of the Sex Situation

Woman wants monogamy:
Man delights in novelty.
Love is woman's moon and sun;
Man has other forms of fun.
Woman lives but in her lord;
Count to ten, and man is bored.
With this the gist and sum of it,
What earthly good can come of it?

DOROTHY PARKER

Be quiet, Sir! Begone, I say!
Lord bless us! How you romp and tear!
There!
I swear!
Now you have left my bosom bare!
I do not like such boisterous play,
So take that saucy hand away.
Why now, you're ruder than before –
Nay, I'll be hang'd if I comply –
Fye!
I'll cry!
Oh, – I can't bear it – I shall die! –
I vow I'll never see you more!
But – are you sure you've shut the door?

ANON (1785)

If intercourse causes thrombosis,
While continence gives you neurosis,
I'd prefer to expire
In the flames of desire
Than live on in a mess of psychosis.

ANON

SEX IS HEREDITARY.
IF YOUR PARENTS
DIDN'T HAVE IT, THE
CHANCES ARE YOU
WON'T EITHER.

'Will the gentleman who endowed the new biology mistress with the undesirable term "Sex Kitten" kindly step out here.'

CARL GILES

From: Napoleon Bonaparte, Emperor of the French; First Consul for Life; First Citizen of France; King in absentia of the United Kingdom of Great Britain and Ireland; Commander-in-Chief of the Imperial Grand Army of France; Commander of the First Military District; Commander of the Second Military District; Commander of the Third Military District; Colonel-in-Chief of the Old Guard; Head of the Deuxième Bureau; Controller of the Troisième Bureau; Commander of the Légion d'Honneur; Chief of the Imperial Order of St. Anthony; holder of the Médaille Militaire with oak leaves; holder of the award for meritorious service (with branches).

To: The Empress Josephine of all France; Queen in absentia of the United Kingdom of Great Britain and Ireland; Grand Dame of the Imperial Order of St. Anthony.
Tilsit, Saturday

Tonight, Josephine
Boney

From: The Empress Josephine of all France. Queen in absentia of the United Kingdom and Ireland; Grand Dame of the Imperial Order of St. Anthony.

To: Napoleon Bonaparte, Emperor of the French; First Consul for Life; First Citizen of France; King in absentia of the United Kingdom of Great Britain and Ireland; Commander-in-Chief of the Imperial Grand Army of France; Commander of the First Military District; Commander of the Second Military District; Commander of the Third Military District; Colonel-in-Chief of the Old Guard; Head of the Deuxième Bureau; Controller of the Troisième Bureau; Commander of the Légion d'Honneur; Chief of the Imperial Order of St. Anthony; holder of the Médaille Militaire with oak leaves; holder of the award for meritorious service (with branches).

Sorry, headache.
Josephine

MICHAEL GREEN

Ahem ... ask your father

THE FACTS OF LIFE

(Peter is sitting in a smart domestic drawing room. Enter Dudley, as a schoolboy.)

PETER (COOK): Is that you, Roger?

DUDLEY (MOORE): Yes, father.

PETER: There's a pot of tea in here for you, if you'd like some.

DUDLEY: That's very kind of you Sir, but I've just come in from rugger and I'm a bit grubby. I think I ought to go and have a shower first, Sir.

PETER: Well pour me a cup, there's a good chap, would you?

DUDLEY: Certainly Sir. Yes of course.

PETER: Thank you. How was school today?

DUDLEY: Oh, much as usual, thank you Sir, but I caught someone having a crafty smoke behind the wooden buildings. Had to give him rather a ticking off. Such a filthy habit you know Sir.

PETER: It's a filthy habit, Roger.

DUDLEY: There we are, Sir. Now if you'll excuse me.

PETER: Roger?

DUDLEY: Yes Sir?

PETER: Sit down. Roger, your mother and I were having a bit of a chat the other day and she thought it might be a good idea if I was to have a bit of a chat with you.

DUDLEY: A bit of a chat, Sir?

PETER: A bit of a chat, yes, Roger. Just a bit of a chat.

DUDLEY: What about, Sir?

PETER: Well, there's nothing to be worried about, Roger. It's just that, well, to be perfectly frank, how old are you?

DUDLEY: Well, to be perfectly frank, Sir, I'm coming up to eighteen.

PETER: Just coming up to eighteen?

DUDLEY: Well, on the verge.

PETER: On the verge of eighteen. Yes, well, I thought it might be a good idea to have a bit of a chat now, because I remember from my own experience that it was when I was just, you know, coming up to eighteen ...

DUDLEY: On the verge.

PETER: On the verge of it, that I first began to take a serious interest in the, in the opposite, the opposite number. Now I don't know, Roger, if you know anything about the method whereby you came to be brought about?

DUDLEY: Well Sir, some of the boys at school say very filthy things about it, Sir.

PETER: This is what I was worried about, and this is why I thought I'd have a bit of a chat, and explain absolutely frankly and openly the method whereby you and everybody in this world came to be. Roger, in order for you to be brought about, it was necessary for your mother and I to do something. In particular, it was necessary for your mother to sit on a chair. To sit on a chair, which I had recently vacated and which was still warm from my body. And then something very mysterious, rather wonderful and beautiful happened, and sure enough, four years later, you were born. There was nothing unhealthy about this, Roger. There's nothing unnatural. It's a beautiful thing in the right hands, and there's no need to think less of your mother because of it. She had to do it, she did it, and here you are.

DUDLEY: I must say it's very kind of you to tell me. One thing, actually, slightly alarms me. I was sitting in this very chair yesterday, Sir, and I vacated it, and the cat sat on it while it was still warm. And should we have it destroyed?

PETER: It's a lovely chair, Roger.

DUDLEY: The cat, Sir.

PETER: Destroyed? Oh no, Roger, you don't understand. This thing of which I speak can only happen between two peole who are married, and you're not married.

DUDLEY: Not yet anyway, Sir.

PETER: Not to the cat, in any case. Well, Roger, now you have this knowledge about chairs and warmth, I hope you'll use it wisely. And take no notice of your school friends, or what Uncle Bertie may say.

DUDLEY: Dirty Uncle Bertie they call him at school, Sir.

PETER: Dirty Uncle Bertie and they're right, Roger. Your Uncle Bertie is a dirty, dirty man. He's been living with us now for forty years, and it does seem a day too much. You know, if it hadn't been for your mother, Roger, I don't know where we'd have been. She's the only person who can really cope with Uncle Bertie. She's the only one who can really deal with him. I don't know if you realise this, Roger, but your mother even has to sleep in the same bed as Uncle Bertie, to prevent him getting up to anything in the night. If only there were more people like your mother, Roger.

DUDLEY: Well, I'm very pleased that you have told me this, Sir, because, as I say, I'm very glad that I don't have to believe all those filthy things that the boys at school say. And only yesterday Uncle Bertie said to me ...

PETER: Take no notice of Uncle Bertie, Roger. He's a sick, sick man and we should feel sorry for him.

DUDLEY: Well, I'll try, Sir. I wonder if I should take a cup of tea up to mother.

PETER: I wouldn't do that, Roger. She's upstairs at the moment, coping with Uncle Bertie.

DUDLEY: Poor Uncle Bertie.

PETER: Poor Uncle Bertie.

PETER COOK

PEOPLE & PLACES

PETER DREDGE

Funny foreigners

In Italy for thirty years under the Borgias they had warfare, terror, murder, bloodshed – they produced Michelangelo, Leonardo da Vinci and the Renaissance. In Switzerland they had brotherly love, five hundred years of democracy and peace, and what did they produce? The cuckoo clock.

HARRY LIME'S FINAL SPEECH, written allegedly by ORSON WELLES, in the film *THE THIRD MAN*

T. PARKES

I speak Esperanto like a native.

SPIKE MILLIGAN

Q. Where are the Seychelles?
A. On the sey shore.

What were the names of the two Mexican fire-fighting brothers? Hose A and Hose B.

Gesticulation: Any movement made by a foreigner.

BEACHCOMBER

The people who live in Paris are called Parasites.

SCHOOLBOY HOWLER

The French will only be united under the threat of danger. Nobody can simply bring together a country that has 265 cheeses.

CHARLES DE GAULLE

STREETS FULL OF WATER, PLEASE ADVISE.

ROBERT BENCHLEY, telegram on arriving in Venice

In America

A farmer was building a haystack to feed his cattle in the coming winter. Having run low on hay the previous winter, he decided to build it higher. After a while he sent his son to the Indian reservation to ask the chief what the winter would be like. The chief looked up and pronounced, 'Bad winter.' The son told his dad, whereupon the farmer built his haystack higher. Later the farmer sent his son to the reservation again for a weather update.

The chief looked up, gazed into the distance and pronounced, 'Bad, cold, snow.' The boy returned to his father with this information. The farmer built his haystack even higher. One more time, he sent his son back to the chief for the latest forecast. The chief looked up and surveyed the horizon. Then he announced, 'Winter cold, snow, heap bad.' The boy was so impressed he asked the old man how he could predict such things. The chief looked up, gazed into the distance and said, 'White man build big haystack.'

On the sixth day, God turned to the angel Gabriel and said, 'Today I am going to create a land called Canada. It will be a land of outstanding natural beauty, snow-capped mountains, beautiful blue lakes, forests of elk and moose, silver rivers full of salmon. With pure, clear air. I will make the country rich in oil and the people there shall prosper. They will be called Canadians, and become known as the friendliest people on earth.' 'Don't you think,' asked Gabriel, 'that you're being a bit over generous to one country?' 'Wait,' said God. 'You haven't yet seen the neighbours I'm going to land them with.'

I have just returned from Boston. It is the only thing to do if you find yourself up there.
FRED ALLEN

In America, there are two classes of travel – first class and with children.
ROBERT BENCHLEY

In the United States there is more space where nobody is than where anybody is. That is what makes America what it is.
GERTRUDE STEIN

The difference between Los Angeles and yoghurt, is that yoghurt has real culture.
TOM TAUSSIK

BARBER (MICHAEL PALIN): ... I didn't want to be a barber anyway. I wanted to be a lumberjack. Leaping from tree to tree as they float down the mighty rivers of British Columbia ...
(He is gradually straightening up with a visionary gleam in his eyes)
The giant redwood, the larch, the fir, the mighty scots pine.
(He tears off his barber's jacket, to reveal tartan shirt and lumberjack trousers underneath; as he speaks the lights dim behind him and a choir of Mounties is heard faintly in the distance)
The smell of fresh-cut timber! The crash of mighty trees! *(Moves to stand in front of back-drop of Canadian mountains and forests)* With my best girlie by my side ... *(A frail adoring blonde, the heroine of many a mountains film, or perhaps the rebel maid, rushes to his side and looks adoringly into his eyes)*
We'd sing ... sing ... sing. *The choir is loud by now and music as well.*

BARBER *(Singing)*: I'm a lumberjack and I'm OK,
I sleep all night and I work all day.
Lights come up to his left to reveal a choir of Mounties.

MOUNTIES CHOIR: He's a lumberjack and he's OK,
He sleeps all night and he works all day.

BARBER: I cut down trees, I eat my lunch,
I go to the lavatory.
On Wednesday I go shopping,
And have buttered scones for tea.

MOUNTIES CHOIR: He cuts down trees, he eats his lunch,
He goes to the lavatory.
On Wednesday he goes shopping,
And has buttered scones for tea.
He's a lumberjack and he's OK,
He sleeps all night and he works all day.

BARBER: I cut down trees, I skip and jump,
I like to press wild flowers.

I put on women's clothing
And hang around in bars.

MOUNTIES CHOIR: He cuts down trees, he skips and jumps,
He likes to press wild flowers.
He puts on women's clothing
And hangs around in bars ...?

During this last verse the choir has started to look uncomfortable but they brighten up as they go into the chorus.

MOUNTIES CHOIR: He's a lumberjack and he's OK,
He sleeps all night and he works all day.

BARBER: I cut down trees, I wear high heels,
Suspenders and a bra.
I wish I'd been a girlie,
Just like my dear Mama.

MOUNTIES CHOIR *(Starting lustily as usual but tailing off as they get to the third line)*
He cuts down trees, he wears high heels,
(Spoken rather than sung) Suspenders ... and a bra? ...
They all mumble. Music runs down. The girl looks horrified and bursts into tears. The choir start throwing rotten fruit at him.

GIRL (CONNIE BOOTH): Oh Bevis! And I thought you were so rugged.

MONTY PYTHON'S FLYING CIRCUS

All abroad!

'Two separate worlds, please.'
ED ARNO

An old English gentleman **checked in at a hotel** in Mexico. The receptionist, looking at his registration card, said pleasantly in English, '**Ah – you are a foreigner.**' 'Certainly not!' said the gentleman. 'I'm English!'

Holidaying in Arizona, a group of tourists spot a cowboy lying by the side of the road **with his ear to the ground. 'What's going on?' they ask. 'Two horses – one grey, one chestnut – are pulling a wagon carrying two men,' the cowboy says.** 'One man's shirt is red, the other's black. **They're heading east.' 'Wow!' says one of the tourists. 'You can tell all that just by listening to the ground?' 'No.' replies the cowboy. 'They just ran over me.'**

'Henry, you <u>must</u> see this!'
'Describe it to me.'
RICHARD DECKER

A Frenchman with a parrot perched on his shoulder **walked into a bar. The barman said,** 'Wow, that's really lovely. **Where did you get him?' 'In France,' the parrot replied. 'They've got millions of 'em over there.'**

'Coo-ee, darling! I'm just going to take the car out to the right-hand side of the road, for our holiday in France.'
FRANK R. GREY

A Russian spy was sent to Wales to make contact with a local sleeper, and he was told the password he had to use was, 'The eagles will fly tomorrow.' So he arrived at his destination, a small Welsh village, knocked on the door of a cottage and said to the woman who opened it, 'The eagles will fly tomorrow.' Immediately she said, 'No, you've come to the wrong house, love. You want number 8, other side of the road. That's where Jones the Spy lives.'

Two men are visiting London for the first time. They see a sign reading, 'Suits £15, Shirts £2, Trousers £3'. 'Wow,' says one. 'We should snap up some of these bargains then sell them at a profit when we get home.' His friend agrees and they go into the shop. 'Twenty suits, 50 shirts and 30 pairs of trousers, please,' says one of the men. 'You're not from round here, are you?' commented the assistant. 'No, I'm not,' answered the man. 'How did you know?' 'This is a dry-cleaner's,' the assistant replies.

Coming from the Soviet Union, I was not prepared for the huge variety of products available in UK supermarkets. On my first shopping trip, I saw powdered milk – you just add water and you get milk. Then I saw powdered orange juice – you just add water and you get orange juice. Then I saw baby powder and I thought to myself, What a country!

YAKOV SMIRNOFF

Ze Crazy Ingleeesh!

In the United Kingdom everything seems designed to put the invader off the track, in time of peace as much as in time of war. The camouflaging of street names and house numbers is, of course, a classic weapon employed by General Staffs the world over to disorient enemy parachutists. But the English have adapted it to peacetime purposes with an uncompromising rigour.

For any foreigner with a merely average memory it is next to impossible to keep engraved on it the full address of an Englishman living in the country. He may well succeed in retaining a part of –

Major W. Marmaduke Thompson
The Tower
Rough Hill Road
Marlborough Heights
Ploughbury
Hampshire

but, considering that none of this is pronounced as it is written, is it surprising that the visitor ends up by mislaying a good half of it?

The first thing I learned, on reaching Ploughbury, was that **Ploughbury was not there, but a little farther on at a place called Fortescue.** Coming to some heights – those of Marlborough as I ascertained from a passer by – I was lucky enough to run into a nameless lane which, I was courteously informed, was Rough Hill Road. This lane was bordered on each side by some fifty brick bungalows indistinguishable from one another save by the floral decoration in front of them.

In most countries, when they finish a house, **architects move on a little farther and build another that is different.** But in England, when they've finished one house, without wasting an inch of space, they promptly stick an identical one right next to it - with the same bricks, the same bay window, the same little garden, the same doorway and the same furniture. In fact, only when he sees his wife's face – and even then assuming he hasn't stopped at the local on the way – can an Englishman be sure he's really home.

PIERRE DANINOS, *THE LAND OF HIDE AND SEEK*

PEOPLE & PLACES
Travel in hope

'The trouble these days is that the jet-set is full of the people that I originally joined the jet-set to get away from!'
KEN PYNE

A skinflint wanted to take his children for a ride in a plane on the cheap. At the aerodrome, the man was shocked to find that the flight would cost £100. He tried haggling with the pilot, who eventually came up with a suggestion. 'I'll take you up for half an hour and as long as you don't cry out, I won't charge you a penny. But if you make so much as a sound I'll charge double.' Agreeing to the terms, they all jumped into the plane and took off. The pilot tried nosedives, tailspins, barrel rolls and every daredevil trick in the book, but none of his passengers made a single sound. 'You win,' said the pilot as they came in for landing. 'There's no charge. I'm amazed that you managed not to scream.' 'Well, I did come close once or twice,' admitted the father. 'Especially when you looped the loop and the kids fell out.'

'And this is us getting the tube to Heathrow.'
ROBERT THOMPSON

I am a traveller,

you are a tourist,

they are trippers.

ANON

It's hot ... too damn hot!

MAD DOGS AND ENGLISHMEN

In tropical climes there are certain times
   of day
When all the citizens retire
To tear their clothes off and perspire.
It's one of those rules that the greatest
   fools obey,
Because the sun is much too sultry
And one must avoid its ultry-violet ray.

Papalaka papalaka papalaka boo,
Papalaka papalaka papalaka boo,
Digariga digariga digariga doo,
Digariga digariga digariga doo.

The native grieve when the white men
   leave their huts,
Because they're obviously definitely nuts!

Mad dogs and Englishmen
Go out in the midday sun,
The Japanese don't care to.
The Chinese wouldn't dare to,
Hindoos and Argentines sleep firmly from
   twelve to one.
But Englishmen detest a siesta.
In the Philippines
There are lovely screens
To protect you from the glare.
In the Malay States
There are hats like plates
Which the Britishers won't wear.
At twelve noon
The natives swoon
And no further work is done.
But mad dogs and Englishmen
Go out in the midday sun.

It's such a surprise for the Eastern eyes
   to see
That though the English are effete,
They're quite impervious to heat,
When the white man rides every native
   hides in glee,
Because the simple creatures hope he
Will impale his solar topee on a tree.

Bolyboly bolyboly bolyboly baa,
Bolyboly bolyboly bolyboly baa,
Habaninny habaninny habaninny haa,
Habaninny habaninny habaninny haa.

It seems such a shame
When the English claim
The earth
That they give rise to such hilarity
   and mirth.

Mad dogs and Englishmen
Go out in the midday sun.
The toughest Burmese bandit
Can never understand it.
In Rangoon the heat of noon
Is just what the natives shun.
They put their Scotch or Rye down
And lie down.
In a jungle town
Where the sun beats down
To the rage of man and beast
The English garb
Of the English sahib
Merely gets a bit more creased.
In Bangkok
At twelve o'clock
They foam at the mouth and run,
But mad dogs and Englishmen
Go out in the midday sun.

Mad dogs and Englishmen
Go out in the midday sun.
The smallest Malay rabbit
Deplores this stupid habit.
In Hongkong
They strike a gong
And fire off a noonday gun
To reprimand each inmate
Who's in late.
In the mangrove swamps
Where the python romps
There is peace from twelve till two.
Even caribous
Lie around and snooze;
For there's nothing else to do.
In Bengal
To move at all
Is seldom, if ever done.
But mad dogs and Englishmen
Go out in the midday sun.

NOËL COWARD

PEOPLE & PLACES
Holiday hilarity

A girl in an office was extolling the virtues of her holiday destination to her friend. 'You ought to come with me. It's this great resort in Turkey. I had a terrific time last year – and I won the beauty contest.'
'No, thanks,' said her friend. 'I prefer crowded places.'

I stayed in this hotel in Majorca that overlooked the sea. Sadly, it also overlooked hygiene, good service and edible food.

A young lady is sunbathing on the hotel roof. Seeing she is alone, she discreetly peels off her swimsuit. In minutes, the manager rushes up. 'Madam, please cover yourself!' 'But there's no one else here,' she complains. 'And I am lying face down.' 'I know,' says the man. 'You're on the dining room skylight.'

Visiting a pub, a tourist was fascinated by a stuffed lion's head mounted on a plaque above a door behind the bar. 'Is there a story behind that magnificent trophy?' asked the tourist. 'That lion killed my wife,' replied the landlord grimly. 'Were you on safari?' 'No,' said the landlord. 'It fell on her head.'

While on holiday, a Swiss man asks two locals for some directions. 'Entschuldigung, sprechen sie Deutsch?' he asks. But the two locals look at him blankly. 'Excusez moi, parlez-vous Français?' he tries again. But the locals just continue to stare. 'Hablan ustedes Español?' Still nothing. The Swiss tourist is very unimpressed and drives off. 'You know,' says one local to the other, 'we should really try to learn a foreign language.' 'Why?' replied the other. 'He knew three and it didn't do him any good.'

Business on the Costa Brava is so bad this year that some of the hotels are stealing towels from their guests.

COLIN WHEELER

'Skimped a bit on the lifeboats, haven't they.'
DAVID MYERS

DO YOU SPEAK FRANGLAIS?

Into the face of the young man who sat on the terrace of the Hotel Magnifique at Cannes there had crept a look of furtive shame, the shifty hangdog look which announces that an Englishman is about to talk French. One of the things which Gertrude Butterwick had impressed upon Monty Bodkin when he left for this holiday on the Riviera was that he must be sure to practise his French, and Gertrude's word was law. So now, though he knew that it was going to make his nose tickle, he said:

'Er, garçon.'

'M'sieur?'

'Er, garçon, esker-vous avez un spot de l'encre et une pièce de papier – notepaper, vous savez – et une enveloppe et une plume?'

'Bien, m'sieur.'

The strain was too great. Monty relapsed into his native tongue. 'I want to write a letter,' he said. And having, like all lovers, rather a tendency to share his romance with the world, he would probably have added 'to the sweetest girl on earth', had not the waiter already bounded off like a retriever, to return a few moments later with the fixings. 'V'là, sir! Zere you are, sir,' said the waiter. He was engaged to a girl in Paris who had told him that when on the Riviera he must be sure to practise his English. 'Eenk – pin – pipper – enveloppe – and a liddle bit of bloddin-pipper.'

'Oh, merci,' said Monty, well pleased at this efficiency. 'Thanks, Right-ho.'

'Right-ho, m'sieur,' said the waiter.

P.G. WODEHOUSE, *THE LUCK OF THE BODKINS* (1935)

Scene Eight **French Farmhouse**

It is very late at night. The farmhouse is very run down, but with pretty possibilities, charming but rough. There are insects, mice, etc. It is very dusty, stocked as a holiday home – odd puzzles, games, packs of cards, lots of books, old furniture, original sink and kitchen, old gas cooker. There is the sound of a car pulling up outside. Headlights switch off. Farmhouse door opens, and Patsy and Ed stagger in through pouring rain with luggage. Patsy is scraping a squashed snail off her shoe. They switch on the light, and stand aghast. It is not quite what they had in mind. Patsy tries her best.

PATSY: It's gorgeous.

EDINA: After eight hours in that car with you, Pats, the local pissotière looked rather attractive. But this?! Shut up.

PATSY: Oh, shut up and sit down.

EDINA: Eight hours, Patsy. Well, that kind of knocks your ideas of wild nightlife in St Tropez on the head.

PATSY: It only took that long because you, Eddy, insisted on retracing the whole bloody route back to the airport every time I gave you a bloody instruction.

EDINA: We wouldn't have had to if you hadn't insisted that every village we'd been through was called Clochmerle.

PATSY: We'd been round in so many bloody circles, thanks to you, we might only be ten minutes from St Tropez.

EDINA: *(Sulkily)* I don't think so, Patsy. The sky lost that comforting orange glow a long way back, babe. *(She is wandering around inspecting the kitchen. She picks up a pan, screams and drops it.)* Cockroaches! Oh, my god,

and a mouse. Oh, my god. Oh, my god!

PATSY: Don't worry, darling. Where did they go?

She grabs a broom. There is a great deal of banging and flapping.

EDINA: Don't kill them. I'm a Buddhist. I could come back as one of those.

PATSY: Out they go. I think the cockroach had a coronary, darling.

EDINA: *(Slamming door shut)* Oh, god …

PATSY: Let's have a drink and fix something to eat.

EDINA: There are four pieces of old pasta and half a packet of French toast that defies eating at the best of times.

PATSY: *(Opens some drinks she's had from the plane.)* Here.

EDINA: I'm never going abroad again. Everywhere is riddled, infested with insects. They follow me everywhere from Tuscany to the Caribbean. Insects, insects, centipedes, snakes, mosquitoes, cockroaches. I look at pictures of luxurious mansions in Morocco and LA and I think, 'Yes, but how big are your spiders?' You never see a picture of Jane Seymour with a centipede hanging off her tiara. They bite me, Pats. They never bite you.

PATSY: The last one that bit me had to check in to the Betty Ford clinic.

EDINA: God, I hate France.

PATSY: *(Trying to make the best of it)* Look, Eds, we're in Provence. Everybody is coming to Provence. Tomorrow we'll stroll into the local village and buy croissants, fresh ground coffee, and local vino, a light white wine. We'll crack open whole baguettes and stuff them with Camembert and Brie. We'll wander to local markets and sniff melons. We'll sit outside in big straw hats, long shirts, slacks, and espadrilles. We'll look like Ava Gardner, and … *(She can't think of an Edina equivalent.)* … her companion.

There is a roll of thunder and the lights go out.

EDINA: Straw dogs!

PATSY: Don't panic. I've got a lighter.

EDINA: *(Ranting)* Why does this always happen? Only abroad! The suggestion of a thunderstorm and all the lights go out. Let's all join Europe so that the lights can go out – Sieg Heil … the Federal State!

PATSY: Shut up, Eddy. *(Lights a lighter. Lights a candle.)* What is the matter with you? You need a joint. We both need a joint.

EDINA: I haven't got any. Saffy flushed it. Everything. Haven't you got some?

PATSY: I was counting on you. I've got a bit of coke and some ecstasy.

EDINA: No one's taking ecstasy any more. *(Swigs the brandy.)* Let's go to bed.

CONTINUED OVERLEAF

Scene Ten **Farmhouse kitchen**

It is morning. A beautiful day makes the whole place look better. Sun is streaming through the windows. Patsy is standing looking out of the door. Edina enters spraying a huge can of fly spray, clutching a dustpan and brush.

EDINA: I'm sorry about the ozone layer, but this is a matter of survival. Pats, you go down the village. You know what we need.

PATSY: I don't know what we need.

EDINA: Darling! Bread, croissant, café, ouefs, milk, lots of lovely French things. I'll write it down for you. We need … *(Writes)* Bread …

PATSY: From the, er …?

EDINA: Baker, the painerie.

PATSY: Blancemangerie?

EDINA: No, franagerie. No, potage. No, that's soup. Oh, you'll see it. It'll be in the window. Boucherier is butcher, isn't it?

PATSY: Mangerie?

EDINA: No, look, ask. Où es c'est possible de comprends des pains? Right! What's milk?

PATSY: Let – late.

EDINA: Where do we get that from?

PATSY: Delicatessen?

EDINA: Vegetables à la grocerie. Right?

PATSY: You go.

EDINA: Oh all right. Will you ring and let Saffy and Bubble know we're here.

PATSY: I've tried. I can't work out the bloody code.

EDINA: What is it from LA? It must be the same.

PATSY: It doesn't work, and there isn't a book.

EDINA: Ring the operator.

PATSY: And say what?

EDINA: What's the code for England, Londra.

PATSY: I'll try when you've gone.

EDINA: I'm off.

PATSY: Got money?

EDINA: Yes, I've got a few five-hundred franc notes.

PATSY: Is that enough?

EDINA: Five-hundred pounds, Pats. *(Thinks)* I've got cards, too. I should be all right.

Edina ties on a huge straw hat over her Vivienne Westwood smock and leggings, and sets off …

JENNIFER SAUNDERS

PEOPLE & PLACES
Seaside sauciness

A crab and a lobster are secretly courting. Soon, the lobster tires of the lying and tells her father, who forbids her to see the crab. 'It'll never work,' he shouts. 'Crabs walk sideways and we walk straight!' 'Please,' she begs. 'Just meet him once. I know you'll like him.' Her father finally agrees and she runs off to share the good news. The crab is so excited he decides to surprise his beloved's family. He practises and practises until he can finally walk straight. On the big day he walks the entire way to the lobster's house as straight as he can. Standing on the porch, the lobster dad shouts to his daughter, 'I knew it. Here comes that crab and he's drunk!'

"I should like a swim, but I don't want to get my truncheon wet!"

"Sea Bathing is so good for my Arthritis"
"Well, you ain't got it under the water, you know!"

DONALD MCGILL

Discussing his recent summer holiday, one man says to his friend,
'I've just come back from a week on a caravan site in Poole.'
'In Dorset?' asked the other.
'Yes,' replied his friend. 'I would recommend it to anyone.'

MONTY PYTHON AND THE HOLY GRAIL –
ARTHUR OF THE BRITONS GETS THE BIRD

EXTERIOR. CASTLE WALLS. DAY.

Mist. Several seconds of it swirling about. Silence. Possibly, atmospheric music. Superimpose 'England AD 787'. After a few more seconds we hear hoofbeats in the distance. They come slowly closer. Then out of the mist comes KING ARTHUR followed by a SERVANT who is banging two halves of coconuts together. ARTHUR raises his hand.

ARTHUR: Whoa there!

SERVANT makes noises of horses halting, with a flourish. ARTHUR peers through the mist. Cut to shot from over his shoulder: castle (e.g. Bodium) rising out of the mist. On the castle battlements a SOLDIER is dimly seen. He peers down.

SOLDIER: Halt! Who goes there!

ARTHUR: It is I, Arthur, son of Uther Pendragon, from the Castle of Camelot, King of all Britons, defeater of the Saxons, Sovereign of all England.

Pause.

SOLDIER: Get away!

ARTHUR: I am ... And this is my trusty servant, Patsy. We have ridden the length and breadth of the land in search of Knights who will join our Court at Camelot. I must speak with your lord and master.

SOLDIER: What? Ridden on a horse?

ARTHUR: Yes.

SOLDIER: You're using coconuts.

ARTHUR: ... What?

SOLDIER: You're using two empty halves of coconuts and banging them together.

ARTHUR: *(Scornfully)* So? We have ridden since the snows of winter covered this land, through the Kingdom of Mercia.

SOLDIER: Where did you get the coconuts?

ARTHUR: Through ... we found them.

SOLDIER: Found them? In Mercia. The coconut's tropical.

ARTHUR: What do you mean?

SOLDIER: Well, this is a temperate zone.

ARTHUR: The swallow may fly south with the sun, or the house martin or the plover seek hot lands in winter, yet these are not strangers to our land.

A moment's pause.

SOLDIER: Are you suggesting coconuts migrate?

ARTHUR: Not at all. They could be carried.

SOLDIER: What? A swallow carrying a coconut?

ARTHUR: It could grip it by the husk ...

SOLDIER: It's not a question of where he grips it, it's a simple matter of weight – ratios ... a five-ounce bird could not hold a one-pound coconut.

ARTHUR: Well, it doesn't matter. Go and tell your master that Arthur from the Court of Camelot is here.

A slight pause. Swirling mist. Silence.

SOLDIER: Look! To maintain velocity a swallow needs to beat its wings four hundred and ninety-three times every second. Right?

ARTHUR: *(Irritated)* Please!

SOLDIER: Am I right?

ARTHUR: I'm not interested.

SECOND SOLDIER *(Who has loomed up on the battlements)*: It could be carried by an African swallow.

FIRST SOLDIER: Oh yes! An African swallow maybe ... but not by a European swallow. That's my point.

SECOND SOLDIER: Oh yes, I agree there.

ARTHUR: *(Losing patience)* Will you ask your master if he wants to join the Knights of Camelot?

FIRST SOLDIER: But then of course African swallows are non-migratory.

SECOND SOLDIER: Oh yes.

ARTHUR raises his eyes heavenwards and nods to PATSY. They turn and go off into the mist.

FIRST SOLDIER: So they wouldn't be able to bring a coconut back anyway.

The SOLDIERS' voices recede behind them.

SECOND SOLDIER: Wait a minute! Suppose two swallows carried it together?

FIRST SOLDIER: No, they'd have to have it on a line.

Stillness. Silence again.

MONTY PYTHON'S FLYING CIRCUS

PEOPLE & PLACES
Best of British

A young Scotsman left home and moved into his own flat. After a few weeks his parents rang to find out how he was. 'What are your neighbours like?' **asked his mother.** 'A bit strange,' he replied. 'On one side there's a man who keeps banging his head against the wall **and on the other,** a woman who just lies on the floor crying and moaning.' 'I'd keep yourself to yourself if I were you,' **advised his mother. 'Oh I do,' the man replied. 'I just stay in my room all day and play my bagpipes.'**

Did you hear about the Scotsman who had just washed his kilt and couldn't do a fling with it?

British modesty: Saying that, although we are superior to other peoples, we never mention that superiority.
BEACHCOMBER

I don't know what London's coming to – the higher the buildings the lower the morals.
NOËL COWARD

The shortest way out of Manchester is notoriously a bottle of gin.
WILLIAM BOLITHO

HOW TO SURVIVE IN LONDON

Keep out of throngs and public places where multitudes of people are – for saving your purse. The fingers of a number go beyond your sense of feeling. A tradesman's wife of the Exchange one day, when her husband was following some business in the city, desired him he would give her leave to go see a play, which she had not done in seven years. **He bade her take his apprentice along with her** and go, but especially to have a care of her purse, which she warranted him she would. Sitting in a box among some gallants and gallant wenches and returning when the play was done, **she returned to her husband and told him she had lost her purse.**

'Wife,' quoth he, 'did I not give you warning of it? How much money was there in it?'

Quoth she, 'Truly, four pieces, six shillings, and a silver toothpicker.'

Quoth her husband, 'Where did you put it?'

'Under my petticoat, between that and my smock.'

'What,' quoth he, 'did you feel nobody's hand there?'

'Yes,' quoth she, 'I felt one's hand there, but I did not think he had come for that.'

So much for the guard of the purse.

HENRY PEACHAM,
THE ART OF LIVING IN LONDON (1642)

FAWLTY TOWERS –
SEE TORQUAY, AND DIE

Mrs Richards – a deaf and batty guest at Fawlty Towers hotel – wants to make a complaint to the manager.

BASIL: Good morning, madam – can I help you?

MRS RICHARDS: Are you the manager?

BASIL: I am the *owner*, madam.

MRS RICHARDS: What?

BASIL: I am the owner.

MRS RICHARDS: I want to speak to the manager.

BASIL: I am the manager too.

MRS RICHARDS: What?

BASIL: I am the manager as well.

MANUEL: Manaher! Him manaher!

BASIL: Shut up!

MRS RICHARDS: Oh … you're Watt.

BASIL: … I'm the *manager*.

MRS RICHARDS: Watt?

BASIL: I'm … the … manager.

MRS RICHARDS: Yes, I know, you've just told me, what's the matter with you? Now listen to me. I've booked a room with a *bath*. When I book a room with a bath I expect to *get* a bath.

BASIL: You've *got* a bath.

MRS RICHARDS: I'm not paying seven pounds twenty pence per night plus VAT for a room without a bath.

BASIL: *(Opening the bathroom door) There* is your bath.

MRS RICHARDS: You call *that* a bath? It's not big enough to drown a mouse. It's disgraceful. *(She moves away to the window.)*

BASIL: *(Muttering)* I wish you were a mouse, I'd show you.

MRS RICHARDS: *(At the window, which has a nice view)* And another thing – I asked for a room with a view.

BASIL: *(To himself)* Deaf, mad and blind. *(Goes to window)* This is the view as far as I can remember, madam. Yes, this is it.

MRS RICHARDS: When I pay for a view I expect something more interesting than that.

BASIL: That is Torquay, madam.

MRS RICHARDS: Well, it's not good enough.

BASIL: Well ... may I ask what you were hoping to see out of a Torquay hotel bedroom window? Sydney Opera House perhaps? The Hanging Gardens of Babylon? Herds of wildebeeste sweeping majestically ...

MRS RICHARDS: Don't be silly. I expect to be able to see the sea.

BASIL: You *can* see the sea. It's over there between the land and the sky.

MRS RICHARDS: I'd need a telescope to see that.

BASIL: Well, may I suggest you consider moving to a hotel closer to the sea. Or preferably *in* it.

MRS RICHARDS: Now listen to me; I'm not satisfied, but I have decided to stay here. However, I shall expect a reduction.

BASIL: Why, because Krakatoa's not erupting at the moment?

JOHN CLEESE AND CONNIE BOOTH

Native nonsense

There was an old man on the Border,
Who lived in the utmost disorder;
He danced with the cat, and made tea in his hat,
Which vexed all the folks on the Border.

There was an Old Man of Dundee,
Who frequented the top of a tree;
When disturbed by the crows, he abruptly arose,
And exclaimed, I'll return to Dundee.'

There was a Young Lady of Ryde,
Whose shoe-strings were seldom untied;
She purchased some clogs, and some small spotty dogs,
And frequently walked about Ryde.

There was an Old Man of the Coast,
Who placidly sat on a post;
But when it was cold, he relinquished his hold,
And called for some hot buttered toast.

There was an Young Lady of Hull,
Who was chased by a virulent Bull;
But she seized on a spade, and called out – 'who's afraid!'
Which distracted that virulent Bull.

EDWARD LEAR, *A BOOK OF NONSENSE* (1845)

FROST OVER CHRISTMAS –
DO YOU KNOW HENDON AT ALL?

A party, JOHN (CLEESE) and RONNIE (CORBETT) stand with glasses, RONNIE is chatty and JOHN pleasantly tolerant ...

RONNIE: What do you do?

JOHN: I'm the world's leading authority on Impressionist painting.

RONNIE: Oh, yes? I'm an accountant ... chartered accountant. *(Pause)* Where do you ... er ... live?

JOHN: I live in a converted monastery in the Outer Hebrides.

RONNIE: Really? How interesting ... I live in Hendon. *(Pause)* Is your wife here tonight?

JOHN: No ... she's in Vietnam ... fighting.

RONNIE: How fascinating ... Do you know Hendon at all?

JOHN: I passed through it once ... when I was being kidnapped by Russian agents.

RONNIE: Really? Well, I never! Where were they taking you?

JOHN: Oh, they had a frigate waiting for me in the Thames estuary.

RONNIE: *(Excitedly)* Really! Then you must have gone down Ulverston Road! Past our house! D'you remember just after the baths?

JOHN: Well, I wouldn't know – they'd drugged me pretty heavily with hypertalcin metrathecane.

RONNIE: Good heavens ... and what does that do?

JOHN: It paralyses the memory.

RONNIE: Does it affect your eyesight?

JOHN: Oh, yes. You're totally unconscious.

RONNIE: Oh ... then you probably didn't see our house. It's number 37 on the corner ... You must drop in sometime.

JOHN: Well, that's very kind of you, but I'm afraid I won't be able to. I'm going to prison.

RONNIE: Really? Not anywhere in Hendon, I suppose?

JOHN: No, it's in Guatemala. It's just a currency offence I committed when I was over there investigating a man-eating cactus they'd discovered.

RONNIE: You went all the way to Guatemala to see cactuses?

JOHN: Yes. I had some pretty horrible adventures. I was nearly trampled to death by a herd of rogue buffaloes.

RONNIE: Just looking for cactuses. If only I'd known ... they've just had a display of them at Hendon Central Library. *(Pause)* You know it's really fascinating talking to you, because it's not everyone that's interested in Hendon.

JOHN: I'll show you something that'll interest you. *(JOHN pulls out a huge prayer mat or shawl.)* Have you seen one of these before?

RONNIE: No, no, I haven't.

JOHN: D'you know what it is?

RONNIE: *(Quite caught up by now)* No.

JOHN: It's a Tibetan prayer shawl. Do you know how I got it?

RONNIE: *(Engrossed)* No, I don't.

JOHN: It was given to me by the chief slave-girl of the High Commander of the Tibetan Army. Oh! She was a beauty – her hair was black as a raven's wings, and one evening at the feast of Ramsit Asi, the all-powerful God of Light, when 10,000 bullocks are sacrificed on the mountain, she crept into my room, filling it with a delicious fragrance, and she cast aside her tribal robe and her black hair spilled over her delicate pale skin ... as she climbed into my bed ...

RONNIE: Really?

JOHN: Mmmmmmm ... *She* came from Hendon.

MICHAEL PALIN
AND TERRY JONES

people & places

I do beg your pardon, I'm British

This actually did happen to a real person, and the real person was me. This was April, 1976, in Cambridge. I had gone to catch a train. I was a bit early so I went to get myself a newspaper, a cup of coffee and a packet of biscuits. I went and sat at a table. I want you to picture the scene. It's very important that you get this clear in your mind: here's the table, newspaper, cup of coffee, packet of biscuits. There's a guy sitting opposite me, perfectly ordinary-looking guy wearing a business suit, carrying a briefcase. It didn't look like he was going to do anything weird. What he did was this: he suddenly leant across, picked up the packet of biscuits, tore it open, took one out and ate it.

Now this, I have to say, is the sort of thing the British are very bad at dealing with. There's nothing in our background, upbringing or education that teaches you how to deal with someone who in broad daylight had just stolen your biscuits. You know what would happen if this had been South Central Los Angeles. There would have very quickly been gunfire, helicopters coming in, CNN, you know ... But in the end, I did what any red-blooded Englishman would have done: I ignored it.

I stared at the newspaper, took a sip of coffee, attempted a clue in the crossword, couldn't do anything, and thought, what am I going to do? In the end I thought, nothing for it, I'll just have to go for it, and I tried very hard not to notice the fact that the packet was already mysteriously opened. I took out a biscuit for myself. I thought, that's settled him. But it hadn't, because a moment or two later he did it again. He took another biscuit. Having not mentioned it the first time, it was somehow even harder to raise the subject the second time around. 'Excuse me, I couldn't help but notice ...' I mean, it doesn't really work.

We went through the whole packet like this. When I say the whole packet I mean there were only about eight biscuits but it felt like a lifetime. I took one, he took one, I took one, he took one. Finally, when we got to the end, he stood up and walked away. Well, we exchanged meaningful looks, then he walked away and I breathed a sigh of relief and sat back. A moment or two later, the train was coming in, so I tossed back the rest of my coffee, stood up, picked up the newspaper, and underneath the newspaper ... were my biscuits.

The thing I like particularly about this story is the sensation that somewhere in England there has been wandering round for a quarter of a century a perfectly ordinary guy with the exact same story; only he doesn't have the punchline.

DOUGLAS ADAMS, *THE SALMON OF DOUBT: HITCHHIKING THE GALAXY ONE LAST TIME*

BLACKADDER'S LODGINGS

Blackadder is working and fed up. It is a gloriously sunny day outside, and the roar of a crowd, which annoys Blackadder even more, shows there is some kind of public holiday going on.
  Percy pops his head round the door. He is dressed in merry gear, with horns on his head and looking suspiciously like a morris dancer. He is very happy and excited.

PERCY: Coming?

BLACKADDER: No.

PERCY: It'll be a once-in-a-lifetime experience.

BLACKADDER: No it won't.

Blackadder slams the door in Percy's face. Another knock. Percy reappears.

PERCY: Everybody's going.

BLACKADDER: Don't exaggerate, Percy. I'm not going. Mrs Miggins from the pie shop isn't going.

PERCY: My lord, you are cruel. You know perfectly well that Mrs Miggins is paralysed from the nose down. And besides, she is honouring the occasion in her own special way by baking a great commemorative pie in the shape of an enormous ... pie.

BLACKADDER: What an imagination that woman has.

PERCY: Oh, come on, Edmund. The greatest explorer of our age is coming home. The streets have never been so gay. Women are laughing, children are singing. Oh, look, look, there's a man being indecently assaulted by nine foreign sailors and he's still got a smile on his face.

CONTINUED OVERLEAF

BLACKADDER: Look, Percy, the return of Sir Walter 'Oo what a big ship I've got' Raleigh is a matter of supreme indifference to me.

Now that is too much for Percy.

PERCY: If you're not careful, all the children will dance about outside your window singing 'sour puss' and 'grumpy face'. And you wouldn't want that, would you?

BLACKADDER: I believe I could survive it. Now Percy, get out before I cut your head off, scoop out the insides and give it to your mother as a vase.

He guides Percy out and slams the door on him.

What a clot. The most absurdly dressed creature in Christendom.

Baldrick enters. He has also made an effort to look nautical, with two little oars sticking out of his hat like antlers.

With one exception.

BALDRICK: My lord?

BLACKADDER: Baldrick, you look like a deer.

BALDRICK: Thank you, my lord. You look a bit of a duckie yourself.

BLACKADDER: Oh, God. What do you want?

BALDRICK: I was wondering if I might have the afternoon off.

BLACKADDER: Of course not. Who do you think you are? Wat Tyler? You can have the afternoon off when you die. Not before.

BALDRICK: But I want to cheer brave Sir Walter home. Oh, dear sir, on a day like today, I feel so proud to be a member of the greatest kingdom in the world.

BLACKADDER: And doubtless many other members of the animal kingdom feel the same way, Baldrick.

There is another roar from the street.

Oh, look, will you shut up. Bloody explorers, ponce off to Mumbo Jumbo land, come home with a tropical disease, a sun-tan and a bag of brown lumpy things, and Bob's your uncle, everyone's got a picture of them in the lavatory. I mean, what about the people who do all the work?

BALDRICK: The servants.

BLACKADDER: No, me. I'm the people who do all the work. I mean, look at this, what is it?

He picks up a potato.

BALDRICK: I'm surprised you've forgotten, my lord.

BLACKADDER: I haven't forgotten. It's a rhetorical question.

BALDRICK: No. It's a potato.

BLACKADDER: Look, to you it's a potato, to me it's a potato, but to Sir Walter bloody Raleigh it's country estates, fine carriages, and as many girls as his tongue can cope with. He's making a fortune out of the things: people are smoking them, building houses out of them. They'll be eating them next.

BALDRICK: Stranger things have happened.

BLACKADDER: Well, exactly.

BALDRICK: That horse becoming pope.

BLACKADDER: For one.

There is a knock on an outer door.

Oh, God.

Baldrick goes to open the door.

Probably some berk with a parrot on his shoulder selling plaster gnomes of Sir Francis Drake and his Golden Behind.

A child is heard from outside.

CHILD: Soar puss, grumpy face, sour puss, grumpy face, sour puss, grumpy face.

BLACKADDER: Right. That does it. *Blackadder shoots an arrow out of the window, as Melchett enters. The child screams, seriously wounded.*

CHILD: Mummy!

BLACKADDER: And another thing. Why aren't you at school?

MELCHETT: Ah, Blackadder: started talking to yourself, I see?

BLACKADDER: Yes, it's the only way I can be sure of intelligent conversation. What do you want?

MELCHETT: Well, I just looked in on my way to the palace to welcome Sir Walter home. I wondered if you'd care to accompany me?

BLACKADDER: I don't think I'll bother, actually. Three hours of bluff seaman's talk about picking the weevils out of biscuits and drinking urine is not my idea of entertainment.

MELCHETT: As you wish. *(To Baldrick)* Servant, my hat.

Baldrick exits. Melchett opens a little silver box he is carrying and offers its contents to Blackadder.

Potato?

They are raw.

BLACKADDER: No thanks. I don't.

RICHARD CURTIS AND BEN ELTON

MONEY MATTERS

I wish
I could afford
to be broke

EASIER
OVERDRAFT

MEL CALMAN

Don't bank on it!

I'd love to work in a bank. They've got the two things I really like in life – money and holidays.

A woman with a £50 note stuck in each ear goes into a building society and says she has an appointment with the manager. 'Oh yes,' says the manager when he is informed of the woman's arrival. 'She's got £100 in arrears.'

**A man walks into a bank and asks to cash a cheque.
The cashier says, 'Yes, that's fine, but you'll have to identify yourself.'
The man looks in the mirror and says, 'Yes, that's me all right.'**

'I'm having an out-of-money experience.'
BERNARD SCHOENBAUM

'Give me all the money, or you're geography!' said the armed robber to the cashier. 'Don't you mean history?' queried the cashier. 'Don't change the subject!' snapped the robber.

CHARLES PEATTIE AND RUSSELL TAYLOR

Lots of lovely cash!

MONTY PYTHON – THE MONEY PROGRAMME

Opening title sequence and signature tune for 'The Money Programme'. Set with presenter and two guests. Close up on presenter.

PRESENTER (ERIC IDLE): Good evening and welcome to 'The Money Programme'. Tonight on 'The Money Programme', we're going to look at money. Lots of it. On film and in the studio. Some of it in nice piles, others in lovely clanky bits of loose change, some of it neatly counted into fat little hundreds, *(Starting to get excited)* delicate fivers stuffed into bulging wallets, nice crisp clean cheques, pert pieces of copper coinage thrust deep into trouser pockets, romantic foreign money rolling against the thigh with rough familiarity, *(Starting to get over-excited)* beautiful wayward curlicued banknotes, filigree copperplating cheek by jowl with tumbling hexagonal milled edges, rubbing gently against the terse leather of beautifully balanced bank books. *(Collects himself)* I'm sorry. But I love money. All money. I've always wanted money. *(Getting worked up again)* To handle. To touch. The smell of the rain-washed florin. The lure of the lira.

(Standing on the desk) The glitter and the glory of the guinea. The romance of the rouble. The feel of the franc, the heel of the Deutschmark, the cold antiseptic sting of the Swiss franc, and the sun-burned splendour of the Australian dollar.

(Sings to piano accompaniment) I've got ninety thousand pounds in my pyjamas.
I've got forty thousand French francs in my fridge.
I've got lots and lots of lira.
Now the Deutschmark's getting dearer.
And my dollar bills would buy the Brooklyn Bridge.

Five singers (male) in Welsh (women's) national costume come on. A Welsh harpist joins them.

ALL: There is nothing quite as wonderful as money,
There is nothing quite as beautiful as cash,
Some people say it's folly
But I'd rather have the lolly
With money you can make a smash.

PRESENTER: There is nothing quite as wonderful as money
There is nothing like a newly minted pound

ALL: Everyone must hanker
For the butchness of a banker
It's accountancy that makes the world go round.

PRESENTER: You can keep your Marxist ways
For it's only just a phase.

ALL: For its money, money, money,
Makes the world go round.

(A shower of paper notes descends.)

Money, money, money, money, money, money!

MONTY PYTHON'S FLYING CIRCUS

Cooking the books

A woman went to the doctor, who broke to her the dreadful news that she only had six months to live. 'That's terrible, doctor. What should I do?'
'I suggest you marry an accountant.'
'Why? Will that make me live longer?'
'No. But it will seem longer.'

'My company is looking for a new accountant.'
'But didn't you just hire one last week?'
'Yes, and that's the one we're looking for.'

'We are neither hunters nor gatherers. We are accountants.'

S. GROSS

'I'm so sorry, but I've decided to find a new accountant.'

NAF

A firm had advertised for a new accountant and they reduced the candidates to a shortlist of three. At his final interview, the first candidate was asked, 'What's two plus two?'
'Four?' he replied.
At his interview the second was asked the same question, and he also said, 'Four?'
Then the third candidate was invited in and asked, 'What's two plus two?'
He replied, 'What do you want it to be?'
He got the job.

RISING DAMP –
A FOOL AND HIS MONEY

*Interior. Attic flat. Morning.
Alan is reading. Rigsby backs into room
clutching the cat. He peers cautiously
around the door.*

ALAN: *(Stares)* What's the matter,
Rigsby?

RIGSBY: I'm trying to avoid Miss Jones.

ALAN: I don't believe it!

RIGSBY: She's got a collecting tin. I
could hear her rattling it in the hall. If
I hadn't had my plimsolls on she'd have
caught me.

ALAN: So you've come to hide up here.
I always knew you were mean, Rigsby.

RIGSBY: I'm not mean – it's just that I'm
a bit short this week, that's all. It isn't
as if she's the first – they've already
been round for 'our feathered friends'.

ALAN: I bet they didn't get anything.

RIGSBY: What do you mean? Who goes
out there every winter and breaks the
ice on the bird bath? Who lavishes his
bacon rind on them? *(Frowns)* Not that
they appreciate it. They just sit in a line
waiting for me to wax the Cortina.
You'd think if I was going to feed one
end they'd show a bit of respect at the
other. The trouble is everyone takes
advantage of my generous nature.

ALAN: Your generous nature! You
haven't got a generous nature. You
spent all last Christmas heating up
pennies for the carol singers.

RIGSBY: That's a lie.

ALAN: And if you're so generous – why
do you always cross the road when you
see a flag seller?

RIGSBY: Yes – well, there's an
explanation for that. I had a very nasty
experience with a flag seller. I had a
lifeboat flag stuck straight through my
chest – set up an infection. They owe
me a few deep sea rescues that lot do.
Mind you, animals have always been
my main concern. I was quite big in
the Tailwaggers at one time.

ALAN: I didn't know that.

RIGSBY: Oh yes – there are quite a few
tails wagging today – thanks to me.
Remember that dog down the road?
That skulking, vicious brute – no one
would go near him. Who befriended
him? Who put his hand out to that
animal?

ALAN: You did, Rigsby. He bit you,
didn't he?

RIGSBY: *(Frowns)* Yes, well, you don't
expect gratitude – you do it because it
has to be done.

ALAN: What's Ruth collecting for
anyway?

RIGSBY: *(Confidentially)* I'm not sure –
but I think it's people.

ALAN: *(Laughs)* Ah, that explains it.

RIGSBY: What do you mean?

ALAN: Well, you don't like people.

RIGSBY: I've got nothing against people –

ALAN: Oh, you'd give to animals because they're soft and cuddly –

RIGSBY: I give to cancer.

ALAN: Only because you think you might get it.

RIGSBY: No, I don't.

ALAN: What about the time you came up here clutching your throat? Thought you'd got a growth. You were nearly wetting yourself – it was only your adam's apple.

RIGSBY: Look, I've got nothing against people but I'm a poor man. I can only give so much – and she'll expect more for people.

ALAN: You don't give that much, Rigsby. I notice you always cover the money with your fingers when you put it in. You don't let anyone see it.

RIGSBY: Of course I don't. You're not supposed to. That's your bad breeding showing that is. Just because you go around making an exhibition of yourself – covering people with flour, smashing up pianos, seeing how many you can squeeze into a phone box. At least I've got a bit of dignity.

ALAN: Well, you don't look very dignified at the moment – skulking up here.

RIGSBY: I'm not skulking, I'm skint. Look at me. I'm the one she should be collecting for. I've hardly got a button left on this jacket.

ALAN: I wondered what you'd been putting in the tins.

ERIC CHAPPELL

Coming into money

A miser called his doctor, lawyer and minister to his death bed. 'When I die I want to take my money with me,' said the miser. 'So I'm going to ask each of you to take one of these envelopes, each containing £15,000 in cash, and throw them into the grave at my funeral.' The men did as they were told, but later the minister confessed that he had kept £5000 for the church and thrown in the rest. 'I'm building a new surgery,' admitted the doctor, 'so I kept £10,000 and only threw in £5000.' 'I'm ashamed of you both!' scolded the lawyer. 'I threw in a cheque for the full amount.'

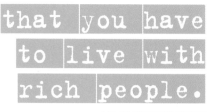

It is the wretchedness of being rich that you have to live with rich people.

LOGAN PEARSALL SMITH

DESPITE WINNING THE LOTTERY, THEY STILL REMEMBERED THEIR OLD FRIENDS

STEVE BEST

SHE: **Do you only love me because my Daddy left me a fortune?**

HE: **No. I'd love you whoever had left you the fortune.**

THESE SYMPTOMS YOU'RE COMPLAINING OF, BRIDGET... ARE YOU SURE?

I DON'T WANT TO BELIEVE IT, PENNY, BUT THEY ALL POINT TO ONE THING...

THE NAUSEA AND LISTLESSNESS, THE THROWING UP IN THE MORNINGS, THE HOT FLUSHES AND RAPID BREATHING... THE NEED TO GO TO THE LOO FREQUENTLY... OBVIOUSLY IT'S TOO EARLY TO SAY BUT...

BUT YOU THINK YOU AND CLIVE MAY HAVE A LITTLE ONE ON THE WAY?

YES...

AND FROM THE SEVERITY OF HIS SYMPTOMS MY GUESS IS THAT CLIVE KNOWS IT'S GOING TO BE HIS TINIEST WEENIEST LITTLE CHRISTMAS BONUS EVER...

OH DEAR.

CHARLES PEATTIE AND RUSSELL TAYLOR

An insurance salesman was trying to persuade a young wife to take out a policy on her husband's life **and working round to the subject rather gingerly. She didn't seem to understand, so he tried a more direct approach. 'Look at it this way.** If your husband died tomorrow, what would you get?' **'Oh,' she said, 'probably a budgie.'**

One of the shortest wills ever written read:
'Being of sound mind, I spent all my money.'

A woman left her husband because he had a will of his own – and it wasn't made out to her.

The rich man and his daughter are soon parted.
KIN HUBBARD

'Hello. Oh, sorry. I must have dialled my salary by mistake.'
MATT

Looking for Mr Right

It is a truth universally acknowledged, that a single man in possession of a good fortune, must be in want of a wife.

However little known the feelings or views of such a man may be on his first entering a neighbourhood, this truth is so well fixed in the minds of the surrounding families, that he is considered as the rightful property of some one or other of their daughters.

'My dear Mr. Bennet,' said his lady to him one day, 'have you heard that Netherfield Park is let at last?'

Mr. Bennet replied that he had not.

'But it is,' returned she; 'for Mrs. Long has just been here, and she told me all about it.'

Mr. Bennet made no answer.

'Do not you want to know who has taken it?' cried his wife impatiently.

'*You* want to tell me, and I have no objection to hearing it.'

This was invitation enough.

'Why, my dear, you must know, Mrs. Long says that Netherfield is taken by a young man of large fortune from the north of England; that he came down on Monday in a chaise and four to see the place, and was so much delighted with it that he agreed with Mr. Morris immediately; that he is to take possession before Michaelmas, and some of his servants are to be in the house by the end of next week.'

'What is his name?'

'Bingley.'

'Is he married or single?'

'Oh! single, my dear, to be sure! A single man of large fortune; four or five thousand a year. What a fine thing for our girls!'

'How so? how can it affect them?'

'My dear Mr. Bennet,' replied his wife, 'how can you be so tiresome! You must know that I am thinking of his marrying one of them.'

'Is that his design in settling here?'

'Design! nonsense, how can you talk so! But it is very likely that he *may* fall in love with one of them, and therefore you must visit him as soon as he comes.'

'I see no occasion for that. You and the girls may go, or you may send them by themselves, which perhaps will be still better, for as you are as handsome as any of them, Mr. Bingley might like you the best of the party.'

'My dear, you flatter me. I certainly *have* had my share of beauty, but I do not pretend to be any thing extraordinary now. When a woman has five grown up daughters, she ought to give over thinking of her own beauty.'

'In such cases, a woman has not often much beauty to think of.'

'But, my dear, you must indeed go and see Mr. Bingley when he comes into the neighbourhood.'

'It is more than I engage for, I assure you.'

'But consider your daughters. Only think what an establishment it would be for one of them. Sir William and Lady Lucas are determined to go, merely on that account, for in general you know they visit no new comers. Indeed you must go, for it will be impossible for *us* to visit him, if you do not.'

'You are over scrupulous surely. I dare say Mr. Bingley will be very glad to see you: and I will send a few lines by you to assure him of my hearty consent to his marrying which ever he chuses of the girls; though I must throw in a good word for my little Lizzy.'

'I desire you will do no such thing. Lizzy is not a bit better than the others; and I am sure she is not half so handsome as Jane, nor half so good humoured as Lydia. But you are always giving *her* the preference.'

'They have none of them much to recommend them,' replied he; 'they are all silly and ignorant like other girls; but Lizzy has something more of quickness than her sisters.'

'Mr. Bennet, how can you abuse your own children in such a way? You take delight in vexing me. You have no compassion on my poor nerves.'

'You mistake me, my dear. I have a high respect for your nerves. They are my old friends. I have heard you mention them with consideration these twenty years at least.'

'Ah! you do not know what I suffer.'

'But I hope you will get over it, and live to see many young men of four thousand a year come into the neighbourhood.'

'It will be no use to us, if twenty such should come since you will not visit them.'

'Depend upon it, my dear, that when there are twenty, I will visit them all.'

Mr. Bennet was so odd a mixture of quick parts, sarcastic humour, reserve, and caprice, that the experience of three and twenty years had been insufficient to make his wife understand his character. *Her* mind was less difficult to develope. She was a woman of mean understanding, little information, and uncertain temper. When she was discontented she fancied herself nervous. The business of her life was to get her daughters married; its solace was visiting and news.

JANE AUSTEN, *PRIDE AND PREJUDICE*

money matters

MONEY MATTERS

Money madness

Money couldn't buy you friends, but you get a better class of enemy.

SPIKE MILLIGAN

Jack stumbled into the house. 'What's wrong?' asked his wife. 'I had a great idea,' he gasped, smiling proudly. 'I ran all the way home behind the bus and saved myself 75 pence.' His wife frowned. 'That's just like you, Jack, always thinking small,' she said, shaking her head. 'Why didn't you run behind a taxi and save yourself £10?'

The patient walked into the doctor's surgery: 'You've got to help me, Doc. It's my ear. There's something in there.' 'Let's have a look,' said the GP. 'My goodness, you're right. There's money inside.' The doctor proceeded to pull out a fifty-pound note. 'I don't believe it,' the practitioner exclaimed, 'there's more in there.' Out came another fifty, a twenty and some tens. Finally all the notes had been removed. The doctor counted the money: 'One thousand, nine hundred and ninety pounds.' 'Ah, yes, that sounds about right,' nodded the patient. 'I knew I wasn't feeling two grand.'

'It's my fervent hope, Fernbaugh, that these are meaningless statistics.'

LEO CULLUM

The safest way to double your money is to fold it over once and put it in your pocket.

KIN HUBBARD

141

'Mmm, I just love to run my fingers through a man's wallet.'
EDWARD MCLACHLAN

CUSTOMER: Look, I bought this shirt yesterday and when I got it back home I found this huge great rip in the back. I want my money back.
SHOP ASSISTANT: I'm afraid we don't give refunds, sir.
CUSTOMER: But the notice in your window says, 'MONEY REFUNDED IF NOT SATISFACTORY'.
SHOP ASSISTANT: It certainly does, sir, but there was nothing wrong with your money.

I have enough money to last me the rest of my life, unless I buy something.
JACKIE MASON

REG SMYTHE, *ANDY CAPP*

The boy done good!

Members of the Literary Society, meeting to discuss the village play, have heard William Brown whistling outside the window. They think his whistle is just the thing to imitate the 'wind' for their latest theatrical performance.

William was proud of his whistle and flattered to be thus asked to perform in public. He paused a minute to gather his forces together, drew in his breath, then emitted a sound that would have done credit to a factory syren.

Miss Georgine Hammersley screamed. Miss Gwladwyn, who was poised girlishly on the arm of her chair, lost her balance and fell on to the floor. Mrs Bruce Monkton-Bruce clapped her hands to her ears with a moan of agony and Miss Greene-Joanes lay back in her chair in a dead faint, from which, however, as no one took any notice of her, she quickly recovered. William, immensely flattered by this reception of his performance, murmered modestly:

'I can do a better one still this way,' and proceeded to put a finger into each corner of his mouth and to draw in his breath for another blast.

With great presence of mind, Mrs Bruce Monkton-Bruce managed to put her hand across his face just in time.

'No, William,' she said brokenly, 'not like that – not like that –'

'I warn you,' Miss Greene-Joanes, in a shrill, trembling voice, 'I shall have hysterics if he does it again. I've already fainted,' she went on, in a reproachful voice, 'but nobody noticed me. I won't be answerable for what happens to me if that boy stays in the room a minute longer.'

'Send him away,' moaned Miss Featherstone, 'and let's *imagine* the wind.'

'Let's leave it to chance,' pleaded Miss Greene-Joanes. 'I can't bear it again. There – there may be a *natural* wind that night. It's quite possible.'

'William,' said Mrs. Bruce Monkton-Bruce, weakly, 'it was a gentle whistle we wanted to hear. A whistle like – like – like the wind in the distance. A *long* way in the distance, William.'

William emitted a gentle, drawn-out, mournful whistle. It represented perfectly the distant moaning of the wind. His stricken audience recovered and gave a gasp of amazement and delight.

'That was *very* nice,' said Mrs Bruce Monkton-Bruce.

William, cheered and flattered by her praise, said: 'I'll do it a bit nearer than that now,' and again gathered his forces for the effort.

'No, William,' said Mrs Bruce Monkton-Bruce again stopping him just in time. 'That's as near as we want. That's *just* what we want … Now, William, we are going to get up a little play, and during the play the wind is supposed to be heard right in the distance – a long, *long* way in the distance, William. The wind is supposed to be a *very* distant one indeed, William. Perhaps for a very great treat we'll let you make that wind, William.'

William's mind worked quickly. The apparently insoluble problem was still with him. He saw a means, not to solve it indeed, but to make it a little less insoluble. Assuming his most sphinxlike expression he said unblushingly, unblinkingly:

'Well, of course – that'll take up a good deal of my time. I dunno *quite* as I can spare all that time.'

They were amazed at his effrontery and at the same time his astounding and unexpected reluctance to accept the post of wind-maker increased the desirability of his whistle in their eyes.

'Of course, William,' said Mrs Bruce Monkton-Bruce in cold reproach, 'if you don't want to help in a good cause like this –'. Wisely she kept the exact nature of the good cause vague.

'Oh, I don' mind *helpin'*,' said William; 'all I meant was that it'd probably be takin' up a good deal of my time when I might be doin' useful things for other people. F'rinstance, I often pump up my uncle's motor tyres for him.' William's face became so expressionless as to border on the imbecile as he added: 'He always gives me sixpence for doing that.'

There was a short silence and then Mrs Bruce Monkton-Bruce said with great dignity:

'We will, of course, be pleased to give you sixpence for being the wind and any other little noises that may come into the play, William.'

'Thank you,' said William, concealing his delight beneath a tone of calm indifference. Sixpence ... it was something to start from. William was such an optimist that with the first sixpence the whole fund seemed suddenly to be assured to him … He could do something else for someone else and get another sixpence and that would be a shilling, and, well, if he kept on doing things for people for sixpence he'd soon have enough money to buy the football.

Optimistically he ignored the fact that most people expected him to do things for them for nothing.

RICHMAL CROMPTON, *WILLIAM—THE GOOD* **(1928)**

More money madness

Travelling on a plane was a man who was proud of his intelligence. When he discovered that the person sitting next to him was a student, he suggested they think up some riddles to pass the time. 'If you can't answer mine, you must give me £5,' he said. 'And if I can't answer yours, I'll give you £5.' 'OK,' said the student. 'But as you're older and wiser than me, it's only fair that if I can't answer I should give you £2.' 'Agreed,' said the man, 'and you can go first.' The student then asked: 'What has six feet on the land and only three feet when swimming?' The man thought for a very long time about this, but reluctantly he had to concede defeat. 'Here's your £5,' he said. 'What's the answer?' 'I don't know,' said the student. 'Here's your £2.'

'Can you keep a secret?'
'Yes, of course I can keep a secret.'
'I want to borrow a hundred quid.'
'Don't worry. It's as if I never heard you.'

'Oh by the way, your long-range investments would have made you a very wealthy man.'
CHARLES BARSOTTI

There are two times in a man's life when he should not speculate: when he can't afford it and when he can.
MARK TWAIN

Money isn't everything...

'The pension fund … I forgot where I buried it!'

LEO CULLUM

A Tax Inspector was surprised to receive a letter from a man which read, 'I've been feeling so bad about under-declaring my tax that I can't sleep, so I'm enclosing a cheque for two thousand pounds. If I find I still can't sleep, I'll send a cheque for the balance.'

'The only reason I made a commercial for American Express was to pay my American Express bill.'

PETER USTINOV

An archaeologist working in the Israeli desert found a casket with a mummy inside, and announced proudly, 'I have just found the three-thousand-year-old body of a man who died of heart failure.' Tests on the mummy proved that the archaeologist's diagnosis had indeed been correct. 'How did you know he died of heart failure?' asked a journalist.
'Simple,' came the reply. 'There was a piece of papyrus in his hand on which was written, "10,000 shekels on Goliath".'

'So it's agreed then, we'll steal from the rich and flog the stuff on eBay.'

PAUL WOOD

…but it's certainly handy if you don't have a credit card.

money matters

Corporal Jones is frantic – he has lost £500 pounds meant for a new servicemen's canteen.

MAINWARING: *(Giving Wilson a glare)* Now, Jones, I want you to tell us calmly and logically everything you did from the moment you received that money yesterday.

JONES: Yes, sir, I'll try, sir.

MAINWARING: And this time, don't let your brain go off at a tangent.

JONES: No, sir, I won't get my brains in a tangle.

MAINWARING: Right, start, and keep calm.

JONES: Yes, sir. Well, Dick Billings brought the money round to my shop just before I closed last night. It was in five pound notes.

MAINWARING: What did you do with it?

JONES: I wrapped it up in a bit of newspaper and took it home with me. When I went to bed, I put the money under my pillow.

MAINWARING: What happened the next morning?

JONES: I woke up *(Mainwaring reacts)* and got out of bed.

WALKER: Which side did you get out?

JONES: The left side.

WALKER: How do you know you didn't get out the right side?

JONES: 'Cos the bed's up against the wall. Shut up, Joe, I'm trying to keep calm, I'm trying to keep calm. I washed, dressed and went downstairs. Then I went upstairs again.

WILSON: This is probably a silly question, but why did you do that?

JONES: To get the money from under the pillow. Please, Mr Wilson, I'm trying to keep calm. I am keeping calm, aren't I, Mr Mainwaring?

MAINWARING: You're doing very well, Jones. Be quiet, Wilson.

JONES: Then I had breakfast and walked round to my shop, and I still had the £500. I opened the shop, wrapped up the previous day's takings in paper, made out a bank slip for the takings and another for the £500, and put it all in a carrier bag. Then I said to the boy Raymond, 'Mind the shop I'm going to the bank.' I think it's working, Mr Mainwaring.

MAINWARING: That's because you're thinking calmly and logically.

JONES: Yes, I'm very calm, I'm very calm. Then I walked across the road to the bank. Young Pikey was there, I said 'Good morning', and paid in the takings.

PIKE: Yes, that's right, Mr Mainwaring.

MAINWARING: What happened next?

JONES: It's all coming back, I'm still quite calm. Then I gave Pike the packet with £500 in it. But it wasn't there.

PIKE: No, it had turned into half a pound of sausages.

JONES: *(Going beserk)* Yes, that's it! I've lost it! I've lost it! Don't panic! Don't panic! I put it somewhere, I know I put it somewhere. I've lost £500! I've lost £500! Don't panic!

JIMMY PERRY AND DAVID CROFT

Loose change

At a dinner in his honour, a wealthy businessman delivered an emotional speech.

'When I first came to this town 50 years ago,' he said, 'I had no car, my only suit was on my back, the soles of my shoes were thin, and I carried all my possessions in a brown paper bag.'

After dinner, a young man nervously approached. 'Sir, I really admire your accomplishments. Tell me, after all these years, do you still remember what you carried in that brown paper bag?'

'Yes,' he replied. 'I had £300,000 in cash and £500,000 in shares.'

The great rule is not to talk about money with people who have much more or much less than you.

KATHARINE WHITEHORN

That money talks **I'll not deny,** I heard it once: **It said, 'Goodbye.'**

RICHARD ARMOUR

If you would know what the Lord God thinks of money, you have only to look at those to whom he gives it.

MAURICE BARING

Money won't buy happiness, but it will pay the salaries of a large research staff to study the problem.

BILL VAUGHAN

i've got enough money to last the rest of my life ... so long as I die by four o'clock this afternoon.

HENNY YOUNGMAN

An old lady sold matches on a street corner for 20p a box. **Every day, a young man would hurry by and throw 20p into her cup** without taking any matches. One day the woman called out to him, 'Just a minute!' 'I know, I know,' he said. **'You're wondering why I leave 20p every day, but never take any matches.'** 'No,' the woman said, 'I wanted to let you know that they'd gone up to 30p.'

'Holy recession, Batman. It's not the same since we lost our company car.'

DAVID HALDANE

TRANSPORTS OF DELIGHT

All at sea

Steward to seasick passenger: 'Do you want me to bring your dinner to the cabin, or shall I just throw it overboard now?'

Excuse me, Madam, the Captain has invited you to come and dine at his table.
Certainly not! I didn't pay all that money for this cruise to end up sitting with the crew.

What do you get if you cross the Atlantic with the Titanic?
About half way.

THE TIP OF THE ICEBERG

RICHARD JOLLEY

'I don't see how sending out flares is going to save us.'
STAN EALES

A young woman stowaway was found on a ship and taken to the captain. 'How long have you been here?' the captain asked. 'Ten days,' replied the woman. 'I'm trying to get to the Far East.' **'And how have you survived all that time?' 'Well, your second officer has been very kind,' explained the woman.** 'He has given me a meal every night and let me sleep in his cabin.' **'Has he demanded anything in return?' 'Well, he's been taking advantage of me,' the woman whispered. 'I'd certainly say he has.' replied the captain. 'This is the Woolwich Ferry.'**

Up, up and away!

How often do jumbo jets crash? Just the once.

'I'm afraid we have a problem here …'
NICK HOBART

'I got my ticket for three dollars over the internet. Are you going to eat that salmon?'
LEO CULLUM

Airplanes aren't really fast and luxurious – it's just that anything would seem fast and luxurious after an hour in an airport bus!
AL BLAKE

'OK, everyone's gone – you can pick it up now.'
NICK HOBART

LORD HIGH-BO

Lord High-Bo, getting tired of trains,
Would binge about in Aero-planes,
A habit which would not have got
Him into trouble, had he not
Neglected what we know to be
The rule of common courtesy.
Past bedroom windows he would sail
And with a most offensive hail
Disturb the privacy of those
About to wash or change their clothes.

HILAIRE BELLOC

It was a woman's first time on a plane. She boarded the aircraft and found herself a window seat in a non-smoking area. After she had settled in, a man came over and insisted that she was in his seat. She ignored him but he continued to hover over her, so she told him to go away. 'OK,' replied the man, 'if that's the way you want it, you fly the plane.'

Flying? I've been to almost as many places as my luggage!

BOB HOPE

EDWARD MCLACHLAN

Off the rails

THE BRITISH CHARACTER.
LOVE OF TRAVELLING ALONE.
PONT

H.M. BATEMAN

There was an old lady
  named Carr,
Who took the three-
  three to Forfar,
For she said, 'I believe
It is likely to leave
Far before the four-four
  to Forfar.'

ANON

The only way to catch a train I ever discovered is to miss the train before.

G.K. CHESTERTON

What do you call an underground train full of professors? A tube of smarties.

STATION
ANNOUNCEMENT:
The train now arriving on Platforms 10, 11, 12 and 13 is coming in sideways.

LETTER TO STATION
MASTER: **Sir, Saturday morning, although recurring at regular and well-foreseen intervals, always seems to take this railway by surprise.**

W.S. GILBERT

CARL GILES

PETER BROOKES

We are sorry to announce ...

We got to Waterloo at eleven, and asked where the eleven-five started from. Of course nobody knew; nobody at Waterloo ever does know where a train is going to start from, or where a train when it does start is going to, or anything about it. The porter who took our things thought it would go from number two platform, while another porter, with whom he discussed the question, had heard a rumour that it would go from number one. The station-master, on the other hand, was convinced it would start from the local.

To put an end to the matter we went upstairs and asked the traffic superintendent, and he told us that he had just met a man who said he had seen it at number three platform. We went to number three platform, but the authorities there said that they rather thought that train was the Southampton express, or else the Windsor loop. But they were sure it wasn't the Kingston train, though why they were sure it wasn't they couldn't say.

Then our porter said he thought that it must be it on the high-level platform; said he thought he knew the train. So we went to the high-level platform and saw the engine-driver, and asked him if he was going to Kingston. He said he couldn't say for certain of course, but that he rather thought he was. Anyhow, if he wasn't the 11.5 for Kingston, he said he was pretty confident he was the 9.32 for Virginia Water, or the 10 a.m. express for the Isle of Wight, or somewhere in that direction, and we should all know when we got there. We slipped half-a-crown into his hand, and begged him to be the 11.5 for Kingston.

'Nobody will ever know, on this line,' we said, 'what you are, or where you're going. You know the way, you slip off quietly and go to Kingston.'
'Well, I don't know, gents,' replied the noble fellow, 'but I suppose *some* train's got to go to Kingston; and I'll do it. Gimme the half-crown.'
Thus we got to Kingston by the London and South-Western Railway.

We learnt afterwards that the train we had come by was really the Exeter mail, and that they had spent hours at Waterloo looking for it, and nobody knew what had become of it.

JEROME K. JEROME, *THREE MEN IN A BOAT* **(1889)**

'Have you been waiting long?'
EDWARD MCLACHLAN

Rules of the road

P.C. 'You were doing forty miles an hour, Sir.'
MOTORIST (whispering). 'Make it seventy; I'm trying to sell him the thing.'
KENNETH BEAUCHAMP

You know, somebody actually complimented me on my driving today. They left a little note on the windscreen, it said, 'Parking Fine'.
TOMMY COOPER

'Why do you paint your getaway car green on one side and yellow on the other?' asked one crook of another. 'Because I like to hear the witnesses contradict each other,' he replied.

'If I park on these double yellow lines and pop over there to post a letter will you give me a ticket?' a driver asked a traffic warden. 'Of course,' replied the warden. 'But these other cars are parked on double yellows,' pleaded the driver. 'I know,' replied the warden, 'but they didn't ask me to book them.'

A policeman looks down at a man in the gutter and asks, 'Are you drunk?' 'Certainly not,' the man replies. 'I'm just holding this parking space for a friend.'

TRANSPORTS OF DELIGHT
Roads scholarship

As already mentioned, intending drivers have to undergo an examination. It is not, however, generally known that in addition to a practical driving test candidates have to do a written paper.

In view of this, and for the benefit of readers who are sitting for their finals, we give below a specimen paper with appropriate answers attached.

EXAMINATION
Parking Limit – Two Hours.
Write on one side of the road only.

(a) Mechanics

1. Your car, except for a tendency to slow down on hills, runs perfectly all day.
   On starting it up next morning, however, you find that it will only move a few inches.
   What would you do?

Answer: Open the garage door.

2. Why is a hand pump included in the toolkit?

Answer: It gives employment.

(b) History

1. Describe the difference between roads made by the Romans and those constructed nowadays.

Answer: The roads made by the Romans have lasted until the present time.

(c) English Grammar

1. What is wrong with the following: 'When I got to the crossroads I hooted and slowed down and looked to see was it safe to cross'?

Answer: It isn't true.

2. What is the feminine of khaki shorts?

Answer: Too tight.

3. 'I have just done a month for having no third-party insurance.' What is wrong with the above sentence?

Answer: Not long enough.

(d) General Knowledge

1. Why is a red light used for danger?

Answer: Because a bright colour that cannot be confused with anything else is essential.

2. Why is a red light used for advertising restaurants, cinemas, drinks, shops, pills and everything else?

Answer: See above.

3. Why does a car ferry require a crew of two?

Answer: One to say 'whoa' while the other says 'come on'.

4. What is the yellow traffic light for?

Answer: To save waiting for the green.

(e) Legal

1. What vehicles are allowed to drive at high speed on either side of the road, across any traffic lights and both ways along one-way streets?

Answer: Those driven by very charming young ladies.

2. A motorist comes suddenly out of a side road, dashes straight across a line of traffic against the lights, moves across the pavement, runs right up the steps of a house, crashes through the door and comes to rest hard up against the bar.
  Is he liable for damages?

Answer: No, not unless he has his car with him.

**FOUGASSE, *YOU HAVE BEEN WARNED,*
A COMPLETE GUIDE TO THE ROAD (1935)**

Driven to distraction

'I said 2x2!'
GILES PILBROW

So I was getting into my car, and this bloke says to me, 'Can you give me a lift?' I said, 'Sure, you look great, the world's your oyster, go for it!'

TOMMY COOPER

A little girl used always to be collected from school by her father, but one day he was ill and her mother fetched her. When they got back home, the father asked his daughter if she'd minded the change of driver. 'No, it was fine,' she replied, 'and we weren't overtaken by a single bastard.'

A motorist locked himself out of his car and a passer-by stopped to help. 'I'll have your door open in no time,' said the stranger, who then began rubbing his bottom up and down on the driver's door. The motorist found this very odd, but before he could comment, all the locks of his car sprang open. 'How amazing!' said the driver. 'How did you manage to do that?' 'Easy,' replied the stranger. 'I'm wearing khaki trousers.'

A woman phoned her husband at work. 'Sorry, darling,' he said. 'I'm really busy at the moment. I haven't got time to chat.' 'This won't take long. It's just that I've got some good news and some bad news.' 'Look, I really am busy,' he repeated. 'So just give me the good news.' 'Well,' she said, 'the air-bag works.'

The quickest way to make your own anti-freeze ..

*'Arthur loves his new job with the fairground – gets
a company car as well.'*

EDWARD MCLACHLAN

Entering a luxury car showroom, a man is grabbed by a salesman and guided round the latest, gleaming convertible sports car. The prospective customer announces that he is interested in purchasing the vehicle and enquires about the price.

The salesman types some figures into his calculator and says, 'That particular model will cost you two pink fluffy notes with rhinos on and seven yellow clown coins, sir.'

'I'm not paying that,' protests the customer, 'it's silly money.'

Natives who beat drums to drive off evil spirits are objects of scorn to smart Americans who blow horns to break up traffic jams.

MARY ELLEN KELLY

.....is to hide her nightie.

'And the wife uses that for popping to the shops.'
ROBERT THOMPSON

The automobile changed our dress, manners, social customs, vacation habits, the shape of our cities, consumer purchasing patterns, common tastes and positions in intercourse.

JOHN KETAS

I took my old car in for an oil change. After one look at it, the mechanic suggested I keep the oil and change the car.

While he was driving through the countryside, a motorist's car broke down by a gate to a field. He got out and lifted the bonnet. **'Your distributor's loose,'** announced a voice. The man looked round in alarm, but could see nobody. He continued to inspect the engine. Again a voice said, **'Your distributor's loose.'** Looking up, he saw a black horse standing by the gate. **'It's definitely your distributor,'** said the horse. Stunned, he checked the distributor and sure enough it was loose. **He quickly did the necessary repairs and drove to the next village.** There he rushed to the nearest pub and ordered a double whisky. 'You won't believe what I've just witnessed,' he confided to the barman and told him about the incident. **'It's a good job it wasn't the white horse you saw,'** said the barman. 'Why's that?' asked the motorist. 'Because he knows nothing about cars.'

MIKE BALDWIN

A woman bought a second-hand car. Three days later she went back to the dealer and asked, 'Do I understand that the guarantee covers everything that breaks?'
'Yes, that's right,' said the dealer.
'In that case,' she said, 'I'd like two bicycles, a pair of wrought-iron front gates, six dozen tulips and a new garage door.'

Teenage son: Dad, there's a problem with the car – water in the carburettor.
Father: Water in the carburettor? Don't be silly.
Son: I promise you there's water in the carburettor.
Father: You don't even know what a carburettor looks like. Where is the car?
Son: In the swimming pool.

'While you're about it, ask him if he knows a good place for lunch.'
RUSSELL BROCKBANK

HUSBAND: That's the third time I've had to replace the clutch on this car.
WIFE: Well, don't blame me. I never use it.

A man read an advertisement in the paper that read: 'Porsche for sale – £100.' He thought either it was a printing error, or the car was just a heap of rust, but still went round to see the vehicle on offer. To his astonishment, he was faced by a brand new model in perfect condition. 'Why on earth are you only charging a hundred pounds?' he asked the woman who showed it to him. 'Simple,' she replied. 'Last week my husband ran off with his secretary. He said: "You can keep the house, but sell the Porsche and send the money on to me."'

TRANSPORTS OF DELIGHT
Yes, we have no petrol

Hollywood, November 24, 1942

I have no desire to evade the gasoline visitation that is about to descend upon us, but don't you think the law is a little unfair to the unfortunate few who happen to own large and well-upholstered automobiles?

Back in the comparatively lush days of '37, a beady-eyed and persistent salesman cajoled me into purchasing an automobile that was considerably longer and heavier than what I originally intended buying. He told me, as he fondly stroked the fender of this shiny monster, that here was a job (they were all called jobs in those days) that would ride like a Pullman. As I wavered, he added as a final clincher, 'Brother, this job has class!' And, from the look in his eye, it was quite evident that this was a commodity he didn't think I had a great deal of. At any rate, dazed by his eloquence and flattery, I soon became the owner of a luxury super-eight.

The salesman didn't lie – it did ride like a Pullman – but he didn't tell me that it was almost as heavy as one and that it sopped up gas as though its insides were lined with blotting paper. A good deal of my time was now spent at gas stations, steadily pouring fuel into this iron camel. It was quite expensive but still not particularly tragic. I had money and gas could be bought at almost every corner.

Then the blow fell – the Government decreed that nonessential workers (and no description ever fitted me so accurately) would be allotted four gallons a week – enough to propel the average motorist sixty miles in any direction. Gargantua or the Frankenstein Eight, as it was now called, laughed heartily at this estimate. He said that if I were to equip him with new spark plugs, adjust his timing, give him a downhill shove and a favoring wind, he might possibly eke out twenty-eight miles on four gallons – but sixty miles! Ridiculous! Who did I think he was – Alsab [*race horse of the 1940s*]?

So here I am, stuck with an iron horse and twenty-eight miles a week while my poor but fortunate friends, who were lucky enough to buy small cars, have practically unlimited mileage. I ask the Government not to discriminate against me. It is unfair and un-American to penalize me because I once was a member of the privileged classes.

This is not a complaint – this is a plea for justice! I willingly drink chicory for breakfast, eat broiled kidneys on meatless Tuesdays, wear cuffless trousers, have my salary frozen in the dead of winter, send my cook to Lockheed, and play dead for the local air raid warden; I buy War Bonds, stamps, entertain at the Service Camps, and know the second stanza of 'The Star-Spangled Banner'. In return, all I ask is a fair measuring stick for my ancient ark. If I can't get that, I hereby petition the authorities to revise the local zoning laws so that I can legally stable a pair of mules in my living room.

GROUCHO MARX

No turning back

No Riderless
Bicycles Allowed

No Eel Fishing
Allowed On
The Clearway

Steep Hill Upwards
(or is it Downwards?)

Hardly Noticeable
Hill Downwards
(or is it Upwards?)

Disintegrating
Lorry Ahead

Beware of
Low-Flying
Motorcycles

Roadmen
Sawing Down Trees

Roadmen
Sawing Up Logs

Is Your
Steering Wheel
Done Up Properly?

Sophia Loren
Ahead

Water Diviner
Ahead

Outdoor Pop Art
Display

Veteran Locomotive
Rally On The Move

Unusual Roadman
Ahead

?

RUSSELL BROCKBANK

Car owners of the world unite: you have nothing to lose but your manners – and someone else's life.
COLIN MACINNES

Two lions were lying in a safari park watching the tourists drive past in their cars.
'I've heard that tinned humans are almost as good as fresh,' says one lion to the other.

Stopping at a ford, a motorist asked an old man sitting nearby how deep the water was. 'Only a few inches,' said the man. Seconds later the car was bonnet-deep. 'Funny,' said the old man. 'That water only goes halfway up our ducks.'

IF YOU CAN READ THIS, I'VE LOST MY CARAVAN.
BUMPER STICKER

One for the road

THERE WAS AN OLD MAN OF DARJEELING,
WHO BOARDED A BUS BOUND FOR EALING.
HE SAW ON THE DOOR:
'PLEASE DON'T SPIT ON THE FLOOR',
SO HE JUMPED UP AND SPAT ON THE CEILING.

ANON

There are two classes of pedestrians in these days of reckless motor traffic: the quick and the dead.

LORD DEWAR

I always like to begin a journey on Sundays because I shall have the prayers of the church to preserve all that travel by land or by water.

JONATHAN SWIFT

A drunk stumbled out of the Devereux Hotel, fell into a cab and said to the driver, 'Take me to the Devereux Hotel.'
'We're there,' said the cabbie.
'All right,' said the drunk, taking a ten pound note out his wallet. 'Only next time don't drive so fast.'

STEVE BEST

'There's no use in crying over it, Charlie.'
NORMAN THELWELL

At the local golf course, the eighth fairway ran beside a main road. A new member was going round the course with the club professional.

On the eighth tee he sliced his shot. The ball sailed into the road, striking a passing motorcyclist on his crash helmet before bouncing off to shatter the windscreen of a passing bus. Swerving wildly, the bus collided with a lorry travelling in the opposite direction, causing it to spill its load all over the road. Three cars piled into the resulting chaos.

The horrified golfer turned to the professional, saying, 'What'll I do? What'll I do?' 'Well,' replied the professional, 'next time keep your hand a little further down the shaft.'

Local councillors had just bought a new fire engine for their village and were discussing what to do with the old one. 'I've got an idea,' said one councillor. 'Why not keep it for false alarms?'

QUIET FUN

My son, Augustus, in the street, one day,
Was feeling quite exceptionally merry.
A stranger asked him; 'Can you show me, pray,
The quickest way to Brompton cemetery?'
'The quickest way? You bet I can,' said Gus,
And pushed the fellow underneath a bus.
Whatever people say about my son,
He does enjoy his little bit of fun.

HARRY GRAHAM

'Don't worry, darling, I've set something up so the kids won't get bored on the trip.'
NAF

'Gosh, that is a very large piece of shrapnel, Grandad.'

ROBERT THOMPSON

WAR & PEACE

Opening shots

**Walking into an army surplus store, a man asked if they had any camouflage jackets.
'Yes, we have,' came the reply, 'but we can't find them.'**

'I think it's a heat-seeking missile.'
EDWARD MCLACHLAN

They were doing **medical examinations for army entry** and a man came in with one leg nine inches shorter than the other. The Medical Officer said, **'Yes, fine. You're in.'**
'Wait a minute,' said the man. 'I've got one leg nine inches shorter than the other.'
'Don't worry,' said the M.O. 'Where you're going, the ground won't be level.'

The Swiss have an interesting army – 500 years without a war, pretty impressive. Also pretty lucky for them. Ever see that little Swiss army knife they have to fight with? Not much of a weapon there – corkscrews, bottle openers. 'Come on, buddy, let's go. You get past me, the guy behind me, he's got a spoon! Back off, I've got the toe clippers right here!'

JERRY SEINFELD

I'M DESPERATELY TRYING TO FIGURE OUT WHY KAMIKAZE PILOTS WORE HELMETS.

DAVE EDISON

WAR & PEACE
Don't mention the war
IT'S THE OFFICE QUIZ NIGHT

Interior. Wernham Hogg function room. Night.

People have teamed up and are sitting at tables nursing drinks. Gareth is in charge.

GARETH: *(Through microphone)* Can I have everyone –

(Feedback)

Ooh, bit of feedback. Umm, can I have everyone's attention please? Welcome to the Seventh Annual Wernham Hogg Quiz Night. Current champions are this team here – The Dead Parrots.

They raise their arms like champions. Finch and Brent go into a Monty Python routine.

FINCH: Bereft of life ...!

BRENT: ... he sleeps!

FINCH: If you hadn't nailed him to the perch, he would be ...

HOW HANCOCK WON THE WAR

HANCOCK: Did I ever tell you about the time we got drunk in Naples?

SID: Everybody got drunk in Naples.

HANCOCK: Not like we got drunk. Roaring stiff we were. We couldn't stand up. Up to here in Chianti we were. Standing on top of Vesuvius pouring in bottles of vino redo. Nearly put it out. It was just the same in battle, too. Tough. Tough? Savage is more the word. *(He growls)* There we were, dug in just outside Anzio, when the order came through – retreat on all fronts. I looked at Smudger, just like I'm looking at you today, and I said, 'Which way's Berlin?' He said, 'That way.' *(Points)* I said, 'Right, that's the way we're going.'

So we were off. Me, Smudger, Ginger, and Chalky. Well when the Germans realised we meant business they threw everything at us. They brought up their eighty-eight millimetres. Well that did it. We assembled our twenty-five pounders. Twenty-five pounders against eighty-eight millimetres. The only chance we had was to try and shoot their shells down before they landed. Or better still, put one down the barrel of their guns and hit their shell just as it was coming out, thus putting them out of action. So we moved forward. And then what do you think? Old Smudger had forgotten the shells. There was only one thing for it ... hand grenades. We pulled the pin out with our teeth

BRENT AND FINCH: ... pushing up the daisies!

GARETH: Ha ha. That's Monty Python. Ha ha. Question one. Alright.

DAWN: Wait! Hang on ... David ...

GARETH: We haven't got ...

BRENT: Oh yeah, er ... Tim's birthday today. He's thirty years young, as I like to say.

Everyone applauds.

BRENT: So what better way to celebrate than a battle of wits? So, let the game ...

DAWN: Speech!

Tim gets up to make a speech, but Gareth continues regardless and so Tim sits down again, embarrassed.

GARETH: Okay, question one. In the mid-nineteen-sixties, the US Army replaced all existing infantry guns with the M16 rifle and which fixed-rate repeat-fire machine gun?

TIM: You what?!

GARETH: Just write down the answer if you know it!

People confer. Brent and Finch confidently scrawl down their answer.

BRENT: Next!

GARETH: Okay, question two. In the song '19' by Paul Hardcastle, he told us that the average age of a soldier in the Vietnam War was nineteen. Hardcastle also told us the average age of a soldier in the Second World War. What was it?

TIM: Gareth, are all these gonna be about war?

GARETH: No, I've got loads of ... I've got one on tennis, one on the Suez canal ... loads. Okay, question three. Which canal links the Mediterranean with the Red Sea?

RICKY GERVAIS AND STEPHEN MERCHANT

(He mimes this) ... rushed forward ... chickety snitch ... and threw them *(Brings arm over as if throwing one).* What an explosion ... right on their ammo dump. I've still got a piece of metal inside me.

SID: You have?

HANCOCK: Yes, I swallowed the pin. *(Pats his stomach)*
It's still there. I can always tell when it's going to rain.

SID: It's a pity you didn't swallow the hand grenade.
What a load of old codswallop.

RAY GALTON AND ALAN SIMPSON,
HANCOCK'S HALF HOUR

WAR & PEACE
Ancient aggressions

SIR ROLAND TRIED TO CONVINCE THE SCEPTICS OF THE POTENTIAL OF HIS LIGHTWEIGHT "MINI-SHIELD".......

GLEN BAXTER

An old soldier was telling a rather bored young man about his military ancestry. 'Do you know, my great-grandfather fought with Wellington in 1810, my grandfather fought with Redvers Buller in 1870, my father fought with Kitchener in 1916, and I fought with Monty in 1942.' 'Oh dear,' the young man drawled, 'your family doesn't seem to have been able to get along with anyone.'

INFAMY! INFAMY! THEY'VE ALL GOT IT IN FOR ME.

KENNETH WILLIAMS, *CARRY ON CLEO*

'Aw c'mon, Genghis – we need one more to make up a horde!'
BILL TIDY

'X, IX, VIII, VII, VI, V, IV, III …'
RICHARD DECKER

During the Middle Ages, a knight and his men returned to their king's castle after a very busy week's fighting. The knight said to the king: **'Sire, I have been busy on your behalf, robbing and pillaging all day, burning the villages of your enemies to the east.'** The king looked confused. 'But I don't have any enemies to the east.'
'Ah,' said the knight, 'well, I'm afraid you have now.'

There was a warship in the Roman navy full of galley-slaves, and one day one of them died at his bench. Immediately all the guards got out their whips and started lashing the other galley-slaves. 'Hey, this is a bit much!' shouted one. 'What've we done? What's this all about?' 'Tradition on this ship,' the chief guard replied. 'Whenever someone dies we always have a whip-round.'

'Sorry, didn't we tell you? We changed it to best out of three …'
NICK NEWMAN

Battling Britons

BRITAIN CONQUERED AGAIN

The withdrawal of the Roman legions to take part in Gibbon's Decline and Fall of the Roman Empire (due to a clamour among the Romans for pompous amusements such as bread and circumstances) left Britain defenceless and subjected Europe to that long succession of Waves of which History is chiefly composed. While the Roman Empire was overrun by waves not only of Ostrogoths, Vizigoths and even Goths, but also of Vandals (who destroyed works of art) and Huns (who destroyed everything and everybody, including Goths, Ostrogoths, Vizigoths and even Vandals), Britain was attacked by waves of Picts (and, of course, Scots) who had recently learnt how to climb the wall, and of Angles, Saxons and Jutes who, landing at Thanet, soon overran the country with fire (and, of course, the sword).

IMPORTANT NOTE

The Scots (originally Irish, but by now Scotch) were at this time inhabiting Ireland, having driven the Irish (Picts) out of Scotland; while the Picts (originally Scots) were now Irish (living in brackets) and *vice versa*. It is essential to keep these distinctions clearly in mind (and *verce visa*).

HUMILIATION OF THE BRITONS

The brutal Saxon invaders drove the Britons westward into Wales and compelled them to become Welsh; it is now considered doubtful whether this was a Good Thing. Memorable among the Saxon warriors were Hengist and his wife (? or horse), Horsa. Hengist made himself King in the South. Thus Hengist was the first English King and his wife (or horse), Horsa, the first English Queen (or horse). The country was now almost entirely inhabited by Saxons and was therefore renamed England, and thus (naturally) soon became C. of E. This was a Good Thing, because previously the Saxons had worshipped some dreadful gods of their own called Monday, Tuesday, Wednesday, Thursday, Friday and Saturday.

HENRY V. AN IDEAL KING

On the death of Henry IV Part II, his son, Prince Hal, who had won all English hearts by his youthful pranks – (such as trying on the crown while his father lay dying, and hitting a very old man called Judge Gascoigne) – determined to justify public expectation by becoming the *Ideal English King*. He therefore decided on an immediate appearance in the Hundred Years War, making a declaration that all the treaties with France were to be regarded as dull and void.

Conditions in France were favourable to Henry since the French King, being mad, had entrusted the government of the country to a dolphin and the command of the army to an elderly constable. After capturing some breeches at Harfleur (more than once) by the original expedients of disguising his friends as imitation tigers, stiffening their sinews, etc., Henry was held up on the road to Calais by the constable, whom he defeated at the utterly memorable battle of AGINCOURT (French POICTIERS). He then displaced the dolphin as ruler of Anjou, Menjou, Poilou, Maine, Touraine, Againe and Againe, and realising that he was now too famous to live long expired at the ideal moment.

CHARLES I AND THE CIVIL WAR

With the ascension of Charles I to the throne we come at last to the Central Period of English History (not to be confused with the Middle Ages, of course), consisting in the *utterly memorable Struggle between the Cavaliers (Wrong but Wromantic) and the Roundheads (Right but Repulsive)*.

Charles I was a Cavalier King and therefore had a small pointed beard, long flowing curls, a large, flat, flowing hat and *gay attire*. The Roundheads, on the other hand, were clean-shaven and wore tall, conical hats, white ties and *sombre garments*. Under these circumstances a Civil War was inevitable.

The Roundheads, of course, were so called because Cromwell had all their heads made perfectly round, in order that they should present a uniform appearance when drawn up in line.

Besides this, if any man lost his head in action, it could be used as a cannon-ball by the artillery (which was done at the Siege of Worcester).

W.C. SELLAR AND R.J. YEATMAN, *1066 AND ALL THAT* (1930)

WAR & PEACE
On parade

Behind the Scenes at Wellington Barracks
H.M. BATEMAN

An officer was walking across a parade ground when he saw a cigarette stub on the tarmac with a private standing nearby.
'You, soldier,' he bellowed. 'Is that yours?'
'No, all right, sir,' said the private. 'You have it – you saw it first.'

A military policeman was on duty round the Southampton docks, when he found a sailor lying on the ground with blood all over his face. He picked the man up and asked, **'Could you describe the person who attacked you?'** 'That's what I was doing when he attacked me,' replied the sailor.

'Sir, sir,
we've run out
of ammunition.'
'We mustn't let the
enemy know that.
Whatever you do,
keep firing.'

A soldier on sentry duty fell asleep while he was standing up, and woke to find his commanding officer standing in front of him, looking furious. With great presence of mind, the soldier said, 'Amen.'

OFFICER: Now come on, you. This won't do. You're meant to be firing this rifle at the target and none of your shots are hitting it. Have you any idea where they're going?
RECRUIT: No, sir. All I know is that they're leaving this end all right.

'You, soldier, are you happy in the army?'
'As happy as can be expected, I suppose, sir.'
'And what were you before you joined?'
'A lot happier.'

Soldier Freddy
was never ready,
But Soldier Neddy,
unlike Freddy
Was always ready
and steady,

Thats why,
When soldier Neddy
Is outside Buckingham Palace on guard in the
pouring wind and rain
being steady and ready,
Freddie —
is home in beddy

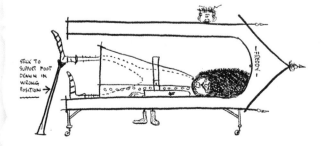

SPIKE MILLIGAN

Taste for action

DAD'S ARMY – JONES THE BUTCHER JOINS UP

JONES: Left, right, left, right – halt! Evening Mr Mainwaring. Evening, Mr Wilson. You know me, don't you?

MAINWARING: Mr Jones, the butcher in the High Street, isn't it?

JONES: That's right.

WILSON: *(To Mainwaring)* Don't you think perhaps Mr Jones is a little old, sir?

JONES: Old! Here, who are you calling old? Just let me get near some of them Jerry parachutists, I'll sort 'em out.

He gestures with a sharpener, hanging from his wrist.

MAINWARING: There, you see, it's keenness that counts Wilson, not age.

JONES: That's the ticket, sir. I'm as keen as mustard.

WILSON: Any previous military experience?

JONES: Ah, now you're talking. Signed on as a drummer boy, I did, in 1884, saw service later in the Sudan, them Fuzzie Wuzzies, they was the boys, they come at you with them long knives, zip you right open. *(He makes a ripping noise.)* It soon shows if you've got any guts or not.

Close up of Wilson looking sick.

JONES: Yeah, them Fuzzie Wuzzies – the only people who ever broke the British square not like them Jerries. Yeah, they couldn't punch puddin', they couldn't. They don't like the old cold steel, you see, they don't like it up 'em.

Jones has now worked himself up into a frenzy and is feeling faint.

MAINWARING: I think you'd better sit down. Get him a chair, Wilson.

JONES: Thank you, sir. *(Sitting down)* Not as young as I was you know. *(He realises his mistake and jumps up again.)* Mind you, I can still give them the old cold ...

MAINWARING: Yes, yes quite so. I think you've proved your point. Sign there. When did you leave the Army?

Jones signs on table top.

JONES: Nineteen fifteen, sir. Invalided out. The old minces, you know. Couldn't get the focus. *(He points to eyes.)*

A war of words

MAINWARING: That, presumably, is why you signed the table.

JONES: Not that they would have stopped me, you know, with the old bayonet – right up there with the old cold steel.

MAINWARING: Yes, well, thank you very much, Mr Jones. That will be all.

JONES: *(Putting a parcel on the table)* Oh, by the way, I've brought along a couple of pounds of steak – compliments of the house.

Mainwaring and Wilson look interested.

JONES: Just one more thing, what about my stripe?

WILSON: Your stripe?

JONES: Yes, I mean I was a Lance Corporal for 14 years. I can keep it, can't I?

MAINWARING: No, Jones, I'm afraid not.

JONES: Well, in that case, I'll take the steak.

He picks it up.

MAINWARING: No, wait a minute, we will be looking for N.C.O.s, you know, Wilson, and it could well be that Jones' past military experience could stand us in very good steak … stead.

WILSON: I think so too, sir.

MAINWARING: That will be all then, Lance Corporal Jones.

JONES: T.T.F.N. Right turn. Quick march. Left, right. Left, right.

JIMMY PERRY AND DAVID CROFT

Disarmament: Conversations between politicians about the next war.
BEACHCOMBER

Military intelligence is a contradiction in terms.
GROUCHO MARX

Sometimes I think war is God's way of teaching us geography.
PAUL RODRIGUEZ

When the military man approaches, the world locks up its spoons and packs off its womankind.
GEORGE BERNARD SHAW

War does not determine who is right; war determines who is left.
ANON

Men love war because it makes them look serious. Because it is the one thing that stops women laughing at them.
JOHN FOWLES

A prisoner of war is a man who tries to kill you and fails, and then asks you not to kill him.
WINSTON CHURCHILL

Peace is a period of unrest and confusion between two wars.
ANON

WAR & PEACE
Going over the top!

'During the war, the patrol I was with was ambushed. One of the enemy soldiers came up to me, put his gun right up against my chest and pulled the trigger.'

'But how on earth did you survive? The bullet must have gone straight through your heart.'

'Well, yes, it would have done, except for the fact that at the time my heart was in my mouth.'

My only regret during the war was that I only had one life to give for my country. I'd have felt a lot safer if I'd had two.

'In my regiment we used to shoot first and ask questions later,' said the elderly Colonel. **'Mind you, we never got many answers.'**

The resident bore was once again pontificating in the Naval Club. 'Worst thing that happened to me was during the war in the Pacific. **My troopship was torpedoed and I had to live for a fortnight on a tin of beans.'** 'Good heavens!' exclaimed an awestruck listener. 'How on earth did you manage to stay on?'

'It's desperate, sir – we're down to our last poet!'

NEIL BENNETT

The Politician Who Addressed the Troops
H.M. BATEMAN

The final push

BLACKADDER GOES FORTH — GOODBYEEE ...

Scene one: the trench and dug-out.

It is night, it is pouring with rain and the shelling is constant. Blackadder and George have just inspected the troops in the trench. They are ankle-deep in mud.

GEORGE: Care for a smoke, sir?

BLACKADDER: No, thank you.

George offers Baldrick a cigarette.

GEORGE: Private?

BALDRICK: Thank you, sir.

He eats it. Suddenly George gets emotional.

GEORGE: Oh, dash and blast all this hanging about, sir. I'm as bored as a pacifist's pistol. When are we going to see some action?

BLACKADDER: Well, George, I strongly suspect your long wait for certain death is nearly at an end. Surely you must have noticed something in the air?

GEORGE: Well yes, of course, but I thought that was Private Baldrick.

BLACKADDER: Unless I'm much mistaken, soon we will at last be making the final big push, the one we've been *so* looking forward to all these years.

GEORGE: Hurrah with highly polished brass knobs on. About time!

The field phone rings: it is on Baldrick's back. Blackadder picks it up.

BLACKADDER: Hullo, Somme Public Baths. No running, shouting or piddling in the shallow end. Oh, it's you, Darling. Tomorrow at dawn. Oh, excellent. See you later then. Bye!

He hangs up.

Gentlemen — our long wait is nearly at an end. Tomorrow morning, General 'Insanity' Melchett invites you to a mass slaughter. We're going over the top.

GEORGE: Huzzah and hurrah! God Save the King, Rule Britannia and boo sucks to Harry Hun!

BLACKADDER: Or to put it more precisely, you're going over the top. I'm going to get out of it.

Blackadder and George move to the dugout.

GEORGE: Oh, come on, Cap! May be a bit risky — but it's sure as bloomin' 'ell worth it, guv'nor.

Blackadder undresses while George dresses for battle.

BLACKADDER: How can it possibly be worth it? We've been sitting here since Christmas 1914, during which time millions of men have died, and we've moved no further than an asthmatic ant with heavy shopping.

GEORGE: No, but this time I'm pos we'll break through — it's ice-cream in Berlin in fifteen days.

BLACKADDER: Or ice-cold in No Man's Land in fifteen seconds. No, the time has come to get out of this madness once and for all.

GEORGE: What madness is that?

BLACKADDER: Oh, for God's sake, George, how long have you been in the army?

GEORGE: What, me? Oh, I joined up straight away – 10 August 1914. What a day that was. Myself and the fellows leap-frogging down to the Cambridge recruiting office, then playing tiddly-winks in the queue. We'd hammered the hell out of Oxford's tiddly-winkers only the week before and here we were off to hammer the Boche. A crashingly superb bunch of blokes, fine, clean-limbed – even our acne had a strange nobility about it.

BLACKADDER: Yes, and how are all the boys now?

GEORGE: Well, Jocko and the Badger bought it at the first Ypres, unfortunately – quite a shock that. I remember Bumfluff's housemaster wrote and told me that Sticky had been out for a duck and the Gubber had snitched a parcel sausage-end and gone goose-over-stumps frog-side.

BLACKADDER: Meaning?

GEORGE: I don't know, sir, but I read in *The Times* that they'd both been killed.

BLACKADDER: And Bumfluff himself?

GEORGE: Copped a packet at Gallipoli with the Ozzies. So did Drippy and Strangely Brown – I remember we heard on the first morning of the Somme when Titch and Mr Floppy got gassed back to Blighty.

BLACKADDER: Which leaves?

GEORGE: Gosh, yes – I suppose I'm the only one of the Trinity's Tiddlers still alive. Cor blimey – there's a thought, and not a jolly one.

BLACKADDER: My point exactly, George.

GEORGE: I might get a bit mis if it wasn't for the thought of going over the top tomorrow. Permission to get weaving, sir.

BLACKADDER: Permission granted.

George exits to trench.

Baldrick.

BALDRICK: Captain B?

BLACKADDER: This is a crisis, a large crisis. In fact, if you've got a moment, it is a twelve-storey crisis with a magnificent entrance hall, carpeted throughout; twenty-four-hour porterage and an enormous sign on the roof saying, 'This is a Large Crisis'. And a large crisis requires a large plan. Get me a ruler, two pencils and a pair of underpants.

RICHARD CURTIS AND BEN ELTON

Do you want to see my war wound?

The Milligan had suffered from his legs terribly. During the war in Italy. While his mind was full of great heroisms under shell fire, his legs were carrying the idea, at speed, in the opposite direction. The Battery Major had not understood.

'Gunner Milligan? You have been acting like a coward.'

'No sir, not true. I'm a hero wid coward's legs, I'm a hero from the waist up.'

'Silence! Why did you leave your post?'

'It had woodworm in it, sir, the roof of the trench was falling in.'

'Silence! You acted like a coward!'

'I wasn't acting sir!'

'I could have you shot!'

'Shot? Why didn't they shoot me in peacetime? I was still the same coward.'

'Men like you are a waste of time in war. Understand?'

'Oh? Well den! Men like *you* are a waste of time in peace.'

'Silence when you speak to an officer,' shouted the Sgt. Major at Milligan's neck.

All his arguments were of no avail in the face of military authority. He was court martialled, surrounded by clanking top brass who were not cowards and therefore biased. 'I may be a coward. I'm not denying dat sir,' Milligan told the prosecution. 'But you can't really *blame* me for being a coward. If I am, then you might as well hold me responsible for the shape of me nose, the colour of me hair and the size of me feet.'

'Gunner Milligan,' Captain Martin stroked a cavalry moustache on an infantry face. 'Gunner Milligan,' he said. 'Your personal evaluations of cowardice do not concern the court. To refresh your memory I will read the precise military definition of the word.'

He took a book of King's Regulations, opened a marked page and read 'Cowardice'. Here he paused and gave Milligan a look.

He continued: 'Defection in the face of the enemy. Running away.'

'I was not running away sir. I was retreating.'

'The whole of your Regiment were advancing, and you decided to retreat?'

'Isn't dat what you calls personal initiative?'

'Your action might have caused your comrades to panic and retreat.'

'Oh, I see! One man retreating is called running away, but a whole Regiment running away is called a retreat? I demand to be tried by cowards!'

A light, commissioned-ranks-only laugh passed around the court. But this was no laughing matter. These lunatics could have him shot.

'Have you anything further to add?' asked Captain Martin.

'Yes.' said Milligan. 'Plenty. For one ting I had no desire to partake in dis war. I was dragged in. I warned the Medical Officer. I told him I was a coward, and he marked me A.1. for Active Service. I gave everyone fair warning! I told me Battery Major before it started, I even wrote to Field Marshal Montgomery. Yes, I warned everybody, and now you're all acting surprised?'

Even as Milligan spoke his mind, three non-cowardly judges made a mental note of Guilty.

SPIKE MILLIGAN, *PUCKOON* (1963)

ALAN: … They say men who really saw action never talk about it, Rigsby.

RIGSBY: Well, you know why, don't you? Because nobody listens anymore. *(Busy with brush)* They're not interested – they want to forget. A few poppies on Armistice Day and that's about it. The parades are getting shorter every year. They can't even keep quiet for the two minutes silence. They'd sooner hold a Pop Festival any day. I often wondered what we saved this country for. What's happened to the old traditions? What happened to British grit?

PHILIP: *(Drily)* I think you're sweeping most of it under the carpet, Rigsby.

RIGSBY: I was one of the first, mate. I didn't take any notice of old Chamberlain – 'In my hand I have a piece of paper.' We all knew what he could do with that. I was there when they were needing them not feeding them. And I saw action. If you don't believe me – what about this? *(He bares his chest)* What do you think this is?

ALAN: *(Peers)* It looks like your nipple.

RIGSBY: What? *(Looks down)* Oh, wrong side. *(He opens his shirt wider)* What do you think that is?

ALAN: That's your other nipple.

RIGSBY: That's shrapnel, mate. If that moves another inch I'll be the last casualty of World War II.

Ruth enters. Rigsby hurriedly buttons his shirt.

RIGSBY: Ah, here's someone who'll remember what it was like. You went without during the war didn't you, Miss Jones. There was no orange juice for you was there?

RUTH: *(Winces)* I was only a baby, Mr Rigsby.

RIGSBY: But you must remember it. The ration books, the gas masks, Potato Pete and Doctor Carrot and Victory Pie.

RUTH: Well, I was very small.

RIGSBY: Still, you made sacrifices. Not like these two – they don't know what it's like to go without.

ALAN: I wouldn't say that.

RUTH: I hardly remember. I mean, I was still in my pram.

RIGSBY: Ah, but it was the people's war, Miss Jones. Everyone suffered.

RUTH: Well, it was some years before I saw a banana.

RIGSBY: *(Triumphantly)* There you are, you see.

RUTH: And mother always insisted we were machine gunned coming from the vicarage. She was pushing me in my pram and this Messerschmitt dived very low. She saw the pilot quite clearly – in fact she swore it was someone she'd met in Germany before the war. What she'd said to make him go to those lengths I can't imagine.

ERIC CHAPPELL

The madness of it all

WORLD WAR II – STALAG 541
ESCAPE CLUB REUNION ANNUAL DINNER

MCLACHLAN

'Here they come!'
EDWARD MCLACHLAN

I'm going to Vietnam at the request of the White House. President Johnson says a war isn't really a war without my jokes.
BOB HOPE

Representatives of the army, the navy and the air force were called upon to speak at a dinner. Proud of their traditions, the army and the navy kept referring to the air force as the Cinderella of the forces. When it was the turn of the air force representative to speak, he began: 'I know very little about Cinderella, except that she had two ugly sisters.'

A soldier serving abroad received a 'Dear John' letter from his girlfriend, breaking off their engagement. She also asked if he could send her photo back. So he collected all the unwanted photos of girls from the entire regiment and sent them to her with a note saying, 'Sorry, can't remember which one you were. Please keep yours and send back the others.'

185

Did you know that the Royal Corps of Signals experimented with **crossing a carrier-pigeon with a woodpecker.** They wanted to get a bird that would knock on the door before delivering a message.

'She likes military men. She's just married a second lieutenant.' 'Why?' 'The first one got away.'

The Perfect Camouflage Artist

Before

After

FOUGASSE

A war correspondent visiting Afghanistan for a second time noted that, since the fall of the Taliban, **wives who used to walk ten paces behind their husbands were now walking ten paces in front.** The journalist asked one of the men if this was a sign of growing equality. 'No,' the man replied. 'Landmines.'

HAMMOND OUTLINED THE RUDIMENTS OF HIS DARING ESCAPE PLAN

GLEN BAXTER

ROUND THE HORNE – WE'LL MEET AGAIN SOME SUNNY DAY

KENNETH (HORNE): Here now is an excerpt from one of the great films of that period, starring Dame Celia Molestrangler and ageing juvenile Binkie Huckaback.

Tape: 'White Cliffs of Dover'

BETTY (MARSDEN): Oh, Charles – I thought you'd never get here.

HUGH (PADDICK): It wasn't easy, but I pulled it off. (I managed to swing a forty-eight.)

BETTY: How strong you are.

HUGH: Oh, Fiona, how I love you in these gay, madcap, antic, hoydenish, exuberant moods of yours. You just twinkle.

BETTY: Only for you, Charles. Only for you. Come – sit here by me – tell me, Charles, is it bad?

HUGH: At the Front?

BETTY: At the Front.

HUGH: Pretty bad. At the front. Not too good at the back. But the sides he's done it beautifully.

BETTY: You're pulling my leg, Charles.

HUGH: I'm sorry, darling, I thought it was mine. *(Hollow laugh)*

BETTY: Is it – hell – the trenches?

HUGH: Yes. The trenches are hell. The buck and wing's not too good either, but fortunately they're not too particular in ENSA.

BETTY: *(Tinkling laugh)*

HUGH: Oh, it tickles you does it? Perhaps I should have shaved it off. How I love to hear you laugh, Fiona – it's everything most wonderful. It's a rainbow after rain, the first cuckoo of spring, a field of corn in the sunlight, the dappled dancing of moonbeams on a mountain lake; it's jam and crumpets in front of the fire, it's Christmas Day, it's like a fairy tinkling in an enchanted glade, a sunset over the Cairngorms, the Taj Mahal by moonlight, it's – it's … I don't have the words for it.

BETTY: I know.

HUGH: I know you know.

BETTY: I know you know I know.

HUGH: Yes, I know.

BETTY: Oh, Charles – I want to make you happy for these few brief, fleeting moments that we're together. How can I make you happy?

HUGH: You know, Fiona.

BETTY: Yes – I know I know. Kiss me, Charles – kiss me –

HUGH: Oh, Fiona – if only this could go on forever. Tell me, Fiona – have you ever loved like this before?

BETTY: Not like this. Not quite like this. Not on the top of a 73 bus.

BARRY TOOK AND MARTY FELDMAN

Church Hall. Day. Platoon standing in group. Mainwaring and Wilson enter either side of platform.

MAINWARING: A good morning's work, men. A first class exercise in the art of camouflage. Now, pay attention, men. The subject of my lecture today is communications. In the event of an invasion, enemy paratroopers will try to seize the following points. *(He points to the diagram on the board.)* The gasworks, here ... The railway bridge, here ... The telephone exchange, here ... and the water reservoir, here. With all these points out of action, the town would be crippled. No gas, no trains, no telephones, and no water. After all, not many of us can last very long without water to drink.

FRAZER: I've managed it for years.

MAINWARING: In short, all these parts of the town are absolutely vital. So the object of the exercise is ...

JONES: To stop the enemy getting his hands on our vital parts!

MAINWARING: Er – well, yes. *(Turns to board.)* Now we shall post two men at each one of these points. In the event of an attack, one of the men will run to the nearest telephone box and phone me at the church hall here.

FRAZER: Excuse me, sir. If one of the men is running to phone you, what happens to the man who's left behind?

WALKER: He'll be running the other way.

MAINWARING: This is not a matter for levity, Walker. No, the man who is left behind will pin the enemy down with constant, withering fire.

JONES: It's going to be a bit difficult to keep up a constant, withering fire, sir – we've only got five rounds each.

MAINWARING: You'll just have to make every shot tell. Now, you will see on the map here that I have pinpointed the nearest telephone box to all these strategic points. *(He points.)* The railway bridge – the nearest phone box is a hundred yards away, here ... The gasworks – there's one here, fifty yards away. And the water reservoir, there's one here, just outside the gates. Now the problem is the telephone exchange, unfortunately the nearest phone box is over half a mile away. So there could be a considerable delay in summoning help.

WILSON: Perhaps it would save time, sir, if we used one of the phones in the exchange.

MAINWARING: What? Oh, yes, of course ... Well done, Wilson.

The men exchange looks.

MAINWARING: Now, as soon as I get a call I shall relieve you at the head of a swift mobile attacking force. By the way, make sure that all your bicycles are in good working order.

FRAZER: There is only one thing, sir.

MAINWARING: What's that, Frazer?

FRAZER: What happens if the phone box is out of order?

MAINWARING: Well, in that case, as usual, we shall have to improvise.

JIMMY PERRY AND DAVID CROFT

Banzai!

KAMIKAZE

A bunch of Japanese in plain military uniform – all with headbands. A COMMANDER enters.

ALL: Hai!

COMMANDER: Hai! You all know the purpose of this mission?

ALL: To die for the Emperor!

COMMANDER: Your task?

ALL: To seek out and destroy the American fleet in the Pacific!

COMMANDER: It is ...?

ALL: A kamikaze mission!

COMMANDER: This will include the deaths of each and every one of you.

ALL: *(A little disconsolate)* Ah so!

(The COMMANDER rounds on one slightly shifty-looking character.)

COMMANDER: Including you.

YAMAMOTO: Me, sir?

COMMANDER: Yes, you sir – you are a kamikaze pilot. What are you?

YAMAMOTO: A kamikaze pilot, sir!!

COMMANDER: And how many missions have you flown?

YAMAMOTO: Nineteen, sir.

COMMANDER: Nineteen suicide missions.

YAMAMOTO: That's right, sir. I pride myself on being the longest-serving suicide pilot in the Japanese Airforce.

COMMANDER: I'm sorry, Yamamoto, but can you not see there is a slight contradiction here?

YAMAMOTO: In what way?

COMMANDER: Well, suicide pilots are meant to commit suicide.

YAMAMOTO: That's right, sir. The problem is that in my case things just keep going wrong.

COMMANDER: Let me look at your card. First mission, 1944, January.

YAMAMOTO: That's right, sir.

COMMANDER: 'Turned back with tickly throat.'

YAMAMOTO: That's right. I wasn't going to die for my Emperor when I wasn't at the peak of my fitness.

COMMANDER: Second mission. 'Suspected toothache ... return home.'

YAMAMOTO: That's right, sir. And as you can see, I was right.

COMMANDER: Third mission. 'Severe toothache ... return home.'

YAMAMOTO: That's right, sir! Then I was all ready to go, when I started having trouble with my headband.

COMMANDER: So I see. Mission six.

'Headband too tight came back with headache.'

YAMAMOTO: That's right, sir.

COMMANDER: Mission seven. 'Forgot headband.' *(YAMAMOTO shrugs shoulders.)* Mission eight. 'New headband slips over eyes.'

YAMAMOTO: That's right, sir.

COMMANDER: Then a new problem arises: Mission nine – 'couldn't find target'. Mission ten – 'couldn't find target'. Then it's 'couldn't find target' – 'couldn't find target' – 'vertigo' – 'held up at traffic lights' – 'couldn't find target', 'couldn't find target' and 'couldn't find target'. You do know what we're looking for, don't you?

YAMAMOTO: Uhm ...

COMMANDER: A-meri ...

YAMAMOTO: A-meri ... A Merry Christmas and a Happy New Year!

COMMANDER: American aircraft carriers.

YAMAMOTO: American aircraft carr-

COMMANDER: Yes, look – where exactly have you been looking for these aircraft carriers? I can't help noticing you seemed to have more or less totally ignored the area of the sea.

YAMAMOTO: I think you're being very unfair, sir – I've flown over the sea lots of times, and in fact once I even attacked an aircraft carrier.

COMMANDER: Ah yes – Mission eleven – let's have a look at that, shall we? Took off 0400 hrs.

YAMAMOTO: Good start.

COMMANDER: Climbed to a height of 4000 feet and proceeded to the target area. 0430 – sighted target. Went into a power dive and successfully ... landed on the target.

YAMAMOTO: That's right, sir – I was just about to do it when I was taken short, so I just stopped off for a quick widdle. Unfortunately, by the time I was ready to start again, the element of surprise had gone. But I intend to put that all right today, sir.

COMMANDER: And commit suicide?

YAMAMOTO: Absolutely. That is my duty and that I will do.

COMMANDER: Very well. Goodbye to you all, and God save the Emperor.

ALL: God save the Emperor!!!

COMMANDER: Dismissed.

(Pause as the COMMANDER leaves.)

YAMAMOTO: *(Casually, to one of his comrades)* Look, you haven't got anything for diarrhoea, have you? My tummy's feeling just a little jippy ...

DOUGLAS ADAMS AND CHRIS KEIGHTLEY,
CAMBRIDGE FOOTLIGHTS

'Looks like a case for Mr Sherlock Holmes, Inspector.'
TONY HUSBAND

LAW& ORDER

Call for the police!

FLYING SQUAD: A special contingent of police whose business is to arrive at the scene of a crime shortly after the departure of all those connected with it.

BEACHCOMBER

POLICEMAN: I am going to have to lock you up for the night.

SUSPECT: What charge?

POLICEMAN: There's no charge. It's all part of the service.

EDWARD MCLACHLAN

THEY WERE LATER CHARGED WITH IMITATING A CONSTABLE.

One day some policemen found three hand grenades in the street and decided to take them back to the police station. 'What if one of the grenades explodes?' asked one of the officers. 'It doesn't matter,' reassured another. 'We'll say we only found two.'

STEVE BEST

LAW & ORDER
It's a fair cop

A man went to the police station **determined to speak to the burglar who had broken into his house the night before.** 'You'll get your chance in court,' said the desk sergeant. 'No, you don't understand,' said the man. 'I want to know how he got into the house in the middle of the night without waking my wife. I've been trying to do that for years.'

Noticing that a man's front garden was crammed with shopping trolleys, a policeman asked him for an explanation. 'I just couldn't resist the bargain,' replied the man. 'They're only a pound each at the supermarket.'

A policewoman stopped a car and found that the driver had been drinking. She told him to get out of the vehicle. 'You're staggering,' she said, when he did. 'You're not so bad yourself,' replied the driver.

'It was ...
AAAAAAAGGGGGGGHHHHH ...'.

'George Herbert
AAAAAAAGGGGGGGHHHHH?
We have reason to believe ...'
EDWARD MCLACHLAN

A slight Misunderstanding
With the Till
H.M.BATEMAN

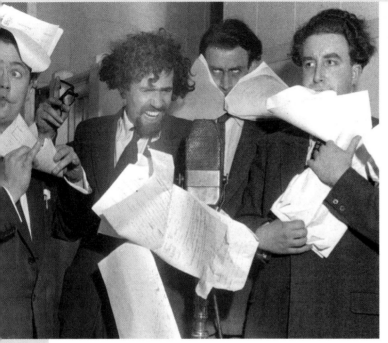

CRUN: She was struck down from behind.

SEAGOON: And not a moment too soon – congratulations, sir.

CRUN: I didn't do it.

SEAGOON: Coward – hand back your OBE. Now tell me who did this felonious deed. What's happened to her?

CRUN: It's too dark to see – strike a light.

SEAGOON: Not allowed in blackout.

MINNIE: Strike a dark light.

SEAGOON: No madam, we daren't – why, only twenty-eight miles across the Channel the Germans are watching this coast.

F.X. Whoosh – splosh – batter pudding hitting Minnie.

MINNIE: Ooooooooooooooohohohohohohoho hohohohohohohohohohohoho …

CRUN: No, I've never heard of him.

MINNIE: Help, Henery – I've been struck down from behind. Helpp.

CRUN: Mnk – oh dear dear. *(Calls)* Police – English Police – Law Guardians???

MINNIE: Not too loud, Henry, they'll hear you.

F.X. Police whistle

SEAGOON: *(Approaching)* Can I help you, sir?

CRUN: Are you a policeman?

SEAGOON: No, I'm a constable.

CRUN: What's the difference?

SEAGOON: They're spelt differently.

MINNIE: Ohhhhhh.

SEAGOON: Oh! What's happened to this dear old silver-bearded lady?

CRUN: Don't be a silly-pilly policeman – they can't see a little match being struck.

SEAGOON: Oh, alright.

F.X. Match striking – quick whoosh of shell – shell explodes.

SEAGOON: Any questions?

CRUN: Yes – where are my legs?

SEAGOON: Are you now aware of the danger from German long-range guns?

CRUN: Mnk ahh! I've got it – I have the answer – just by chance I happen to have on me a box of German matches.

SEAGOON: Wonderful – strike one – they won't fire at their own matches.

CRUN: Of course not – now …

F.X. Match striking and flaring – whoosh of shell – shell burst.

CRUN: … Curse … the British!!!

SPIKE MILLIGAN

LAW & ORDER
Caught in the act

The contents of the Queen's Speech come under scrutiny and are deemed to have been designed to suit a General Election in the spring.

PETER BROOKES

After a morning stroll, the three bears headed for the kitchen to see if their breakfast had cooled down. 'Somebody's eaten my porridge!' wailed baby bear. 'Somebody's eaten my porridge!' exclaimed mother bear. 'Forget the porridge!' roared father bear. 'Who's taken the TV and video?'

A man was attacked and left bleeding in a ditch. **Two sociologists passed by** and one said to the other, 'We must find the man who did this – he needs help.'

A woman was in the supermarket when her friend rushed in. 'Quick, quick! Out to the car park! There's a man trying to steal your car!' The woman rushed out, but was soon back again. 'Did you catch him?' asked her friend. 'No, but I got his number.'

Library:

The room where the

We had gay burglars the other night. They broke in and rearranged the furniture.
ROBIN WILLIAMS

Policeman: (producing notebook)
Name, please.
Motorist: Aloysius Alastair
Cyprian …
Policeman: (putting book away)
Well, don't let me catch you again.
H.M. BROCK

A thief went into a fast food restaurant and held a gun to the manager's head. 'Hand over everything in the till!' he demanded.
'To take away?' asked the manager.

A shoplifter was caught red-handed trying to steal a watch from a jeweller's. The shoplifter pleaded with the manager not to call the police **and said that he would happily buy the watch. After a bit of thought, the manager agreed.** 'That'll be five hundred pounds then.' **'Oh dear,' said the shoplifter, 'that's more than I was intending to spend. Could you show me something a bit cheaper?'**

'Curiosity.'
JAMES STEVENSON

murders take place.

HAND UP YOUR STICKS!

A nervous, first-time robber is standing outside a bank, rehearsing his lines …

THIEF: *(Practising)* Hands up, this is a hold-up. This is a hold-up, hands up. Hold up your hands, this is a stick-up. Stick up your hands, this is a hold-up. Give me the money. Oh, I must get that right. Give me the money. Hands up, this is a stick-up, give me the money. Hands up, this is a stick-up, give me the money. Hands up, this is a stick-up, give me the money. Oh yes, that's it, hands up, this is a stick-up, give me the money. Hands up, this is a stick-up, give me the money. Hands up, this is a stick-up, give me the money. *(Runs into bank.)* Hold hands, this is an up stick, I mean, up sticks, this is a handle.

CASHIER: I beg your pardon?

THIEF: I mean this is a stick-up, a hold-stick.

CASHIER: A hold-stick?

THIEF: I mean a hand-stick.

CASHIER: Oh, I see, you mean this is a hold-up.

THIEF: Yes, that's right, this is a hold-up, yes. Up with your hands and give me the money.

CASHIER: How?

THIEF: What do you mean, how?

CASHIER: How do I give you the money with my hands up?

THIEF: Well, you put your hands up and give me the money. No, you give me the money and then put your hands – Oh, I don't know. Work it out for yourself, but give me the money.

CASHIER: No, I don't think I will.

THIEF: Come on.

CASHIER: Why should I?

THIEF: I've got a gun, stupid …

CASHIER: Yes.

THIEF: … and it's loaded …

CASHIER: Yes.

THIEF: … with real bullets, and if I fire, you'll be dead, all sprawled on the floor, dead.

CASHIER: Well, go on, then, shoot me.

THIEF: Do you mean that?

CASHIER: Yes.

THIEF: What, cross your heart and hope to die?

CASHIER: Cross my heart and hope to die.

THIEF: Oh, stop messing about. Give me the money.

CASHIER: No.

THIEF: But you don't understand. I don't want to shoot you.

CASHIER: No, I know that.

THIEF: You see, you're supposed to be terrified by my threat …

CASHIER: I see.

THIEF: I waggle the gun …

CASHIER: Uh-huh.

THIEF: … you give me the money …

CASHIER: Hm.

THIEF: … and then I run out with the bag.

CASHIER: Of course.

THIEF: But if I take the wrong one, you call me back and give me the right one.

CASHIER: Yes.

THIEF: All right then, shall we do it again?

CASHIER: Right.

THIEF: Close your eyes. I won't go all the way out. I'll just go a little way. *(Goes out and comes back.)* Hold up your hands and give me your money. *(A bell sounds.)* Oh, what did you do that for? That's the alarm bell.

CASHIER: I know.

THIEF: The police'll be round here any minute.

CASHIER: Well, you'd better be quick.

THIEF: They'll take me away and put me in prison.

CASHIER: Well, hurry up and go away then.

THIEF: What, without the money?

CASHIER: Yes, hurry. They'll be here any moment.

THIEF: No, I won't go.

CASHIER: Get out, you idiot, I don't want you to go to prison.

THIEF: I know you don't.

CASHIER: Well, go away then.

THIEF: But I'm not going.

CASHIER: Go *on*.

THIEF: No.

CASHIER: Go on.

THIEF: No.

CASHIER: Go on.

THIEF: Shan't.

CASHIER: All right then, take the money.

THIEF: Thanks. *(Runs off.)*

PETER COOK, *PIECES OF EIGHT*

LAW & ORDER
Letter of the law

It ain't no sin if you crack a few laws now and then, just so long as you don't break any.

MAE WEST

Lawyer, n. One skilled in circumvention of the law.

Litigation, n. A machine which you go into as a pig and come out of as a sausage.

AMBROSE BIERCE, *THE DEVIL'S DICTIONARY* (1911)

Thieves respect property; they merely wish the property to become their property that they may more perfectly respect it.

G.K. CHESTERTON

5-1   © Jim Unger/dist. by United Media, 2002

'Not a lot of clues. We only found one footprint.'
JIM UNGER

law & order

LAW & ORDER

Crime capers

'How do you kill a circus?'

'Go for the juggler.'

'*An interesting case, eh, Sergeant?*'
EDWARD MCLACHLAN

Harold and David are out hunting when David suddenly collapses and stops breathing. Desperately, Harold searches for a pulse but can't find one. He whips out his mobile phone, dials 999 and blurts, 'My friend has just dropped dead! What should I do?' A soothing voice at the other end says, 'OK, OK. Just relax. First, let's make sure he's really dead.' After a brief silence the operator hears a shot ring out. Then Harold comes back to the phone. 'OK,' he says nervously, 'what do I do next?'

In the news the other day – first a lorry carrying brand new file folders was hijacked, then a van loaded with Post-it notes was stolen. Detectives believe the robberies were the work of organised crime.

ERIC: Excuse me, can you see a policeman round here?

ERNIE: No.

ERIC: Okay, stick 'em down!

ERNIE: You mean stick 'em up!

ERIC: Don't confuse me – I'm nervous enough as it is. Just give me your watch.

ERNIE: But it isn't worth anything. Its only value is sentimental.

ERIC: Let's have it anyway – I feel like a good cry. I'll never forget my mother's words to me when I first went to jail.

ERNIE: What did she say?

ERIC: Hello, son.

ERNIE: What were you in for?

ERIC: Well, I'd started in a small way – picking midgets' pockets.

ERNIE: How could you stoop so low?

ERIC: Stoop? I was up on tiptoe! I was very young. I can remember it to this day, being hustled into the back door of the court with my nappy over my head to avoid the photographers.

FRED METCALF

CARL GILES

ALAN (BENNETT): The great train robbery of over three million pounds continues to baffle the British police.

PETER (COOK): Good evening.

ALAN: However, we have here with us in the studio this evening ...

PETER: Good evening.

ALAN: Sir Arthur Gappy, the First Deputy Head of New Scotland Yard, and I'm going to ask him a few questions about the train robbery.

PETER: Good evening.

ALAN: Good evening. Sir Arthur. I'm going to ask you a few questions about the train robbery.

PETER: Good – the very thing we are investigating. In fact, I would like to make one thing quite clear at the very outset and that is, when you speak of a train robbery, this involved no loss of train, merely what I like to call the contents of the train, which were pilfered. We haven't lost a train since 1946, I believe it was – the year of the great snows when we mislaid a small one. Trains are very bulky and cumbersome, making them extremely difficult to lose as compared with a small jewel, for example, or a small pearl which could easily fall off a lady's neck and disappear into the tall grass. Whereas a huge train with steam coming out is very ...

ALAN: I think you have made that point rather well, Sir Arthur. Who do you think may have perpetrated this awful crime?

PETER: Well, we believe this to be the work of thieves, and I'll tell you why. The whole pattern is very reminiscent of past robberies where we have found thieves to have been involved. The tell-tale loss of property – that's one of the signs we look for, the snatching away of the money substances – it all points to thieves.

ALAN: So you feel that thieves are responsible?

PETER: Good heavens, no! I feel that thieves are totally irresponsible. They're a ghastly group of people, snatching away your money, stealing from you ...

ALAN: I appreciate that, Sir Arthur, but ...

PETER: You may appreciate it, but I don't. I'm sorry I can't agree with you. If you appreciate having your money snatched away from you I will have to consider you some sort of odd fish ...

ALAN: You misunderstand me, Sir Arthur, but who in your opinion is behind the criminals?

PETER: Well, we are – considerably. Months, days, even seconds ...

ALAN: No, I mean who do you think is the organising genius behind the crime?

PETER: Of course, now you're asking me who is the organising genius behind the crime.

ALAN: You are a man of very acute perception, Sir Arthur.

PETER: Yes. Through the wonderful equipment known as 'Identikit' – do you know about that?

ALAN: Yes, I believe it's when you piece together the face of the criminal.

PETER: Not entirely, no – it's when you piece together the appearance of the face of the criminal. Unfortunately we're not able to piece together the face of the criminal – I wish we could. Once you have captured the criminal's face the other parts of the criminal's body are not too far behind, being situated immediately

below the criminal's face ... anyway through this wonderful equipment of 'Identikit', we have pieced together a remarkable likeness to the Archbishop of Canterbury.

ALAN: So His Grace is your number one suspect?

PETER: Let me put it this way. His Grace is the man we are currently beating the living daylights out of down at the Yard.

ALAN: And he is still your number one suspect?

PETER: No, I'm happy to say that the Archbishop, God bless him, no longer resembles the picture we built up. A change, I think, for the better.

ALAN: I see. I believe I'm right in saying that some of the stolen money has been recovered?

PETER: Yes, that's right.

ALAN: And what is being done with this?

PETER: We're spending it as quickly as we can. It's a short life, but a merry one. Goodnight.

ALAN BENNETT AND PETER COOK

I blame the kids

'Look, he's taking his first steps.'
ROB BAINES

Police arrested two kids yesterday, one was drinking battery acid, the other was eating fireworks. They charged one and let the other one off.
TOMMY COOPER

Walking past a playground surrounded by a tall fence, a man heard some children chanting, 'thirteen, thirteen,' very loudly. His curiosity got the better of him and he peeked through a knot-hole in the fence. Someone promptly poked him in the eye and he fell over. 'Fourteen, fourteen,' the chant continued.

A five-year old boy got lost in a shopping mall. Remembering what his mother had told him to do in these circumstances, he went up to a policeman and said, 'Constable, did you happen to see a lady without a boy like me?'

See you in court

CHRISTMAS OATH

Scene: a courtroom. The ACCUSED enters the dock. CLERK OF THE COURT leans over to him.

CLERK: Would you read what is on the card?

ACCUSED: *(After brief look at Clerk)*
May every Christmas wish
    come true
And joy this day be yours,
With mistletoe upon the tree
And holly on the doors –

CLERK: *(In angry whisper)*
The other side.

ACCUSED: Oh! I swear to tell the truth, and nothing but the truth –
love Denis and Mabel.
MICHAEL PALIN

DAVE WHAMOND

CLIENT: Can you tell me what your fees are?
LAWYER: Certainly. I charge £250 to answer three questions.
CLIENT: That's a bit steep, isn't it?
LAWYER: Yes, now what's your final question?

A man was sent to court for drunk and disorderly conduct. The judge enquired where the defendant worked. **'Here and there,' he replied. 'And what do you do for a living?' 'This and that,' came the answer.** The judge turned to a policeman and instructed him to take the man straight to jail. **'Wait,' implored the accused, 'when will I come out?' 'Sooner or later.'**

WHAT DO YOU CALL A JUDGE WITH NO THUMBS?

'And that m'lud concludes the case for the prosecution.'
KEN PYNE

Two scientists were discussing their latest research methods. One said, 'We've introduced something new in all our laboratories. Now we don't use rats for experiments. We use lawyers.'
The other one said, 'Lawyers instead of rats? What's the advantage in that?'
And the first one replied, 'Well, you do kind of get attached to rats.'

DAVID AUSTIN

... JUST HIS FINGERS.

law & order

Alan Partridge is interviewing an unconventional lawyer.

ALAN: Right. Indeed. Now, you are –

NICK: Great.

ALAN: – you are a very different kind of lawyer.

NICK: That's right. What I say is, the law is an ass and I kick it.

ALAN: Very good, very clever. Yeah. Now, you've done all sorts of things in court, you once abseiled into court –

NICK: Uh-huh.

ALAN: – you once did a partial strip –

NICK: That's right.

ALAN: – and you once simulated a heart attack.

NICK: Yeah.

ALAN: The one that was in the press recently is the man who robbed the –

NICK: Mickey Hall. Basically what happened was he robbed a building society, and I felt that there were mitigating circumstances, and so when it came to the summing up, I kind of went in there with all the jewellery on, all the gear and had a baseball cap on with 'justice' written on it, and I just got them to dim all the lights, one centre spot on me and I went:

(Raps) Ladies and gents, jury. Everybody in the court, hear me one and all, I'm here to plead the case of a guy called Mickey Hall. When he went into the Woolwich on that fateful day, he was an innocent man, he didn't blow no one away. Yeah, he pulled a gun, but the gun was fake, on that piece of evidence I stake – my claim. Society's to blame. Look at its face.

I rest my case –

ALAN: Very good.

NICK: I rest my case, I rest my case.

(Applause) Said it three times and I just very slowly, very dramatically walked

backwards into my seat, sat down. The atmosphere was electric. Could've heard a pin drop.

ALAN: Amazing. What happened?

NICK: He got five years.

ALAN: Well, good for you! Great, well, he won't be doing that again in a hurry, now would he?

NICK: I was defending him, Alan. I lost the case.

ALAN: Yeah, it puzzles me, that law. How can you defend a man who, let's say, has been arrested for murder?

NICK: Well, 'cos he may be innocent.

ALAN: Well, with the greatest respect, the police are hardly likely to arrest him if he's innocent, are they?

NICK: With slightly less respect, haven't you heard of wrongful arrest?

ALAN: No.

NICK: Guildford four, Birmingham six –

ALAN: Well, yes, but that's different. Now, they are innocent –

NICK: Be very careful, Alan. You're on air.

ALAN: No, I think we should go into it –

NICK: No, if I was your lawyer, I would advise you very strongly now to shut your mouth.

ALAN: Why?

NICK: These people will sue and put an injunction on your show and you'll never broadcast again.

ALAN: *(Long pause)* Where did you get your shirt from?

ARMANDO IANNUCCI, STEVE COOGAN AND PATRICK MARBER

I want to see my lawyer

How many lawyers does it take to change a light bulb?

How many can you afford?

An American tourist was having a guided tour of Westminster Abbey. The guide pointed to one monument and said, 'There lies a famous, honest man and a most celebrated lawyer.'
'Gee,' said the American. 'Back in the States we'd never put two bodies in the same grave.'

'I'm a criminal lawyer.'
'Thank you for being so frank.'

Wanting to sue an airline for damaging his luggage, a man spoke to a solicitor. He was told his case wasn't strong enough.

'Now you're in big trouble. Here comes my solicitor.'
BUD GRACE

Crime and punishment

Two women were in a bar trying to find boyfriends, but weren't having much luck. About to give up and go home, they spotted a man sitting alone and one of them went over for a chat. 'You look really unhappy,' she said arriving at his table. 'I am,' he groaned. 'I've just wasted 20 years of my life in prison.' 'Twenty years?' gasped the woman. 'What did you do?' 'I poisoned my wife,' admitted the man. 'And then I chopped her up.' Looking across the bar to her friend, the woman mouthed, 'He's single.'

Before a burglary trial the judge explained to the defendant, 'You can let me try your case, or you can choose to have a jury of your peers.' The man thought for a moment. 'What are peers?' he asked. 'They're people just like you – your equals.' 'Forget it,' retorted the defendant. 'I don't want to be tried by a bunch of thieves.'

When a businessman discovered that his safe had jammed, he called the nearby prison and asked whether any of the inmates might know how to open it. Soon, a convict and a prison officer turned up at the office. The criminal spun the dials, listened intently and calmly opened the safe door. 'I'm much obliged,' said the businessman. 'How much do I owe you?' 'Well,' replied the prisoner, 'the last time I opened a safe I got £20,000.'

'My big regret is that I didn't start earlier. I'da been out by now.'
CHON DAY

Sitting in the electric chair waiting to be put to death, a convict gets hiccups. 'Do you have any last requests?' the warden asks. 'Yes,' replies the convict. 'Could you do something to scare me?'

'They __all__ are. That's what he's in for.'
CLAUDE SMITH

Convicts last night escaped from
Dartmoor in a cement mixer.

Police are looking for a group
of hardened criminals.

'See what I mean Ahmed, it's not the deterrent it used to be.'
JEREMY BANX

Doing time

PORRIDGE – HEARTBREAK HOTEL

Fletcher's cell. He has just turned off a radio request programme that Lennie was listening to.

LENNIE: … I'd written in, like. For a record. For Denise.

FLETCHER: Denise?

LENNIE: My fiancée.

FLETCHER: Oh yes, that Denise, of course, yes.

LENNIE: Just wanted to convey my undying feelings of affection and devotion. 'Everlasting Love', that was the record I asked for.

FLETCHER: You should have asked for 'My Ding-a-Ling'.

LENNIE: I been listening all week, but it ain't been on yet. Not fair. You'd think my needs were greater than an almond sorter's from Dundee.

FLETCHER: Hang about. Did you write this on prison notepaper?

LENNIE: Yes. If you remember I gave you me last sheet of Basildon Bond.

FLETCHER: That's it then.

LENNIE: Why? Are they biased against prisoners?

FLETCHER: P'raps not officially. But I don't recall ever having heard a prisoner's request on the air. Forces yes. Aircraft carriers or ack-ack batteries, but never heard nothing from no one from the nick.

LENNIE: It's a disgrace. We have a rotten enough life in here without having our requests refused. That's

discrimination that is. And five five and a halfpenny stamps up the spout.

FLETCHER: You can see it from their point of view. The public what pay their radio licence faithful every year. Take offence, wouldn't they? Sitting down to Sunday lunch with their beloved *Family Favourites*. Suddenly they read out a card with a Parkhurst postmark. Says could Tommy 'Mad Dog' Hollister please have 'Clair de Lune'. *(Mackay enters.)*

MACKAY: 'Clair de Lune'?

FLETCHER: Oh. Yeah, it's French, Mr Mackay. French for 'By the light of the silvery moon'.

MACKAY: I thought for a moment, Fletcher, you were having a cultural conversation.

LENNIE: P'raps you could tell us the ruling, Mr Mackay.

MACKAY: The ruling, Godber?

FLETCHER: Miss Lonelyloins here, lovelorn Lennie, he wants to know whether the BBC plays prisoners' requests?

MACKAY: No. The answer to that is no, on the grounds that it caused embarrassment.

LENNIE: Embarrassment?

MACKAY: To the prisoners' families. The family might have excused his absence by telling the neighbours that the felon in question was abroad, or working on a North Sea oil rig.

LENNIE: Oh I see.

MACKAY: No doubt your wife, Fletcher, has told your friends that you're on a five-year safari. *(He laughs.)*

FLETCHER: *(Reading paper)* No, no. She tells them I'm doing missionary work in Scotland.

MACKAY: No, Godber. The practice was also open to abuse. There was nothing to stop prisoners sending messages in code across our airways.

FLETCHER: Ah, that's a point – yeah, that's a point. Listen to some heartwarming Christmas message from some poor lag. To his beloved wife and family and little Tiny Tim. Could he please hear Harry Secombe with 'The Impossible Dream'. Translated what he really meant was 'Nobby, have the ladder round the back of E Wing, Boxing Day – and bring me a mince pie.'

LENNIE: Oh it's a good idea, that.

MACKAY: It's an abuse of privilege, Godber. Which is why I'm here.

FLETCHER: Oh, I thought it was a social call.

MACKAY: Six rolls of soft toilet paper have disappeared from the Governor's closet – the Governor's own personal water closet.

FLETCHER: Oh dear. Would you Adam and Eve it? What next?

MACKAY: Knowing you, Fletcher, probably the seat.

DICK CLEMENT AND IAN LA FRENAIS

HE TOOK EVERY GAME OF CRICKET VERY SERIOUSLY.

STEVE BEST

GAMES & SPORTS

SPORTING NONSENSE

It's gold or nothing ... and it's nothing.
He comes away with a silver medal.
DAVID COLEMAN

Most of these athletes will have
a favourite lead leg, which is
either left or right.
MIKE WHITTINGHAM

Is there something that sticks out that
makes you an exceptional pole-vaulter?
ADRIAN CHILES

And here's Moses Kiptanui, the 19-year-
old Kenyan who turned 20 a few weeks
ago.
DAVID COLEMAN

GRIZELDA

The race is not always to
the swift nor the battle
to the strong, but that's
the way to bet.
DAMON RUNYON

**Jogging is very
beneficial. It's good
for your legs and
your feet.** It's also
very good for the
ground. It makes
it feel needed.
SNOOPY

EDWARD
MCLACHLAN

Football crazy

Walking along a pier on holiday, a young couple spotted a sign on a caravan saying: 'Chief Running Bear Memory Man – All Questions Answered'.

'Come on, I bet I can fox him,' the husband boasted. Inside, they found a wizened old man in a headdress. 'Who won the Preston North End v. Millwall third-round FA Cup game in 1938?' the husband demanded.

'Preston,' the chief replied.

'He's right,' said the husband. 'What was the score?'

'1-0. Malcolm McDermott scored in the ninetieth minute,' replied the chief.

'That's amazing,' said the husband and walked off shaking his head in disbelief.

Many years later, for their silver wedding anniversary, the couple revisited the resort and came across the same caravan.

On entering, the husband was surprised to find the old chief still alive and, raising his hand in mock Indian greeting, he said, 'How.'

'It was a header,' came the reply.

Two flies were playing football in a saucer. One said to the other, 'Have to do better than this. Come on, we're playing in the cup next week.'

REG SMYTHE, *ANDY CAPP*

Studies of dolphins have shown they have the same intellectual level as the average man.
STEVE BEST

The crowds were gathering on Mount Olympus to watch a football match between the gods and mortals. As the teams ran out on to the pitch, the manager of the mortals asked the manager of the gods, 'Who's that character that's half-human and half-horse?' 'Oh,' replied the gods' manager, 'that's our centaur forward.'

'Dad!' called a boy. 'I think I've been selected for the school football team.'

'That's good,' replied his father, 'but why aren't you sure?'

'Well, it hasn't been announced officially, but I overheard the coach saying that if I were in the team I'd be a great drawback.'

'What do you mean, "here comes the opening ceremony"? That was months ago.'
PETER KING

Playing in a football match, a chicken scored two goals. 'You're playing very well,' the referee said. 'Do you train hard?' 'Yes, I do,' replied the chicken. 'But it's not easy. I'm a lawyer and don't have much free time.' With that the referee immediately pulled out the red card and ordered the chicken off the pitch. 'Why did you do that?' demanded the chicken's team-mates. 'Professional fowl,' said the referee.

GAMES & SPORTS
... the second half

The world's worst football team was playing the world's second-worst team and an away supporter asked a local resident for directions to the ground. 'Go up this street and you'll see two queues,' said the local. 'Don't get in the long one, though,' he warned. 'That's for the chip shop.'

WORK ON STONEHENGE SLOWED DRAMATICALLY
AFTER THE FIRST THREE STONES WERE IN POSITION
STEVE BEST

FOOT IN MOUTH

Kilmarnock versus Partick Thistle, match postponed ... that, of course, is a latest score.
FRANK BOUGH

That chance was too easy. If it had been harder he probably would have scored.
DENIS LAW

It was Forest's night on Tuesday, but it looks like being Liverpool's night this afternoon.
PETER JONES

Sporting Lisbon in their green and white hooped shirts ... they look like a team of zebras.
PETER JONES

For nearly all the season we've been in the top half of the table and for most of the season better than that.
ALAN CURBISHLEY

After a goalless first half, the score at half-time is 0-0.
BRIAN MOORE

If you can get through the first round you have a good chance of getting into the next one.
NIGEL WORTHINGTON

... 1-0 is not a winning score, by any means ...
IAN HALL

He is the man who has been brought on to replace Pavel Nedved. The irreplaceable Pavel Nedved.
CLIVE TYLDESLEY

I was inbred into the game by my father.
DAVID PLEAT

What I said to them at half-time would be unprintable on the radio.
GERRY FRANCIS

Let's get physical

ETHEL

I don't understand Ethel.
I don't, I don't really.
She's one of my very best friends,
Just about the best, nearly.
She's an awfully nice girl, Ethel is,
Dainty and refined,
I mean she'd never do or say
Anything unkind.
But get her inside a stadium
And she seems to go out of her mind.

'KILL HIM!' she yells, 'KNOCK HIS
    BLOCK OFF!'
At ice hockey or football or what.
'KILL 'EM!' she yells, turning purple,
'KILL THE PERISHING LOT!'
'SH-SH!' I say, 'ETHEL!'
'SH-SH!' and I die of shame.
'KILL HIM AND BASH HIS TEETH IN HIS
    FACE!'
She says,
And calls him a dirty name.

I don't understand Ethel,
I don't, I don't truly.
She is always gentle and sweet,
Never a bit unruly.
She's an awfully shy girl, Ethel is,
Wouldn't say boo to a goose.
You wouldn't think she ever could
Suddenly break loose.
But get her inside a stadium
And her face turns a terrible puce.

'THROW HIM OUT OF THE WINDER!'
    she yells,
And her eyes go a terrible red.
'SWIPE 'EM!' she says, looking cheerful,
'SWIPE 'EM UNTIL THEY'RE DEAD!'
'SH-SH!' I say, 'ETHEL!'
'SH-SH!' and I nearly die,
'SWIPE HIM AND GRIND HIS FACE IN
    THE MUD!'

She says,
'AND PUT YOUR THUMB IN HIS EYE!'

I don't understand Ethel,
I don't, I don't, really.
She's one of my very best friends,
Just about the best, nearly.
She's an awfully quiet girl, Ethel is,
That's why I never see
What makes her carry on like that,
Noisy as can be.
Then last Saturday down at the stadium
Well … it suddenly happened to me.

'BREAK HIS SILLY NECK!' I yells,
    'IRON HIM OUT!'
Well, Ethel was startled at that.
'IRON HIM!' I says, feeling
    lovely,
'IRON HIM UNTIL HE'S FLAT!'
'OOH', I says, 'ETHEL!'
'OOH', and I did feel
    queer.
Then she grinned,
    and we both of
    us gave a yell
'BITE A BIT OUT OF
    HIS EAR!'

JOYCE GRENFELL

Hit for six

SILLY POINTS
Clearly the West Indies are going to play their normal game, which is what they normally do.

TONY GRIEG

That was a sort of parson's nose innings – good in parts.

CHARLES COLVILLE

He's taking the bull by the horns here, and throwing everything at it.

BOB WILLIS

The batman's Holding, the bowler's Willey.

BRIAN JOHNSTON

We didn't have metaphors in our day.
We didn't beat about the bush.

FRED TRUEMAN

'Hey, you've forgotten ... oh it probably won't make any difference.'
MATT

The Game of Cricket
I wish you'd speak to Mary, Nurse,
She's really getting worse and worse.
Just now when Tommy gave her out
She cried and then began to pout
And then she tried to take the ball
Although she cannot bowl at all.
And now she's standing on the pitch,
The miserable little Bitch!

HILAIRE BELLOC

Cricket is a game which the British, not being a spiritual people, had to invent in order to have some concept of eternity.

LORD MANCROFT

(with apologies to Samuel Taylor Coleridge)

An Ancient It is an Ancient Cricketer
Cricketer And he stoppeth one of three.
goeth in to The others whistle past his ear
bat. Or strike him on the knee.

The pavilion gate is open wide
And he is last man in.
With creaking joints he walketh forth,
Thirty to make to win.

He sendeth a His bat is in his skinny hand,
catch to first There are three slips thinks he.
slip, who He snicks a ball up to the first,
droppeth it. Eftsoons the catch drops he.

His A chance! A chance! Another chance!
opponents The Cricketer giveth three.
beat their The fielding captain beats his breast
bosoms. And curseth him roundly.

The field was there, the field was here,
So thick upon the ground;
They crouched and growled, appealed
   and howled
The Cricketer's bat around.

Fielders, fielders, everywhere,
About his bat did creep.
Fielders, fielders everywhere,
Nor anyone in the deep.

The Cricketer God save thee, Ancient Cricketer!
doth fear he Have mercy on thy soul!
hath an hole Like many men before thee gone,
in his bat. Thy bat must have an hole.

Yet still the Cricketer batteth on,
A full half-hour bats he.
He doth not score a single run
Though he trieth mightily.

Although he 'Tis done! 'Tis done! The game is won
scoreth no And well and truly fought,
runs, the The Cricketer limpeth happily in
Cricketer Although his score was nought.
helpeth his
side to win.

He batteth best, who scoreth most,
And hath but little luck.
Yet though the Cricketer made no runs
It was a noble duck.

MICHAEL GREEN, *BOOK OF COARSE SPORT* (1965)

EDWARD MCLACHLAN

Nets have been rigged up in the yard, with a coconut matting wicket. Stumps have been put into a wooden block. Walker is batting with cigarette in mouth. Mainwaring is bowling to him, watched by the squad.

MAINWARING: Now watch this one very carefully, Walker.
Mainwaring bowls. Walker steps across the wicket and cuts it hard round to leg.

MAINWARING: Yes, well that was an easy one, but I want to give you a tip, Walker. *(He goes to the wicket and takes the bat.)* Now, you can all pay attention to this, because you'll all profit by it. Now, whether you play forward to a good-length ball, thus *(He demonstrates.)* or play back to – Wilson, pay attention.

WILSON: I thought I'd just skip …

MAINWARING: This is just as much for your benefit as anybody else's. Or play back a short ball, thus *(He demonstrates.)* it is absolutely essential that you play with a straight bat, thus. Do you understand?

WALKER: Why?

MAINWARING: Why?

WALKER: Yeh, why do you have to do that?

MAINWARING: Because it's the correct way. If you slash at it in any old ugly fashion, you'll miss the ball.

WALKER: Well, I hit it, didn't I?

MAINWARING: That was luck. Send me up a good-length, straight one, Pike.

PIKE: Very good, Mr Mainwaring. I wouldn't stand there, Walker, that's just about where I shall be putting it.
Pike starts to bowl.

MAINWARING: All right, just a minute.
Pike stops.

MAINWARING: Now, take particular note how I watch the ball all the way from the bowler's hand, right on to the bat.
Pike bowls – Mainwaring misses.

PIKE: Sorry, Mr Mainwaring.

MAINWARING: This sun's a damn nuisance, isn't it?

WILSON: You seem to lose sight of the ball somewhere between the bowler's arm and the bat, sir.

MAINWARING: Let's see you have a go, Godfrey.
Godfrey approaches.

GODFREY: Oh, oughtn't I to have pads on?

MAINWARING: No, we're not bowling fast ones.

GODFREY: It's just that my legs chip awfully easily.

MAINWARING: Get on with it. Send him one down.
Pike starts to bowl.

MAINWARING: Just a moment.
Pike stops.

MAINWARING: Oh no, no, that won't do at all. Haven't you ever played before, Godfrey?

GODFREY: Well, when I was at the Civil Service Stores I used to play for the Gentleman's Outfitting Department.

MAINWARING: Really?

GODFREY: We used to have a match against the Tobacco and Cigarette Department. I christened it the Gentlemen versus the Players.

MAINWARING: Indeed.

GODFREY: I was quite a wag in those days.

MAINWARING: Yes. Now, get your left hand round the front more. Left shoulder more round, head down – look up more. Feet a little more apart, right arm straight. *(Godfrey is now in excruciating position.)* Now, relax. Right, bowl him one, Pike.

PIKE: *(Walking to his place)* Shall I give him a googly one, or an easy one like I gave to you?

MAINWARING: Just bowl, Pike.
Pike runs up a bit, but is stopped just before delivering the ball.
Mainwaring falls.

MAINWARING: Just a moment, I think we can all learn something from the faults in Pike's bowling action. His arm doesn't go over nearly high enough, the whole action should be as if you are about to turn a cartwheel. Line up and we'll all try it.

GODFREY: *(Still crouching)* Shall I remain poised for action, sir?

MAINWARING: No, no, no. Just take it easy for a moment, Godfrey. Now, all together – over – and over – and over, come along, Wilson, pretend you're doing a cartwheel.

WILSON: I've never done a cartwheel.

MAINWARING: What about when you were a child?

WILSON: I just didn't do that sort of thing.

MAINWARING: Extraordinary. Right, that's enough of that. Now, let's see what happens when we put it into practice.
Enter Jones. He has come straight from the shop in his straw hat, apron, etc.

JONES: Sorry I'm late, sir, I was in the middle of coupon counting and then the sausages came.

MAINWARING: I don't want excuses, Jones, a parade is a parade and you should be here on time.

JONES: I've shoved a pound in your left-hand drawer, sir, as usual.

MAINWARING: Yes, well, thank you, Jones, but watch it in future. Right, let's resume our batting practice.

JONES: I would like to volunteer to do some of that, sir. Let me be the striker, sir.

MAINWARING: Oh, yes, all right, get on with it. Take over from Godfrey.
Jones goes to wicket.

MAINWARING: Now, notice how I grip the ball, the forefinger is along the seam and slightly to the left. As the ball leaves my hand notice the wrist action so, that's very good, Godfrey, and the final flick with the finger that will bring the ball in just outside the off stump. This will probably fox you a bit, Jones. *(He bowls.)*
Jones clouts it – they watch the ball over the wall and there is a crash of glass.

MAINWARING: Pike, go and ask the Vicar if we can have our ball back.

JIMMY PERRY AND DAVID CROFT

A good walk spoiled

**Give me my golf clubs, fresh air and a
beautiful partner, and you can keep my
golf clubs and the fresh air.**
JACK BENNY

If you drink, don't drive. Don't even putt. DEAN MARTIN

There's a man playing golf and his caddie spends ages finding him the right club.
'Oh, come on!' **says the man.** 'You must be the worst caddie in the world.'
'I doubt it,' says the caddie. 'That would be too much of a coincidence.'

*'It's a vital approach shot. I'd use a seven iron and try and
hook it into the prevailing easterly wind and hope to drop
it above the pin because it's a pretty fast green and there's
that big sand trap to the front left. But you'll probably just
belt it straight into the trees as usual.'*
DUNCAN MCCOSHAN

A golfer was losing badly in his club championships when he hit his ball into the
rough. Bending down to retrieve it, he came face to face with a leprechaun. 'Would
you like some help with your game?' it asked. 'Yes, please,' replied the man
excitedly. 'OK,' said the leprechaun. 'There's just one condition. Every time you call
upon me for assistance, you will lose one year of your sex life.' The player agreed
and won the championship by two strokes. Getting into his car to go home, the
man found the leprechaun sitting on the dashboard with a notebook and pencil.
'I assisted you ten times during the game,' the leprechaun reminded him. 'You
know the rules. Now, what's your name?' 'Father O'Flattery,' replied the golfer.

GOLF'S GIFT TO THE WORLD

To the philosophical students of golf like myself (said the Oldest Member) perhaps the most outstanding virtue of this noble pursuit is the fact that it is a medicine for the soul. Its great service to humanity is that it teaches human beings that, **whatever petty triumphs they may have achieved in other walks of life, they are after all merely human. It acts as a corrective against sinful pride.** I attribute the insane arrogance of the later Roman emperors almost entirely to the fact that, **never having played golf, they never knew that strange chastening humility which is engendered by a topped chip-shot. If Cleopatra had been outed in the first round of the Ladies' Singles, we should have heard a lot less of her proud imperiousness ...**

P.G. WODEHOUSE, *HEART OF A GOOF* (1926)

GOLFER: This is a terrible golf course. I've never played on a worse one.

CADDIE: This isn't the course. We left that more than an hour ago.

Two members of a golf club set out one morning for a round. Several hours later they returned to the club house; at last, one of them returned, carrying the other, who was quite dead, over his shoulders.

'What a terrible experience,' said the club secretary.

'I'll say,' said the survivor. 'Poor old Carruthers – he passed away on the fairway of the third, and from then on it was pick him up, put him down, play my stroke, pick him up, put him down, play my stroke ...'

THEY INSTINCTIVELY KNEW THE SAFEST PLACE WHEN HE WAS ABOUT TO PLAY HIS SHOT.

STEVE BEST

Making a splash

Some friends rented a boat and went fishing on a lake. After they'd caught their fill and were heading back to the dock, one man asked, 'Did you mark the spot where we got all these fish?' 'Of course,' his friend said. 'I put a big white X on the side of the boat where we caught them.' 'You idiot!' the first man shouted in disgust. 'What makes you think we'll be able to get this boat tomorrow?'

JACK ZIEGLER

Colin and Keith fly to Scotland for a fishing trip. They rent a boat, rods and tackle. After two weeks, they've caught just one small salmon. 'Keith, do you realise this pathetic little fish cost us about £500 apiece?' says Colin. 'Blimey,' Keith replies. 'At that rate, it's lucky we only caught one.'

Saint Peter halted a man at the gates of heaven. 'You've told too many lies to be admitted here,' he said gloomily. 'Have a heart,' replied the man. 'You were a fisherman yourself.'

A knowledge of where the fish are likely to be located can save hours of frustration ...

and the ability to handle the catch is essential.
NORMAN THELWELL

THE ANGLER'S PRAYER

Lord,
I am sitting here,
In inclement weather
And conditions of
Great personal inconvenience,
For all sorts of reasons:
To get away from the fumes, the smoke,
    the noise,
The rat race, the boss, the bank manager,
    the tax inspector,
The wife, the kids, the mother-in-law,
But ostensibly to catch fish.

The fish are slow in coming.
Possibly because they have been annihilated
By the four tons of toxic rubbish
Dumped upriver
By the factory
Last Tuesday.

At the end of this day,
Having had nary a nibble,
And feeling at odds
With the world,
I shall stumble from the meadow
Into the shelter and warmth
Of a well-appointed
Hostelry.

There I shall sup
More than is good
For my health, pocket or equilibrium.
Telling the while,
To whomever will listen,
The most outrageous
And unprincipled
Variations on the truth.

After which,
Having been ejected
By a landlord
Who no longer loves me,
Either for my money
Or considerable personal charm,
I shall wend my weary way home,
Holding deep philosophical conversations
With passing tomcats, stray dogs,
Lamp posts and policemen,
None of whom have much sympathy
With the piscatorial ethos.

'Oh no! Synchronised Ladies of the Lake!'
NICK NEWMAN

Meanwhile,
Back at the cottage small,
Will be waiting
The Little Woman,
Light of My Life and Moon of My Desire,
With a feast
Long since past
Its prime.
Armed as a shield maiden
Of old Teutonic legend,
With a hairy great rolling pin,
Lethal-looking poker,
Substantial tin tray,
Or any combination of these,
The Light of My Life
Will bend one or all
Over my
Already throbbing
Swede.

If this, Lord,
Is what fishing
Is all about,
I give up.

Never again.
Under any circumstances.
Nothing would tempt me.
Wild horses would not drag me.
I'd rather die.
So there.   Amen.

P.S. Could You please make it a bit warmer
    for this Saturday?

CLIFF PARKER, *HOOK, LINE AND STINKER*

Horsing around

Horse sense is good judgment
which keeps horses from
betting on people.

W.C. FIELDS

**'I went to a party last night, and
we played Jockey's Knock.'
'What's that?'
'It's like Postman's knock, only
with more horseplay.'**

'Anybody here ride the last horse in the last race?'
CARL GILES

The Body Beautiful
What Three Months of Riding Can Do

Before …

after …
NORMAN THELWELL

'Betting on horses is a funny old game,' says a man to his friend. 'You win one day and lose the next.' 'Why not bet every other day?' advises his friend.

Hunter Trials

It's awf'lly bad luck on Diana,
    Her ponies have swallowed their bits;
She fished down their throats with a
      spanner
    And frightened them all into fits.

So now she's attempting to borrow.
    Do lend her some bits, Mummy, *do*;
I'll lend her my own for tomorrow,
    But today *I'll* be wanting them too.

Just look at Prunella on Guzzle,
    The wizardest pony on earth;
Why doesn't she slacken his muzzle
    And tighten the breech in his girth?

I say, Mummy, there's Mrs Geyser
    And doesn't she look pretty sick?
I bet it's because Mona Lisa
    Was hit on the hock with a brick.

Miss Blewitt says Monica threw it,
    But Monica says it was Joan,
And Joan's very thick with Miss Blewitt,
    So Monica's sulking alone.

And Margaret failed in her paces,
    Her withers got tied in a noose,
So her coronets caught in the traces
    And now all her fetlocks are loose.

Oh, it's me now. I'm terribly nervous.
    I wonder if Smudges will shy.
She's practically certain to swerve as
    Her Pelham is over one eye.

    •   •   •

Oh wasn't it naughty of Smudges?
    Oh, Mummy, I'm sick with disgust.
She threw me in front of the Judges,
    And my silly old collarbone's bust.

JOHN BETJEMAN

KNOWING ME, KNOWING YOU –
PARTRIDGE MEETS HIS BOXING MATCH

ALAN: Now, Terry: sport. You have managed boxers, wrestlers, snookers – snookerers?

TERRY: Snooker players.

ALAN: Snooker players. Bowling … crown green and tenpin; that didn't work … but you first made your name way back in the 70s with that fabulous champion boxer Billy O'Rourke.

TERRY: Billy 'the Blitz' O'Rourke.

ALAN: Billy the Blitz. Why did they call him 'the Blitz'?

TERRY: Because when he come at you it was like a blitzkrieg.

ALAN: You can say that again. Was he German?

TERRY: No, he's London Irish. Out of Kilburn.

ALAN: But, he could take a punch, couldn't he? At the end of some of those fights he looked like a bloomin' cauliflower.

TERRY: And the other geezer looked like mashed potatoes.

Terry and Alan laugh.

ALAN: Mashed potatoes! Oh. Billy 'the Blitz' O'Rourke. Sadly, of course, no longer with us.

TERRY: Oh, Billy's still alive.

ALAN: Well, technically. Now Terry, you come from a very humble background. But now you mix with the great and the good. You're a little Cockney whelk, sitting on a plate of oysters. Do you ever think to yourself, how did I get here on top of this … plate of … oysters?

TERRY: Well, well, of course I do, Alan. I mean, it's a combination of determination, perseverance and a good head for business.

ALAN: Of course. And, if I may so, (*sings*) wi' a little bit, wi' a little bit, wi' a little bit o' bloomin' luck. Is that fair?

TERRY: (*Looking annoyed*) Well, you know, if you like, yeah. No, you and me, Alan, we're the same. No, we're two working-class boys, no education, no qualifications, but through sheer determination we have made it to the top of the tree.

ALAN: Well, I've got to pick you up on a couple of points there. I did go to East Anglia Polytechnic and I've got a couple of pretty good A levels.

TERRY: Yeah, well, you know what I mean.

ALAN: Yeah, I know, and very quickly, as regards working class, my parents did own their home and we holidayed now and again in Spain. So I don't think that's quite right. But, erm, I imagine you know Spain quite well, what with all your connections?

TERRY: Yeah, yeah, I've got a villa out there. It's cut into the cliff, overlooking the Med. Blindin'.

ALAN: Lovely. Well, you would, wouldn't you. Just in case.

TERRY: Just in case what?

ALAN: You know, just in case you need to go on holiday – quickly.

TERRY: (Laughs) I think you're leading me down a dark alley.

ALAN: (Laughs) I see – the last place I'd like to be with you is down a dark alley.

TERRY: Why's that?

ALAN: Sorry?

TERRY: Why's that?

ALAN: I just wouldn't.

ARMANDO IANNUCCI, STEVE COOGAN
AND PATRICK MARBER

'All right, I'll go over the strategy just once more: get in there and smash his face to a pulp.'
HECTOR BREEZE

I'll never forget my first fight ... all of a sudden I found someone I knew in the fourth row. It was me.

HENNY YOUNGMAN

A boxing fan had to miss a big fight because he was working nights, so he asked his wife to watch for him and tell him the result. After work he rushed home eagerly.
'Who won?' he asked.
'Oh,' said his wife, 'nobody. One of the men got hurt in the first round and they had to stop.'

All good sports

I'm afraid I play no outdoor games at all, except dominoes. I have sometimes played dominoes outside French cafés.

OSCAR WILDE

Stepping on the toes of the woman he had asked to dance, a man tried to think of an excuse for his lack of talent. 'I'm so sorry,' he told her, 'but I'm a little stiff from badminton.' 'Quite frankly,' she replied curtly, 'I don't care where you're from.'

SCHWADRON

BERYL COOK

Caesar was watching Christians being thrown to the lions. 'One good thing about this sport,' he said, 'is that we're never bothered by spectators running on to the pitch.'

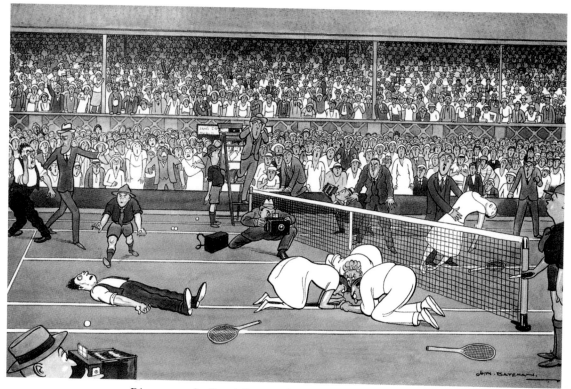

Discovery of a Dandelion on the Centre Court at Wimbledon
H.M. BATEMAN

CRAZY COMMENTRY
Without picking out individuals, I thought Gary Stanley did very well indeed.
ANON

At this stage of the race being in front is a double-edged coin.
BBC2

Jamie Quarry of Scotland lies in second place. Meanwhile, the leading Briton is in fifth place.
BBC NEWS 24

At an exhibition of the world's best swordsmen, the third-placed fencer took the stage. A fly was released and with a flash of his sword the fencer cut the insect in half. The crowd cheered. Then the second-placed man sliced a fly into quarters. A hush fell in anticipation of the world's greatest swordsman.

His blade came down in a mighty arc – but the insect continued on its way. The crowd was aghast – but the swordsman continued to smile.

'What are you so happy about?' someone shouted out. 'You missed.'

'The fly lives, yes,' replied the swordsman. 'But he'll never have kids!'

Indoor games

We play the game of 'Cutlets'. When we had all sat on each other's laps, Gowing said: 'Are you a believer in the Great Mogul?'

August 20. I am glad our last day at the seaside was fine, though clouded overhead. We went over to Cummings' (at Margate) in the evening, and as it was cold, we stayed in and played games; Gowing, as usual, overstepping the mark. He suggested we should play 'Cutlets', a game we never heard of. He sat on a chair, and asked Carrie to sit on his lap, an invitation which dear Carrie rightly declined.

After some species of wrangling, *I* sat on Gowing's knees and Carrie sat on the edge of mine. Lupin sat on the edge of Carrie's lap, then Cummings on Lupin's and Mrs. Cummings on her husband's. We looked very ridiculous, and laughed a good deal.

Gowing then said: 'Are you a believer in the Great Mogul?' We had to answer all together: 'Yes – oh, yes!' (three times). Gowing said: 'So am I,' and suddenly got up. The result of this stupid joke was that we all fell on the ground, and poor Carrie banged her head against the corner of the fender. Mrs. Cummings put some vinegar on; but through this we missed the last train, and had to drive back to Broadstairs, which cost me seven-and-sixpence.

GEORGE AND WEEDON GROSSMITH,
DIARY OF A NOBODY (1892)

Gowing said: 'So am I,' and suddenly got up.

CHESSMANSHIP

The prime object of gamesmanship in chess must always be, at whatever sacrifice, to build up your reputation. In our small chess community in Marylebone it would be mock modesty on my part to deny that I have built up for myself a considerable name without ever actually having won a single game.

Even the best players are sometimes beaten, and that is precisely what happens to me. Yet it is always possible to make it appear that you have lost your game *for the game's sake*.

'Regardez la Dame' Play

This is done by affecting anxiety over the wiseness of your opponent's move. An occasional 'Are you sure you meant that?' or 'Your castle won't like that in six moves' time' works wonders.

By arrangement with another gamesman I have made an extraordinary effect on certain of our Marylebone Chess Club Rambles by appearing to engage him in a contest without board. In the middle of a country lane I call out to him 'P to Q3', then a quarter of an hour later he calls back to me 'Q to QB5'; and so on. 'Moves', of course, can be invented arbitrarily.

Junior Member: I can't think how you do it.
Self: Do what?
Junior Member: Play chess without the pieces. Do you have a *picture* of the board in your brain ... or what is it?
Self: Oh, you mean our little game? I am actually up at the moment. Oh, you mean how do we do it? Oh, I've always been able to 'see' the board in that way, ever since I can remember.

MORRIS BISHOP

Once a month, a woman played cards with her friends. Because she returned home late, she often accidentally woke up her husband. One night, to avoid disturbing him, she undressed in the living room and tiptoed nude into the bedroom. Her husband was reading in bed. He looked up from his book and gasped, 'My God! Did you lose everything?'

GREAT FAILURES OF OUR TIME
No.16 The first Yo-Yo.
GLEN BAXTER

ARTS & ENTERTAINMENT

It's a bit chocolate-boxy

PHILIP THOMPSON

PAINTER: So tell me, what's your opinion of my painting?

CRITIC: It's worthless.

PAINTER: I know, but I'd like to hear it, anyway.

THEY TRIED EVERYTHING TO STOP THE MEN TALKING ABOUT SPORT.

STEVE BEST

GEOFF THOMPSON

'Excuse me, but is that a Constable over the fireplace?' 'Yes, he's sitting up there because his boots are damp.'

Van Gogh
With hand signals
And a polite cough
He bid twelve million
For a Vincent Van Gogh
For that sort of money
I'd cut my right ear off

SPIKE MILLIGAN

It was Tom's first brush with modernism.
GLEN BAXTER

Call that art?

An artist had just seduced his beautiful young young model in his studio. 'Do you know,' he said, 'you're the first model I've ever made love to.'

'I bet,' said the girl. 'Who were your other models?'

'Let me see ... A vase of flowers, a melon, a dead pheasant and a kipper.'

DAVE WHAMOND

A burglar broke into the house of a modern artist and, while he was stealing all of the valuables, the owner surprised him. Though the burglar got away, the artist had a good look at him and produced a lightning sketch. Police started looking for a man with seven green legs and two poached eggs on his head.

COLIN WHEELER

An inexperienced assistant in an art gallery accidentally dropped a priceless painting, tearing the canvas.

'You imbecile!' the director stormed at him. 'That picture is over four hundred years old.'

'Oh,' said the assistant. 'Lucky it wasn't a new one.'

'*Art, art, art – when are we going to get some engineers?*'
EDWARD MCLACHLAN

A beautiful girl went to see an artist. '**Can you paint me in the nude?**' she asked. 'Certainly,' he replied. 'But I'll have to keep my socks on – must have somewhere to put the brushes.'

I went to the museum where they had all the heads and arms from the statues that are in the other museums.

STEVEN WRIGHT

TERRY GILLIAM

THE LAST SUPPER – WITH A DIFFERENCE

An impressive PAPAL PERSON sits on a ritzy throne in the middle of a large Catholic sort of room. We hear a cry of 'Michelangelo to see the Pope'. An ATTENDANT enters.

ATTENDANT: Michelangelo to see you, Your Holiness.

POPE: Show him in.
(Michelangelo enters.)

MICHELANGELO: Evening, Your Grace.

POPE: Good evening, Michelangelo. I want to have a word with you about this *Last Supper* of yours.

MICHELANGELO: Oh, yes?

POPE: I'm not happy with it.

MICHELANGELO: Oh dear. It took hours.

POPE: Not happy at all.

MICHELANGELO: Do the jellies worry you? No, they add a bit of colour, don't they? Oh, I know, you don't like the kangaroo.

POPE: What kangaroo?

MICHELANGELO: I'll alter it, no sweat.

POPE: I never saw a kangaroo!

MICHELANGELO: Well, it's right at the back, but I'll paint it out, no problem. I'll make it into a disciple.

POPE: Ah!

MICHELANGELO: All right now?

POPE: That's the problem.

MICHELANGELO: What is?

POPE: The disciples.

MICHELANGELO: Are they too Jewish? I made Judas the most Jewish.

POPE: No, no it's just that there are twenty-eight of them.

MICHELANGELO: Well, another one would hardly notice, then. So I'll make the kangaroo into a disciple …

POPE: No!!

MICHELANGELO: All right, all right … we'll lose the kangaroo altogether – I don't mind, I was never completely happy with it …

POPE: That's not the point. There are twenty-eight disciples.

MICHELANGELO: Too many?

POPE: Of course it's too many!

MICHELANGELO: Well, in a way, but I wanted to give the impression of a huge get-together… you know, a real Last Supper. Not any old supper, but a proper final treat … a real mother of a blow out …

POPE: There were only twelve disciples at the Last Supper.

MICHELANGELO: Supposing some of the others happened to drop by?

POPE: There were only twelve disciples altogether.

MICHELANGELO: Well, maybe they'd invited some friends?

POPE: There were only twelve disciples and Our Lord at the Last Supper. The Bible clearly says so.

MICHELANGELO: No friends?

POPE: No friends.

MICHELANGELO: Waiters?

POPE: No!!

MICHELANGELO: Cabaret?

POPE: No!

MICHELANGELO: But, you see, I like them. They fill out the canvas. I mean, I suppose we could lose three or four of them, you know, make them …

POPE: (Loudly, ex cathedra) There were only twelve disciples and Our Lord at the Last …

MICHELANGELO: I've got it. I've got it!!! We'll call it … The Penultimate Supper.

POPE: What?

MICHELANGELO: There must have been one. I mean, if there was a last one, there must have been one before that, right?

POPE: Yes, but …

MICHELANGELO: Right, so this is the Penultimate Supper. The Bible doesn't say how many people were at that, does it?

POPE: Er, no, but …

MICHELANGELO: Well, there you are, then.

POPE: Look!! The Last Supper is a significant event in the life of Our Lord. The Penultimate Supper was not … even if they had a conjuror and a steel band. Now I commissioned a Last Supper from you, and a Last Supper I want!

MICHELANGELO: Yes, but look …

POPE: With twelve disciples and one Christ!

MICHELANGELO: One?

POPE: YES, ONE.
(Michelangelo is momentarily speechless.)
Now will you please tell me what in God's name possessed you to paint this with three Christs in it?

MICHELANGELO: It works, mate!!!

POPE: It does not work!

MICHELANGELO: It does, it looks great! The fat one balances the two skinny ones!

POPE: (Brooking no argument) There was only one Saviour …

MICHELANGELO: I know that, everyone knows that, but what about a bit of artistic licence?

POPE: (Bellowing) One Redeemer!!!

MICHELANGELO: (Shouting back) I'll tell you what you want, mate … you want a bloody photographer, not a creative artist with some imagination!!

POPE: I'll tell you what I want – I want a Last Supper, with one Christ, twelve disciples, no kangaroos, by Thursday lunch, or you don't get paid!!!

MICHELANGELO: You bloody fascist!!

POPE: Look, I'm the bloody Pope, I am! I may not know much about art, but I know what I like …

JOHN CLEESE

Last picture show

At a gallery, a couple went to look at some paintings. One of the pictures was of a beautiful naked woman with only a little foliage covering the appropriate areas. The wife thought the picture was in bad taste and moved on quickly, but the husband lingered, completely transfixed. 'What are you waiting for?' called his wife. 'Autumn?'

"YOU'RE WASTING YOUR TIME, MONET ONLY PAINTS THE LILIES."

STEVE BEST

'Bloody hell, Mavis! The bus leaves in ten minutes.'

BUD GRACE

Florence

Sept. 4, 1503

Dear Leonardo,

I am afraid I shall have to rearrange the sitting I was due to have tomorrow morning. I have to go to the surgeon to have my teeth examined, so I will postpone the sitting until the evening, when I will have completed my appointment with him. He says he may have to take out one of my front teeth but it should not make much difference to my expression.

Yours sincerely,

Lisa

MICHAEL GREEN, *TONIGHT JOSEPHINE, AND OTHER UNDISCOVERED LETTERS*

Life class in a nudist colony.
REA IRVIN

CHARLES E. MARTIN

arts & entertainment

Interior. Ruth's room. Rigsby leads Brenda into the room.

RIGSBY: Here we are then.

BRENDA: Well, what is it?

RIGSBY: I just wanted a quiet chat. I like to take a personal interest in all my tenants.

They sit down on the settee.

BRENDA: I suppose you're like a father to them.

RIGSBY: No, not exactly, no, but I like to get to know them.

BRENDA: Well, what do you want to know?

RIGSBY: For example, why did you want to leave your present place?

BRENDA: It's the landlord. He was trying it on.

RIGSBY: Typical. A woman's not safe anymore.

BRENDA: He thinks he can try it on because I'm a model.

RIGSBY: A model. Of course, I should have realised. The poise, the elegance, the daring use of colours. Furs? Paris originals?

BRENDA: I'm not that sort of a model.

RIGSBY: Oh, the commercial. The chocolate one. That desert scene – those two Arabs wrestling in the rays of the dying sun and you on your silk cushions, full of Eastern promise – your eyes glittering.

BRENDA: That's not me. I'm an artist's model. And just because I take my clothes off for a living some men try to take advantage. You should see the photographic club – I can feel their eyes burning into me. Half of them haven't even got film in their cameras.

RIGSBY: How disgraceful. I can see what you mean. I've an artistic bent myself. I can understand exactly how you feel. I can admire the perfection of the female form without having to throw a leg over it. It's no more than a good sunset to me. Talking about the artistic trade, I'm quite handy with the camel hairs myself – and you've got this English rose quality. I'd love to get you down on canvas …

ERIC CHAPPELL

I joined him in front of the portrait.

'Looks good, Jeeves, what?'

'Yes, sir.'

'Nothing like a spot of art for brightening the home.'

'No, sir.'

'Seems to lend the room a certain – what shall I say –'

'Yes, sir.'

The responses were all right, but his manner was far from hearty, and I decided to tackle him squarely. I mean, dash it. I mean, I don't know if you have ever had your portrait painted, but if you have you will understand my feelings. The spectacle of one's portrait hanging on the wall creates in one a sort of paternal fondness for the thing: and what you demand from the outside public is approval and enthusiasm – not the curling lip, the twitching nostril, and the kind of supercilious look which you see in the eye of a dead mackerel. Especially is this so when the artist is a girl for whom you have conceived sentiments deeper and warmer than those of ordinary friendship.

'Jeeves,' I said, 'you don't like this spot of art.'

'Oh, yes, sir.'

'No. Subterfuge is useless. I can read you like a book. For some reason this spot of art fails to appeal to you. What do you object to about it?'

'Is not the colour-scheme a trifle bright, sir?'

'I had not observed it, Jeeves. Anything else?'

'Well, in my opinion, sir, Miss Pendlebury has given you a somewhat too hungry expression.'

'Hungry?'

'A little like that of a dog regarding a distant bone, sir.'

I checked the fellow.

'There is no resemblance whatever, Jeeves, to a dog regarding a distant bone. The look to which you allude is wistful and denotes Soul.'

'I see, sir.'

P.G. WODEHOUSE, *VERY GOOD, JEEVES*,
'THE SPOT OF ART' (1930)

GREGORY

'*What I do as an artist is take an ordinary object – say a lamppost – and by urinating on it transform it into something that is uniquely my own.*'
ALEX GREGORY

Film funnies

A fan club is a group of people who tell an actor he's not alone in the way he feels about himself.

JACK CARSON

'Are you the motion-picture reviewer of this newspaper?'
CARL ROSE

Two goats were behind a studio lot in Hollywood, eating an old movie film. One says to the other, 'Pretty good, huh?' And the other says, 'Yes, but not as good as the book.'

Outside the cinema, a man queued up to see Titanic. 'I'm sorry, sir,' **said the usher as he approached the front of the line.** 'Women and children first.'

A couple were returning to their cinema seats after a trip to the confectionary counter. 'Did I step on your toes on the way out?' the husband asked the man at the end of the row. 'You certainly did,' the man responded angrily. 'All right,' the husband said to his wife. 'This is our row.'

They're making a new film about Moses. It's not finished yet, but apparently the baby looks just great in the rushes.

Television is more interesting than people. If it were not, we should have people standing in the corners of our rooms.

ALAN COREN

Luckily Rudolph Valentino's films were silent.
STEVE BEST

SIMON BOND

India – backpacker Dave is having a highly uncomfortable ride on a rickety bus travelling from Delhi to Simla …

The one advantage of being at the back was that you were further away from the Hindi musicals playing at the front of the bus. In the course of the trip, the same film was played four times, and although I could only see the screen when I was in mid air, by the end of the journey I'd watched most of the film piecemeal, and could just about follow the story.

As far as I could tell it was about a guy who wants to marry a sexy girl, but his parents want him to marry an ugly girl. Just when he's about to marry the ugly girl, he discovers that the sexy girl has been kidnapped by an ugly man who wears black leather and scowls at the camera. The hero rushes out on a horse in search of the kidnapped sexy girl, and has a punch-up in the desert with the ugly man. He's about to save the sexy girl when it emerges that the ugly girl is in cahoots with the ugly man, and she has somehow tied the father to a chair in the sand and is in the process of pouring petrol all over him. The ugly girl pulls out a box of matches, and they all pause to sing a song. Just then, fifty blokes in black jump out from behind a bush that wasn't there until they jumped out from behind it and start shooting at the hero, who hides behind a small wooden box. Eventually, he comes out, holding a white handkerchief, but when the ugly man in black comes to gloat (which he does in song) the hero trips him up, steals his gun, and shoots all the fifty men in black who jumped out from behind the magically appearing bush.

The father, whose petrol seems to have dried off, frees himself from the chair and has a comedy fight with a fat man who appears to serve no purpose. The sexy girl points out to the hero that the ugly girl is escaping through the desert just as the father defeats the fat man by putting a bucket on his head. The hero, the father and the sexy girl then all sing a song in which the father seems to give his blessing to their marriage. Meanwhile, the ugly girl on the horizon shakes her fist, and says something which can only be a vow of revenge. A few seconds later, just as she is on the point of dying of thirst, she comes across a lonely hut on top of a sand-dune. She knocks on the door and is welcomed by a man who tries to seduce her (in song). She is unimpressed by his advances until she notices that in the corner of the room is a mini-laboratory, containing what appears to be a half-finished nuclear bomb. Together they hatch a plan.

After that, the plot became a bit too difficult to follow. As far as I could tell, in the end the sexy people married each other, the ugly people got blown up, and the fat people ended up with buckets on their head.

Now that's what I call quality entertainment.

WILLIAM SUTCLIFFE, *ARE YOU EXPERIENCED?*

Stage frights

'They want a couple of stalls.'
RONALD SEARLE

Young girl after seeing a performance of Peter Pan.
'Mummy, what was Captain Hook's name before he lost his hand?'

'I left the theatre to become an architect.'
'So are you now drawing better houses?'

On a stage comedy: 'Some laughter was heard in the back rows. Someone must have been telling jokes back there.'

ROBERT BENCHLEY

For an actress to succeed she must have the face of Venus, the brains of Minerva, the grace of Terpsichore, the memory of Macaulay, the figure of Juno and the hide of a rhinoceros.

ETHEL BARRYMORE

Long experience has taught me that in England nobody goes to the theatre unless he or she has bronchitis.

JAMES AGATE, *EGO 6*

One of my chief regrets during my years in the theatre is that I couldn't sit in the audience and watch me.

JOHN BARRYMORE

'...if you want "to be", press 1, ... if you want "not to be" press 2....'

SIMON DREW

TECHNIQUE. The amount of genuine acting which a Coarse player will be called upon to do is limited. To start with he will merely be called upon to register certain simple emotions. The only emotions that need be used are as follows:

1. RAGE   4. JOY
2. PLEASURE   5. PAIN
3. LOVE   6. HATE

And even in this simple list the same expression may serve for two emotions (see pictures). Once a player is able to register these stock emotions successfully he can introduce subtleties by mixing two emotions.

ABOVE All-purpose Coarse expression: love, joy, pleasure, hope etc.

RIGHT All-purpose Coarse expression (female): hate, grief, etc. Can be used to indicate physical illness such as indigestion or approaching death.

For instance, to portray a woman who although badly injured has succeeded in saving her lover from death, one merely mixes emotions 3, 4 and 5. To portray a man like Othello, furious with the object of his devotion, is simply a matter of mixing emotions 1, 3 and 6.

Have no truck with any director who requires impossible subtleties of feeling. If he says 'I want you to give me that underlying sense of insecurity' simply hand him the list and ask him to tick off the required emotion.

STAGE FIGHTS. A skilled actor can make a piece of wood seem like a sword. A Coarse Actor can make a sword seem like a piece of wood. The pattern of a Coarse sword fight is traditional. Grunting is substituted for sword-play and both contestants spend much time circling round apparently trying to grunt each other to death. It helps if they grunt on different notes, otherwise it becomes monotonous. The actual circling is done with bent knees in a kind of waddle. Under no circumstances should the sword be pointed at the opponent. It is always held with a slight slope backwards, towards one's own side. That way there's no danger of anyone getting hurt (or of the fight looking realistic).

If action is called for, blows are aimed at the opponent's weapon and never at the person. Usually this is done to pattern: clash swords at shoulder level, clash at knee height, clash again at shoulder height in a figure of eight motion. Sometimes one swordsman is out of time and the other has to wait, or even prompt the other as to what to do. Actors have been seen to mouth 'Stab me' at their opposite number.

But far the best way of fighting is simply to lock hilts (or shields)

LEFT Traditional way of killing: The Royal Shakespeare Armpit Death.

BELOW A pleasant and harmless alternative method of sword-fighting. Both contestants locked in this position grunting occasionally. To terminate the fight, one of the characters should drop dead.

and rock to and fro, grunting. This gives the actor a chance to rest and look round the audience for his mother or girl friend. Occasionally a daring director will allow a character to beat his opponent's shield with his sword but Coarse Actors are usually so scared they don't hold their shields over their bodies but raise them high in the air so the opponent has to jump up and down to hit them.

Another variation is for an actor to swipe at the legs of his opponent, who escapes by jumping over the sword. Not advisable. Usually the actor jumps too soon and has landed before the blow is struck or else he jumps too late with fatal results. Indeed, last time I saw that happen the offended swordsman lost his temper and the fight started in earnest and was carried on in the wings, where shouts and cries of pain punctuated the next scene.

Most sword fights end in death. The usual way of simulating this is the traditional Royal Shakespeare Armpit Death. The loser holds out one arm horizontal, a sword is passed under the armpit, and he lowers the arm trapping it. His opponent then makes great play of pulling out the sword (it is best to avoid putting a foot on your opponent's stomach) and the loser dies horribly.

A simple alternative is for both actors to lock hilts or shields and for one of them to drop dead suddenly. There is a third death, in which the fight moves off-stage, there is a cry of pain in the wings, and the winner returns with red toothpaste all over him. Coarse Actors should favour Method Three – it is less dangerous.

MICHAEL GREEN, *THE ART OF COARSE ACTING*

The Mastermind set. CONTESTANT is sitting in the big chair, MAGNUS fires the questions.

MAGNUS (RONNIE BARKER): So on to our final contender. Your name, please.

CONTESTANT (RONNIE CORBETT): Good evening.

MAGNUS: Thank you. In the first heat your chosen subject was Answering Questions Before They Were Asked. This time you have chosen to answer the question before last each time – is that correct?

CONTESTANT: Charlie Smithers.

MAGNUS: And your time starts now. What is palaeontology?

CONTESTANT: Yes, absolutely correct.

MAGNUS: Correct. What's the name of the directory that lists members of the peerage?

CONTESTANT: A study of old fossils.

MAGNUS: Correct. Who are David Owen and Sir Geoffrey Howe?

CONTESTANT: Burke's.

MAGNUS: Correct. What's the difference between a donkey and an ass?

CONTESTANT: One's a Social Democrat, the other's a member of the Cabinet.

MAGNUS: Correct. Complete the quotation. 'To be or not to be …'

CONTESTANT: They're both the same.

MAGNUS: Correct. What is Bernard Manning famous for?

CONTESTANT: 'That is the question.'

MAGNUS: Correct. Who is the present Archbishop of Canterbury?

CONTESTANT: He's a fat man who tells blue jokes.

MAGNUS: Correct. What do people kneel on in church?

CONTESTANT: The Most Reverend Robert Runcie.

MAGNUS: Correct. What do tarantulas prey on?

CONTESTANT: Hassocks.

MAGNUS: Correct. What would you use a ripcord to pull open.

CONTESTANT: Large flies.

MAGNUS: Correct. What did Marilyn Monroe always claim to wear in bed?

CONTESTANT: A parachute.

MAGNUS: Correct. What was the next new TV station go on the air after Channel Four?

CONTESTANT: Chanel Number Five.

MAGNUS: Correct. What do we normally associate with Bedlam?

CONTESTANT: Breakfast television.

MAGNUS: Correct. What are jockstraps?

CONTESTANT: Nutcases.

MAGNUS: Correct. What would a jockey use a stirrup for?

CONTESTANT: An athletic support.

MAGNUS: Correct. Arthur Scargill is well known for what?

CONTESTANT: He puts his foot in it.

MAGNUS: Correct. Who was the famous clown who made millions laugh with his funny hair?

CONTESTANT: The leader of the mineworkers' union.

MAGNUS: Correct. What would a decorator use methylene chlorides to make?

CONTESTANT: Coco.

MAGNUS: Correct. What did Henri de Toulouse-Lautrec do?

CONTESTANT: Paint strippers.

MAGNUS: Correct. What is Dean Martin famous for?

CONTESTANT: Is he an artist?

MAGNUS: Yes – what kind of artist?

CONTESTANT: Er – pass.

MAGNUS: Yes, that's near enough. What make of vehicle is the standard London bus?

CONTESTANT: A singer.

MAGNUS: Correct. In 1892 Brandon Thomas wrote a famous long-running English farce – what is it?

CONTESTANT: British Leyland.

MAGNUS: Correct. Complete the following quotation about Shirley Williams: 'Her heart may be in the right place, but her …'

CONTESTANT: Charley's Aunt.

MAGNUS: Correct, and you have scored 22 and no passes!

DAVID RENWICK

Face the music and dance

The owner of a pet shop is asked for a bird that can talk and sing. He shows the customer a scrawny-looking bird with a price tag of £2000. 'How can it be worth that much?' enquires the customer. 'That bird can sing the complete works of Elgar,' says the owner. 'Or you could try this one.' He reveals a second bird, even thinner than the first, costing £3000. 'Come off it,' says the customer. 'What's so special about this one?' 'It can reproduce all of Verdi's operas note perfect,' replies the owner. 'But I have one other that might interest you.' The third bird is in a sorry state, bald, rheumy-eyed and weak with age. The customer looks at the price tag. '£10,000?' he says. 'What does it do?' The owner shakes his head. 'To tell you the truth, we don't know yet. But the other two call him "Maestro".'

JORODO

Two dogs and a cat wanted to go to a classical music recital, but were told that it was for musicians only. 'That's all right,' said one dog and pointed to the other. 'He Bach; I Offenbach and,' indicating the cat, 'he Debussy.'

An American maestro was so furious when the clarinettist in the orchestra he was conducting ruined a slow passage in a piece of music that he took out a gun and shot the man. He was arrested, convicted and sent to the electric chair for his crime. The lever was pulled three times, but with no effect. He survived, because he was a bad conductor.

A musical glossary:
Jazz Five men on the same stage playing different tunes.
Blues Played exclusively by people who woke up this morning.
World Music A dozen different types of percussion going on at once.
Opera People singing when they should be talking.
Rap People talking when they should be singing.
Classical Discover the other 45 minutes from the TV advert.
Folk Endless songs about shipwrecks in the 19th century.

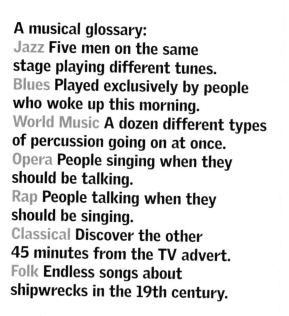

WHILST DOING A LONG OVERDUE CLEAROUT AT THE OFFICES OF IRELAND'S OLDEST AND MOST RESPECTED SCHOOL OF DANCE, MRS O'HARA MADE A TERRIBLE DISCOVERY.......

EDWARD MCLACHLAN

Two cowboys staggered out of the zoo with their clothes in shreds. 'Now I'm telling yuh,' said one to his partner, 'that's the last time I go lion dancing.'

GERARD HOFFNUNG

ROUND THE HORNE – FOLK HERO

KENNETH (HORNE): We move on now to trends in music. It's time again to meet folk-singer Rambling Syd Rumpo, one of the all-time grates – and I think you'll agree nobody grates like Rambling Syd.

KEN W (WILLIAMS): Hello me deario, chirrup chirrup for the fox be away with a goose and the fly be on the termutt.

KENNETH: Well, what can you expect if you leave it out all night? Now what are you going to sing for us today?

KEN W: Well, I was a-rummaging in my ganderbag for a gladsome ditty to bend your ear-oh with. It's a song of the Royal Scottish Pretender –

KENNETH: Bonnie Prince Charlie?

KEN W: No, this were an old Scotch tramp called McWhirter. He pretended to be Queen Frederika in order to get free orange juice. You can't drink metal polish straight, you know.

KENNETH: It does tend to dull the palate.

KEN W: Anyway, we fell to chatting by the wayside and over a rude meal of hedgehog pâté, washed down with a simple, unpretentious bottle of paraffin rosé, he sung me it. It tells the story of a simple Highland lass, who one day espies a man in a kilt sitting up an oak tree. 'Hello,' quoth she to herself, 'it's Bonnie Prince Charlie' – well she could tell it wasn't Mary Queen of Scots.

KENNETH: Of course. A different tartan.

KEN W: Yes. So anyway, she takes him in and hides him, and gives him sustenance for three months. But lackaday, there's a sorry end to this tale that will wring your withers.

KENNETH: Good. They haven't been wrung for years.

KEN W: It turns out that he isn't Bonnie Prince Charlie after all but a cabinet maker from Huddersfield called Alf Posselswaite.

KENNETH: How tragic.

Guitar vamp

KEN W: And to this very day, almost six months later, the Highlanders still sing the Posselswaite Lament, which goes after this fashion.

(Sings in minor key – slowly and sadly.)

Ye mucky doon a braw me lummock

A scorpit beastie through the rye

For there's a tatty bogel in me trussoch

Over the sea to Skye –

Pull away

Pull away me sporran

Till the seas run dry –
ooooooooooooooooooh!

BARRY TOOK AND MARTY FELDMAN

SMASHIE: Fab-four-tastic! That was the, err. Beatles, err – I love the Beatles. don't you? – with 'Eight Days A Week'.

NICEY: There's only seven days in a week, mate.

SMASHIE: Right, thanks, mate.

NICEY: Don't mention it.

SMASHIE: Erm, but I think you'll find that's what the Beatles – I love the Beatles, don't you? – were saying –

NICEY: I don't care what the Beatles – I love the Beatles, don't you? – were saying, mate, there's only seven days in a week. Never longer, never shorter. It's the law!

SMASHIE: Right!

NICEY: Right, starts on a Monday, goes through to a Sunday, with a Wednesday, Friday type stuff in the middle, and the weekend on the end.

SMASHIE: I love the weekend, don't you mate?

NICEY: Me too, mate.

SMASHIE: Right, well one thing I do know, is that err, today, is err, Tuesday which is quite literally, err – Tuesday.

NICEY: I love Tuesdays, don't you mate?

SMASHIE: Certainly do, mate. It's one of the best between Monday and Wednesday type days we've got.

NICEY: It's the only between Monday and Wednesday type day we've got, mate. It may not have the glamour

and excitement of a Saturday, or the mournfulness of a Monday morn, but it's our Tuesday, the good, old-fashioned, honest to goodness, down to earth, great British Tuesday, and if those Eurocrats, Bureaucrats and other Bonkerscrats try and take our Tuesday away from us, they'll have to get past me first. And if they think I'm gonna start me show by saying Bonjourno doodle-doo, and Guten Morgen mongous, they've got another think coming.

SMASHIE: I don't think they are gonna do that, mate. It'd be frogadobadabu-lously bonkers, mate. Because what makes a nation is not its borders or its monetary system, no, it's its radio stations, such as Radio Fab F.M., and the people who work therein. Such as you, Nicey. You are what makes Britain great.

NICEY: Thanks mate. *(Pause)* Err, so are you, mate.

HARRY ENFIELD AND PAUL WHITEHOUSE

Words, words, words ...

'*But ov wat use wil this dicshunary of yours be, Dr Johnson?*'
FRAN

He is a writer whose books will be read long after Shakespeare, Jane Austen and Dickens are forgotten. But not until then.

'I once wrote for *The New Yorker*.'
'Did you? What happened?'
'What do you think? They sent me a copy.'

The dubious privilege of a freelance writer is he's given the freedom to starve anywhere.
S.J. PERELMAN

Shakespeare walks into a pub and orders a beer.

'I can't serve you,' says the barman. 'You're bard.'

'I'm afraid he's got Odes, Mrs Keats.'
N. BENNETT

Don't read science fiction books. It'll look bad if you die in bed with one on the nightstand. Always read stuff that will make you look good if you die in the middle of it.

P.J. O'ROURKE

If you want to get rich from writing, write the sort of thing that's read by persons who move their lips when they're reading to themselves.

DON MARQUIS

'We like the plot, Miss Austen, but all this effing and blinding will have to go.'
JOHN TAYLOR

'I've been laughing ever since I picked up your book. Some day I'm going to read it.'

GROUCHO MARX

Prince George's Chambers. There is a knock at the door.

PRINCE GEORGE: Enter!

Blackadder opens the door for Dr Johnson. He is sixty, fat and pompous.

BLACKADDER: Dr Johnson, your Highness.

PRINCE GEORGE: Ah, Dr Johnson. Damn cold day.

JOHNSON: Indeed it is, sir. But a very fine one for I celebrated last night the encyclopaedic implementation of my premeditated orchestration of demotic Anglo-Saxon.

The prince nods sagely for a good while, then …

PRINCE GEORGE: No. Didn't catch any of that.

JOHNSON: I simply observed, sir, that I am felicitous, since during the course of the penultimate solar sojourn, I terminated my uninterrupted categorisation of the vocabulary of our post-Norman tongue.

PRINCE GEORGE: Don't know what you're talking about but it sounds damn saucy, you lucky thing! I know some fairly liberal-minded girls but I've never penultimated them in the solar sojourn or, for that matter, been given any Norman tongue.

BLACKADDER: I believe, sir, that the Doctor is trying to tell you that he is happy because he has finished his book. It has taken him ten years.

PRINCE GEORGE: *(Sympathetically)* Yes, well, I'm a slow reader myself.

JOHNSON: Here it is, sire. *(He produces a sheaf of manuscript.)* A very

cornerstone of English scholarship. This book contains every word in our beloved language.

BLACKADDER: Every single one, sir?

JOHNSON: Every single one, sir.

BLACKADDER: In that case, sir, I hope you will not object if I also offer the Doctor my most enthusiastic contrafibularatories.

JOHNSON: What, sir?

BLACKADDER: Contrafibularatories, sir. It is a common word down our way.

Johnson takes a pencil from behind his ear. He is furious.

JOHNSON: Damn!

He starts writing in the dictionary.

BLACKADDER: Oh. I'm sorry, sir. I am anaspeptic, phrasmotic, even compunctious to have caused you such periconbobulations.

JOHNSON: What, what, what?

He's now frantic, scribbling down all these new words.

PRINCE GEORGE: Look, what *are* you on about? This is beginning to sound a bit like dago talk to me.

BLACKADDER: I'm sorry, sir. I merely wished to congratulate Dr Johnson on not having left out a single word. *(He smiles at Johnson, Johnson glares.)* Shall I fetch the tea, my lord?

PRINCE GEORGE: Yes, yes – and get that damn fire up here, will you.

BLACKADDER: *(Smoothly)* Certainly, sir. I shall return … interphrastically.

A smug nod and he leaves.

PRINCE GEORGE: So, Dr Johnson. Sit ye

down. Now, this book of yours. Tell me, what's it all about?

JOHNSON: It is a book about the English language, sir.

PRINCE GEORGE: I see. And the hero's name is what?

JOHNSON: There is no hero, sir.

PRINCE GEORGE: No hero? Well! Lucky I reminded you! Better put one in pronto. Call him George, that's a good name for a hero. What about heroines?

JOHNSON: There is no heroine, sir – unless it is our Mother Tongue.

PRINCE GEORGE: Ah – the mother's the heroine. Nice twist. So how far have we got then? Old Mother Tongue is in love with George the hero … Now what about murders? Mother Tongue doesn't get murdered, does she?

JOHNSON: No, she doesn't! No one gets murdered! Or married! Or in a tricky situation over a pound note!

PRINCE GEORGE: Well, now, look Dr

Johnson, I may be as thick as a whale omelette, but even I know that a book's got to have a plot.

JOHNSON: *Not this one*, sir. It is a book that tells you what English words mean.

PRINCE GEORGE: But I *know* what English words mean. I *speak* English. You must be a bit of a thicko!

That is it. Johnson is seriously angry. He rises to his feet.

JOHNSON: Perhaps you would rather not be patron of my book, sir, if you can see no value in it whatsoever!

PRINCE GEORGE: Perhaps so, sir, since it sounds to me as though being patron of this complete cowpat of a book will set the seal once and for all on my reputation as an utter turnip head.

JOHNSON: It is a reputation well deserved, sir! Farewell.

He marches towards the double doors and flings them open.

RICHARD CURTIS AND BEN ELTON

On a modern poet:
'He regularly tortured the English language but had not yet succeeded in forcing it to reveal its meaning.'

BEACHCOMBER

'Do you like Kipling?'
'I don't know, you naughty boy, I've never kippled.'
DONALD MCGILL

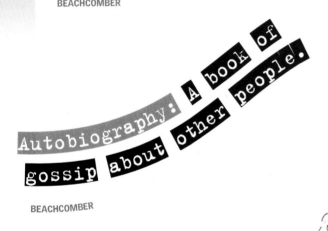

Autobiography: A book of gossip about other people.

BEACHCOMBER

'And what is this I've found under your mattress?'
MEYRICK JONES

The pen is mightier than the sword, and considerably easier to write with.

MARTY FELDMAN

Tony goes over to the shelves. A woman is choosing a book from the Crime section. Tony stops and looks at the title. He shakes his head, pulls out another book, and hands it to her. Gives her the thumbs up and carries on. He stops a little further on and starts examining the titles on the Crime shelves. He apparently can't find what he's looking for so he moves on to the next section which is marked 'Greek Philosophy'. He starts searching for some books, then snaps his fingers and beckons. The Librarian comes up.

LIBRARIAN: Can I help you?

TONY (HANCOCK): Yes, I'm looking for Sir Charles Bestead's complete history of the Holy Byzantine Empire.

LIBRARIAN: *(Impressed)* Oh, you want to borrow it?

TONY: Yes please.

LIBRARIAN: I'm so pleased. We don't get much call for it. I'm so pleased there are still men of culture left. It's a magnificent edition.

TONY: Oh yes, yes, most useful.

LIBRARIAN: I do hate to see it neglected.

TONY: Oh I often borrow it, I find it most helpful.

LIBRARIAN: I think I've misjudged you, haven't I? Is there anything else I can get for you?

TONY: Yes er ... Plato's *Republic*, the complete translation of Homer's *Iliad*, and Ulbricht's *Roman Law* ... The Wilkinson edition, of course.

LIBRARIAN: Of course. A very wise choice. You've chosen probably the four best books in the library.

TONY: I agree ... have you got them?

LIBRARIAN: Of course, I'll get them.

LIBRARIAN: *(Going off)* The first time in four years there's been any call for these.

He finds the four volumes, all great big books about six inches thick. He goes back to Tony.

LIBRARIAN: There we are. It's times like this that make my job worth while.

TONY: Thank you very much, they're the ones.

LIBRARIAN: You can have all these on one ticket.

TONY: Oh, that's most kind of you.

He puts them on the floor at the Crime section, then stands on them, stretches up, and takes down a book from a higher shelf.

TONY: Ah, that's the little beauty I'm after. *Lady Don't Fall Backwards.*
(He steps off the books.)
Thank you very much. I won't need those any more for now. Keep them handy though, they're just the right height.

The Librarian picks up the books lovingly.

RAY GALTON AND ALAN SIMPSON, *HANCOCK'S HALF HOUR*

arts & entertainment

KNOWING ME, KNOWING YOU –
WILL THE REAL SHERLOCK HOLMES PLEASE STAND UP

ALAN: Knowing me, Alan Partridge, knowing you, Lawrence Camley, ah-haa. Welcome.

LAWRENCE: Ah-haa.

ALAN: Glad to have you on the show. Now, I've got to say, first reaction to your book – don't drop it on me foot!

LAWRENCE: Yes, it is a heavy book, but if I may be so bold there are, of course, certain literary precedents. One thinks of Proust's *A La Recherche du Temps Perdu*, Dante's *Divina Commedia*, Chaucer's *Canterbury Tales*, which I'm reliably informed could cripple one. Maybe that's what happened to Lord Byron?

ALAN: Why, what happened to him?

LAWRENCE: He had a clubbed foot.

ALAN: Right. Ha ha! *The Soul of Time*, that's the name of your book. Sounds a bit deep, is it?

LAWRENCE: Well, it's a serious novel. I deal with the great contemporary themes. But I like to think there are one or two jokes in it.

ALAN: Oh, great. Go on, tell us a joke. Ha ha ha! We like to start the show with a joke. It's always great to get it off on –

LAWRENCE: I see I've got myself in sticky mud already. They're not jokes in the traditional Knock-Knock sense. They're more comic vignettes woven into the general fabric and architecture of the novel.

ALAN: It's more funny-peculiar than funny-ha-ha then, is it? What I want to ask you is, and this is a question I've been dying to ask you, if you were stuck in a lift, what one book would you have with you?

LAWRENCE: Well, I would actually choose – for sheer bloody-minded entertainment value – I would be stuck in a lift with *The Hound of the Baskervilles*.

ALAN: I don't believe it, Sherlock Holmes. Now you're making sense. I am his number one fan. I've read all his books.

LAWRENCE: Yes, I've read them.

ALAN: I've read all of them. Have you read all of them?

LAWRENCE: Probably not all of them.

ALAN: I've read all of them. All of them. I love Sherlock Holmes. I've got all his books, leather-bound. What I thought was great about Sherlock Holmes was that not only was he a supersleuth, he was also a hard worker. Not only did he go out and solve the crimes, he came home and wrote it all down. Fantastic. That's why I admire him.

LAWRENCE: Yes. I've always thought it was a shame that Conan Doyle had to kill him off.

ALAN: No, I think you'll find it was Moriarty that killed him.

LAWRENCE: Yes, I know, but ultimately of course it was Conan Doyle.

ALAN: No, it was Moriarty, it was definitely –

LAWRENCE: Yes, I know, in the books it was Moriarty, but of course the ultimate responsibility was Conan Doyle's.

ALAN: Yep, hang on. As far as I know, Moriarty acted alone. Or did he? This is interesting. You think that there was some sort of conspiracy involving this shadowy Doyle figure? All right, OK, fair enough. Who solved all the cases?

LAWRENCE: Sherlock Holmes.

ALAN: Exactly.

LAWRENCE: Yes, but the cases were fictional too, it's all make-believe.

ALAN: All right. Who lived on Baker Street?

LAWRENCE: I don't know.

ALAN: Moriarty?

LAWRENCE: No!

ALAN: Did the Doyle live there?

LAWRENCE: The Dail – the Dail is the Irish Parliament.

ALAN: The Irish Parliament! This conspiracy's getting bigger. You can't trust anyone these days. You've got the Doyle, Moriarty, the Irish Parliament! On that bombshell, I think we'll move on.

LAWRENCE: No, no, no. I'm sorry, Alan, I'd like to let this go, but I really can't. Sherlock Holmes did not exist.

ALAN: He did.

LAWRENCE: Look. If he had existed, how would he have been able to describe in intimate detail the circumstances of his own death?

ALAN: *(Long pause)* The Nobel Prize for Literature. You never won it. What went wrong?

**ARMANDO IANNUCCI, STEVE COOGAN
AND PATRICK MARBER**

BARRY FANTONI

In a library, a man asked where he might find the books on suicide. **'Second row down on the left,'** replied the assistant. The man proceeded to the shelf but couldn't find what he was looking for. Returning to the enquiry desk he explained, 'I've had a good look, but I can't find anything on suicide.' **'I didn't think you would,'** the assistant replied knowingly. **'They never bring them back.'**

I'm so old
I can
remember
Socialism :

MEL CALMAN

THE
POLITICAL
WORLD

Right royal fun

This Earl of Oxford, making of his low obeisance to Queen Elizabeth, happened to let a Fart, at which he was so abashed and ashamed that he went to travel, 7 years. On his return the Queen welcomed him home, and said, My Lord, I had forgot the Fart.

JOHN AUBREY (1626-97), *BRIEF LIVES*

George the Third
Ought never to have occurred
One can only wonder
At so grotesque a blunder.

E. CLERIHEW BENTLEY

TUESDAY

I receive my Prime Minister, a Mr Blair. He informs me of his plans for revitalising the National Health Service and modernising the railway system.

'This is all very interesting indeed,' I say.

'Thank you,' he says.

'You've obviously put a tremendous amount of thought into it,' I say.

'Yes,' he says.

'Railways are still very popular,' I tell him. 'They are particularly useful if people want to get from A to B and for one reason or another they don't have their driver.'

'You've hit the nail on the head,' he says.

CRAIG BROWN, *THE DIARY OF HM QUEEN ELIZABETH II*

Anne when in good humour was meekly stupid, and when in bad humour was sulkily stupid.

THOMAS MACAULAY on Queen Anne

DIDN'T YOU KNOW, ALL SWANS ARE PROTECTED BY THE QUEEN?

ROBERT THOMPSON

I blame the government

When a member of parliament died, an eager candidate rang to put himself forward as successor. 'Sorry to hear of the recent death of Tom Atkins,' he said. 'Is there any chance of my taking his place?' 'Sure,' replied the national agent. 'If the undertaker has no objection.'

'Good luck, Minister – and when you lie, remember to look straight into the cameras.'
HUGH BURNETT

**How many MPs does it take to change a light bulb?
Twenty-one. One to change it and twenty to form a fact-finding committee to learn more about how it's done.**

'The Republicans stole the election.'
'No, they didn't.'
'Yes, they did.'
'No, they paid cash for it.'

He can best be described as one of those orators who, before they get up, do not know what they are going to say; when they are speaking, do not know what they are saying; and, when they have sat down, do not know what they have said.
WINSTON CHURCHILL on Lord Charles Beresford

'Of course, the world must realise I'm only the head of a caretaker government.'
EDWARD MCLACHLAN

How long does a US Congressman serve? – Until he gets caught.

PETER BROOKES

Silly season

We don't want to go back to tomorrow, we want to go forward.

DAN QUAYLE

I was recently on a tour of Latin America, and the only regret I have was that I **didn't study Latin harder** at school so I could converse with those people.

DAN QUAYLE

Rarely is the question asked:
Is our children learning?

GEORGE W. BUSH

Now we are going to get unemployment to go up and I think we're going to succeed.

RONALD REAGAN

PETER BROOKES

I believe that people would be alive today if there were a death penalty.

NANCY REAGAN

If we don't succeed, we run the risk of failure.

DAN QUAYLE

It's no exaggeration to say that the undecideds could go one way or another.

GEORGE BUSH

I have orders to be awakened at any time in the case of a national emergency, even if I'm in a cabinet meeting.

RONALD REAGAN

THERE also happened in this reign the memorable Charta, known as Magna Charter on account of the Latin *Magna* (great) and Charter (a Charter); this was the first of the famous Chartas and Gartas of the Realm and was invented by the Barons on a desert island in the Thames called Ganymede. By congregating there, armed to the teeth, the Barons compelled John to sign the Magna Charter, which said:

Utter Incompetence

1. That no one was to be put to death, save for some reason – (except the Common People).
2. That everyone should be free – (except the Common People).
3. That everything should be of the same weight and measure throughout the Realm – (except the Common People).
4. That the Courts should be stationary, instead of following a very tiresome mediaeval official known as the *King's Person* all over the country.
5. That 'no person should be fined to his utter ruin' – (except the King's Person).
6. That the Barons should not be tried except by a special jury of other Barons who would understand.

Magna Charter was therefore the chief cause of Democracy in England, and thus a Good Thing for everyone (except the Common People).

W.C. SELLAR AND R.J. YEATMAN, *1066 AND ALL THAT* (1930)

MEL CALMAN

'Frank is into unofficial strike action ... Harry is into working to rule ... Bob is into picketing ... and Walter here is into impotent rage!'
KENNETH MAHOOD

Getting agitated

'My mother is such an alarmist!' complained **the teenager. 'One cough and she thinks I have bronchitis. A headache and she's sure it's a brain tumour. One little lie and she thinks I'm destined for politics.'**

'Gentlemen, gentlemen! Disorder, please, disorder.'
WILLIE RUSHTON

'You ordered the house red, didn't you?'
NEIL DISHINGTON

An old man who's been a lifelong Socialist is on his deathbed, and his son – also a lifelong Socialist – asks his father if there's anything he's left undone, anything he'd like to do before his life is over. And the old man says, 'Yes, I'd like you to organise for me to become a **member of the Conservative Party.'** The son is shocked. 'You can't do that. It goes against everything you've stood for all your life.' **'Maybe so,'** says the old man. 'But if someone has got to die, I'd rather it was one of theirs than one of ours.'

'Even the illiterates are forming revolutionary groups, now …'
RAY LOWRY

Too bad all the people who know how to run the country are busy driving cabs and cutting hair.

GEORGE BURNS

ON COMMUNISTS

WHAT is a Communist? One who has yearnings
For equal division of unequal earnings;
Idler or bungler, or both, he is willing
To fork out his penny and pocket your shilling.

EBENEZER ELLIOTT

CHARLES PEATTIE AND RUSSELL TAYLOR

Politics, politics

In crime, you take the money and run; in politics, you run first and then take the money.

Why don't politicians like golf?
Because it's too much like their work –
trapped in one bad lie after another.

Q: Why should politicians be buried 100 feet deep?
A: Because deep down, they're really good people.

First politician: Did you hear my last speech?
Second politician: I certainly hope so.

A politician is a man who approaches every question with an open mouth. OSCAR WILDE

It is now known that men enter local politics solely as a result of being unhappily married.

C. NORTHCOTE PARKINSON

CHARLES PEATTIE AND RUSSELL TAYLOR

'I think I may say, without fear of contradiction …'
CARL ROSE

A politician is an animal that can **sit on a fence** and keep both ears to the ground.

H.L. MENCKEN

A statesman is a successful politician who is dead.

THOMAS B. REED

Politics – the gentle art of getting votes from the poor and campaign funds from the rich, by promising to protect each from the other.

OSCAR AMERINGER

'This is the voice of Moderation, I wouldn't go so far as to say we have actually seized the radio station.'
JOHN HANDELSMAN

It's election time

CAPTION: 'ELECTION NIGHT SPECIAL'
Cut to linkman sitting at desk.

LINKMAN (JOHN CLEESE): *(Very excited)* Hello and welcome to 'Election Night Special'. There's great excitement here as we should be getting the first result through any minute now. We don't know where it'll be from ... it might be from Leicester or from Luton. The polling's been quite heavy in both areas ... oh, wait a moment ... I'm just getting ... I'm just getting a loud buzzing noise in my left ear. Excuse me a moment. *(He bangs ear and knocks a large bee out.)* Uuggh! *(Cheering from crowd)* Anyway, let's go straight over to James Gilbert at Leicester. Shot of returning officer in front of a group consisting half of grey-suited, half of silly-dressed candidates and agents. The silly ones are in extraordinary hats, false noses etc.*

VOICE-OVER (MICHAEL PALIN): Well, it's a straight fight here at Leicester ... On the left of the Returning Officer *(Camera shows grey-suited man)* you can see Arthur Smith, the Sensible candidate and his agent, *(Camera pans to silly people)* and on the other side is the silly candidate Jethro Walrustitty with his agent and his wife.

OFFICER (TERRY JONES): Here is the result for Leicester. Arthur J. Smith ...

VOICE-OVER: Sensible Party.

OFFICER: 30,162 ... Jethro Q. Walrustitty ...

VOICE OVER: Silly Party.

OFFICER: 32,108.

Cheering from the crowd. Cut back to the studio.

LINKMAN: *(Even more excited)* Well,

there's the first result and the Silly Party have held Leicester. What do you make of that, Norman?

Cut to Norman. He is very excited.

NORMAN (MICHAEL PALIN): Well, this is largely as I predicted except that the Silly Party won. I think this is mainly due to the number of votes cast. Gerald?

Cut to Gerald standing by 'swingometer' – a pivoted pointer on a wall chart.

GERALD (ERIC IDLE): Well, there's a swing here to the Silly Party ... but how big a swing I'm not going to tell you.

Cut to George also standing by a swingometer.

GEORGE (TERRY JONES): Well, if I may ... I think the interesting thing here is the big swing to the Silly Party and of course the very large swing back to the Sensible Party ... and a tendency to wobble up and down in the middle because the screw's loose.

Cut to Alphonse.

ALPHONSE (GRAHAM CHAPMAN): No, I'm afraid I can't think of anything.

Cut to Eric.

ERIC (TERRY GILLIAM): I can't add anything to that. Colin?

Cut to Colin.

COLIN (IAN DAVIDSON): Can I just butt in at this point and say this is in fact the very first time I've ever appeared on television.

Cut to linkman.

LINKMAN: No, no, we haven't time, because we're going straight over to Luton.

Cut to Luton Town Hall. There are sensible, silly and slightly silly candidates.

VOICE-OVER: Here at Luton, it's a three-cornered fight between Alan Jones – Sensible Party, in the middle, Tarquin Fin-tim-lin-bin-whin-bim-lin-bus-stop-F'tang-F'tang-Olé-Biscuitbarrel – Silly Party, and Kevin Phillips-Bong – the Slightly Silly candidate.

OFFICER (ERIC IDLE): Alan Jones …

VOICE-OVER: On the left, Sensible Party.

OFFICER: 9,112 … Kevin Phillips-Bong …

VOICE-OVER: On the right, Slightly Silly.

OFFICER: Nought … Tarquin Fin-tim-lin-bin-whin-bim-lin-bus-stop-F'tang-F'tang-Olé-Biscuitbarrel …

VOICE-OVER: Silly.

OFFICER: 12,441.

VOICE-OVER: And so the Silly Party has taken Luton.

Quick cut to linkman.

LINKMAN: A gain for the Silly Party at Luton. The first gain of the election, Norman?

Cut to each speaker in close-up throughout the scene.

NORMAN: Well, this is a highly significant result. Luton, normally a very sensible constituency with a high proportion of people who aren't a bit silly, has gone completely ga-ga.

LINKMAN: Do we have the swing at Luton?

GERALD: Well, I've worked out the swing, but it's a secret.

LINKMAN: Er, well, ah, there … there *isn't* the swing, how about the swong?

NORMAN: Well, I've got the swong here in this box and it's looking fine. I can see through the breathing holes that it's eating up peanuts at a rate of knots.

CONTINUED OVERLEAF

LINKMAN: And how about the swang?

ALPHONSE: Well, it's 29% up over six hundred feet but it's a little bit soft around the edges about …

LINKMAN: What do you make of the nylon dot cardigan and plastic mule rest?

VOICE (off): There's no such thing.

LINKMAN: Thank you, Spike.

NORMAN: Can I just come in here and say that the swong has choked itself to death.

GEORGE: Well, the election's really beginning to hot up now.

ERIC: I can't add anything to that.

COLIN: Can I just add at this point this is in fact the second time I've ever appeared on television?

LINKMAN: I'm sorry, Sasha, we're just about to get another result.

A large number of candidates in Harpenden Town Hall.

VOICE-OVER (TERRY JONES): Hello, from Harpenden. This is a key seat because in addition to the official Silly candidate there is an independent Very Silly candidate *(In large cube of polystyrene with only his legs sticking out)* who may split the silly vote.

OFFICER (JOHN CLEESE): Mr Elsie Zzzzzzzzzzzz. *(Obvious man in drag with enormous joke breasts)*

VOICE-OVER: Silly.

OFFICER: 26,317 … James Walker …

VOICE-OVER: Sensible.

OFFICER: 26,318.

VOICE-OVER: That was close.

OFFICER: Malcolm Peter Brian Telescope Adrian Umbrella Stand Jasper Wednesday *(Pops mouth twice)* Stoatgobbler John Raw Vegetable *(Sound effect of horse whinnying)* Arthur Norman Michael *(Blows squeaker)* Featherstone Smith *(Blows whistle)* Northgot Edwards Harris *(Fires pistol, which goes 'whoop')* Mason *(Chuff-chuff-chuff)* Frampton Jones Fruitbat Gilbert *(Sings)* We'll Keep a Welcome In The *(Three shots, stops singing)* Williams If I Could Walk That Way Jenkin *(Squeaker)* Tiger-draws Pratt Thompson *(Sings)* 'Raindrops Keep Falling On My Head' Darcy Carter *(Horn)* Pussycat 'Don't Sleep In The Subway' Barton Mannering *(Hoot, 'whoop')* Smith.

VOICE OVER: Very Silly.

OFFICER: Two.

VOICE OVER: Well, there you have it. A Sensible gain here at Driffield. *Back to the studio.*

LINKMAN: Norman.

NORMAN: Well, I've just heard from Luton that my auntie's ill er, possibly, possibly gastro-enteritis – Gerald.

GERALD: Er, well, if this were repeated over the whole country it'd probably be very messy. Colin.

COLIN: Can I just butt in and say here that it's probably the last time I shall ever appear on television.

LINKMAN: No, I'm afraid you can't, we haven't got time. Just to bring you up to date with a few results, er, that you may have missed. Engelbert Humperdinck has taken Barrow-in-Furness, that's a gain from Ann Haydon-Jones and her husband Pip. Arthur Negus has held Bristols. That's not a result, that's a bit of gossip. Er … Mary Whitehouse has just taken umbrage. Could be a bit of trouble there. And apparently Wales is not swinging at all. No surprise there. And … Monty Python has held the credits.

Roll credits.

MONTY PYTHON'S FLYING CIRCUS

Vote for me!

Mr. Pickwick, with his usual foresight and sagacity, had chosen a peculiarly desirable moment for a visit to the borough. Never was such a contest known. The Honourable Samuel Slumkey, of Slumkey Hall, was the Blue candidate; and Horatio Fizkin, Esq., of Fizkin Lodge, near Eatanswill, had been prevailed upon by his friends to stand forward on the Buff interest. The Gazette warned the electors of Eatanswill that the eyes not only of England, but of the whole civilised world, were upon them; and the Independent imperatively demanded to know, whether the constituency of Eatanswill were the grand fellows they had always taken them for, or base and servile tools, undeserving alike of the name of Englishmen and the blessings of freedom. Never had such a commotion agitated the town before.

It was late in the evening when Mr. Pickwick and his companions, assisted by Sam, dismounted from the roof of the Eatanswill coach. Large blue silk flags were flying from the windows of the Town Arms Inn, and bills were posted in every sash, intimating, in gigantic letters, that the Honourable Samuel Slumkey's committee sat there daily. A crowd of idlers were assembled in the road, looking at a hoarse man in the balcony, who was apparently talking himself very red in the face in Mr. Slumkey's behalf; but the force and point of whose arguments were somewhat impaired by the perpetual beating of four large drums which Mr. Fizkin's committee had stationed at the street corner. There was a busy little man beside him, though, who took off his hat at intervals and motioned to the people to cheer, which they regularly did, most enthusiastically; and as the red-faced gentleman went on talking till he was redder in the face than ever, it seemed to answer his purpose quite as well as if anybody had heard him.

The Pickwickians had no sooner dismounted than they were surrounded by a branch mob of the honest and independent, who forthwith set up three deafening cheers, which being responded to by the main body (for it's not at all necessary for a crowd to know what they are cheering about), swelled into a tremendous roar of triumph, which stopped even the red-faced man in the balcony.

'Hurrah!' shouted the mob in conclusion.

'One cheer more,' screamed the little fugle-man in the balcony, and out shouted the mob again, as if lungs were cast iron, with steel works.

'Slumkey for ever!' roared the honest and independent.

'Slumkey for ever!' echoed Mr. Pickwick, taking off his hat.

'No Fizkin!' roared the crowd.

'Certainly not!' shouted Mr. Pickwick.

'Hurrah!' And then there was another roaring, like that of a whole menagerie when the elephant has rung the bell for the cold meat.

'Who is Slumkey?' whispered Mr. Tupman.

'I don't know,' replied Mr. Pickwick in the same tone. 'Hush. Don't ask any questions. It's always best on these occasions to do what the mob do.'

'But suppose there are two mobs?' suggested Mr. Snodgrass.

'Shout with the largest,' replied Mr. Pickwick.

Volumes could not have said more.

CHARLES DICKENS, *PICKWICK PAPERS* **(1837)**

The mother-in-law

My mother-in-law had her photograph taken and complained to the photographer that it didn't do her justice.
'You don't need justice,' he said. 'You need mercy.'

'Why are you so miserable?' a man asked his friend who was drinking in the pub to drown his sorrows. 'I had a terrible row with my mother-in-law,' the friend replied, 'and she vowed that she wouldn't speak to me for a whole week.' 'That's no reason to be miserable. You should be celebrating your good fortune.' 'No,' said the friend with a choked sob. 'The row happened last week ... so today's the last day.'

I said to my mother-in-law, 'My house is your house.' She said, 'Get the hell off my property.'

JOAN RIVERS

The wife's mother said, 'When you're dead, I'll dance on your grave.' I said, 'Good, I'm being buried at sea.'

LES DAWSON

The Man Who Dared to Differ from his Mother-in-law
H.M. BATEMAN

Meet the family

THE LADS HAD A WAY OF DEALING
WITH BORING OLD RELATIVES

GLEN BAXTER

Following the birth of our fourth child, I noticed that our seven-year-old eldest son was unusually quiet. He asked if there were going to be any more babies. Fearing he was resentful of his new sister, I gently assured him that each baby brought more love to the rest of the family. He looked surprised and said, 'I asked because there is only room for six toothbrushes on our holder.'

A wife who'd been married many times rushed up to her husband, who had also been married many times. 'Come quickly!' **she said.** 'My kids and your kids are beating up our kids!'

The children despise their parents until the age of forty, when they suddenly become just like them – thus preserving the system.

QUENTIN CREWE

My mother loved children – she would have given anything if I'd been one.

GROUCHO MARX

Many a family tree needs trimming.

KIN HUBBARD

'Now read me the part again where I disinherit everybody.'

PETER ARNO

THE ROYLE FAMILY — SMILE!

Living room. Mam has been trying unsuccessfully to take a photo of Dad, Denise, David, Antony, Mary and Joe.

MARY: Let me take one of just the family.

Mary and Mam change places but Joe still stands in picture.

MARY: Say cheese.

ALL: *(Half-heartedly)* Cheese.

MARY: I can't turn it on.

MAM: *(Rescuing the camera)* It's the end of the film, Mary.

MARY: I think I've clicked twice on that last one.

DAD: Is it twenty-four or a thirty-six?

MAM: I don't know.

DAD: Well what number is it on?

MAM: I don't know, it's rewound.

MARY: It's a nice camera that, Barbara.

MAM: It's from Argos ... we got that for ... what did we get that for, Jim?

DAD: For taking bloody photographs.

CAROLINE AHERNE, CRAIG CASH AND HENRY NORMAL

God gives us our relatives; thank God we can choose our friends.

ETHEL WATTS MUMFORD

ADRIAN RAESIDE

Extended family

Proudly showing off his newborn triplets, a father asks his friend what he thinks of them. 'Well, if I were you,' replies his friend, 'I'd keep *that* one.'

'Damn flowers – never a bottle of Scotch.'
CARL GILES

I come from a big family. There were twenty-three of us. I didn't know what it was like to sleep on my own until I got married.

Do your kids a favour – don't have any.
ROBERT ORBEN

WIFE: It must be time to get up, darling.
HUSBAND: What on earth makes you say that?
WIFE: The baby's fallen asleep.

'Hello, NASA, how much would it cost to put a rocket up my teenage son's backside?'
ROBERT THOMPSON

ERNIE: Well, the festive season is here again. Are you doing anything special?

ERIC: Not really. We're having my mother-in-law for lunch on Christmas Day.

ERNIE: How nice.

ERIC: Yes, I prefer chicken myself but times are hard. And I'm getting the wife a surprise present.

ERNIE: What is it?

ERIC: A packet of cigarettes.

ERNIE: That's not much of a surprise.

ERIC: It is – she's expecting a fur coat.

ERNIE: And what am *I* getting from you this Christmas?

ERIC: Close your eyes and what do you see?

ERNIE: Nothing.

FRED METCALF

Two young boys were spending Christmas Eve at their grandparents' house. That night, after they had hung up their stockings, they knelt down and began to pray. The youngest one shouted at the top of his voice: **'I pray for a brand new computer games console!'** His older brother complained: 'Stop shouting – God isn't deaf!' **'No, but Grandma is,'** answered his little brother.

'Yes, darling, Mummy has to keep her hands lovely in case she ever wants to go back to brain surgery.'
MERRILY HARPUR

THE ROYLE FAMILY — TEA AND LACK OF SYMPATHY

Tea-time – living room. Dad, Denise, Mam and Antony are eating at the table.

MAM: Mary next door's got a microwave.

DENISE: Me and Dave's going to have a microwave … do you think I should get a food processor?

DAD: What for? Just stick to the chip pan love.

DENISE: We're not going to have chips every night.

MAM: What are you going to have then?

DENISE: I don't know, we might have pasta and stuff like that.

DAD: Pasta my arse.

MAM: Have you told Dave this?

DENISE: Yeh.

DAD: And he still wants to marry you?

DENISE: He's not marrying me for what I'm like in the kitchen.

ANTONY: It's what you're like in the bedroom.

DAD: Hey, cut it out.

DENISE: *(To Antony)* Who threw you nuts? *(To Mam)* What I'm going to do is … I'm going to make lasagne and I'm going to stick it in the freezer so he can heat it up when he gets home.

MAM: Look at you Denise … you've got it all mapped out. I wish I was like you. You know, when I was your age we knew nothing.

Mam, Denise, Dad and Antony sitting round the table after tea.

MAM: *(To Denise)* Oh your nana's coming for the day, Sunday.

DENISE: Who's going to pick her up?

MAM: Your dad can go and get her on the bus.

DAD: Why can't she get the bus on her own?

MAM: She's eighty-two.

DAD: She should know the way then.

MAM: You're going.

DAD: She manages to get the bus to bingo every week.

MAM: You'd go if it was your mother.

DAD: I'd have a job, she's been dead fifteen years.

MAM: Ah. She'll be looking forward to coming all week.

ANTONY: All she does when she comes here is watch telly.

MAM: Well it's nice for her to watch telly in someone else's house. It's company for her.

DAD: If I get like that, shoot me.

ANTONY: Who's got a gun?

CAROLINE AHERNE, CRAIG CASH AND HENRY NORMAL

THE TWINS

In form and feature, face and limb,
I grew so like my brother
That folks got taking me for him
And each for one another.
It puzzled all our kith and kin,
It reach'd an awful pitch;
For one of us was born a twin
And not a soul knew which.

One day (to make the matter worse),
Before our names were fix'd,
As we were being washed by nurse,
We got completely mix'd.
And thus, you see, by Fate's decree,
(Or rather nurse's whim)
My brother John got christened *me*,
And I got christened *him*.

This fatal likeness even dogg'd
My footsteps when at school,
And I was always getting flogg'd –
For John turn'd out a fool.
I put this question hopelessly
To everyone I knew –
What *would* you do if you were me,
To prove that you were *you*?

Our close resemblance turned the tide
Of my domestic life;
For somehow my intended bride
Became my brother's wife.
In short, year after year the same
Absurd mistakes went on;
And when I died – the neighbours came
And buried brother John!

H.S. LEIGH

'Of course your daddy loves you. He's on Prozac
– he loves everybody.'
LEO CULLUM

'Don't trample on a young girl's hopes and
dreams, Ray'
DANNY SHANAHAN

DREAM PARENTS

ROZ CHAST

HOME LIFE
Mr and Mrs

A magician accidentally turned his wife into a sofa and his children into a pair of armchairs. They were rushed to hospital, and a while later **the worried sorcerer rang to check their condition. 'Comfortable,' said the doctor.**

CORK

Why do most men die before their wives? Because they want to.

Out walking in the woods, a woman found a frog in a trap. The frog promised to give her three wishes if she freed him. So she did. The frog said he had failed to mention that there was just one condition: whatever she wished for, her husband would also receive, but ten times better. As her first request, the woman said she wanted to be the most beautiful woman in the world. The frog pointed out that this would make her husband an Adonis to whom all women would flock. 'That's OK,' replied the woman, 'because I'll be beautiful too and he'll only have eyes for me. For my second wish, I'd like to become the richest woman in the world.' The frog reminded her that her husband would be ten times richer. 'That's fine,' explained the woman, 'because what's his is mine.' 'And for your final wish?' asked the frog. 'Well,' said the woman, 'I'd like a mild heart attack.'

I was cleaning the attic the other day with the wife. Filthy, dirty and covered with cobwebs ... but she's good with the kids.

TOMMY COOPER

'That's the cooker, deepfreeze, washing machine, spin-drier, dishwasher and husband.'
MICHAEL HEATH

After a hard day at work Trevor comes home, flops down in front of the television and says to his wife, **'Quick! Get me a can of lager before it starts.'** She rolls her eyes and brings him a beer. A quarter of an hour later he bellows, 'Fetch me another can, darling. It's going to start any minute now.' His wife is furious. 'Is that all you're going to do tonight? Sit in front of that television drinking beer? You have to be the world's laziest, most –' He interrupts her with a heavy sigh. **'Well,' he grimaces, 'looks like it's started.'**

HUSBAND: Put your coat on, love. I'm going down the pub.

WIFE: You mean you're taking me out for a drink?

HUSBAND: Don't be silly, woman. I'm turning off the central heating.

ANDY CAPP

SLAP AND TICKLE

The scene is a front cloth of a street with, on the right, three steps leading to the front door of a neat little house. The HUSBAND and WIFE come out – he is wearing a business suit, bowler hat, etc. and carrying a little bag.

WIFE: Well, goodbye, dear.

HUSBAND: Goodbye.

WIFE: Be home in good time for dinner.

HUSBAND: I always am.

WIFE: Have you got everything?

HUSBAND: Yes, everything. Goodbye. *(He kisses her and walks off left.)*
(When she has waved to him she goes into the house and comes out again with a pail of water and a scrubbing brush – she kneels down with her back to the audience and proceeds to scrub the steps. The HUSBAND comes on again left tapping his pockets, obviously having forgotten something. He sees his wife, smiles and, meaning to surprise her, creeps up behind her and gives her a playful slap.)*

WIFE *(Without turning her head)* Only half a pint this morning, Mr Jones.

Black out.

NOËL COWARD, *THE ORDER OF THE DAY*

Every morning a man passed by a house and saw a woman hitting her husband over the head with a French loaf. When one day he saw the woman was using a **fruit cake instead of bread,** he was curious and knocked on the door of the house. 'Don't you usually beat your husband with a French loaf?'he asked the woman when she answered the door. 'Yes,' she replied. 'But it's his birthday today.'

My wife will buy anything marked down. Last year she bought an escalator.
HENNY YOUNGMAN

ANDY CAPP

RUPERT FAWCETT

Wife: I need a new dress. I haven't had any new clothes for ages.
Husband: What's wrong with the dress you've got?
Wife: It's too long and impractical and besides, this veil keeps on getting in my eyes.

'My wife's a liar,' a man confided to his best friend in the pub.
'How do you know that?'
'Because she didn't come home last night, and when I asked where she'd been, she said she spent the night with her sister Gloria.'
'So?'
'So she's a liar. I spent the night with her sister Gloria.'

A husband and wife had four boys. The oldest three had red hair, pale skin and were tall, while the youngest son had black hair, dark eyes and was short. After a long illness, the father took to his deathbed. He turned to his wife and whispered: 'Darling, before I die, be honest with me – is our youngest boy my child?' The wife gently replied, 'I swear on everything that's holy that he is your son.' With that, the husband passed away peacefully. His wife dabbed her eyes and muttered, 'Thank God he didn't ask about the others.'

'Well the children are grown up, married, divorced and remarried. I guess our job is done.'
LEO CULLUM

My grandparents have been married for more than 50 years, and they still hold hands. If they didn't, they'd kill each other.

Walking into his living room one day after work, a man finds toys and clothes strewn all over the sofa and chairs. Next he goes into the kitchen and sees piles of washing and more mess everywhere. 'What happened?' the shocked man asks his wife. 'You know how you always come home and ask me what I did all day?' **replies his wife. 'Well, today I didn't do it.'**

'I didn't say anything, that was yesterday.'
CHON DAY

First woman: Working full time and doing housework really gets me down. At the end of the day, I come home and wash the clothes and dishes. Tomorrow I have to wash the kitchen floor and the front windows ...
Second woman: What about your husband?
First woman: Absolutely not. He can wash himself.

Men who have pierced ears are better prepared for marriage. They've experienced pain and bought jewellery.

RITA RUDNER

ERNIE: Why don't you wash your face – I can see what you had for breakfast this morning.

ERIC: Really? What did I have?

ERNIE: Bacon and eggs.

ERIC: Wrong – that was yesterday morning. My wife was doing the cooking this morning so I settled for cornflakes. It's the only thing she can do.

ERNIE: You must get sick of them.

ERIC: I do. I've had so much cornflakes since I got married, I go soggy in the bath.

ERNIE: Did you have to teach her how to prepare cornflakes?

ERIC: I did. When we first got married she used to spoil them every time.

ERNIE: How?

ERIC: She used to boil them in the bag.

ERNIE: Are things much different now?

ERIC: Oh yes – I now know what it means to go home at night to a three-course slap-up supper.

ERNIE: Really?

ERIC: It means I've gone home to the wrong house, that's what it means.

FRED METCALF

For sale: Twenty-volume encyclopedia. Excellent condition. No longer needed. Wife knows everything.

**WIFE: If you ever spent a Sunday with me instead of on that damned golf course, I think I'd drop down dead.
HUSBAND: Stop trying to bribe me.**

'Why are you asking for a divorce?' the judge enquired. 'Because all my husband wants to do is make love,' the woman said. 'Most women would be pleased about that!' 'They are!' the woman shot back. 'That's why I want a divorce.'

Basil has hired the cheap but incompetent builder O'Reilly, rather than Sybil's choice, Stubbs – with dire consequences.

SYBIL: I am going to make you regret this for the rest of your life, Basil.

BASIL: Well, fair enough, I suppose. But I think Stubbs is partly to blame …

SYBIL: *(Screaming)* BASIL!!!

BASIL: … Yes, dear?

SYBIL: Don't you *dare*!!! Don't you dare give me any more of those pathetic lies!!

BASIL: Oh! Right.

SYBIL: What do you *take* me for? Do you really think that I would believe this shambles was the work of professional builders, people who do it for a living?

BASIL: … No, not really, no

SYBIL: Why did I *trust* you, Basil? *Why* did I let you make the arrangements?! I could have *seen* what was going to happen. *Why* did I do it?

BASIL: … Well, we all make mistakes, dear.

SYBIL: *(Slapping him hard)* I am *sick to death* of you!!! You never learn do you? You *never, ever learn*!!! We've used O'Reilly three times this year, and each time it's been a *fiasco*!! That wall out there is *still* not done! You got him to change a washer in November and we didn't have any running water for two weeks!!

BASIL: *(Reasonably)* Well, he's not really a plumber, dear.

SYBIL: Well, why did you *hire* him?! … Because he's *cheap*!

BASIL: Oh, I wouldn't call him cheap, Sybil.

SYBIL: Well, what *would* you call him, then?

BASIL: Well … cheap … *ish* …

SYBIL: And the reason he's 'cheap-ish' is he's *no bloody good*! *(Kicks Basil's shin.)*

BASIL: *(Hopping about)* Oh Sybil, you do exaggerate. I mean, he's not *brilliant* …

SYBIL: Not brilliant!?!?!? He belongs in a *zoo*!!! *(Kicks his other shin.)*

BASIL: *(In some discomfort)* Sybil, you never give anyone the benefit of the doubt.

O'Reilly, refreshed by a quick drink in the bar, emerges into the lobby.

SYBIL: He's *shoddy*, he doesn't care, he's a *liar*, he's *incompetent*, he's *lazy*, he's nothing but a *half-witted thick Irish joke*!!!

BASIL: Hallo, O'Reilly … How funny! We were just talking about you … and then we got onto *another* Irish builder we used to know – Oh God, he was awful!

SYBIL: I was talking about *you*, Mr O'Reilly.

BASIL: *Were* you, dear?

I thought you were … *(He puts his hand on Sybil's arm to calm her; she slaps it away.)*

O'REILLY: *(Turning on his gentle Irish charm)* Now come, come, Mrs Fawlty …

SYBIL: *(Walking over to him)* I'm coming.

O'REILLY: *(Winningly)* Oh dear me, what have I done now?

SYBIL: *(Pointing to his work)* That and that.

O'REILLY: Not to worry. I'm putting it right.

SYBIL: … Not to worry?

O'REILLY: You've heard of the genius of the lamp, Mrs Fawlty? Well, that's me.

SYBIL: … You think I'm joking, don't you?

BASIL: *(More to himself than O'Reilly)* Oh *don't* smile.

SYBIL: … Why are you smiling, Mr O'Reilly?

O'REILLY: Well, to be perfectly honest, Mrs Fawlty, I like a woman with spirit.

SYBIL: Oh, *do* you? Is *that* what you like?

O'REILLY: I do, I do.

SYBIL: Oh, good. *(She picks up a golfing umbrella.)*

BASIL: Now, Sybil! That's enough.

She hits him with it, steps up to the now apprehensive O'Reilly, and whacks him. He steps back.

SYBIL: Come on, then – give us a smile.

She wallops him. He collapses under a flurry of blows, emitting a charming gentle Irish cry of distress.

JOHN CLEESE AND CONNIE BOOTH

Marriage guidance

Marriage is a wonderful invention; but then again, so is a bicycle puncture repair kit.

BILLY CONNOLLY

The critical period in matrimony is breakfast time.

A.P. HERBERT

Marriage is a wonderful institution, but who wants to live in an institution.

GROUCHO MARX

A girl must marry for love, and keep on marrying until she finds it.

ZSA ZSA GABOR

Husbands are like fires – they go out when unattended.

ZSA ZSA GABOR

How many husbands have I had? You mean apart from my own?

ZSA ZSA GABOR

A WORD TO HUSBANDS

To keep your marriage brimming,
With love in the loving cup,
Whenever you're wrong, admit it;
Whenever you're right, shut up.

OGDEN NASH

HOME LIFE
Home sweet home

'Could I speak to the landlord, please?'
'Speaking.'
'It's about the roof ...'
'Yes?'
'We'd like one.'

HOUSEHOLDER: *But hang it all, I can't see why that bomb next door should make you want to raise my rent!*
LANDLORD: *Don't you perceive, my dear Sir, that your house is now semi-detached?*
H.M. BROCK

'Forget the porridge! Someone's been screwing around with the pre-set TV channels!'
NAF

'We've managed to furnish one of the rooms in our house simply by collecting soap coupons.'
'Furnished one room by collecting soap coupons? Aren't you going to furnish the other six rooms?'
'No – they're full of soap.'

Did you hear about the family who was evicted from their tree house? The bank says they didn't pay their mortgage, but the family says it's a mix-up because they recently switched branches.

The British Character – Strong tendency to become doggy
PONT

'I hate it when you get bored.'
NAF

'I bought a second hand carpet in mint condition.'
'You mean it was as good as new?'
'No, I mean it had a hole in it.'

Three sisters, aged 92, 94 and 96, live together. One night the 96-year-old runs a bath. She puts one foot in and pauses. 'Was I getting in the tub or out?' she yells. The 94-year-old shouts back, 'Don't know. I'll come and see.' She starts up the stairs and stops. 'Was I going up or coming down?' she calls out. The 92-year-old is sitting at the kitchen table having tea, listening to her sisters. She shakes her head and says, 'I do hope I never get that forgetful,' and knocks on wood for good measure. Then she yells, 'I'll come up and help both of you as soon as I see who's at the door.'

While her husband is watching TV, a wife asks him if he could fix the hall light. He responds angrily. 'Do I have "electrician" printed on my forehead?' His wife asks him to repair the taps in the kitchen. The husband replies, 'Do I have "plumber" printed on my forehead?' 'Fine,' says the wife, 'but could you at least mend the front steps?' 'Mend the front steps?' retorts her spouse. 'Do I have "builder" printed on my forehead?' **With that he storms out of the house. Later that night he returns to find the front steps have been fixed. The hall light works and the taps have been repaired. 'Wow,' says the husband to his wife. 'How did all these things get mended?'** 'After you left,' she began, 'I sat outside crying and a nice young man stopped to ask me what was wrong, so I told him. He offered to do all the repairs and all I had to do in return was sleep with him or bake him a cake.' 'Great,' said the husband. 'What kind of cake did you bake?' 'Bake a cake?' replied the wife. 'Do I have "Delia Smith" printed on my forehead?'

HOME LIFE
Come into the garden

I was clipping my hedge with electric cutters the other day when my friend popped his head over to say, 'Peep-Bo.' He only got as far as 'Peep'.

WIFE: When are you thinking about mowing the lawn?
HUSBAND: When I've finished thinking about putting up the shelves.

Steven asked his gardener to kill a mole that was ruining his lawn. 'Did you catch that mole?' Steven enquired the next day. 'Yes, sir,' replied the gardener. 'And did you kill it?' Steven asked. 'I did,' replied the gardener. 'I buried it alive.'

Ad from a Cape Town newspaper:
Gardeners should waste no time. Tie your pants in now before the south-easters blow.

Did you hear about the psychiatrist who had a new garden gate made from overwrought iron?

'Damn! Just because we've built a waterfeature, the Brownlows have to go one better!'
ADEY BRYANT

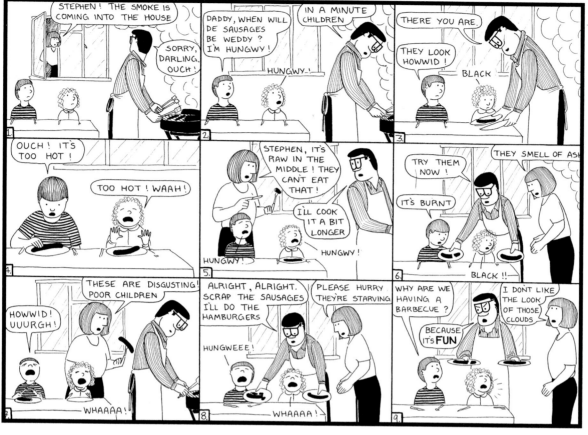

RUPERT FAWCETT

Love your neighbour, yet don't pull down your hedge.

BENJAMIN FRANKLIN

'I see you had a word with Jenkins about his untidy mowing.'

NOEL FORD

Home improvements

Oh dear, Mr Pooter has bought some paint ...

April 25.

In consequence of Brickwell telling me his wife was working wonders with the new Pinkford's enamel paint, I determined to try it. I bought two tins of red on my way home. I hastened through tea, went into the garden and painted some flower-pots. I called out Carrie, who said: **'You've always got some new-fangled craze;'** but she was obliged to admit that the flower-pots looked remarkably well. Went upstairs into the servant's bedroom and painted her washstand, towel-horse, and chest of drawers. To my mind it was an extraordinary improvement, but as an example of the ignorance of the lower classes in the matter of taste, our servant, Sarah, on seeing them, evinced no sign of pleasure, but merely said **'she thought they looked very well as they was before.'**

April 26.

Got some more red enamel paint (red, to my mind, being the best colour), **and painted the coal-scuttle,** and the backs of our *Shakespeare*, the binding of which had almost worn out.

April 27.

Painted the bath red, and was delighted with the result. Sorry to say Carrie was not, in fact we had a few words about it. She said I ought to have consulted her, and she had never heard of such a thing as a bath being painted red. I replied: **'It's merely a matter of taste.'**

Fortunately, further argument on the subject was stopped by a voice saying, 'May I come in?' It was only Cummings, who said, 'Your maid opened the door, and asked me to excuse her showing me in, as she was wringing out some socks.' **I was delighted to see him, and suggested we should have a game of whist with a dummy,** and by way of merriment said: '*You* can be the dummy.' Cummings (I thought rather ill-naturedly) replied: 'Funny as usual.' He said he couldn't stop, he only called to leave me the *Bicycle News*, as he had done with it.

I painted the washstand in the servant's bedroom.

Another ring at the bell; it was Gowing, who said he 'must apologise for coming so often, and that one of these days *we* must come round to *him*.' I said: 'A very extraordinary thing has struck me.' 'Something funny, as usual,' said Cummings. 'Yes,' I replied; 'I think even *you* will say so this time. It's concerning you both; for doesn't it seem odd that Gowing's always *coming* and Cummings' always *going*?' Carrie, who had evidently quite forgotten about the bath, went into fits of laughter, and as for myself, I fairly doubled up in my chair, till it cracked beneath me. I think this was one of the best jokes I have ever made.

Then imagine my astonishment on perceiving both Cummings and Gowing perfectly silent, and without a smile on their faces. After rather an unpleasant pause, Cummings, who had opened a cigar-case, closed it up again and said: 'Yes – I think, after that, I *shall* be going, and I am sorry I fail to see the fun of your jokes.' Gowing said he didn't mind a joke when it wasn't rude, but a pun on a name, to his thinking, was certainly a little wanting in good taste. Cummings followed it up by saying, if it had been said by anyone else but myself, he shouldn't have entered the house again. This rather unpleasantly terminated what might have been a cheerful evening. However, it was as well they went, for the charwoman had finished up the remains of the cold pork.

April 28

At the office, the new and very young clerk Pitt, who was very impudent to me a week or so ago, was late again. I told him it would be my duty to inform Mr. Perkupp, the principal. To my surprise, Pitt apologised most humbly and in a most gentlemanly fashion. I was unfeignedly pleased to notice this improvement in his manner towards me, and told him I would look over his unpunctuality. Passing down the room an hour later, I received a smart smack in the face from a rolled-up ball of hard foolscap. I turned round sharply, but all the clerks were apparently riveted to their work. I am not a rich man, but I would give half-a-sovereign to know whether that was thrown by accident or design. Went home early and bought some more enamel paint – black this time – and spent the evening touching up the fender, picture-frames, and an old pair of boots, making them look as good as new. Also painted Gowing's walking-stick, which he left behind, and made it look like ebony.

April 29, Sunday.

Woke up with a fearful headache and strong symptoms of a cold. Carrie, with a perversity which is just like her, said it was 'painter's colic', and was the result of my having spent the last few days with my nose over a paint-pot. I told her firmly that I knew a great deal better what was the matter with me than she did. I had got a chill, and decided to have a bath as hot as I could bear it. Bath ready – could scarcely bear it so hot. I persevered, and got in; very hot, but very acceptable. I lay still for some time.

On moving my hand above the surface of the water, I experienced the greatest fright I ever received in the whole course of my life; for imagine my horror on discovering my hand, as I thought, full of blood. My first thought was that I had ruptured an artery, and was bleeding to death, and should be discovered, later

CONTINUED OVERLEAF

on, looking like a second Marat, as I remember seeing him in Madame Tussaud's. My second thought was to ring the bell, but remembered there was no bell to ring. **My third was, that there was nothing but the enamel paint,** which had dissolved with boiling water. I stepped out of the bath, perfectly red all over, resembling the Red Indians I have seen depicted at an East-End theatre. I determined not to say a word to Carrie, but to tell Farmerson to come on Monday and paint the bath white.

GEORGE AND WEEDON GROSSMITH,
THE DIARY OF A NOBODY (1892)

I looked like Marat in the bath, in Madame Tussaud's.

Piano, n. A parlor utensil for subduing the impenitent visitor. It is operated by depressing the keys of the machine and the spirits of the audience.

AMBROSE BIERCE, *THE DEVIL'S DICTIONARY* (1911)

I installed a skylight in my apartment ... The people who live above me are furious.

STEVEN WRIGHT

I was doing some decorating, so I got out my step-ladder. I don't get on with my real ladder.

HARRY HILL

Old? The only thing that kept the house standing was the woodworm holding hands.

JERRY DENNIS

TRY IT THE OTHER WAY 'ROUND

It were just striking tea-time, last
    Tuesday but two
When the chap from next door
    gave a knock.
He said, 'Quick!'
I said, 'Where?'
He said, 'Here!'
I said, 'Who?'
He said, 'You!'
I said, 'Crikes … That's a shock.'

Upstairs on his landing, where both
    of us flew,
Was his wardrobe jammed tight
    in the door.
Well we pushed it and shoved it but
    all we could do
Was too wedge the thing more than
    before.

We hammered the doors off and
    hacked out the drawers
But it wouldn't go anywhere near.
Then at midnight we heard a 'rat tat'
    and a pause
And a voice shouted, 'What's all this 'ere?'

It was Constable Bright, he said,
    'What's all this din?'
He said, 'Come on, it's not very nice.'
Then he took in the scene, tucked in
    his chin
And said, 'Listen now, take my advice.'

He said, 'Try it the other way 'round.'
He said, 'Try it but don't make a sound.
If I hear one squeak … if you so much
    as speak,
I'll have you inside for the rest of
    the week.'

As it lifted it jarred on the paintwork
Rasped out as clear as could be.
He said, 'Caught ya!' and laughed …
    I said, 'Don't be daft'
'It's those onions I had for my tea.'

I said, 'Try it the other way 'round.
There's a way and it's got to be found.'
Said the copper, 'That's true … push 'ard
    and you too,
And I'll whip out me truncheon and lever
    it through.'

Well the wardrobe went in like a
    charmer
Said my neighbour, 'It's in, there's no
    doubt,
We could put up the flag but there's
    only one snag
I've been struggling to get the thing out!'

The Constable got on his bike in
    disgust
And by taking the wardrobe apart,
The two of us pushed and we shoved
    and we just
Got it wedged like it was at the start.

It was dawn when the man from next
    door paid a call
'This brickwork's too flimsy!' he said.
'And by banging that wardrobe so
    hard on the wall …
You keep knocking my wife out of bed!!!'

He said, 'Try it the other way 'round,
There's a theory I'd like to propound.
If we all get inside … with the weight
    it might slide
And I think you might find, you'll get
    quite a nice ride.'

'Oh, I can't live with this!' said the
    neighbour
'It's a fact I'd be willing to prove.'
He said, 'Is it wedged tight?' I said,
    'Yes!' he said, 'Right!
Let's leave it … I'll bloody well move!!!'

RONNIE TAYLOR, performed by Al Read

HOME LIFE
Need some work done?

THE PLUMBER

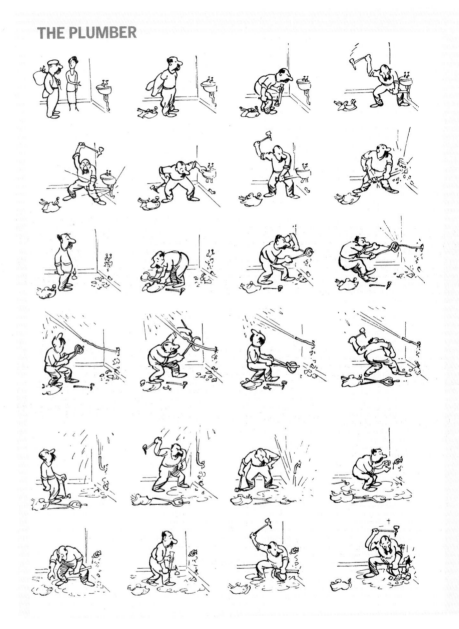

Travelling through the jungle, a missionary came across a native pounding a drum. **'Why are you doing that?'** the missionary asked. 'Because we don't have any water,' replied the native. **'Oh, I see. You're praying for rain,'** concluded the missionary. 'No,' said the native, 'I'm sending for the plumber.'

In a crowd of workmen, how do you recognise the plumber?

H.M. BATEMAN

A bricklayer, a carpenter and an electrician argued about who was on the earth first. 'We built the Pyramids of Giza,' said the bricklayer, 'so we must have been here first.' 'No,' said the carpenter. 'We built Noah's Ark long before that.' Hearing this, the electrician chuckled to himself. 'What's so funny?' asked the carpenter. 'On the first day of creation God said, "Let there be light,"' explained the electrician. 'And we'd already laid the cables.'

He's the one wearing a drip-dry shirt, drainpipe trousers and pumps.

Do come and see what we've done with the house

DESIGN FOR LIVING

When I started making money, when
  I started making friends,
We found a home as soon as we were
  able to.
We bought this little freehold for about
  a thousand more
Than the house our little house was
  once the stable to.
With charm, and colour values, wit,
  and structural alteration,
Now designed for graceful living, it
  has quite a reputation …

We're terribly House and Garden
At Number Seven B,
We live in a most amusing mews
Ever so very Contemporary!
We're terribly House and Garden;
The money that one spends
To make a place that won't disgrace
Our House and Garden friends!

We planned an uninhibited interior decor,
Curtains made of straw,
We've wall-papered the floor!
We don't know if we like it, but at least
  we can be sure
There's no place like home sweet home.

It's fearfully Maison jardin
At Number Seven B,
We've rediscovered the Chandelier
Très très very Contemporary!
We're terribly House and Garden,
Now at last we've got the chance,
The garden's full of furniture
And the house is full of plants!

Oh, it doesn't make for comfort
But it simply has to be;
'Cos we're ever so terribly up to date
Contemporary-ry!

Have you a home that cries out to your
  every visitor:
'Here lives somebody who is Exciting to
Know!' No?

Why not …
collect those little metal bottle-tops and nail
  them upside down to the floor? This will
  give a sensation of walking on little
  metal bottle-tops, turned upside down
  and nailed to the floor.

Why not …
get hold of an ordinary Northumbrian
  Spoke-shaver's Coracle, paint it in
  contrasting stripes of Telephone Black
  and White-White, and hang it up in the
  hall for a guitar-tidy for parties?

Party time!

Why not …
keep, on some convenient shelving, a
little cluster of clocks; one for each
member of the family, each an
individual colour? I like to keep mine
twenty minutes fast, don't you?

Why not …
drop in one evening for a Mess of
Pottage? My speciality.
Just aubergine and carnation petals –
but with a six shilling bottle of Mule
du Pape, a feast fit for a king!
I'm delirious about our new cooker
fitment with the eye-level grill. This
means that without my having to
bend down the hot fat can squirt
straight into my eye!

We're frightfully House and Garden
At Number Seven B,
The walls are patterned with shrunken
heads,
Ever so very Contemporary!
Our search for self-expression
Leaves us barely time for meals;
One day we're taking Liberty's in,
The next we're down at Heal's!

With little screens and bottle lamps
and motifs here and there,
Mobiles in the air,
Ivy everywhere!
You mustn't be surprised to find a
cactus in the chair,
But we call it home sweet home.

Oh, we're terribly House and Garden
As I think we said before,
But though Seven B is madly gay –
It wouldn't do for every day –
We actually live in Seven A,
In the house next door!

MICHAEL FLANDERS AND DONALD SWANN

'Remind me darling … is it my turn to drink too much
and ruin the evening by storming off in a huff, or yours?'
RICHARD JOLLEY

'Jean … if you could fill in this questionnaire on how
you've enjoyed the evening.'
TONY HUSBAND

**'I've had a perfectly
wonderful evening.
But this wasn't it.'**
GROUCHO MARX

WORK, WORK, WORK

"It's agreed, then, 5-to-4, that we disagree."

MIKE TWOHY

Computer capers

ROBERT THOMPSON

'What sound does a dog make?' my friend, who is a teacher, asked her class. 'Woof, woof,' came the reply. 'And a cat?' 'Meow,' said the children. 'And what sound does a mouse make?' she asked. 'Click,' chorused the class.

How many computer programmers does it take to change a light bulb? None. It can't be done – it's a hardware problem.

A woman was sitting in the lounge reading the paper, when her husband rushed past into the hall, looked at the doormat and then went back to his study. A little later he did the same thing. Five minutes passed and the husband stormed into the hall for the third time. 'Is something wrong, dear?' the woman asked. 'Yes there is!' he replied furiously. 'My stupid computer keeps telling me "You've got mail".'

'Hi, my name's alan-smith@freenet.com.'
NAF

Labouring the point

Anyone can do any amount of work, provided it isn't **the work he is supposed to be doing at that moment.**

ROBERT BENCHLEY

So I was in my car, and I was driving along, and my boss rang up and said, 'You've been promoted'. And I swerved. And then he rang up a second time and said, 'You've been promoted again'. And I swerved again. He rang up a third time and said, 'You're managing director'. And I went into a tree. And a policeman came up and said, 'What happened to you?' And I said, 'I careered off the road'.

TOMMY COOPER

I used to sell furniture for a living. The trouble is, it was my own.

LES DAWSON

After a long course of psychiatric treatment, the patient was cured. 'So,' said the psychiatrist, 'your life's in front of you now. What are you going to do with it?'
'Well,' said the patient, 'I've got very high academic qualifications, so I can really take my pick of jobs. I might try the Law, Politics, Advertising, PR, Television, the City. On the other hand, I might go back to being a teapot.'

'Do you know, I can never remember whether to spell 🐦🐦🐦 with an 🐦 or an 🐦.'

RONALD SEARLE

'Can you hang on a sec! I think I just took another picture of my ear.'
ROBERT LEIGHTON

I like work: it fascinates me. I can sit and look at it for hours.

JEROME K. JEROME

I wonder about unemployed blacksmiths. Do they stand around talking about possible jobs, saying, 'Yes, I've got a few irons in the fire'?

JERRY SEINFELD

'I'd much rather work in Los Angeles than New York. For a start, you get paid three hours earlier.'

'This is going to be kind of a working lunch.'
ARNIE LEVIN

SEAGOON: Napoleon's piano – the story starts in the bad old days, back in April 1955. It was early one morning. Breakfast had just been served at Beauleigh Manor – I was standing at the window, looking in. With the aid of a telescope, I was reading the paper on the breakfast table – when suddenly an advertisement caught my eye. It said –

GRYTPYPE-THYNNE: *(Distort)* Will pay anybody five pounds to remove piano from one room to another. Apply, The Bladders, Harpyapipe, Quants.

SEAGOON: In needle nardle noo time I was at the address and with the aid of a piece of iron and a lump of wood – I made this sound.

F.X. Three knocks with iron knocker on solid oak door.

MORIARTY: Sapristi Knockoes – when I heard that sound I ran down the stairs and with the aid of a door knob and two hinges I made *this* sound.

F.X. Door knob being heavily agitated followed by fast squeaky hinges as door opens.

SEAGOON: Ah, good morning.

MORIARTY: Good morning? Just a moment.

F.X. Furious dialling.

MORIARTY: Hello, Air Ministry Roof? Weather report. Yes? Yes, thank you.

F.X. Phone down.

MORIARTY: You're perfectly right – it *is* a good morning.

SEAGOON: Thanks. My name is Neddie Seagoon.

MORIARTY: What a memory you have.

SEAGOON: Needle nardle noo. I've come to move the piano.

MORIARTY: *(Insane laugh)* Come in.

SEAGOON: *(Laughs similarly)* Thanks.

MORIARTY: You must excuse the mess but we've got the Socialists in.

GRYTPYPE-THYNNE: *(Approach)* Oh Moriarty, can I borrow a shoe? Mine's worn out – oh, you have company.

MORIARTY: Ahh ah – these three men are called Neddie Seagoon. He's come in answer to our ad.

GRYTPYPE-THYNNE: Ohhhh – come in – sit down. Have a gorilla.

SEAGOON: No thanks, I'm trying to give them up.

GRYTPYPE-THYNNE: Splendid. Now, Neddie, here's the money for moving the piano – there, five pounds in fivers.

SEAGOON: Five pounds for moving a piano? Ha ha – this is money for old rope.

GRYTPTPE-THYNNE: Is it? I'd have thought you'd have bought something more useful.

SEAGOON: Oh no – I have simple tastes. Now, where's this piano?

GRYTPYPE-THYNNE: Just a moment. First, would you sign this contract in which you guarantee to move the piano from one room to another for five pounds.

SEAGOON: Of course I'll sign – have you any ink?

GRYTPYPE-THYNNE: Here's a fresh bottle.

SEAGOON: *(Drinks)* … ahhhhhhhh. Gad, I was thirsty.

MORIARTY: Sapristi Nuckoes – do you always drink ink?

SEAGOON: Only in the mating season.

MORIARTY: Shall we dance?

Old 1929 scratchy Guy Lombardo record of 'Lover' waltz.

SEAGOON: You dance divinely.

GRYTPYPE-THYNNE: Next dance please! Now, Neddie, just sign the contract on the side of this horse.

SEAGOON: Certainly.

F.X. Stratching of pen under Seagoon as he speaks next line.

SEAGOON: Neddie – Seagoon – A.G.G.

MORIARTY: What's A.G.G. for?

SEAGOON: For the kiddies to ride on … get it? A gee-gee – ha ha ha ha –

(Agonised silence)

GRYTPYPE-THYNNE: You're *sure* you won't have a gorilla?

SEAGOON: No thanks, I've just put one out. Now, which room is this piano in?

GRYTPYPE-THYNNE: Ahemm. It's in the Louvre.

SEAGOON: Strange place to put a piano.

GRYTPYPE-THYNNE: We refer to the Louvre Museum, Paris.

SEAGOON: What what what what what? Ahhhh, I've been tricked – ahhhh.

F.X. Thud of unconscious body hitting ground.

MORIARTY: For the benefit of people without television – he's fainted.

SPIKE MILLIGAN

WORK, WORK, WORK
Second interview

My brother-in-law ...
I wish he would learn
a trade, **so we'd know
what kind of work he
was out of.**

HENNY YOUNGMAN

**Work is the greatest thing in the
world,** so we should always save
some of it for tomorrow.

DON HEROLD

Work is the refuge of people who have nothing better to do.

OSCAR WILDE

'I'm ecstatic! I made a million
pounds profit last month?'
'Honestly?'
'Now why do you have to go
and spoil everything?'

**'I used to be a dresser in a strip
club for twenty pounds a week.'**
'Twenty pounds a week? That's
not very much.'
'No, but it was all I could afford.'

RUPERT FAWCETT

'I'm working from home today.'
VICTORIA ROBERTS

Executive

I am a young executive. No cuffs than mine are cleaner;
I have a Slimline brief-case and I use the firm's Cortina.
In every roadside hostelry from here to Burgess Hill
The *maîtres d'hôtel* all know me well and let me sign the bill.

You ask me what it is I do. Well actually, you know,
I'm partly a liaison man and partly P.R.O.
Essentially I integrate the current export drive
And basically I'm viable from ten o'clock till five.

For vital off-the-record work – that's talking transport-wise –
I've a scarlet Aston-Martin – and does she go? She flies!
Pedestrians and dogs and cats – we mark them down for slaughter.
I also own a speed-boat which has never touched the water.

She's built of fibre-glass, of course. I call her 'Mandy Jane'
After a bird I used to know – No soda, please, just plain –
And how did I acquire her? Well to tell you about that
And to put you in the picture I must wear my other hat.

I do some mild developing. The sort of place I need
Is a quiet country market town that's rather run to seed.
A luncheon and a drink or two, a little *savoir-faire* –
I fix the Planning Officer, the Town Clerk and the Mayor.

And if some preservationist attempts to interfere
A 'dangerous structure' notice from the Borough Engineer
Will settle any buildings that are standing in our way –
The modern style, sir, with respect, has really come to stay.

JOHN BETJEMAN

Meet the boss

BOSS: And why did you leave your last job?

SECRETARY: Well, to be quite frank, my boss's wife objected to the fact that I let him make love to me.

BOSS: Oh. So when would you be able to start ... tomorrow?

SECRETARY: The Invisible Man's outside.
BOSS: Tell him I can't see him.

The timid little clerk was terribly afraid of his boss, so one day when he felt ill and a colleague suggested he go home, he said, 'Oh, I couldn't do that. The boss would fire me.'
'Don't be silly,' said his friend. 'He'll never know. He's not even in today.'
So the little clerk went home. When he got to his house, he looked through the window and there was his boss, passionately kissing his wife. Racing back to the office, he rushed up to his friend.
'A fine friend you are, giving me that advice!' he shouted. 'I nearly got caught.'

**EMPLOYEE: I went to church and prayed for a raise.
BOSS: Don't let me ever catch you going over my head again.**

SCOTT ADAMS

spoken to old man Derwent in years. The man's a recluse. It's hopeless I tell you. Marjorie's won. And she hasn't even fired a shot. (Drinks)

STEPHEN: Listen to me, Peter. Marjorie may have won the war, but she hasn't won the battle.

HUGH: Dammit John, you're up to something. I've seen that look before.

STEPHEN: You're damn right I'm up to something.

HUGH: Dammit.

STEPHEN: What?

HUGH: What are you up to?

STEPHEN: Something. I'm up to something.

HUGH: I thought so.

STEPHEN: I want you on my team for this, Peter.

HUGH: Dammit John, I'm yours, you know that.

STEPHEN: I haven't finished. It's absolutely mandatory that you buy into my way of working. Things could get a little hairy during the next forty-eight. (Drinks)

HUGH: You know me, John. Hairy is as hairy does.

STEPHEN: Good to hear. Call O'Neill for me, will you? Get him to postpone the meeting.

HUGH: What shall I tell him? (Drinks)

STEPHEN: (Shouting) Tell him any damn thing you like – just buy me some time!

HUGH: Dammit John, it's good to have you back.

STEPHEN: You'd better save the pretty speeches for later, Peter, we've a long night ahead of us. (Drinks)

HUGH: Just like old times, eh, John?

STEPHEN: Sure, Peter, sure.

HUGH: (Dialling) You know it's funny. I drove through High Wycombe just the other day ... (into phone) Hello? Peter here. Get me O'Neill.

STEPHEN: And fast.

HUGH: And fast. (Pause) Say again? Dammit.

STEPHEN: What?

HUGH: O'Neill's out of town and can't be reached.

STEPHEN: Dammit to hell and back.

HUGH: Right. Damn blast and double damn.

STEPHEN: Damn.

HUGH: Want me to try Amsterdam?

STEPHEN: No.

HUGH: But ...

STEPHEN: Come on Peter, you're not thinking straight. Amsterdam's too obvious. Marjorie was never obvious. That's why I loved her.

HUGH: (Drinks) By God here's a turn-up. I never thought I'd hear an old warhorse like you talk about love.

STEPHEN: Love's nothing to be afraid of, Peter. You don't need a Harvard MBA to know that the bedroom and the boardroom are just two sides of the same ballgame. I wonder –

HUGH: Try me. Shoot.

STEPHEN: Put it together. A block of part-paid ordinaries funnelled through Geneva. A carefully staged release of IDL preference stock through the back door, underpinned by a notional rights issue. Who'll be wincing then? (Drinks)

HUGH: Dammit John, it's starting to add up. Want me to try Sydney?

CONTINUED OVERLEAF

STEPHEN: Come on Peter, stay awake. He'll be in Australia by now.

HUGH: Dammit sideways. Wait a minute. Will they trace it back to us?

STEPHEN: A ploy like that? It'll have Seagrove's handwriting all over it, John.

HUGH: And back again. But that still leaves us with Marjorie.

STEPHEN: Dammit

HUGH: *(Whispered mysteriously)* What's she *after*?

STEPHEN: No point in asking that, Peter. I gave up trying to understand Marjorie a long time ago.

HUGH: Yeah. Women.

STEPHEN: Marjorie isn't women, Peter.

HUGH: No, of course not, John. Forgive me. I meant no offence.

STEPHEN: Something I've always wondered. How did you keep Nancy so long?

HUGH: I've never been Nancy, John.

STEPHEN: No, your wife.

HUGH: Oh Nancy. You know. Rough with the smooth. You work at it. Do your best. Never enough time. Keep on grafting, long hours, you think you know but of course you don't, cover all the angles, they talk about stress, I tell them I'm married to it.

STEPHEN: Am I right in thinking that you have a daughter?

HUGH: Yup. Henrietta.

STEPHEN: Did he? Did he really? That must have hurt. Hurt like hell on a jetski.

HUGH: You never had kids of your own, I believe?

STEPHEN: You're wrong, Peter. You're so wrong.

HUGH: Oh, I beg your pardon.

STEPHEN: We're sitting in my children at this moment.

HUGH: I may have misheard that, John.

STEPHEN: The company, Peter.

HUGH: Oh right.

STEPHEN: I gave everything to this company. *(Suddenly shouting)* Dammit New York should have rung by now!

HUGH: Relax, John. It's still early.

STEPHEN: I know, Peter. But it's not going to stay early for long.

Stephen goes to the window.

HUGH: New York'll come through, John. I know they will.

STEPHEN: *(Looking out of the window)* I hope so. There are six million people out there, Peter.

HUGH: Really? What do they want?

STEPHEN: Who knows? Peter?

HUGH: Yeah.

STEPHEN: I say we go with it.

HUGH: Agreed.

STEPHEN: If New York rings, we give them affirmative.

HUGH: I'll tell Susan.

STEPHEN: Now let's get the hell out of here.

HUGH: Sure?

STEPHEN: Yeah. I don't think even we two can sustain this level of high intensity work without coming down for a space.

HUGH: Dammit you're right.

STEPHEN: Besides, I could use a drink.

STEPHEN FRY AND HUGH LAURIE

It can't be good for you!

SINCE YOU WON'T GO AWAY, I'LL MAKE YOU AN INTERN.

GREAT! WHAT'S AN INTERN?

YOU'LL SPEND YOUR DAY IN A HIGH-TRAFFIC CUBE TRYING TO LOOK BUSY. YOUR MAIN FUNCTION IS TO MAKE THE REST OF US GLAD WE'RE NOT YOU.

HOW DID PEOPLE EVER LOOK BUSY BEFORE COMPUTERS?

SCOTT ADAMS

A man was given the job of painting white lines down the middle of the road. **The first day he did ten miles; the second day he did four miles; the third day he did less than a mile. His foreman was furious. 'How come you're doing less each day?'** 'Because each day I get further away from the can of paint.'

'We've got to draw a line on unethical behaviour and then get as close to that line as possible.'
W.B. PARK

WELCOME TO SALES TRAINING.

AS YOU KNOW, OUR COMPANY MAKES OVER-PRICED, INFERIOR PRODUCTS. WE TRY TO COMPENSATE BY SETTING HIGH SALES QUOTAS.

WE DON'T <u>ASK</u> YOU TO ACT ILLEGALLY, BUT IT'S PRETTY MUCH THE ONLY WAY TO REACH QUOTA. OKAY, THAT'S IT FOR TRAINING. ANY QUESTIONS?

12-16

SCOTT ADAMS

ABSOLUTELY FABULOUS – PATSY'S OFFICE

The office is much as Patsy left it – not very tidy. Items of clothing, cigarette stubs in ashtray, large wardrobe unit to one side filled with free samples of clothing, tights, make-up, etc. Huge bunches of flowers around, some dying, some fresh. Bottle of champagne on desk with glasses. There are some unvased bunches of flowers on desks. Edina and Patsy enter.

PATSY: This is it.

EDINA: As you left it, by the look of things. Now, let's not be long.

PATSY: (*Looks through bunches of flowers. Selects some, chucks one bunch directly in the bin.*) Nobody gets flowers from that florist any more. Bloody cheek. (*Looks at label of another bunch.*) Oh, Gucci. Only the second time I've been bunched by them. About bloody time.

EDINA: (*Looking at cupboard*) Is this the samples?

PATSY: Help yourself.

Edina rifles through the clothes and products. She finds a blazer she likes.

EDINA : Oh, nice. Look, Armani. (*The name is written on the sleeve.*)

PATSY: Only Emporio.

EDINA: Darling, I can felt-pen that bit out.

Patsy has opened champagne – she pours.

PATSY: Is my Chanel still in there?

EDINA: *(Produces Chanel suit on hanger.)* This one?

PATSY: Yes, my little baby. I think I'll put it on if there's a meeting. It frightens the editors. I'm the only one with Chanel couture. Let them kiss my buttons.

Magda the editor enters.

MAGDA: Patsy Stone.

PATSY: Hallo, Mag. You know Eddy?

MAGDA: Yeah. Look are you coming to this meeting?

PATSY: If I must.

MAGDA: Good. We need to drum up some more advertising revenue. It's not looking good this month. We've lost Swiss Watches, Nivea, Lanson, two lingeries, one showergel, and all my tampons have dropped out.

EDINA: Oh, dear.

MAGDA: If it wasn't for three-page Estée Lauder and bloody Rive Gauche, we'd be looking pretty thin this month.

EDINA: It won't be long this meeting, will it?

MAGDA: Five mins at the most. I've got three lunches and a tights launch to get to by two o'clock. And this, with my late-working breakfast with Marie Helvin still floating about here. *(Indicates top of her stomach.)* I'll see you there in two minutes. *(She exits.)*

PATSY: All right. Chuck me the Chanel, Eds.

JENNIFER SAUNDERS

'Do you think the directors ever pretend to be us?'
HECTOR BREEZE

Bob was a slow worker and found it difficult to hold down a job. After a visit to the job centre, he was offered work at the local zoo. When he arrived for his first day, the head keeper, aware of Bob's reputation, told him to take care of the tortoise section. Later, the keeper dropped by to see how Bob was getting on and found him standing by an empty enclosure. 'Where are the tortoises?' he asked Bob. 'I can't believe it,' said Bob. 'I just opened the door and then – whoosh!'

'Have a seat. There are 342 email messages ahead of you.'
CAROLE CABLE

Late shift

'That's an excellent suggestion, Miss Triggs. Perhaps one
of the men here would like to make it.'
RIANA DUNCAN

GARAGE MECHANICS
COURSE
INTRODUCTION
DEALING WITH
CUSTOMERS

'Now, repeat after me – "oh dear,
oh dear, oh dear!"'
GERARD WHYMAN

'I like your looks, Ramsey. You're hired.'
ALAIN

Some factory workers
were in the habit of
returning to work only
after the siren had
signalled the end of
lunch. Angry, the
foreman asked his
colleagues to write
down any solutions
they had and put them
in the suggestions box.
The next day, the
foreman opened the box
to find a single piece of
paper. It read: 'The last
person back after lunch
should sound the siren.'

IT'S INCREDIBLE...

I KNOW THE CHESTER-PERRY ORGANISATION HAVE GAINED CONTROL OF ME BUT I NEVER REALISED TO WHAT EXTENT...

THIS TEA IS DELICIOUS!

GULP!

EVEN MY TASTE BUDS HAVE BEEN BRAINWASHED....

FRANK DICKENS

A man had a problem getting up in the mornings and he was always late for work. He was getting into such bad trouble about it, that he went to the doctor. The doctor prescribed him a pill to take at bedtime. After taking the pill, the man slept soundly, woke up refreshed, had a leisurely breakfast and went into work.

'Good morning,' he said to his boss. 'I feel great. I think my timekeeping problems are a thing of the past.'

'Great,' said his boss. 'Where were you yesterday?'

Tarzan came home from a hard day's work and said, 'Jane, it's a jungle out there.'

SCOTT ADAMS

WORK, WORK, WORK
Let's split up into teams

THE OFFICE – TRAINING DAY

Interior. Training room. Day. Staff are filing back in. Rowan (the trainer) is talking to an employee.

We zoom past him to Tim, who is lost in thought, staring out of a window.

Someone taps him. He blinks out of his trance, and goes back into the training room.

The words 'Team Building' appear on the overhead projector.

ROWAN: Right, this next exercise is all about forward planning and teamwork. And I'm gonna need to put you into pairs for this, so, Gareth, if you could go with Tim.

TIM: *(Annoyed)* Ohhh God.

GARETH: Alright, smartass, I wouldn't want to be stuck with you in a situation either.

TIM: *(Sarcastic)* What? A situation? Who *would* you rather be with on a desert island then Gareth, with some whittling wood and berries?

Gareth muses on this.

GARETH: Daley Thompson.

Rowan puts a picture on the overhead projector.

ROWAN: Okay, let me give you the

problem. A farmer, not pictured, has a chicken, a bag of grain and a fox and he needs to get them from one side of the river to the other. But, and here's the rub, his boat is only big enough to take one item at a time. So I want you to work out in what order he takes them across the river.

BRENT: Remember, you can't use –

ROWAN: *(Interrupting)* Five minutes, okay?

Cut to two employees discussing the problem.

DIFFERENT EMPLOYEE: He can't take the fox first because then the chicken will eat the seed –

Brent walks into the shot deliberately and gives them encouraging looks.

Cut to Tim.

TIM: *(Thinking aloud)* Okay, he can't take the grain first because he can't leave the fox and chicken together –

GARETH: *(Patronising)* Fox and the chicken, together? Bloodbath!

TIM: Yeah I know. *(Musing)* You can't leave the chicken with the grain.

GARETH: *(Sarcastic)* 'Er hello, I'm a chicken – thank you Tim for leaving me with my favourite food.'

TIM: Yes, I was saying, Gareth, you can't do that, alright?

GARETH: How big is this chicken, that it's the same size as a bag of grain?

TIM: I don't know, big chicken.

GARETH: Yeah, how big?

TIM: Big, it's a super-chicken.

GARETH: What's the farmer doing with a fox? The fox is the farmer's worst enemy. He should just drown the fox in the river.

TIM: Gareth, it's a puzzle. You know, it's just a puzzle.

GARETH: Yeah, well it's stupid. Doesn't mean anything. What are we learning from this?

TIM: It's not about learning. It's just a problem to be solved.

GARETH: Put the grain on a wall.

TIM: There's not a wall.

GARETH: There's always walls.

TIM: Not here there isn't.

GARETH: What, it's just nothing? It's just a farm and a river? Get his wife to help.

TIM: He ain't got a wife.

GARETH: All farmers have wives.

TIM: Not this one. He's gay.

GARETH: Well, then he shouldn't be allowed near animals, should he?

RICKY GERVAIS AND STEPHEN MERCHANT

PETS
& OTHER
ANIMALS

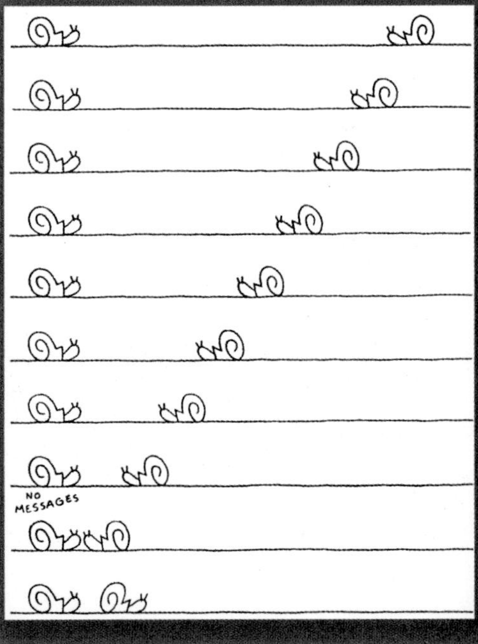

NO MESSAGES

CHARLES BARSOTTI

Here kitty, kitty

A house is never perfectly furnished for enjoyment unless there is a child in it rising three years old, and a kitten rising three weeks.

ROBERT SOUTHEY

The proud owner of a cat had taught it a simple trick. 'I bet neither of your cats could do that,' she said to a friend. One week later her friend invited her round, claiming to have taught one of her cats a trick. 'I'll show you the video,' she said. They settled themselves in front of the TV, but the film just showed a cat eating and scratching. 'What's so special about that?' asked the first woman. 'The other cat's holding the camera,' replied her friend.

We've got a cat called Ben Hur. We called it Ben till it had kittens.

SALLY POPLIN

LIFE IS FUN WHEN YOU KNOW YOU'VE GOT NINE OF THEM

STEVE BEST

'What's the matter, dear? Cat got your tongue?'
FRANK COTHAM

Two cats met in the street.
'Meow,' said the first cat.
**'Woof,' said the second cat.
The first one tried again.**
'Meow.'
'Woof,' said the second cat.
'Cats don't say "woof",'
**said the first one.
'Sorry,' said the other. 'I'm a stranger around here.'**

Don't stroke these cats

'Oh yes, we can change your spots. It's quite an operation, but we can do it.'
MICHAEL HEATH

REMEMBER, PHIL: CATCH AND RELEASE.

ANIMALS FOR THE ETHICAL TREATMENT OF PEOPLE

PETER STEINER

A Christian was thrown into an arena with a lion. As the animal leapt at him, he whispered in its ear and it slunk away. Asked what he had said to the lion, the Christian replied: 'I told him he'd have to make an after-dinner speech.'

A large lion and a small lamb strolled into a café. The lamb ordered a cup of tea and a plate of spaghetti.
'What about your friend?' said the waitress, indicating the lion. 'Isn't he hungry?'
'If he was hungry,' said the lamb curtly, 'do you think I'd be sitting next to him?'

ERNIE: Did you have to go deep into the jungle?

ERIC: Certainly, we went to places where the hand of man has never set foot. Deep, deep in the jungle, where the young girls all wear grass skirts and the young men spend all their time saving up for lawnmowers.

ERNIE: Did you meet any wild animals?

ERIC: Yes – one day we came face to face with a ferocious lion.

ERNIE: Did it give you a start?

ERIC: I didn't need one. But I'd read a book about lions so I knew exactly which steps to take.

ERNIE: What?

ERIC: Long ones. I ran to the nearest tree and climbed up it.

ERNIE: What about your wife?

ERIC: She wasn't so lucky. The lion seized her in his jaws and carried her off.

ERNIE: Good heavens! What did she do?

ERIC: She cried out 'Shoot! Shoot!'

ERNIE: And did you?

ERIC: I couldn't.

ERNIE: Why?

ERIC: I'd run out of film.

ERNIE: Did you get down from the tree?

ERIC: No, you get down from a swan – you get wood from a tree.

FRED METCALF

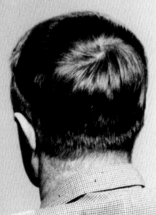

It's a dog's life

Noticing a 'Talking Terrier' for sale in a pet shop, a man went to have a look. After chatting to the dog, he bought it and took it to the pub. 'I bet everyone five pounds,' he said to a group of his friends, 'that this dog can talk.' But the dog didn't say a word and the man had to pay up.

The next day the terrier was very chatty, so his owner returned to the pub and increased the bet to ten pounds. After three hours of silence, he admitted defeat and went home. 'You're a waste of money!' the man shouted at his dog. 'Give me one good reason why I shouldn't return you to the pet shop.' The dog replied, 'Think of the odds we'll get tomorrow ...'

A dog goes into a job centre and asks for help in finding work. 'With your rare talent,' says the assistant, 'I'm sure we can get you something in the circus.' 'The circus?' echoes the dog. 'What would the circus want with a plumber?'

DOG SHOW
WORKING DOGS SECTION

WINNER

ROBERT THOMPSON

DOGS THAT LOOK LIKE THEIR OWNERS COMPETITION

3 1 2

TONY HUSBAND

WHAT IS IT, LASSIE?! WHAT IS IT, GIRL?? IS IT TIMMY? HAS HE FALLEN IN THE ABANDONED MINE SHAFT?!!

DEERING
WWW.CREATORS.COM
4-22

LASSIE

WHY LASSIE NEVER GETS FED

JOHN DEERING

DAVE COVERLY

Outside of a dog, books are a man's best friend: inside of a dog, it's too dark to read.

GROUCHO MARX

I poured spot remover on my dog. Now he's gone.

STEVEN WRIGHT

A dog went into a telegram office, took out a blank form and wrote, 'Woof, woof, woof, woof, woof, woof, woof, woof, woof.' The clerk studied the form and said, **'There are only nine words here. You could send another "woof" for the same price.'** The dog said, 'But that would be silly.'

I took my dog to a flea circus; and he stole the show.

When we take our dog on a car journey, we carry his drinking water in a gin bottle. On one occasion we stopped at a pub for lunch and let him out of the car.

Pouring some water from the bottle into his bowl, I noticed a man watching with fascination. He came over to me and whispered, 'I hope that you're not going to let him drive!'

'Sounds to me like you've had a stroke.'
ROBERT THOMPSON

'Leave me if you must, Marjorie, but to run away with my best friend, that's what really hurts.'
RIANA DUNCAN

To his dog, every man is Napoleon; hence the constant popularity of dogs.
ALDOUS HUXLEY

MY MUM'S DOG

Yorkie won't go for a walkie
the only order he'll obey is stay
the only trick he does is sit
he's a rip off

JOHN HEGLEY

Visiting his new girlfriend in her tenth-floor flat, the young man became impatient. His sweetheart was taking so long to finish her make-up that the man decided to pass the time by playing football with her poodle. Unfortunately, the dog became a little over-exuberant and chased the ball out of the window. At that moment the girl appeared. Noticing a dismayed expression on her boyfriend's face, she asked him if everything was all right. 'Yes,' he replied, 'but I was wondering if your poodle had been showing any signs of depression recently.'

'I've really had it with my dog: he'll chase anyone on a bike.' 'So what are you going to do – leave him at the dog's home? Give him away? Sell him?' 'No, nothing that drastic. I think I'll just confiscate his bike.'

'My dog's cross-eyed,' says a man to the vet. 'Is there anything you can do for it?' 'Let's have a look at him,' says the vet. He picks up the dog and examines it at length. 'Hmm,' he says. 'I'm going to have to put him down.' 'Just because he's cross-eyed?' exclaims the man. 'No,' says the vet, 'because he's heavy.'

'I thought I told you to stay out of sight while the judges were around.'
CARL GILES

The noblest of dogs is the hot dog; for it feeds the hand that bites it. LAURENCE J. PETER

Q: Where would you find a dog with no legs?
A: Exactly where you left it.

'I sometimes think we spoil that dog.'
TONY HUSBAND

At morning surgery a doctor received the most haggard looking patient he had ever seen. 'I can't sleep,' said the patient. 'The dogs in the street outside my window bark all night long and it's driving me mad!' 'There now,' said the doctor soothingly. 'Try these new sleeping pills.' A week later the patient was back, looking even more tired and distressed. 'Didn't the pills work?' asked the doctor. 'No,' sobbed the patient. 'I've been up every night chasing those damn dogs and even if I catch one, it just won't swallow the pill.'

To look at Montmorency you would imagine that he was an angel sent upon the earth, for some reason withheld from mankind, in the shape of a small fox-terrier. There is a sort of Oh-what-a-wicked-world-this-is-and-how-I-wish-I-could-do-something-to-make-it-better-and-nobler expression about Montmorency that has been known to bring the tears into the eyes of pious old ladies and gentlemen.

When first he came to live at my expense, I never thought I should be able to get him to stop long. I used to sit down and look at him, as he sat on the rug and looked up at me, and think: 'Oh, that dog will never live. He will be snatched up to the bright skies in a chariot, that is what will happen to him.'

But, when I had paid for about a dozen chickens that he had killed; and had dragged him, growling and kicking, by the scruff of his neck, out of a hundred and fourteen street fights; and had had a dead cat brought round for my inspection by an irate female, who called me a murderer; and had

been summoned by the man next door but one for having a ferocious dog at large, that had kept him pinned up in his own tool-shed, afraid to venture his nose outside the door, for over two hours on a cold night; and had learned that the gardener, unknown to myself, had won thirty shillings by backing him to kill rats against time, then I began to think that maybe they'd let him remain on earth for a bit longer, after all.

… We were, as I have said, returning from a dip, and halfway up the High Street a cat darted out from one of the houses in front of us, and began to trot across the road. Montmorency gave a cry of joy – the cry of a stern warrior who sees his enemy given over to his hands – the sort of cry Cromwell might have uttered when the Scots came down the hill – and flew after his prey.

His victim was a large black Tom. I never saw a larger cat, nor a more disreputable-looking cat. It had lost half its tail, one of its ears, and a fairly appreciable proportion of its nose. It was a long, sinewy-

looking animal. It had a calm, contented air about it.

Montmorency went for that poor cat at the rate of twenty miles an hour; but the cat did not hurry up – did not seem to have grasped the idea that its life was in danger. It trotted quietly on until its would-be assassin was within a yard of it, and then it turned round and sat down in the middle of the road, and looked at Montmorency with a gentle, inquiring expression, that said:

'Yes! You want me?'

Montmorency does not lack pluck; but there was something about the look of that cat that might have chilled the heart of the boldest dog. He stopped abruptly, and looked back at Tom. Neither spoke; but the conversation that one could imagine was clearly as follows:

THE CAT: 'Can I do anything for you?'

MONTMORENCY: 'No – no, thanks.'

THE CAT: 'Don't you mind speaking, if you really want anything, you know.'

MONTMORENCY: *(Backing down the High Street)*: 'Oh, no – not at all – certainly – don't trouble. I – I am afraid I've made a mistake. I thought I knew you. Sorry I disturbed you.'

THE CAT: 'Not at all – quite a pleasure. Sure you don't want anything, now?'

MONTMORENCY: *(Still backing)*: 'Not at all, thanks – not at all – very kind of you. Good morning.'

THE CAT: 'Good morning.'

Then the cat rose, and continued his trot; and Montmorency, fitting what he calls his tail carefully into its groove, came back to us, and took up an unimportant position in the rear.

To this day, if you say the word 'Cats!' to Montmorency, he will visibly shrink and look up piteously at you, as if to say: 'Please don't.'

JEROME K. JEROME,
THREE MEN IN A BOAT (1889)

ERIC: I could never get rid of a dog. I'll never forget having our last one put down.

ERNIE: Was he mad?

ERIC: He was furious! And we'd been such pals. Every day we used to go for a tramp in the woods.

ERNIE: I bet he enjoyed that!

ERIC: He did. Mind you, the tramp was getting a bit fed up. He was such a clever dog, too. The only dog I ever had that could say its own name.

ERNIE: What was it called?

ERIC: Woof. You remember the film *Lassie Come Home*?

ERNIE: Yes.

ERIC: He was in that.

ERNIE: What part did he play?

ERIC: The lead. I was in it too, actually – I had a bit part.

ERNIE: What did you do?

ERIC: I got bit. This dog ran up to me, barking its head off ...

ERNIE: But didn't you know, a barking dog never bites?

ERIC: I did – but the dog didn't.

FRED METCALF

Dog ends

THE DOG

The truth I do not stretch or shove
When I state the dog is full of love.
I've also proved, by actual test,
A wet dog is the lovingest.

OGDEN NASH

CHARLES PEATTIE AND RUSSELL TAYLOR

A dog teaches a boy fidelity, perseverance and to turn round three times before lying down.

ROBERT BENCHLEY

A blind man is walking down the street, accompanied by his guide dog. Approaching a busy junction, the animal leaps into a torrent of traffic, dragging its owner behind him. The screeching of tyres and car horns is ear-splitting, as motorists desperately try to avoid running them down. The pair eventually reach the other side of the street. After a few seconds, the man takes a biscuit from his pocket and offers it to the dog. A passer-by who had observed the incident is amazed: 'Why on earth are you rewarding your dog with a biscuit? He nearly killed you!' The blind man grimaces and replies, 'I'm trying to find out where the mutt's head is, so I can give him a good kick up the backside.'

'Ah look, he wants his dinner.'
ROBERT THOMPSON

Sir Lancelot had fought a bitter battle all day, and didn't want to quit when his horse was killed. Despite the thunder, the lightning and the rain, he managed to stagger to a nearby farmhouse, where he asked the farmer to lend him a horse, so that he could return to the battle.

'I'm afraid I don't have a horse to spare,' said the farmer, 'but I do have a large St Bernard dog you could use.'

Sir Lancelot took one look at the huge shaggy dog and cast his eyes towards the dark and stormy sky.

'Surely,' he said, 'you wouldn't send a knight out on a dog like this.'

Q No one has been able to tell us what kind of dog we have. I am enclosing a sketch of one of his two postures. He only has two. The other one is the same as this except he faces in the opposite direction.
Mrs Eugennia Black

A I think that what you have is a cast-iron lawn dog. The expressionless eye and the rigid pose are characteristic of metal lawn animals. And that certainly is a cast-iron ear. You could, however, remove all doubt by means of a simple test with a hammer and a cold chisel, or an acetylene torch. If the animal chips, or melts, my diagnosis is correct.

JAMES THURBER, *THE THURBER CARNIVAL* (1945)

IAN BAKER

Getting the bird

Noticing his hens weren't laying many eggs, a farmer decided that he must buy a new cockerel. At the supply shop, the assistant offered him a particularly randy cockerel and warned the farmer that the bird was absolutely sex-obsessed. Insisting this was just what he needed, the farmer bought the cockerel and took it home. Back at the farm, the cockerel immediately had his way with all the hens. Still raring to go, he went over to a nearby pond and had his wicked way with the ducks and after that the geese. This behaviour continued throughout the week until the farmer found the cockerel flat out in the yard, with buzzards circling overhead. 'Serves you right, you filthy thing,' said the farmer. Pointing up at the sky the cockerel winked and whispered, 'Shhh.'

It was going to be a long day at the Post Office.
BP

A hen is only an egg's way of making another egg.

SAMUEL BUTLER

A farmer buys a new cockerel for his hen house. The new bird goes up to the old cock and tells him to leave. 'Oh, come on,' says the older bird, 'at least give me a chance. Let's have a race and if I win I can stay.' 'OK,' agrees the young cockerel. 'I'll tell you what. Just to show what a good sport I am, I'll give you a five-yard head start.' The two birds set off and just as the younger one is about to catch up the farmer shoots him dead. 'Can you believe it?' he said to his wife. 'That's the third gay cockerel I've been sold this month.'

'Is there any way of keeping the light on when you're inside?'
NAF

The customer asked the hardware shop assistant for a tin of canary-coloured emulsion. 'I need it to paint my parakeet so I can enter him in a canary contest. He sings so sweetly he's bound to win.' 'Well, you can't do that,' said the assistant. 'The paint will kill him!' 'No it won't,' replied the man. The shop worker insisted: 'Look, I'll bet you a tenner your parakeet dies if you try to paint him!' 'You're on,' said the pet owner. Two days later he came back looking very sheepish, and laid a crisp ten-pound note on the counter. 'So the painting killed him?' enquired the assistant. 'Indirectly,' said the customer. 'He didn't survive the sanding between coats.'

'I didn't realise it was a formal do.'
NEIL DISHINGTON

'We just haven't been flapping them hard enough.'
SAM GROSS

DAVE COVERLY

NOT ONLY, BUT ALSO – RAVENS TAKE FLIGHT

Dudley Moore is interviewing Peter Cook, aka Sir Arthur Streeb-Greebling.

DUDLEY: We are very pleased to have in the studio tonight one of the very few people in the world, if not the only person in the world, who has spent the major part of his life under water attempting to teach ravens to fly.

SIR ARTHUR STREEB-GREEBLING: Good evening.

DUDLEY: Good evening. We're very pleased to welcome to the studio Sir Arthur Greeb-Streebling.

SIR ARTHUR: Streeb-Greebling.

DUDLEY: I beg your pardon.

SIR ARTHUR: You're confusing me with Sir Arthur Greeb-Streebling. Good evening.

DUDLEY: Yes. Good evening. Thank you very much.

SIR ARTHUR: And good Greebling.

DUDLEY: Good Greebling indeed.

SIR ARTHUR: Hello fans.

DUDLEY: Shut up, Sir Arthur.

SIR ARTHUR: Good evening.

DUDLEY: Good evening. Sir Arthur, could you tell us what first led you to this way of life, teaching ravens to fly underwater?

SIR ARTHUR: Well, it's always very difficult to say what prompts anybody to do anything, let alone getting underwater and teaching ravens to fly. But I think it probably all dates back to a very early age, when I was quite a young fellow. My mother, Lady Beryl Streeb-Greebling, you know, the wonderful dancer – a hundred and seven tomorrow and still dancing – she came up to me in the conservatory – I was pruning some walnuts – and she said 'Arthur' – I wasn't Sir Arthur in those days – she said 'Arthur, if you don't get underwater and start teaching ravens

to fly, I'll smash your stupid face off,' and I think it was this that sort of first started my interest in the whole business of getting them underwater.

DUDLEY: How old were you then?

SIR ARTHUR: I was forty-seven. I'd just majored in O Level in Forestry – I got through that – and I was looking about for something to do.

DUDLEY: Yes. Where did you strat your work?

SIR ARTHUR: I think it can be said of me that I have never, ever strated my work. That is one thing I have never done. I can lay my hand on my heart, or indeed anybody else's heart, and say I have never strated my work, never strated at all. I think what you probably want to know is when I started my work. You've misread completely the question.

DUDLEY: Yes, I'm awfully sorry. I did make an error. Where did you start your work?

SIR ARTHUR: Where did I start it? Well, I started almost immediately. My mother had given me this hint. She's a powerful woman, Lady Beryl. She can break a swan's wing with a blow of her nose. Incredible creature.

DUDLEY: Sir Arthur, is it difficult to get ravens to fly underwater?

SIR ARTHUR: Well, I think the word difficult is an awfully good one here. Yes, it is. It's well nigh impossible. The trouble is, you see, God, in his infinite wisdom and mercy, designed these creatures to fly in the air, rather than through the watery substances of the deep. Hence they experience enormous difficulty, as you said, difficulty, in beating their tiny wings against the water. It's a disastrous experience for them.

DUDLEY: How do you manage to breathe?

SIR ARTHUR: Through the mouth and the nose – the usual method, in fact. God gave us these orifices to breathe through and who am I to condemn him? I think you can't breathe through anything else. If you start breathing through your ears, you can't hear yourself speak for the rush to your ears, you can't hear yourself speak. Nose and mouth is what I use, and I trust you do.

DUDLEY: Yes, I most certainly do, of course, but what I was meaning was how do you manage to breathe underwater?

SIR ARTHUR: Well that's completely impossible. Nobody can breathe underwater. That's what makes it so difficult. I have to keep bobbing to the surface every thirty seconds. Makes it impossible to conduct a sustained training programme on the ravens. And they're no better. They can't even be taught to hold their beaks – horrible little animals. There they are, sitting on my wrist. I say 'Fly! Fly, you devils!' And they inhale a face full of water.

DUDLEY: I suppose they drown, do they?

SIR ARTHUR: It's curtains, yes. They drown. Little black feathery figure topples off my wrist, spirals very slowly down to a watery grave. We're knee-deep in feathers off that part of the coast.

DUDLEY: Sir Arthur, have you ever managed to get a raven to fly underwater?

SIR ARTHUR: No. I have never managed to get one to fly underwater. Not at all – not a single success in the whole forty years of training.

DUDLEY: Sounds rather a miserable failure then, your whole life, really, I suppose.

SIR ARTHUR: My life has been a miserable failure, yes.

DUDLEY: How old are you, if that's not a personal question?

SIR ARTHUR: It is a personal question, but I am eighty-three. Remarkably well preserved because of the water, of course, on the face.

DUDLEY: Well I would say then that your life probably has been a bit of a shambles.

SIR ARTHUR: It's a bit late in life, you see, to turn to anything else. I've often thought of taking something else up, you know – a bit more commercial. But it's very difficult when you go round to a firm and they say 'what were you doing before this?' And you say 'well, I was hovering about ten foot underwater, attempting unsuccessfully to get ravens to fly.' They tend to look down their noses at you.

DUDLEY: What a miserable thing.

SIR ARTHUR: A miserable thing indeed.

DUDLEY: Well, thank you very much indeed, Sir Arthur, for telling us your absolute tale of woe. Thank you very much for coming along.

SIR ARTHUR: Thank you and good evening.

PETER COOK

Can you bear it?

'Grizzle, grizzle, grizzle! That's all you do! I'm sick of it.'
NAF

The baby bear was born utterly bald, so its parents named it Fred Bear.

While briefing a group of walkers in Canada, a park ranger warned, 'It's possible that we will encounter a grizzly bear. However, as grizzlies usually avoid contact with humans, I suggest you attach small bells to your rucksacks to signal your approach and give the bears time to retreat.' 'If you do see any grizzly-bear droppings,' he added, 'leave the area at once.' 'But how will we know if they're bear droppings?' one of the walkers queried. 'Easy,' replied the ranger. 'Grizzly-bear droppings are full of small bells.'

'Winnie the __what__?'
JOHN DONEGAN

'This one put up a real fight, but I got him in the end.'
NAF

Insect insanity

WOW! I'VE GOT A BELTER !

ROBERT THOMPSON

Two male centipedes were standing on a corner, eyeing up the local talent as it passed by.
'Hey now, look at that,' cried one of them suddenly as a well-endowed young female strolled by. 'That's what I really call a fine pair of legs, pair of legs, pair of legs ...'

Wandering round a pet shop, a customer asked for an unusual animal. 'I know just the thing,' said the assistant, 'a clever centipede.' 'What does it do?' asked the man. 'Everything that you tell it to,' came the reply. The man took the clever centipede home and asked it to fetch his slippers, which it did. It turned on the television, made him a cup of tea and vacuumed and ironed. The man remembered that he hadn't bought a newspaper, so he sent the clever centipede out for one. One hour later it hadn't returned. He waited another hour, but there was still no sign of the centipede. On going to the door he spotted the centipede on the stairs. 'Where have you been?' he asked. 'Nowhere,' said the centipede. 'I'm still putting my boots on.'

'You slept with her, didn't you?'
DANNY SHANAHAN

A flea went into a pub and ordered a double scotch. And another. And another. And another. He drank them all down and at closing time he hopped unsteadily out into the street, leapt into the air and fell flat on his face. 'Oh, damn,' he said, 'someone's moved my dog.'

Pet shop – going cheap

MONTY PYTHON – THE PARROT SKETCH

Mr Praline walks into a pet shop carrying a dead parrot in a cage. He walks to the counter where the shopkeeper tries to hide below the cash register.

PRALINE (JOHN CLEESE): Hello, I wish to register a complaint ... Hello? Miss?

SHOPKEEPER (MICHAEL PALIN): What do you mean, miss?

PRALINE: Oh, I'm sorry, I have a cold. I wish to make a complaint.

SHOPKEEPER: Sorry, we're closing for lunch.

PRALINE: Never mind that my lad, I wish to complain about this parrot what I purchased not half an hour ago from this very boutique.

SHOPKEEPER: Oh yes, the Norwegian Blue. What's wrong with it?

PRALINE: I'll tell you what's wrong with it. It's dead, that's what's wrong with it.

SHOPKEEPER: No, no it's resting, look!

PRALINE: Look my lad, I know a dead parrot when I see one and I'm looking at one right now.

SHOPKEEPER: No, no sir, it's not dead. It's resting.

PRALINE: Resting?

SHOPKEEPER: Yeah, remarkable bird the Norwegian Blue, beautiful plumage, innit?

PRALINE: The plumage don't enter into it – it's stone dead.

SHOPKEEPER: No, no – it's just resting.

PRALINE: All right then, if it's resting I'll wake it up. *(Shouts into cage)* Hello Polly! I've got a nice cuttlefish for you when you wake up, Polly Parrot!

SHOPKEEPER: *(Jogging cage)* There, it moved.

PRALINE: No he didn't. That was you pushing the cage.

SHOPKEEPER: I did not.

PRALINE: Yes, you did. *(Takes parrot out of cage, shouts)* Hello Polly, Polly *(Bangs it against counter)* Polly Parrot, wake up. Polly. *(Throws it in the air and lets it fall to the floor)* Now that's what I call a dead parrot.

SHOPKEEPER: No, no it's stunned.

PRALINE: Look my lad, I've had just about enough of this. That parrot is definitely deceased. And when I bought it not half an hour ago, you assured me that its lack of movement was due to it being tired and shagged out after a long squawk.

SHOPKEEPER: It's probably pining for the fiords.

PRALINE: Pining for the fiords, what kind of talk is that? Look, why did it fall flat on its back the moment I got it home?

SHOPKEEPER: The Norwegian Blue prefers kipping on its back. Beautiful bird, lovely plumage.

PRALINE: Look, I took the liberty of examining that parrot, and I discovered that the only reason that it had been sitting on its perch in the first place was that it had been nailed there.

SHOPKEEPER: Well of course it was nailed there. Otherwise it would muscle up to those bars and voom.

PRALINE: Look matey *(Picks up parrot)* this parrot wouldn't voom if I put four thousand volts through it. It's bleeding demised.

SHOPKEEPER: It's not, it's pining.

PRALINE: It's not pining, it's passed on. This parrot is no more. It has ceased to be. It's expired and gone to meet its maker. This is a late parrot. It's a stiff. Bereft of life, it rests in peace. If you hadn't nailed it to the perch, it would be pushing up the daisies. It's rung down the curtain and joined the choir invisible. This is an ex-parrot.

SHOPKEEPER: Well, I'd better replace it then.

PRALINE: *(To camera)* If you want to get anything done in this country you've got to complain till you're blue in the mouth.

SHOPKEEPER: Sorry guv, we're right out of parrots.

PRALINE: I see. I see. I get the picture.

SHOPKEEPER: I've got a slug.

PRALINE: Does it talk?

SHOPKEEPER: Not really, no.

PRALINE: Well, it's scarcely a replacement, then is it?

SHOPKEEPER: Listen, I'll tell you what, *(Handing over a card)* tell you what, if you go to my brother's pet shop in Bolton he'll replace your parrot for you.

PRALINE: Bolton eh?

SHOPKEEPER: Yeah.

PRALINE: All right.

He leaves, holding the parrot.

MONTY PYTHON'S FLYING CIRCUS

HOW MUCH ARE THOSE PETS IN THE WINDOW?

The scene is a pet shop. Deric and his wife, Aileen, have gone in for a litter-tray for their cat, Thermal, but are distracted by some sad creatures hoping for a home.

There was a notice scrawled on the pet shop window.

'Closing Down – Everything must go.' Everything had almost gone and the shop echoed emptily like a newly decorated room before the curtains are hung and the carpet laid.

Tatty paper sacks spilled dog biscuits down on to the bare boards and in a cage by the window sat the scruffiest looking budgie I'd ever laid eyes on. He was a sort of yellowy-beige colour and he hadn't seen a comb in years.

He was the kind of budgie who ought to have had a fag hanging out of the corner of his beak and one wing stuffed deep down inside his pocket as he leaned against his mirror, making rude gestures at the passing pigeons. Sellotaped to his cage was the sign, 'Shop-soiled – Half price.'

I wanted to take him home with me, but Aileen said he probably drank meths or took drugs or something and would be a lot more trouble than he was worth.

There was a tortoise in a glass tank with 'Ten per cent off' stuck on its shell, and since its head seemed to be missing I assumed that was the 10 per cent they were talking about. However, the owner assured me that it did actually have a head – it was hibernating.

'Anyway,' he said, 'it was only a joke.'

The puppies were segregated into two distinct lots. A couple of posh ones lolled in a pen by the fishtank and looked suitably bored with life, whilst on the other side of the shop a small herd of runts dashed around and collided with each other under a large sign which read, 'Reduced'.

I wanted to take four puppies as well as the shop-soiled budgie but Aileen talked me out of it once more.

'We came in for a cat litter-tray.'

They didn't have one and so we popped round the corner to see the opposition who were driving them out of business. They had a dozen different litter-trays ranging from a rather basic mini-skip right up to the deluxe model suitable for hauling heavy freight on the Manchester Ship Canal. 'That's the one.'

'It's enormous.'

'He might want to have his friends round every now and then.'

'He won't be cleaning it out – you will.'

'That's true.'

The shopkeeper came over to help. I couldn't see the one I really wanted.

'Maureen Lipman has one with a roof.'

'Does she now?'

'Her cat does.'

'Well she won't have bought it here then.'

'No – she lives in London.'

'Ah well, she'll have bought it down there then.'

'Yes, I suppose she will have.'

As conversations go, it sort of went all limp and not where I wanted it to go at all.

'Which one would you suggest?'

'That one.'

That one was the Kitty Corner Cat Pan complete with its own Litter Enclosure and priced at £8.61. It was finished in a pleasing brown and cream and looked just the thing for today's modern cat. For £1.99 we bought a large bag of Thomas Cat Litter with added Super Blue Deodorant Granules and then lashed out on a dozen tins of Whiskas Supermeat and a box of Brekkies – *prepared with real pilchard*. I had no idea there was so much to owning a cat – if Patrick wanted it back now he was going to have to take out a mortgage.

I hoped Thermal would be pleased – the litter-tray wasn't as spacious as some of those we had seen, but at least there was sufficient room in there for a cosy candle-lit dinner for two and drinks afterwards in the alcove. I thought that was much more romantic.

He loved it, and spent the whole afternoon curled up in one corner, fast asleep.

'He likes it, doesn't he?'

'He's not supposed to sleep in it,' Aileen pointed out. 'It's for crapping in.'

'I can't seem to get that through to him.'

'Show him.'

'Perhaps later.'

DERIC LONGDEN, *THE CAT WHO CAME IN FROM THE COLD*

EDWARD MCLACHLAN

It's like a zoo out there

EXPEL ELEPHANTS

Elephant Elephant
Go away
I don't like Elephants that stay
Twenty-four hours is all I can stand
After that they must be banned
It is very well known
That England is an Elephant-free zone
Pussy-cats and Dogs can stay
But Elephants must go away

SPIKE MILLIGAN

'I don't like the look of this.'
EDWARD MCLACHLAN

What do you give an elephant with diarrhoea? Plenty of room.

"PERSONALLY I WOULDN'T RECOMMEND SPAIN"

STEVE BEST

What do you call
two elephants
on a bicycle?
Optimistic.

What do you call
a donkey with
three legs? A
wonkey.

YEAH, YEAH, I KNOW THEY'RE BAD FOR ME. BUT, HEY, I'M FACING EXTINCTION ANYWAY.

raesidecartoon.com

ADRIAN RAESIDE

Odd things animals.
All dogs look up to you.
All cats look down to you. Only a pig looks at you as an equal.
WINSTON CHURCHILL

I ask people why they have deer heads on their walls. They always say it's because it's such a beautiful animal. I think my mother is attractive, but I have photographs of her.
ELLEN DEGENERES

What do you call a deer with no eyes? No idea.

What do you call a deer with no eyes and no legs? Still no idea.

Did you hear about the hyena who swallowed an Oxo cube? He made himself a laughing stock.

'A complete Brazilian wax? Did it hurt?'
RICHARD JOLLEY

A little boy pestered his reluctant father into taking him to the zoo. 'So how was it?' asked his mother on their return. 'It was great,' replied the boy. 'And Daddy liked it too, especially when one animal came racing home at thirty to one.'

'This is ridiculous, why couldn't we meet them downstream?'
JOSEPH MIRACHI

Crazy creatures

I saw a hyena. I told it a joke. It stopped laughing. I watched leopards changing their spots. They moved from one spot to another. One moved to a guest spot. I saw some striped leopards and spotted zebras. The leopards had played football with the zebras and after the match they changed jerseys. I saw a bison. It was a pudding-bison.

Struck up a conversation with a Chinese girl in the snake house.

'You're a real charmer,' I said.

'That's a lot of cobras,' she said.

One snake was counting the snakes climbing ladders. It was an adder. He was wheeling the pram with a kid in it. It was shaking a snake. It was a rattlesnake. The kid's father was an old goat. He kept trying to butt in.

There was a sudden disturbance. It was the Mad Boar from Boreham Wood. He was boring holes in the road and singing 'The High Top Hat my Feather Boa, fifty years ago'. It upset an old deer who was trying to break into a stag party.

I saw a polar bear. It was trying to balance on a glacier mint. A monkey was filling a jaguar with petrol. I stood by the kerb and watched a pelican crossing. A couple of giraffes were necking in broad daylight. They had a lot of neck. The boxing kangaroo was challenging all comers. He met his match in the Kung Fu Kangaroo. It nearly kicked the stuffing out of him.

The elephants were packing their trunks for the weekend. An old bull elephant was in charge. He kept prodding them with his tusks. He was a hard tusk-master.

I poodled along to the book kiosk for some books on animals. It was chock-full with penguins, corgis and pelicans. They were crowding the shelves so I went back to my car.

I found a snake on the windscreen. It was a wind-screen viper. On the verge I saw a snake in the grass. It was a traffic warden. She was chatty. She told me she came from a long line of wardens. Her grandfather had been a prison warden, her father an air-raid warden and her uncle a church warden.

Personally, I thought she might be a game warden but I was in a hurry to get home.

TOMMY COOPER, *JUST LIKE THAT!*

The Diplomatic Platypus

I had a duck-billed platypus when I was up at Trinity,
With whom I soon discovered a remarkable affinity.
He used to live in lodgings with myself and Arthur Purvis,
And we all went up together for the Diplomatic Service.
I had a certain confidence, I own, in his ability,
He mastered all the subjects with remarkable facility;
And Purvis, though more dubious, agreed that he was clever,
But no one else imagined he had any chance whatever.
I failed to pass the interview, the Board with wry grimaces
Took exception to my boots and then objected to my braces,
And Purvis too was failed by an intolerant examiner
Who said he had his doubts as to his sock-suspenders' stamina.
The bitterness of failure was considerably mollified,
However, by the ease with which our platypus had qualified.
The wisdom of the choice, it soon appeared, was undeniable;
There never was a diplomat more thoroughly reliable.
He never made rash statements his enemies might hold him to,
He never stated anything, for no one ever told him to,
And soon he was appointed, so correct was his behaviour,
Our Minister (without Portfolio) to Trans-Moravia.
My friend was loved and honoured from the Andes to Esthonia,
He soon achieved a pact between Peru and Patagonia,
He never vexed the Russians nor offended the Rumanians,
He pacified the Letts and yet appeased the Lithuanians,
Won approval from his masters down in Downing Street so wholly, O,
He was soon to be rewarded with the grant of a Portfolio,
When, on the Anniversary of Greek Emancipation,
Alas! He laid an egg in the Bulgarian Legation.
This untoward occurrence caused unheard-of repercussions,
Giving rise to epidemics of sword-clanking in the Prussians.
The Poles began to threaten, and the Finns began to flap at him,
Directing all the blame for this unfortunate mishap at him;
While the Swedes withdrew entirely from the Anglo-Saxon dailies
The right of photographing the Aurora Borealis,
And, all efforts at rapprochement in the meantime proving barren,
The Japanese in self-defence annexed the Isle of Arran.
My platypus, once thought to be more cautious and more tentative
Than any other living diplomatic representative,
Was now a sort of warning to all diplomatic students
Of the risks attached to negligence, the perils of imprudence,
And, branded in the Honours List as 'Platypus, Dame Vera',
Retired, a lonely figure, to lay eggs at Bordighera.

PATRICK BARRINGTON from *PUNCH*

WHO LET THE ANIMALS OUT?

The zoo manager (John Cleese) is waiting to see Butterling, the head zoo keeper.

SHEILA: Head keeper to see you, sir.

(Enter KEEPER)

JOHN: Now, when you joined us three weeks ago, Butterling, this was the second largest zoo in the whole of Europe. We had over 6000 animals. All we have left are two hyaenas, a rhinoceros and a ferret with a wooden leg. Where are the others?

KEEPER: I don't know, sir.

JOHN: They're in the main street, Butterling, the main street. All except for the water buffalo.

KEEPER: Where's the water buffalo, sir?

JOHN: In my bathroom. My wife found it there early this morning. She's a nervous woman, Butterling. The police caught her just forty minutes ago. She was over 100 miles away, still running. She doesn't remember anything, and she thinks she's a potato.

KEEPER: I'm sorry, sir.

JOHN: That's all right, I didn't like her anyway. But the town, Butterling, the town! It looks like a National Game Reserve. I mean, Butterling, how does anyone lose giraffes?

KEEPER: People take them, sir.

JOHN: What!

KEEPER: I don't think they mean to steal them, sir. They just borrow them and forget to give them back.

JOHN: You're lying, Butterling. I know all about your little agreement with the sausage factory.

KEEPER: Ohhh!

JOHN: And the aviary, Butterling, my little pride and joy the aviary. What have you done with it?

KEEPER: I put all the birds in one cage, sir.

JOHN: Well?

KEEPER: The vulture's looking very well, sir.

JOHN: Aaaarrghhh! I'm dismissing you as from tomorrow, Butterling. One of the baboons can take over for the time being. Now for the rest of the day, one, get the ferret out of the elephant's cage. It doesn't fool anyone. Two, Butterling, can you impersonate animals?

KEEPER: Yes, sir.

JOHN: Well?

KEEPER: Cluck, cluck, sir.

JOHN: What was that, Butterling?

KEEPER: That was a chicken, sir. Woof, woof.

JOHN: No, don't tell me, Butterling. Let me guess that one. That was a dog.

KEEPER: Thank you very much, sir. Mooooooo!

JOHN: This is a zoo, not a farm, Butterling. Get out. It's five to one. Go and feed the animals. The animal. Oh, and Butterling –

KEEPER: Yes, sir?

JOHN: If there's a potato waiting outside, tell her I love her.

JOHN CLEESE

Q My husband's seal will not juggle, although we have tried everything.

Grace H.

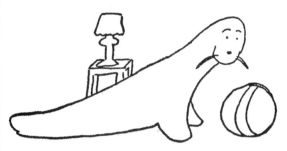

A Most seals will not juggle; I think I have never known one that juggled. Seals balance things, and sometimes toss objects (such as the large ball in your sketch) from one to another. This last will be difficult if your husband has but one seal. I'd try him in plain balancing, beginning with a billiard cue or something. It may be, of course, that he is a non-balancing seal.

JAMES THURBER, *THE THURBER CARNIVAL* (1945)

Hearing that a zookeeper has managed to train a lion to live in the same cage as a lamb, a man pays a visit to see if it's true. Amazingly, the man finds the animals lying next to each other. 'How did you do this?' he asks the keeper. 'Is it a trick?' '**No,**' replies the zookeeper, '**this has been going on for three months now. I don't mind telling you, though,**' he confides, 'we've had to replace the lamb a few times.'

'We shall now sing hymn 35, "The Lord is my Shepherd".'
NAF

GEOFF THOMPSON

Two sheep were talking in a field. 'Baaaaaa!' **said the first.** 'Damn,' **said the second.** 'I was going to say that.'

SPIRITUAL LIFE

SIMON BOND

Holy jokers

The vicar's wife was entertaining some small children to tea. Turning to one little girl she said, 'I understand God has sent you a little brother,' 'Yes,' said the little girl. 'And He knows where the extra money's coming from too. I heard Daddy say so.'

HE STARTED IT!

THE LYING BAST...

BILL TIDY

There was a young lady from Tottenham
Who'd no manners, or else she'd forgotten 'em
At tea at the vicar's
She tore off her knickers
Because, she explained, she felt hot in 'em.

ANON

What do you get when you cross a Jehovah's Witness with an atheist?

Someone who knocks on your door for no apparent reason.

GO TO CHURCH THIS SUNDAY – AVOID THE CHRISTMAS RUSH.

GRAFFITO

NORMAN THELWELL

REV COUNTER

After attending a conference on honesty, four bishops were sharing a train compartment. They agreed to confess their weaknesses to each other. 'Well, I'm drunk most of the time,' said one. 'I just can't stop gambling,' admitted the second. 'I'm always flirting with pretty girls,' said the third. All eyes were on the fourth bishop. 'I'm a terrible gossip,' he said.

A conscientious young vicar was walking through his parish when he met an attractive young woman who had the reputation of being very free with her favours.
He looked at her reprovingly and said, 'I prayed for you last night.'
'Silly – you should have given me a ring,' she said. 'I wasn't doing anything all evening.'

An old lady was very proud of her well-behaved parrot and was showing him off to the vicar. 'And he talks, you know. But none of those rude things that parrots usually say. He's very religious. If you pull his right leg, he recites the Lord's Prayer, and if you pull his left leg, he recites the Twenty-third Psalm.'
'That's remarkable,' said the vicar, 'quite remarkable. And what happens if you pull both legs at once?'
'I fall flat on my back, you stupid old twit,' said the parrot.

A missionary was captured by cannibals and popped into the pot. Thinking that his last hour had come, he was most surprised to see the cannibal chief suddenly sink to his knees and lift up his hands in prayer.
With new hope in his heart, the missionary said, 'Am I to understand that you are a practising Christian?'
'Of course I am,' said the chief. 'And please don't interrupt me while I'm saying grace!'

'Cor! That was a bit of luck … he's just been unfrocked!'
BILL TIDY

REG SMYTHE, *ANDY CAPP*

I once wanted to become an atheist, but I gave up – they have no holidays.

HENNY YOUNGMAN

A man goes on holiday to the Holy Land with his wife and mother-in-law. During the trip, the mother-in-law dies.

The man visits an undertaker, who explains that they can ship the body home, but it'll cost £5000. Or they can bury her in the Holy Land for just £150.

'We'll ship her home,' says the son-in-law.

'Are you sure?' says the undertaker. 'That's an awfully big expense.'

'Look,' says the son-in-law, 'two thousand years ago they buried a bloke here and three days later he rose from the dead. I just can't take that chance.'

'I wish I could pull the birds like you, Brother Francis.'
N. BENNETT

Dearly beloved ...

In church one Sunday the vicar was disappointed to find that his congregation consisted of just one farmer. Wondering whether he should hold the service, he decided to ask the man's opinion. 'If I take a bucket of food to my hens,' said the farmer thoughtfully, 'and only one turns up, I don't send it away hungry.' Moved by this simple analogy, the minister climbed into his pulpit and delivered a vigorous and lengthy sermon. 'Did you enjoy the service?' enquired the vicar when he had finished. 'When only one hen turns up,' the farmer replied testily, 'I don't give it the whole bucket.'

Two church wardens were comparing the sermons of the curate and the vicar. **'Personally, I prefer the curate's,'** said one. **'Why's that?'** asked the other. 'Well, the curate always says "in conclusion" and concludes,' replied the first, 'and the vicar always says "lastly" and lasts.'

'What do you mean, we have to go to church today?'
MARTIN HONEYSETT

Sunday May 17th
My grandma made us get up early and go to church with her. My father was made to comb his hair and wear one of his dead father's ties. Grandma held both our arms and looked proud to be with us. The church service was dead boring. The vicar looked like the oldest man alive and spoke in a feeble sort of voice. My father kept standing up when we were supposed to sit down and vice versa. I copied what grandma did, she was always right. My father sang too loudly, everyone looked at him. I shook the vicar's hand when we were allowed outside. It was like touching dead leaves.

SUE TOWNSEND,
THE SECRET DIARY OF ADRIAN MOLE AGED 13 3/4

'When those among us who failed to remember to put their clocks
forward are comfortably seated I will continue.'
CARL GILES

'On account of the widespread floods we will
omit the verse about soft refreshing rain.'
NORMAN THELWELL

'That was a metaphorical call to gird up
our loins, Miss Thring.'
ALANDE LA NOUGEREDE

CHARLES PEATTIE AND RUSSELL TAYLOR

BEYOND THE FRINGE – TAKE A PEW FOR TODAY'S LESSON

VICAR: The eleventh verse of the twenty-seventh chapter of the book of Genesis, 'But my brother Esau is an hairy man, but I am a smooth man' – 'my brother Esau is an hairy man, but I am a smooth man.' Perhaps I can paraphrase this, say the same thing in a different way, by quoting you some words from the grand old prophet, Nehemiah, Nehemiah seven, sixteen.
'And he said unto me, what seest thou? And I said unto him, lo

(He reads the next four lines twice.)

I see the children of Bebai, Numbering six hundred and seventy-three, And I see the children of Asgad Numbering one thousand, four hundred and seventy-four.'
There come times in the lives of each and every one of us when we turn aside from our fellows and seek the solitude and tranquillity of our own firesides. When we put up our feet and put on our slippers, and sit and stare into the fire. I wonder at such times whether your thoughts turn, as mine do, to those words I've just read you now.

They are very unique and very special words, words that express, as so very few words do, that sense of lack that lies at the very heart of modern existence. That-don't-quite-know-what-it-is-but-I'm-not-getting-everything-out-of-life-that-I-should-be-getting sort of feeling. But they are more than this, these words, much, much more – they are in a very real sense a challenge to each and every one of us here tonight. What is that challenge?

As I was on my way here tonight, I arrived at the station, and by an oversight I happened to come out by the way one is supposed to go in, and as I was coming out an employee of the railway company hailed me. 'Hey, mate,' he shouted, 'where do you think you are going?' That at any rate was the gist of what he said. You know, I was grateful to him because,

you see, he put me in mind of the kind of question I felt I ought to be asking you here tonight. Where do you think you're going?

Very many years ago when I was about as old as some of you are now, I went mountain climbing in Scotland with a very dear friend of mine. And there was this mountain, you see, and we decided to climb it. And so, very early one morning, we arose and began to climb. All day we climbed. Up and up and up. Higher and higher and higher. Till the valley lay very small below us, and the mists of the evening began to come down and the sun to set. And when we reached the summit we sat down to watch this most magnificent sight of the sun going down behind the mountain. And as he watched, my friend very suddenly and violently vomited.

Some of us think Life's a bit like that, don't we? But it isn't. You know, Life – Life, it's rather like opening a tin of sardines. We are all of us looking for the key. Some of us – some of us think we've found the key, don't we? We roll back the lid of the sardine tin of Life, we reveal the sardines, the riches of Life, therein and we get them out, we enjoy them. But, you know, there's always a little piece in the corner you can't get out. I wonder – I wonder, is there a little piece in the corner of your life? I know there is in mine.

So now I draw to a close. I want you when you go out into the world, in times of trouble and sorrow and helplessness and despair amid the hurly-burly of modern life, if ever you're tempted to say, 'Oh, shove this!' I want you then to remember, for comfort, the words of my first text to you tonight …
'But my brother Esau is an hairy man, but I am a smooth man.'

Black out.

PETER COOK, ALAN BENNETT,
JONATHAN MILLER AND DUDLEY MOORE

Vicar enters.

VICAR: Ah, Captain Mainwaring, I wonder if you'd approve the hymns for Sunday – I thought 'Lead Kindly Light', 'Rock of Ages', 'God Moves in a Mysterious Way' and 'Onward Christian Soldiers'.

MAINWARING: They seem all right to me, nothing very controversial.

VICAR: The reason I was asking is because we haven't had an organist since poor Mrs West passed away, so we have to sing unaccompanied, which means the congregation must know the hymns. I give them the first note, of course.

He blows a note on his pitch-pipe.

MAINWARING: Yes, well, I expect we'll manage.

JONES: Permission to interject, sir?

MAINWARING: What is it?

JONES: There's no need for the Vicar to use his pipe, sir.

VICAR: You mean you think I should 'La' it.

MAINWARING: Oh no, we can't have him 'La'ing' it, it's much better for him to use his pipe.

VICAR: I quite agree with you, Captain Mainwaring. I'd much rather do this. *(Blows pipe)* Than this. *(La's)*

JONES: No, no, what I'm trying to say is – the Vicar can use his pipe for the first three hymns, but I can play the organ for 'Onward Christian Soldiers'.

MAINWARING: I didn't know that you played the church organ, Jones.

JONES: I was driven to it by passion, sir.

MAINWARING: Really.

JONES: Yes, sir. You see it all happened many years ago in Leamington-on-Spa. I fell in love with this beautiful lady, well she wasn't really beautiful, sir – bit of an acid face – very acid it was – but what really attracted me to her was her knees.

MAINWARING: Her knees?

JONES: Yes, they were very flat – I'd never seen such flat knees – then I found out why – very religious she was – did a lot of praying – I was mad with lust – I had to find a way to make her look favourable on me. Driven by desire, I practised 'Onward Christian Soldiers' on the organ – day and night I practised, with her flat knees imprinted on my mind, until finally I did it in my repertoire. Flushed with triumph, I went round to her house, but it didn't do me any good, she'd moved to Bournemouth. But I never lost the touch.

JIMMY PERRY
AND DAVID CROFT

It's all in the Bible

'Did Moses ever get better in the end?' asked a little girl when she got back from Sunday School.
'Why, whatever makes you think he was ill?' asked her mother.
'He must have been,' came the reply. 'Didn't God tell him to take the tablets?'

" WHAT DO YOU MEAN ' IT'S A BIT MUDDY ' ? "

STEVE BEST

COLIN WHEELER

I've read the last page of the Bible. It's all going to turn out all right.

BILLY GRAHAM

HEAR THE GOOD NEWS

NEWSREADER: Good even. Here beginneth the first verse of the news. It has come to pass that the seven elders of the seven tribes have now been abiding in Sodom for seven days and seven nights. There seems little hope of any early settlement. An official spokesman said this afternoon, 'Only a miracle can save us now.'

The walls of Jericho today suddenly collapsed, burying one Joshua and his seven-piece brass band who were passing beneath at the time. Scientists are working on the theory that soundwaves from the music may have disturbed the brickwork.

In the Sanhedrin today there was a wailing and gnashing of teeth in the public gallery when a certain Philistine was accused of writing on the wall at Balshazzar's feast a phrase including two four-letter words.

At the weigh-in for the big fight tomorrow, Goliath tipped the scales this even at 15 stone 3 lbs and David at 14 stone 3 lbs. David's manager said this even, 'The odd stone could make all the difference.'

News of a happy event. In Ramoth-Gilead, early this morning, Zebediah begat Naaman.

The news in brief: Lamentations 4, 18-22 and 11 Kings 14, 2-8. And now a look at the weather.

WEATHERMAN: Good even. Well, it's been a pretty rough week in the Holy Land, hasn't it? Anyway, let's have a look at the scroll. Now we've got a plague of locusts moving in here from the north-west. They're going to be in the Tyre and Sidon area about lunchtime tomorrow. Scattered outbreaks of fire and brimstone up here in Tarsus and down here in Hebron. Oh, and possibly some mild thunderbolts, force two to three, in Gath. Down in the south, well, Egypt's had a pretty nasty spell recently. Seventeen or eighteen days ago it was frogs, followed by lice, flies, a murrain on the beasts and last Tuesday locusts, and now, moving in from the south-south-east, boils. Further outlook for Egypt, well, two or three days of thick darkness lying over the face of the land and then death of the first-born. Sorry about that, Egypt.

Up here in the eastern Mediterranean, we've got a pretty big depression. It's been building up here for some time now and that's being brought in towards the land by high almighty winds. So, further outlook in that area – well, continual rain for forty days and forty nights, followed by widespread flooding. So if you've got any gopher, well, I should start building your arks now. Good night.

NEWSREADER: Finally, here are two police messages. Would Moses, last heard of seven months ago on a hiking holiday in the wilderness, go at once to Egypt where his people are anxiously awaiting deliverance. At the crossroads between Sodom and Gomorrah early this morning a Mrs Lot, of no fixed abode, was turned into a pillar of salt. Would anyone who saw the accident or can give any information, please ring Revelation 7777 …

BILL ODDIE AND JOHN CLEESE

GOD: *(Standing on a chair behind Noah, he rings a bell once.)* NOAH.

NOAH: *(Looks up)* Is someone calling me? *(Shrugs and goes back to his work.)*

GOD: *(Ding)* NOAH!!

NOAH: Who is that?

GOD: It's the Lord, Noah.

NOAH: Right … Where are ya? What do ya want? I've been good.

GOD: I want you to build an ark.

NOAH: Right … What's an ark?

GOD: Get some wood and build it 300 cubits by 80 cubits by 40 cubits.

NOAH: Right … What's a cubit?

GOD: Well never mind. Don't worry about that right now. After you build the ark, I want you to go out into the world and collect all the animals of the world, two by two, male and female, and put them into the ark.

NOAH: Right … Who is this really? What's going on? How come you want me to do all these weird things?

GOD: I'm going to destroy the world.

NOAH: Right … Am I on Candid Camera? How are you gonna do it?

GOD: I'm going to make it rain for a thousand days and drown them right out.

NOAH: Right … Listen, do this and you'll save water. Let it rain for forty days and forty nights and wait for the sewers to back up.

GOD: Right …

NARRATOR: So Noah began to build the ark. Of course his neighbors were not too happy about it. Can you imagine leaving for the office at 7am and seeing an ark?

NEIGHBOR: *(Enters whistling, with brief-case.)* Hey! You over there.

NOAH: What do you want?

NEIGHBOR: What is this thing?

NOAH: It's an ark.

NEIGHBOR: Uh huh, well you want to get it out of my driveway? I've gotta get to work. Hey listen, what's this thing for anyway?

NOAH: I can't tell you, ha ha ha.

NEIGHBOR: Can't you even give me a little hint?

NOAH: You want a hint?

NEIGHBOR: Yes, please.

NOAH: Well, how long can you tread water? Ha ha ha.

NEIGHBOR: There's one in every neighborhood. *(Shakes head and leaves.)*

NARRATOR: Well Noah finally got the ark built. Then he had the task of gathering all the animals two by two.

NOAH: Hey, anybody know how to tell the difference between a male and a female mosquito? *(Looking in a box)* I told you rabbits before, only two! *(He puts box in boat.)* Whew, finally the last two animals are on board. Let's get this thing closed up before God asks me to do something else. I'm six hundred years old. I am getting too old for this sort of thing.

GOD: Noah!

NOAH: I knew it. What do you want now?

GOD: You're going to have to take one of those hippos off and get another one.

NOAH: Why?

GOD: 'Cause you got two males. You need a female.

NOAH: I'm too tired to bring anything else on board. You change one of them.

GOD: Come on, you know I don't work like that.

NOAH: But I'm sick and tired of this. I've been working all day everyday like crazy for months now, dawn to dusk. I'm tired of this.

GOD: Noah.

NOAH: Yeah?

GOD: How long can you tread water? Ha ha ha.

NOAH: Yeah, well I got news for you. You keep talking about this flood and I haven't seen a drop of rain. Meanwhile, the whole neighborhood is making fun of me. I told one of my friends I'd been talking to the Lord and he laughed so hard he wet his pants. Do you know I'm the only guy in town with an ark in his yard? People are picketing and calling the health department, strangers walk up to me and say, 'How's it going, Tarzan?' I am sick and tired of all of this, you let me get a pregnant elephant … Do you give me an instruction book? … No!!! Here I am standing under the elephant and brrrrrrrump! Right on top of me! I'm telling you, I've had enough. You're supposed to see all and know all, well have you seen the bottom of that ark? Who's going to clean up that mess? Not me, I tell you. I quit. I'm tired of this. I'm going to let the animals out and burn that ark down. I can't believe you made me do all this … *(God takes a watering can and begins to pour water on Noah's head.)*

NOAH: *(Continues)* I can't believe the mess you got me in and … and … it's raining … This isn't just a shower is it? OK. All right, it's me and you Lord, me and you all the way. I'm with you Lord. Whatever you say …

BILL COSBY

Heavenly bodies

Up in heaven, the pastor was shown his eternal reward. To his disappointment, he was only given a small shack. Down the street he saw a taxi driver being shown a lovely estate with gardens and pools. 'I don't understand it,' the pastor moaned. '**I dedicated my whole life to serving God and this is all I get, yet a cabbie is awarded a mansion?**' 'It's quite simple,' Saint Peter explained. 'Our system is based on performance. **When you preached, people slept; when he drove, people prayed.**'

NICK HOBART

PAUL WOOD

My wife is an angel. Lucky you. Mine's still alive.

I DO BENEFITS FOR all RELIGIONS –

A little boy is being very naughty. 'You won't go to heaven', his mother scolds him, 'if you behave so badly.' 'Yes I will,' replies the little boy. 'I'll just run in and out, slamming all the doors until Saint Peter says, "For goodness sake, Jimmy! Come in or stay out".'

'Buzz off Louise! That was only till death us did part.'
LEE LORENZ

The definition of heaven: a British home, an American salary, Chinese food, a German car and a Latin lover. The definition of hell: a British lover, an American car, a Chinese home, German food and a Latin salary.

'I'm sorry you're disappointed, John, but what exactly did you imagine heaven would be like?'
NAF

On arrival in heaven a woman asked to speak to Saint Paul. 'I've always wondered,' she said to the saint. 'Did you ever get any replies to all those letters you wrote to the Corinthians?'

'You're being reincarnated as a mayfly, Mr Hoskins – have a nice day.'
JEREMY BANX

I'D HATE TO BLOW THE HEREAFTER ON A TECHNICALITY.

BOB HOPE

The man upstairs

Mortal: What does a million years feel like to you?
God: Like one second.
Mortal: What is a million pounds like to you?
God: Like one penny.
Mortal: Can I have a penny?
God: Just a second ...

A builder was hammering a nail into the church roof when he hit his thumb. 'Damn it, I missed!' he shrieked. **The priest heard him, and called up, 'You shouldn't say that on the House of the Lord.'** 'Why?' sneered the builder. 'Will I be struck by a bolt of lightning or something?' **'Yes, you might well be,'** replied the priest. Seconds later, there was a huge flash from the heavens and a bolt of lightning shot down. It just missed the builder, but struck the priest dead. **And a voice from on high boomed out, 'Damn it, I missed!'**

NICK DOWNES

Walking down the street, Betty suddenly collapsed and died. **Being a good woman, she went straight to heaven. Passing through the Pearly Gates, she was surprised to see two imposing figures sitting on thrones.** 'I don't understand,' she said. 'One of you must be God, but who is the other one?' 'I'm God,' said God. 'Surely you've heard of me?' said the second figure. 'I'm Cleanliness.'

THE HITCHHIKER'S GUIDE TO THE GALAXY – THE BIG QUESTION

Arthur Dent has a Babel Fish in his ear – he looks in The Hitchhiker's Guide for an explanation ...

The Babel fish is small, yellow and leech-like, and probably the oddest thing in the Universe ... if you stick a Babel Fish in your ear you can instantly understand anything said to you in any form of language ... Now, it is such a bizarrely improbable coincidence that anything so mindbogglingly useful could have evolved purely by chance that some thinkers have chosen to see it as a final clinching proof of the non-existence of God.

The argument goes something like this: 'I refuse to prove that I exist,' says God, 'for proof denies faith, and without faith I am nothing'. 'But,' says Man, 'the Babel Fish is a dead giveaway isn't it? It proves you exist, and so therefore you don't. QED'. 'Oh dear,' says God, 'I hadn't thought of that' and promptly vanishes in a puff of logic. 'Oh, that was easy,' says Man, and for an encore he proves that black is white and gets killed on the next zebra crossing.

Most leading theologians claim that this argument is a load of dingo's kidneys, but that didn't stop Oolon Colluphid making a small fortune when he used it as the central theme of his best-selling book *Well, That About Wraps It Up For God.*

Meanwhile, the poor Babel Fish, by effectively removing all barriers to communication between different cultures and races, has caused more and bloodier wars than anything else in the history of creation.

ARTHUR (DENT): What an extraordinary book.

DOUGLAS ADAMS

CHARLES BARSOTTI

'Do you believe in the existence of God?' one goldfish asked another. 'Of course,' the second replied. 'Who do you think changes our water?'

Why is it that when we talk to God we're said to be praying, but when God talks to us we're schizophrenic?

LILY TOMLIN

Ooh, you are a devil!

Omen-type music and an echoey, cave-like atmosphere. If you've got a budget, try to introduce some kind of altar, and perhaps a threatening-looking polystyrene rock. Try and zap up the costumes a bit too. But don't worry overmuch – these are not absolutely grade-A satanists.

HIGH PRIEST: Worshippers of Satan, the hour has come to summon our master and unleash the powers of Hell.

ALL: *(Led by HIGH PRIEST)* O Prince of Darkness, the Promised One, the Divine Beast, Lord of Supreme Evil, we who follow you drink to thy power, drink to thy glory, in blood!

(A thunderclap)

The blood of this virgin!!!

HIGH PRIEST: Where's the virgin?

DIABOLIST 1: Sorry?

HIGH PRIEST: The virgin. Where's the virgin? Well, who was responsible for the sacrifice?

DIABOLIST 2: He was.

DIABOLIST 1: It was you.

DIABOLIST 2: You're the virgin monitor.

DIABOLIST 1: Look, the last thing I said to you on Friday after the whist drive was, don't forget, you're bringing the virgin.

(The row continues.)

HIGH PRIEST: Silence!! Well, that's just great, isn't it? No virgin's blood to drink. None of you lot are virgins, I suppose?

DIABOLIST 1: 'Fraid not, no.

DIABOLIST 2: Nope, sorry.

HIGH PRIEST: Thought not. Anyone done it … less than twenty times?

ALL: 'Fraid not …

HIGH PRIEST: Forty times?

ALL: Nope, sorry …

WOMAN DIABOLIST: I don't enjoy it. Does that count?

HIGH PRIEST: Afraid not, no … *(Sighs)*

DIABOLIST 2: Look, can't we just skip the virgin-sacrificing and go on to the group sex?

(General agreement)

HIGH PRIEST: There *has* to be a sacrifice first.

WOMAN DIABOLIST: Well, we could sacrifice a living creature … like a goat.

HIGH PRIEST: Well, stab me, I seem to have come out without my goat, what do you know?

DIABOLIST 2: Any living creature would do, wouldn't it?

HIGH PRIEST: *(Invoking)* O Prince of Darkness, we drink to thy power, we drink to thy omnipotent glory in the blood of this earwig – no, I'm sorry. It feels silly. Besides, it's too small to get the pentangle round its neck.

DIABOLIST 2: Let's just get on to the group sex.

HIGH PRIEST: Will you shut up about group sex? This is a powerful demonic ritual, not an office party. To invoke the powers of darkness we must sacrifice something. Something symbolic. Something potent.

DIABOLIST 1: Well, can we get a move on? Only I go on duty in an hour.

HIGH PRIEST: On duty?

DIABOLIST 1: Yeh, with the wheel-clamping unit … Here, get your hands off me …

HIGH PRIEST: *(Declaiming triumphantly)* We thank you, O Prince of Darkness, for sending us this sacrifice and we drink to thy power in the blood of this … git.

ANDY HAMILTON

SPIRITUAL LIFE
Ghosties and ghoulies

Hoping to get a picture of a ghost that appeared only once every hundred years, a photographer visited a haunted castle. Clutching his camera, he sat in the dark until midnight when the ghost arrived. It turned out to be friendly and even agreed to pose for a snapshot.

The photographer took the picture and dashed home to develop it. But to his dismay he found that nothing could be seen in the photo but darkness. It turned out that the spirit was willing but the flash was weak.

Q: Where do baby ghosts go during the day?
A: The Dayscare Centre.

Q. What do you get when you cross Bambi with a ghost?
A: Bamboo!

Q: Why are ghosts bad at telling lies?
A: Because you can see right through them.

Q: What did the polite ghost say to her son?
A: Don't spook until your spooken to!

Q: Who speaks at the ghosts' press conference?
A: The spooksperson.

'I've given up the ghost.'
ROBERT THOMPSON

Using a medium, a widow contacted her deceased husband and was told he wished to speak to her. 'How are you, darling?' she cried emotionally. 'Wonderful!' came the ghostly reply. **'There's plenty of food, sex and swimming. You know how I always loved the water.'** The widow sighed contentedly, **'I can't wait to join you in heaven, dearest.'** 'I'm not in heaven,' corrected her husband, 'I've come back to earth as a duck.'

A man who lived next door to a pub had a favourite tabby cat. Sadly, the cat was run over by a truck and killed. A year later, at around midnight, the pub landlord was tidying up the empty bar when suddenly the ghost of the cat appeared, holding its severed tail in its paw.

'Can you help me?' asked the cat's ghost. 'I used to live next door to you until I was run over by a truck.'

'Yes, I remember you,' said the landlord. 'You were a very nice cat – the customers really liked you.'

'The thing is,' the cat went on, 'this bit of tail I'm holding was cut off in the accident that killed me, and I've been wandering around with it for a year. I know it's late, landlord, but would you sew it back on for me?'

'No, I'm sorry,' replied the landlord. 'Much as I would like to help you, I'm afraid I can't. You see, I'm not allowed to retail spirits after eleven o'clock.'

'How long have you believed in reincarnation?'
'Ever since I was a young woodlouse.'

'You actually have a choice of sheet colours or patterns, though plain white is consistently our most popular model.'
MARC TYLER NOBLEMAN

SPIRITUAL LIFE
Grim reaper

Mort has become apprenticed to Death. As part of the job, he follows Death to the court of the King, whose time on Earth is nearly up …

The appearance of Death didn't cause much of a stir. A footman by the door turned to him, opened his mouth and then frowned in a distracted way and thought of something else. A few courtiers glanced in their direction, their eyes instantly unfocusing as common sense overruled the other five.

WE'VE GOT A FEW MINUTES, said Death, taking a drink from a passing tray, LET'S MINGLE.

'They can't see me either!' said Mort. 'But I'm real!'

REALITY IS NOT ALWAYS WHAT IT SEEMS, said Death. ANYWAY, IF THEY DON'T WANT TO SEE ME, THEY CERTAINLY DON'T WANT TO SEE YOU. THESE ARE ARISTOCRATS, BOY. THEY'RE *GOOD* AT NOT SEEING THINGS. WHY IS THERE A CHERRY ON A STICK IN THIS DRINK?

'Mort,' said Mort automatically.

IT'S NOT AS IF IT DOES ANYTHING FOR THE FLAVOUR. WHY DOES ANYONE TAKE A PERFECTLY GOOD DRINK AND THEN PUT IN A CHERRY ON A POLE?

'What's going to happen next?' said Mort. An elderly earl bumped into his elbow, looked everywhere but directly at him, shrugged and walked away.

TAKE THESE THINGS, NOW, said Death, fingering a passing canapé. I MEAN, MUSHROOMS YES, CHICKEN YES, CREAM YES, I'VE NOTHING AGAINST ANY OF THEM, BUT WHY IN THE NAME OF SANITY MINCE THEM ALL UP AND PUT THEM IN LITTLE PASTRY CASES?

'Pardon?' said Mort.

THAT'S MORTALS FOR YOU, Death continued. THEY'VE ONLY GOT A FEW YEARS IN THIS WORLD AND THEY SPEND THEM ALL IN MAKING THINGS COMPLICATED FOR THEMSELVES. FASCINATING. HAVE A GHERKIN.

'Where's the king?' said Mort, craning to look over the heads of the court.

CHAP WITH THE GOLDEN BEARD, said Death. He tapped a flunky on the shoulder, and as the man turned and looked around in puzzlement deftly piloted another drink from his tray.

Mort cast around until he saw the figure standing in a little group in the centre of the crowd, leaning over slightly the better to hear what a rather short courtier was saying to him. He was a tall, heavily built man with the kind of stolid, patient face that one would confidently buy a used horse from.

'He doesn't look a *bad* king,' said Mort. 'Why would anyone want to kill him?'

SEE THE MAN NEXT TO HIM? WITH THE LITTLE MOUSTACHE AND THE GRIN LIKE A LIZARD? Death pointed with his scythe.

'Yes?'

HIS COUSIN, THE DUKE OF STO HELIT. NOT THE NICEST OF PEOPLE, said Death. A HANDY MAN WITH A BOTTLE OF POISON. FIFTH IN LINE TO THE THRONE LAST YEAR, NOW SECOND IN LINE. BIT OF A SOCIAL CLIMBER, YOU MIGHT SAY. He fumbled inside his robe and produced an hourglass in which black sand coursed between a spiked iron latticework. He gave it an experimental shake. AND DUE TO LIVE ANOTHER THIRTY, THIRTY-FIVE YEARS, he said, with a sigh.

'And he goes around killing people?' said Mort. He shook his head. 'There's no justice.'

Death sighed. NO, he said, handing his drink to a page who was surprised to find he was suddenly holding an empty glass, THERE'S JUST ME.

He drew his sword, which had the same ice blue, shadow-thin blade as the scythe of office, and stepped forward.

'I thought you used the scythe,' whispered Mort.

KINGS GET THE SWORD, said Death. IT'S A ROYAL WHATSNAME, PREROGATIVE.

His free hand thrust its bony digits beneath his robe again and brought out King Olerve's glass. In the top half the last few grains of sand were huddling together.

PAY CAREFUL ATTENTION, said Death, YOU MAY BE ASKED QUESTIONS AFTERWARDS.

'Wait,' said Mort, wretchedly. 'It's not fair. Can't you stop it?'

FAIR? said Death. WHO SAID ANYTHING ABOUT FAIR?

'Well, if the other man is such a –'

LISTEN, said Death, FAIR DOESN'T COME INTO IT. YOU CAN'T TAKE SIDES. GOOD GRIEF. WHEN IT'S TIME, IT'S TIME. THAT'S ALL THERE IS TO IT, BOY.

TERRY PRATCHETT, *MORT*

Is anybody there?

ROUND THE HORNE – HAVING A CRYSTAL BALL

KENNETH (HORNE): Any survey of the occult would not be complete without a look at the medium – and that's why when I saw an advert in my copy of *Physique Pictorial* – I buy it for the gardening section – it was an advert actually for Bona Seances – I rushed out of my lattie and trolled down there.

F.X. Knock on door. Door opens.

KENNETH: Hello – anybody there.

HUGH (PADDICK): Oh hello. I'm Julian and this is my friend Sandy.

KEN W (WILLIAMS): Or to give us our professional names – I am Madam Bona – and Jule here is the Great Omipaloni – natural sensitive.

KENNETH: I believe you can see into the future.

HUGH: Oh yes. I'm gifted with second vada. I am occupied by your actual mystic forces.

KEN W: He is. Occupied. Frequently. He's got the waves, he's got telepathy. You see, it's a gift with him. Some have got it, some haven't. He's got it – by George he's got it. Go on heartface – cross his palm with silver.

KENNETH: Well, I'm afraid I haven't got any silver on me –

HUGH: Oh, don't worry. You can cross me hand with a Diners Club Card. They trust you up there. Now, how would you like me to prognosticate? Through the tea leaves, a spot of palmistry or would you like Sand here to have a vada in his crystals?

KEN W: I'll have a vada in me crystal. Right. Whip it out of its chamois, Jule. There. There's your actual crystal ball. Now let's see what it foretells – it's cloudy – 'Scuse me I'll just hurr on it. *(Heavy breath)* There, it's clearing – I see a man – it's you – you're in a room – a dark room – but you're not alone – there's two strange weird creatures – one of them is peering into a crystal … Oh sorry it's a reflection, it's us. How mortifying.

HUGH: Don't castigate yourself, Sand. Nantes coming through. Shall we try the Ouija?

KEN W: Yes. Get out your Ouija, Jule. Let's have a palare with the spirits. Come on all sit round and hold hands – you sit next to me, Mr Horne. Jule will be going off.

HUGH: Yes I do, you know. I go right off. Right up the astral plane.

KEN W: He does. Right up there. He's limp for days afterwards. It takes it right out of him. Right, nisht the chat now, he's going

A woman went to a seance in the hope of getting in touch with her late husband who, during his life, had been a waiter in a big restaurant. The lights were dimmed, the medium went into a trance and the table began to make knocking sounds.

'Fred,' she said, 'Fred – is that you? Speak to me.'
'I can't,' said a ghostly voice. 'It's not my table.'

into his trance. Are your vibrations quite favourable? Oh bona.

HUGH: *(Groan)* Yes I'm going off. I'm going one step beyond.

KEN W: You go, Jule. Don't worry about us. We'll be all right on our own. He's going, he's going … he's coming back.

HUGH: *(Groans)*

KEN W: What do you want, Jule?

HUGH: I forgot to leave a note for the milkman.

KEN W: He's going again. He's going. It's coming over him in waves …

HUGH: *(More groans)*

KEN W: … Look at him. He's levitating. He's in touch with what we do not know.

KENNETH: Neither do we particularly want to.

KEN W: He's gone beyond. He's being possessed now by his spirit guide. He's a great butch Red Indian you know – look – look – Geronimo's occupying him now. It's very uncomfortable to be occupied by a Red Indian. And it lowers the value of the property.

HUGH: *(More groans)*

KEN W: Hello – Geronimo – it's Sand here – have you a message for any of us? Speak, Geronimo.

HUGH: *(Haltingly)* Mr. Geronimo is out. Leave your name and number. He will call you when he comes in. This is a recorded message.

Orchestra: Play-off

KENNETH: The flesh was willing but the spirits were a bit weak. But I wonder if it is possible that there is a limbo where strange wraith-like creatures flit about in a twilight world of their own.

KEN W: Mind your own business. We don't ask you how you spend your evenings.

BARRY TOOK AND MARTY FELDMAN

A man hears a bumping sound, looks over his shoulder and sees a coffin bouncing down the street towards him. Frightened, he runs all the way home, opens his front door and locks it behind him. But the coffin smashes through the door. **So the man rushes upstairs and locks himself in the bathroom. But the coffin breaks down this door too and tumbles towards him.** Reaching out for something to fend it off, the man finds some cough mixture and as a last resort, throws the bottle at it. Only then does the coffin stop.

At the AGM of the Clairvoyants' Association they read out the minutes of next year's meeting.

STEPTOE AND SON –
SEANCE IN A WET RAG AND BONE YARD

Albert is very late home and Harold has been waiting up for him.

HAROLD: Where have you been?

ALBERT: I'm not telling you. It's nothing to do with you.

HAROLD: It's everything to do with me. Supposing something was to happen to you. Supposing you was taken ill, or supposing you was knocked down by a bus.

ALBERT: They don't knock me down, they just go through the puddles.

HAROLD: Supposing you was taken to hospital, how would they know who you belonged to?

ALBERT: I've got identification on me. I've got my name inside my socks.

HAROLD: Ugh, who's going to look inside your socks, they'd take them off with a pair of tongs and burn them. Now just tell me where you've been and we'll forget all about it.

ALBERT: Honestly, it's like bleeding Z Cars coming home here. I'm surprised you don't shine a light in my face,

HAROLD: Come on, own up, where have you been?

ALBERT: Oh all right, I suppose you'll break me down eventually, so I might as well tell you. I've been to a spiritualist meeting.

HAROLD: You've been where?

ALBERT: To a spiritualist meeting.

HAROLD: You haven't. Not really?

ALBERT: Yeah. I've been in contact with the dead.

HAROLD: I bet that scared them. What do you mean, you've been in contact with the dead?

ALBERT: I have. I spoke to Dan Leno tonight. And Henry the Eighth.

HAROLD: Dan Leno and Henry the Eighth. What were they doing, a double act? I say, I say, I say, Henry, who was the lady I saw you with last night? That was no lady, that was my fourth wife. Boom boom.

ALBERT: You don't believe me, do you?

HAROLD: Of course I don't believe you.

ALBERT: It's true. I went to a seance. In the Goldhawk Road.

HAROLD: Oh well, that explains it. Henry the Eighth was always up and down the Goldhawk Road. You couldn't keep him away. I think he had a bird down there. So let me get this straight. You're sitting there in a parlour down the Goldhawk Road. In the dark.

ALBERT: Yeah. Six of us. Round a table. Holding hands. And then suddenly … she goes into a trance.

HAROLD: Who does?

ALBERT: The medium. Madame Fontana. And she introduces her spirit guide.

HAROLD: A Red Indian.

ALBERT: How did you know?

HAROLD: They're always Red Indians

ALBERT: Yeah. This one was Geronimo. And he says, through her … I've got somebody here who wants to meet you all. And this voice says …

HAROLD: Good evening everybody. This is Henry the Eighth speaking and tonight is my guest night. And I'd like you to give a big hand to my first guest, your friend and my friend, Dan Leno.

ALBERT: If you're not going to take it seriously, I'm going to bed.

HAROLD: Well, Gordon Bennett, you don't believe in all that nonsense, do you? A voice comes on and says he's Henry the Eighth and you believe him. If he'd said he was Christopher Columbus, you would have believed him.

ALBERT: No, I wouldn't. Cos I met him last week …

RAY GALTON AND ALAN SIMPSON

Two fortune-tellers met on the seafront at Frinton one lovely summer's day. 'Beautiful weather,' said one.
'Yes,' said the other, 'reminds me of the summer of 2034.'

A medium at a seance gets a message for a widower who is sitting at the table. 'Arthur Barker, it's your late wife knocking.'
'Ah,' says the man, 'she hasn't changed a bit.'

A woman at a seance said, 'I want to speak to my departed husband, please.'
'Why?' asked the medium.
'Because he died before I finished telling him what I thought of him.'

The medium at the seance had made contact with the other side.
'It is the spirit of your dear departed wife,' she said to the little man on the other side of the table. The little man just sat there, saying nothing.
'Do you understand?' asked the medium. 'We are in touch with your late wife. Don't you wish to speak to her?'
'Don't worry,' said the little man. 'If it's her, she'll do the talking.'

Laughter makers

These brief biographies give a taste of the lives of 150 of the funniest people, whose jokes, cartoons, witticisms, puns and other assorted frivolities help to fill this book. They are a remarkably diverse crowd. While some have been full of jollity, others have struggled with mental demons, often exploiting their unhappiness to keep us smiling at life's absurdities. What these men and women all share though is the gift of making us laugh.

Adams, Douglas *(1952-2001)*
Creator of the radio and TV series and best-selling book *The Hitchhiker's Guide to the Galaxy*, also made into a feature film in 2005. Adams was notoriously prone to writer's block, producing distressingly little and once saying, 'I love deadlines – I love the whooshing noise they make as they go by'. When he died of a heart attack aged only 49 he left behind an incomplete novel and notebooks that were published posthumously in 2002 as *The Salmon of Doubt*.

Adams, Scott *(1957-)*
Man behind the Dilbert strip cartoon, poking fun at the confusions of office life. The cartoon is syndicated to more than 2000 papers in 65 countries, and over ten million Dilbert books have been sold. Adams also invented Dogbert so that Dilbert would have someone to talk to.

Aherne, Caroline *(1963-)*
Came to fame in the mid 1990s as the TV character Mrs Merton, a spiky Stockport pensioner who poked fun at celebrities while supposedly inverviewing them. In 1998 she helped to create the TV series *The Royle Family*, in which she also played the part of Denise. Aherne has since suffered from periodic bouts of depression that have caused, so far brief, 'retirements'.

Anon *(from the beginning-)*
The most prolific author of humorous verse and prose in English – less prolific as a cartoonist and illustrator. Began writing and talking in the Middle Ages, if not before, and still going strong at the beginning of the 21st century.

Allen, Woody *(1935-)*
Quirky Manhattan-based film-maker renowned for self-deprecating and mordant wit as well as a highly publicised private life. Born Allen Stewart Konigsberg in Brooklyn, he began writing gags at 15, worked as a stand-up comic and wrote his first film script, *What's New Pussycat?*, in 1965. He turned full-time to film acting and directing and won three Oscars. 'I don't want to achieve immortality through my work', he once wrote, 'I want to achieve it by not dying'. ▼

Atkinson, Rowan ▲ *(1955-)*
Rubber-faced actor and comedian who first appeared in Oxford University revues before finding TV fame in 1979 on the series *Not the Nine O'clock News* and then as the swaggering Edmund Blackadder in the historical *Blackadder* spoofs by Richard Curtis and Ben Elton (qqv). He found a worldwide audience with the bungling, disaster-prone Mr Bean.

Ayres, Pam *(1947-)*
Performance poet whose simple rhymes, rhythms, sentiments and humour have endeared her to a huge audience. Ayres shot to fame after appearing on the TV talent show *Opportunity Knocks* in 1975.

Bankhead, Tallulah *(1902-68)*
Notorious American femme fatale and quipster whose best-known stage role was in *The Little Foxes* (1939) and film role in Alfred Hitchcock's *Lifeboat* (1944). Chain-smoker, drinker, cokehead and serial seductress with a propensity for removing her clothes on the slimmest pretext, Bankhead liked to claim that she was 'pure as the driven slush'. She once told actress Joan Crawford, then wife of Douglas Fairbanks Jnr, 'I've had your husband. He's divine. You're next!'

Barker, Ronnie *(1929-2005)*
Comedian and writer best known for TV's *The Two Ronnies* (1971-87) with Ronnie Corbett (qv), and *Porridge*, a 1970s sitcom about prison life in which he played a world-weary lag. Barker officially retired from showbiz in the late 1980s to run a shop in the Cotswolds but returned to act as Winston Churchill's butler in the TV film *The Gathering Storm* (2002). He also published a number of books about saucy postcards.

Barr, Roseanne *(1952-)*
Blousy Salt Lake City waitress whose repartee so amused customers that she became a professional comedienne and was given her her own show, *Roseanne*, in 1987. It ran for eight seasons.

Barrington, Patrick *(1908-90)*
The 11th Viscount Barrington led a varied life as a member of the House of Lords, attaché at HM Embassy in Berlin, barrister, and a polished purveyor of nonsense verse. He was best known for his poems about hippopotami and platypi, often appearing in *Punch* magazine.

Barsotti, Charles *(1933-)*
New Yorker cartoonist with a deceptively simple style and a cast consisting (usually) of an endearing pooch and his master and the king whose kingdom consists of one guard and a telephone.

Bateman, H(enry) M(ayo) *(1887-1970)*
Australian cartoonist who specialised in drawings of people committing faux pas and captioned 'The Man who … '. A famous example is 'The Guardsman who dropped his rifle'. Bateman was the highest-paid humorist in the world in the 1920s and 30s but then escaped to the island of Gozo to paint serious pictures of English and Mediterranean country life.

Baxter, Glen *(1944-)*
Eclectic, whimsical cartoonist who first came to prominence in Holland in 1979 and is known to his many fans as 'The Colonel'. Baxter has produced several books of cartoons, including *The Wonder Book of Sex* and *Blizzards of Tweed*.

Beachcomber (J.B. Morton) *(1893-1975)*
Comic columnist on the *Daily Express* who invented such characters as Mr Justice Cocklecarrot and the seven red-bearded dwarves. Fellow humorist D.B. Wyndham-Lewis recalled Morton's arrival in Fleet Street – 'The door was burst open and a thick-set, furious, bucolic figure all over straw and clay, strode in and banged passionately on the floor with a thick gnarled stick uttering a roar soon known and feared in every pub in Fleet Street: "Flaming eggs! Will no one rid me of this stinking town!"' Morton's surreal humour was a major influence on Spike Milligan (qv), creator of The Goons.

Belloc, Hilaire *(1870-1953)*
Anglo-French poet, essayist and Roman Catholic propagandist best known for his children's nonsense verse, most notably *Cautionary Tales* (1907). Belloc was a close friend and collaborator of G.K. Chesterton (qv) – so close that they were referred to by George Bernard Shaw as 'Chesterbelloc'.

Benchley, Robert *(1889-1945)*
One of the first contributors to *The New Yorker* magazine and a leading member of the Algonquin Round Table, a gathering of New York writers and wits, known as 'The Vicious Circle'. Editor of the *Harvard Lampoon* before the First World War, Benchley later became Managing Editor of *Vanity Fair* but was fired for 'too much larking around'. He was seen as the nicest of the Vicious Circle (possibly the *only* 'nice' member), but his talents were as admired as anyone's. James Thurber (qv), no slouch himself, said that 'one of the greatest fears of the humorous writer is that he has spent three weeks writing something done faster and better by Benchley in 1919'.

Benny, Jack ▼ *(1894-1974)*
Originally a violinist, Benny (born Benjamin Kublesky) soon became a comedian. After several years on Broadway he appeared on radio in the *Ed Sullivan Show*

in the early 1930s with the announcement, 'This is Jack Benny. There will be a short pause for everyone to say, "Who cares?"' Benny's own radio show ran from 1932 to 1955. He then switched to TV in the 60s and continued to perform until his final months.

Bentley, Edmund Clerihew (1875-1956)
Journalist and novelist who wrote *Trent's Last Case* (1913) a prototype of the modern detective story. He also invented an idiosyncratic verse form known as a 'clerihew'. This consists of two rhyming couplets of irregular length and often contains the name of a famous person.

> It was a weakness of Voltaire's
> To forget to say his prayers,
> And one which to his shame
> He never overcame.

Bernard, Jeffrey (1932-97)
An all-time legend in his own lunchtime, Bernard was a vodka-quaffing *Spectator* columnist and London Soho 'character'. His weekly chronicle charting his rake's progress often failed to materialise, replaced by the words 'Jeffrey Bernard is unwell'. He was later immortalised by Peter O'Toole in Keith Waterhouse's play *Jeffrey Bernard is Unwell*.

Best, Steve (1954-)
Liverpool-based cartoonist who taught art to prisoners before drawing full-time from 1990. Best contributes to *Private Eye* but since 1992 has become particularly successful as a producer of greetings cards. His subject matter ranges from sport, art and film to history and wildlife, with a particular affection for frogs. Best's lush watercolours usually pack a surprising killer punchline.

Betjeman, John ▲ (1906-84)
Sardonic Poet Laureate (from 1972) with a sharp eye for dreary architecture and town planning ('Come kindly bombs and fall on Slough'); social foibles ('Phone for the fish-knives, Norman'); and the Cornish countryside as well as churches of all descriptions, and suburbia. He compiled, with the artist John Piper, the *Shell Guides* to the counties of England in the 1930s and 50s.

Bierce, Ambrose (1842-c.1914)
Journalist, aphorist and story-teller who served with distinction in the American Civil War. He started on a San Francisco paper, then worked in London in the 1870s before returning to California with the nickname 'Bitter Bierce'. He became editor of the *Wasp* in 1881 and six years later a columnist on William Randolph Hearst's *Sunday Examiner*. In 1897 he moved to Washington as a Hearst correspondent and later published a collection of venomous definitions entitled

The Cynic's Word Book, later re-christened *The Devil's Dictionary*. After becoming disenchanted with America he moved to Mexico in 1913 and vanished mysteriously, possibly dying in battle.

Bond, Simon (1947-)
Creator of a 'genre defining' series of cartoon anthologies beginning with *101 Uses for a Dead Cat* and continuing with a series of examinations of what to do with feline corpses.

Brockbank, Russell (1913-79)
Canadian-born cartoonist who specialised in aviation, motoring and motor-racing and was Art Editor of *Punch* from 1949 to 1960. His first book, *Round the Bend*, published in 1948, was followed by a number of similar collections with punning titles such as *Bees Under My Bonnet*.

Brookes, Peter (1943-)
Political cartoonist for *The Times*, also known for weekly 'Nature Notes' in which he has depicted Deputy Prime Minister John Prescott as the Unhappypotamus and former US President Bill Clinton as a hornbill ('often flies undone'), and invented a bird called the Rail ('Travels nowhere fast').

Brooke-Taylor, Tim (1940-)
Former president of the Cambridge Footlights in the 1960s who formed the comedy trio, The Goodies, with Graeme Garden and Bill Oddie. A grandfather was a vicar who played football for England and his mother played lacrosse for England, although Brooke-Taylor's great love is cricket, about which he often writes. He has had long-running success in the daft radio show *I'm Sorry I'll Read That Again*.

Brown, Craig *(1957-)*

Old Etonian *Private Eye* parodist and columnist who succeeded Auberon Waugh as the contributor of the 'Way of the World' column in *The Daily Telegraph* after the latter's death in 2001. His books include the memoirs of arch-blimp fogey, *The Agreeable World of Wallace Arnold*.

Burns, George ▼ *(1896-1996)*

Cigar-chomping American comedian (born Nathan Birnbaum) who quipped memorably, 'For forty years my act consisted of one joke. Then she died.' This was a reference to his wife and radio and TV other half, Gracie Allen, with whom he starred in the hugely popular *The George Burns and Gracie Allen Show*, first aired in the US in 1950 and 1955 in Britain. Burns achieved a remarkable age and performed indomitably and crustily almost to the end. Typically crabby Burnsisms include 'There are many ways to die in bed, but the best way is not alone', and 'Happiness is having a large, loving, caring close-knit family – in another city'.

Calman, Mel *(1931-94)*

Best known as *The Times* pocket cartoonist and creator of The Cartoon Gallery in London. He also worked for the *Daily Express*, *The Sunday Telegraph*, *The Observer* and *The Sunday Times* as well as being resident cartoonist on the BBC's *Tonight* programme. Calman's favourite character was a mild put-upon man whom he claimed was 'not autobiographical – at least not totally'. His many anthologies included such typically mordant titles as *It's Only You That's Incompatible!* and *How About a Little Quarrel Before Bed?*

Chapman, Graham *(1941-89)*

Of the original Monty Python team, Chapman was widely reckoned to be the most purely Pythonesque. He took the lead in Python films, playing King Arthur in *Monty Python and the Holy Grail* and Brian in *Life of Brian*. In the Python TV series he was perhaps best known for his role as 'The Colonel', the stuffy staff officer who appears out of nowhere brandishing his pipe and ordering that a sketch must cease because it is too silly. A serious pipe smoker in real life as well as on-screen, Chapman succumbed to cancer at an early age. He admitted his homosexuality late in life and was thereafter an enthusiastic spokesman for gay causes.

Chappell, Eric *(1933-)*

A prolific author of sit-coms, most notably the ever-popular *Rising Damp* starring Leonard Rossiter as the oily landlord Rigsby. Chappell has also written a number of widely performed 'straight' plays.

Chesterton, G(ilbert) K(eith) *(1874-1936)*

The other half, with Hilaire Belloc (qv), of the renowned 'Chesterbelloc' association, Chesterton was best known for his *Father Brown* detective stories featuring a deceptively benign and innocent-looking Roman Catholic priest. He also wrote a number of light verses and some unusual adventure stories of which the oddest was probably *The Napoleon of Notting Hill* (1904), which featured bomb-throwing anarchists in cloaks.

Cleese, John *(1939-)*

Cambridge law graduate and first among equals of the Monty Python team, where he achieved immortality as the strutting exponent of 'silly walks'. Cleese was also hugely popular as the curmudgeonly hen-pecked hotelier Basil Fawlty in *Fawlty Towers* (1975-9), where he headed a brilliant cast including Prunella Scales as his wife Sybil, his own first wife Connie Booth as a skittish waitress and Andrew Sachs as Manuel the cack-handed waiter from Barcelona. He has also enjoyed a number of one-off successes in movies, notably *A Fish Called Wanda* (1988). In a more unexpected and serious vein Cleese founded Video Arts Ltd to produce industrial training films, often starring himself.

Clement, Dick *(1937-)*

With partner **Ian la Frenais** *(1937-)*, author of a series of shrewd, realistic and funny TV series, including the *The Likely Lads* (1964-6), starring Rodney Bewes and James Bolam, and *Porridge* (1974-7), starring Ronnie Barker (qv) as the wily career-criminal Fletcher. The pair have since moved into the writing of film and TV screenplays, such as *The Commitments* (1991) and *The Rotters' Club* (2005).

Connolly, Billy ▼ (1942-)

Anarchic Glaswegian stand-up comic known as 'the big Yin', a specialist in expletive-driven personal invective and ingenious put-downs. Connolly, who started his working life as a Clydeside shipyard welder, also gave a convincing film performance in 1997 as Queen Victoria's favourite ghillie, John Brown. He remains, though, at his best standing up, solo, in front of a live audience.

Coogan, Steve (1965-)

Studied drama at Manchester Polytechnic and began his career doing voice-overs for celebrity characters in TV's *Spitting Image* (1984). Coogan then invented his best-known fictional character, the ghastly radio and TV personality from Norfolk, Alan Partridge. He has also appeared in a number of films, including *24 Hour Party People* (2002) and *Around the World in 80 Days* (2004).

Cook, Peter (1937-95)

The humorist's humorist, a founding father in the early 1960s of *Private Eye* magazine but best known to the public as one of the original *Beyond the Fringe* quartet (with Alan Bennett, Dudley Moore, and Jonathan Miller – qv) and for his TV dialogues with Moore, as Dud and Pete, in which they appeared as two tramps and he frequently made his small partner 'corpse' with his brilliant ad-libs. A self-destructive streak, which included an over-dependence on alcohol, precipitated Cook's premature demise and in the eyes of his more puritan peers prevented the full flowering of his talents. Many of his best performances probably took place in private.

Cooper, Tommy ▼ (1922-84)

Lugubrious stand-up comic and magician who specialised in tricks going wrong. Cooper remains one of Britain's best-loved funny men, immediately identifiable because of his trademark red fez and malleable plasticine face, and renowned for the catchphrase 'Just like that!'. He once said 'When I go I want to be on stage. I want the audience laughing and everyone happy.' One night, during a live performance of ITV's *Live from Her Majesty's* he collapsed on stage. The audience thought this was part of the act but it was a massive heart attack and he died shortly afterwards.

Cope, Wendy (1945-)

Light versifier of skill and originality whose best-known collection is probably *Making Cocoa for Kingsley Amis* (1986). Cope has also been a TV critic for *The Spectator*, edited anthologies and written children's books.

Corbett, Ronnie (1930-)

The (very much) smaller half of the Two Ronnies with Ronnie Barker (qv), which lasted for 12 popular series from the early 1970s. Before that, Corbett contributed a string of character parts to the mid-60s TV satire show *The Frost Report*. He is also the author of *Small Man's Guide* and *Armchair Golf*.

Coren, Alan (1938-)

Clever (first-class Oxford English degree, postgraduate work at Yale and Berkeley) former *Punch* editor, *Times* columnist, day-time TV veteran and *Call My Bluff* expert with the uncanny and unnerving ability to construct elaborate humorous articles out of virtually nothing – the verbal equivalent of building a life-size model of the *QE2* entirely from matchsticks. Coren's anthologies include *Golfing for Cats* and *Something for the Weekend*.

Cosby, Bill *(1937-)*

Comic who achieved ground-breaking stardom as the first man to portray a middle-class Afro-American paterfamilias on a mainline sitcom – *The Cosby Show* (1984-92). Cosby is best-known as a storyteller rather than gagster – a typical example of his work is a conversation piece between God and a skeptical Noah. In later life he suffered the tragedy of his son's murder and saw his popularity decline partly because of – hotly denied – allegations of sexual harassment and partly because of his controversial views on black politics. 'The real pleasure', he has said, 'is trying to please everybody.'

Coward, Noël *(1899-1973)*

Suave and debonair wit, playwright and song-writer with a much imitated (but inimitable) staccato drawl that suited his own words to perfection. Coward's smart, sophisticated plays included *Private Lives* (1930) and *Blithe Spirit* (1941), often conceived as vehicles for his great friend and actress Gertrude Lawrence. In wartime, his screenplays *This Happy Breed* (1944) and *Brief Encounter* (1945) brought wider fame, but thereafter Coward's star waned until he found a new lease of life as a cabaret artist in the 1960s, performing songs such as 'Mad Dogs and Englishmen' and 'The Stately Homes of England'.

Often known as 'The Master' he was, in real life, a past-master of the laconic one-liner as well as the immaculately crafted works that made his fortune and reputation.

Crompton, Richmal *(1890-1969)*

Best known as the creator of the ultimate scruffy but loveable schoolboy William Brown, Crompton (original surname Lamburn) was born in Bury, Lancashire, and was a teacher all her life, though always in girls' schools. She wrote more than 80 books, many of them romantic novels of which she was much prouder than her *Just William* stories about the 11-year old urchin, believed to have been modelled on her younger brother, Jack. William Brown would have thought her romantic novels 'mushy' – they are scarcely remembered, unlike the enduringly popular William books.

Crystal, Billy *(1947-)*

American comedian, actor, producer, director and writer who became a star of the *Saturday Night Live* TV show in 1984. Crystal has hosted many Academy Award Ceremonies and made a number of movies, most memorably playing the role of Harry in *When Harry Met Sally* (1989).

Curtis, Richard *(1956-)*

Writer on the TV series *Not the Nine O'clock News* (1979-82) and *Blackadder* (1983-9) who later turned to writing feature films, beginning with *Four Weddings and a Funeral* (1994), and followed by *Notting Hill* (1999) and *Love Actually* (2003), among others. Their quintessentially upper-middle class British humour is befitting of an old boy of Harrow School and Christ Church, Oxford.

Dangerfield, Rodney *(1921-2004)*

American comic (born Jacob Cohen) with what *Rolling Stone* once described as a 'distinctive wackdoodle voice'. His catchphrase was 'I don't get no respect', 'no respect' being a concept which featured in both his autobiographies, one of which contained the self-revelatory words, 'It ain't easy being me'. He equally characteristically and revealingly once said that he would like to have spoken to his wife during their marriage but didn't want to interrupt.

Daninos, Pierre *(1913-2005)*

French writer who created an archetypal English caricature with his bowler-hatted, rolled umbrella-carrying Major W. Marmaduke Thompson, the epitome of every Frenchman's vision of what 'les rosbifs' are really like. The Major's 'carnets', or diaries, first published in the mid 1950s, sold more than a million copies in France and fuelled long-held prejudice with such lines as 'The cooking of England is like the country itself – surrounded by water.' The diaries first appeared in *Le Figaro*, where Daninos worked as a journalist.

Dawson, Les ▼ *(1931-93)*

Burly, gruff northern comic with rubber lips, a super-mobile jaw made more so after being broken in a boxing match, and a permanently grouchy manner. *The Les*

Dawson Show (1978-89) was once categorised as being distinctive for his 'elaborately styled jokes, cross dressing and intentionally bad piano-playing'. One of his several books was called *Hitler Was My Mother-in-law*.

Dickens, Frank *(1931-)*
Created the Bristow comic strip for *The Sunday Times* in 1960 and has continued to draw this everyday story of mundane city office life at the Chester-Perry organisation, where Bristow is the classic little white-collar man with moustache and bowler hat.

Diller, Phyllis *(1917-)*
Widely regarded as the first modern female stand-up comic, but until age 37 Diller was a discontented Ohio housewife, newspaper columnist and publicist. She then made her debut at San Francisco's Purple Onion Club and wowed audiences with her 'ghastly laugh and self deprecating manner'. Diller won further plaudits playing a nightclub star in the Natalie Wood–Warren Beatty movie *Splendor in the Grass* (1961). Despite having a pacemaker fitted in 1999, she is still working. Her memoirs are entitled *Like a Lampshade in a Whorehouse*.

Dodd, Ken *(1927-)*
Favourite comedian of former Prime Minister Harold Wilson, who was MP for Dodd's home constituency of Huyton in Liverpool, although on stage and screen Dodd always said he came from Knotty Ash. This was also home to his accomplices, the Diddymen, of whom the originals were the Hon Nigel Ponsonby-Smallpiece, who had a caviar allotment and a pond of 18-carat goldfish, and Dicky Mint, a jam-butty mine worker. Dodd began work on Blackpool pier as a support for Morecambe and Wise (qv). The toothy floppy-fringed Dodd also has a mellifluous singing voice, which has gained him several more or less serious top ten hits, including 'Tears', which spent five weeks at number one in 1965. ▼

Elton, Ben *(1959-)*
New-wave stand-up comic in the early 1980s, who turned script-writer and best-selling novelist. The scion of a serious, professor-filled family, Elton studied drama at Manchester University before joining the likes of Rik Mayall and Adrian Edmondson at London's Comedy Store club and going on to write the student-life TV sitcom *The Young Ones* (1982-4) and three series of *Blackadder*. He turned to novel-writing in the 1990s and then, surprising many, to musical librettos, such as *We Will Rock You*, based on the songs of the rock group Queen.

Enfield, Harry *(1961-)*
Began comic career with chums at York University and moved apparently seamlessly to the professional scene. Enfield worked as a stand-up, provided voices for the *Spitting Image* TV satire show, and then got his big break in 1986 appearing as the kebab-shop owner Stavros on *Saturday Live*. His co-writers, and close neighbours on a Hackney council estate, were Paul Whitehouse (qv) and Charlie Higson, who also contributed to his popular sketch shows of the 1990s, such as *Harry Enfield's Television Programme*.

Fantoni, Barry *(1940-)*
London-born jazz musician, cartoonist and academic, intimately associated with *Private Eye* since the 1960s. He took Italian citizenship on becoming Professor of Media Studies at the University of Salerno in 1997.

Feldman, Marty *(1933-82)* ▶
Bug-eyed comic of anarchic tendencies who began as a jazz trumpeter but after meeting kindred spirit, Barry Took (qv), quickly turned to writing comedy with scripts for radio's *Educating Archie*, *The Army Game*, *At Last the 1948 Show*, *Round the Horne* and *The Frost Report*. His strange appearance, the result of a chronic thyroid problem, helped his career as a performer, first as a third of 'Morris Marty and Mitch' and the 'strange little man' in *At Last the 1948 Show* but later in movies, perhaps most memorably as Igor the hunchback in Mel Brooks' classic *Young Frankenstein* (1974). He died aged only 49 after suffering a heart attack while filming a pirate movie called *Yellowhead* in Mexico City.

ffolkes, Michael *(1925-88)*
Feline caricaturist and cartoonist with a sharp pen who made his name (originally Brian Davis) with minute illustrations for Michael Wharton's surreal 'Way of the World' column in *The Daily*

Freshly Dead

6 Months Dead

Telegraph. Ffolkes also contributed larger full-colour pictures for *Playboy* in which he specialised in voluptuous women – a consuming passion in real life together with champagne, large cigars and an open-top Bentley. He occasionally undertook unlikely commissions such as portraits of the Fellows of Balliol College, Oxford.

Fields, W.C. *(1880-1946)* Cantankerous, alcohol-fuelled actor (christened William Claude Dukenfield) who began public life as 'W.C. Fields, the Tramp Juggler' and played a command performance before Edward VII. In 1915 he joined the *Ziegfield Follies* where he stayed for six years, and in 1924 appeared on Broadway as the fraudulent Eustace McGargle in *Poppy*, subsequently filmed by D.W. Griffith. In 1931 Fields moved permanently to Hollywood where he won fame in a series of films, most notably *David Copperfield* (1935) in which he played Mr Micawber. Each of his last four films – *You Can't Cheat an Honest Man*, *My*

Little Chickadee, *The Bank Dick* and *Never Give a Sucker an Even Break* – became comedy classics. He died on Christmas Day, which he affected to loathe along with everything to do with animals and small children. His self-composed epitaph, aimed at the city of his birth, was 'On the whole, I'd rather be in Philadelphia'.

Flanders, Michael *(1922–75)* and **Swann, Donald** *(1923-94)* Flanders was a truly gilded figure at Westminster School, where he composed a revue called *Go To It* with his friend and future collaborator Donald Swann. This promise continued at Oxford, where Flanders, President of the University Dramatic Society, seemed set to be the next Lawrence Olivier or Robert Donat. After joining the Royal Naval Reserve, however, he contracted polio and was confined to a wheelchair for the rest of his life. The handicap effectively ruined his acting career although his voice remained good enough for him to be much in demand as a narrator and broadcaster, and his writing abilities were

unimpaired. Flanders' biggest success was with the 1950s theatre revue *At the Drop of a Hat*, of which the writer Michael Meyer said, 'Flanders' genial yet caustic lyrics and Swann's witty and tuneful music, and the contrast between Flanders' robust exuberance and the prim appearance of Swann, exerted a seemingly universal appeal.'

Fougasse *(1887-1965)* Cyril Kenneth Bird sold his first cartoon to *Punch* in 1916 using the pseudonym 'Fougasse', which variously means a Provençal flat-bread or a dodgy French mine that would sometimes explode and at other times not. Bird became Art Editor of *Punch* in 1937 and Editor from 1949 until retirement in 1953. In wartime the War Ministry sent him to France to research propaganda drawings – his resulting contributions, including the posters 'Careless talk costs lives' and 'Walls have ears', are some of the most memorable Second World War images.

French, Dawn (1957-)

Cuddly comedienne best known for her role in TV's *Vicar of Dibley* (1994-2000) written by Richard Curtis (qv). French, born in Anglesey and unhappily educated at a Plymouth boarding school, met her friend and collaborator Jennifer Saunders (qv) at The Central School of Speech and Drama in London and went on to make the successful TV series *French and Saunders*, first aired in 1987. She is married to fellow comedian Lenny Henry. ▼

Fry, Stephen (1957-)

Jovial polymath, ubiquitous writer and actor, including the part of a portly TV Jeeves alongside the stick-insect Bertie Wooster of Hugh Laurie (qv), as well as producing four *A Bit of Fry and Laurie* TV series and appearing in innumerable advertising campaigns. His colourful early life included three months in prison for stealing credit cards when aged 17, and making a million for re-writing the musical *Me and My Girl* for the West End in 1984. It was in theatreland ten years later that he suffered a breakdown during a production of the play *Cell Mates*, promptly disappearing to the Continent. Fry has since made a move into film directing with *Bright Young Things* (2003).

Galton, Ray (1930-)

Celebrated scriptwriter who has collaborated for more than 50 years with **Alan Simpson** *(1929-)*. The two met while being treated for tuberculosis in the same sanatorium, and in 1954 wrote the first of ten years' worth of *Hancock's Half Hour*, starring Tony Hancock (qv). They later went on to make a fabulous success out of *Steptoe and Son* (1962-74) with Harry H. Corbett and Wilfred Bramble. 'Alan did the typing,' Galton has said, 'and I did the sitting down watching him think, the wandering round the room, the lying on the floor.'

Gervais, Ricky (1961-)

Studied philosophy at London University and then returned with salaried job as Student Union entertainment manager. Gervais' career took off in the 1990s after he hired Stephen Merchant and the two co-authored *The Office*, a hugely successful series on Slough office life presented as if it were a real-life fly-on-the-wall saga. Gervais played David Brent, a desperately self-deluding manager who apparently doesn't realise what a disaster he is. The eagerly awaited follow-up to *The Office* – *Extras* – began its first series in 2005.

Gilbert, W(illiam) S(chwenk) (1836-1911) ▶

Word half of the Gilbert and Sullivan team who wrote the Savoy operas, but also a prolific comic versifier in his own right. Gilbert began life as an unsuccessful barrister and made ends meet by writing humorous verse for *Fun* magazine under the boyhood nickname 'Bab'. Gilbert's first collaboration with Arthur Sullivan was *Trial by Jury* (1871), which, thanks partly to the dynamic management of the D'Oyly Carte Company, proved hugely popular. A succession of witty and tuneful light operas followed, from *HMS Pinafore* in 1878 to *The Gondoliers* in 1889. The partnership ended in acrimony and Gilbert never found another composer to work so brilliantly with his librettos.

Giles, Carl (1916-95)

Cartoonist mainstay of the *Daily Express* during its glory days under the proprietorship of Lord Beaverbrook. After a stint as an animator for the film producer Alexander Korda he was the main cartoonist for the *Express* for more than half a century. John Gordon, an illustrious editor of the *Sunday*

Express, wrote of Giles, 'Far above the trick of cartooning here is a man who loves drawing and lavishes love as well as labour on it.' His cartoons accurately reflected ordinary British life, nearly always through a vivid depiction of the large Giles family centred upon the grumpy Grandma with her keynote umbrella and shapeless dress. Larry, the diminutive mophead with the camera, is said to be based on Giles himself.

Graham, Harry (Col. D. Streamer) *(1874-1936)*
A career army officer with the Coldstream Guards – hence his military pseudonym – Graham wrote a popular account of travelling across Canada with the Governor-General, Lord Minto, whom he served as ADC. In humorous terms he was best known for his *Ruthless Rhymes for Heartless Homes* which more than lived up to their title.

Green, Michael *(1927-)*
Comic writer of coarse genius and man of the theatre, especially amateur, Green is best known for the books *The Art of Coarse Rugby* and *The Art of Coarse Acting*. He began professional life as a general reporter on a local paper in Northampton, about which he has written entertainingly in at least one autobiography, and was for many years an inspiration of the (amateur) Players Theatre in Ealing.

Grenfell, Joyce *(1910-79)*
Actress and comedienne of aristocratic Anglo-American ancestry who composed and performed memorable skits and sketches, notably as a harassed nursery teacher with at least one difficult pupil – 'George, don't do that'. She toured extensively during the Second World War entertaining the troops and enjoyed a long professional association with Stephen Potter, a radio producer and author of *One-Upmanship*, with whom she produced the radio *How To ...* series from the late 1940s. Grenfell was also a memorable gym mistress in the St Trinian's films of the 1950s.

Grossmith, George *(1847-1912)* and **Weedon** *(1853-1919)*
The brothers were together responsible for a single classic of English humour, *The Diary of a Nobody*, which first appeared as instalments in *Punch* in 1892, introducing the world to the character of Mr Pooter, who became a symbol of surburban middle class pretensions. George also began a career as a singer in 1870 and took the chief parts in many Gilbert and Sullivan operas.

Hamilton, Andy *(1954-)*
Regular performer on radio shows such as *News Quiz* and *I'm Sorry I Haven't a Clue*. Hamilton started as a writer in the 1970s on TV shows such as *Not the Nine O'clock News* and *Shelley*, and in 1990 created, with Guy Jenkin, the groundbreaking topical news sitcom *Drop the Dead Donkey*.

Hancock, Tony *(1924-68)*
Depressive, doomed, achingly funny radio and TV performer whose *Hancock's Half Hour* managed the improbable feat of turning the donating of blood and being a ham radio operator into something utterly side-splitting. Later forays into mainstream movies such as *The Punch and Judy Man* were less successful. He committed suicide in Australia.

Heath, Michael *(1935-)* Began as an animator with the Rank Organisation in 1955 before turning to drawing cartoons, contributing regularly to *Punch* for 30 years from 1958. Heath has drawn for *The Sunday Times* since 1967, been Cartoons Editor of *The Spectator* since 1989, and creates the 'Great Bores of Today' series for *Private Eye*.

Hegley, John *(1953-)*
Innovative stand-up performer and comic poet with a particular interest in glasses, dogs and Luton. His six bestselling volumes of poetry include *My Dog is a Carrot* and *The Sound of Paint Drying*.

Hill, Harry *(1964-)*
Master of the absurd, the bespectacled former doctor careers at a cracking pace through riotous streams of consciousness. Live shows create a flurry of intertwining surreal tales – complete with badgers. He followed radio shows such as *Harry Hill's Fruit Corner* with three TV series and *Harry Hill's TV Burp*, which takes a skewed look at each week's TV offerings.

Hoffnung, Gerard *(1925-59)*

Berlin-born Renaissance man who fled to England aged 14 and crammed artistic, musical and broadcasting careers into a tragically short life. Hoffnung was also a wizard of timing as a comic after-dinner or Oxford Union turn.

Honeysett, Martin *(1943-)*

Cartoonist who, after a succession of jobs, including lumberjack and bus driver, turned full-time freelance professional in 1972 with prickly often porcine characters who, he says, 'tend to sag in all the wrong places'. He illustrated *The Queen and I* by Sue Townsend (qv).

Hope, Bob ▼ *(1903-2003)*

Born in Eltham, southeast London, Hope (born Leslie Townes Hope) moved to America with his family when he was four. After a childhood in Cleveland, Ohio, he became as American as apple pie and a national icon. His Broadway debut was in 1927 with *Sidewalks of New York* and the following year he took on the stage name of Bob Hope as well as developing the comedy

monologue routine that led to star billing. His first major Broadway hit was *Ballyhoo* in 1932 by which time he had honed his comic timing and encyclopaedic memory for gags and one-liners. In one of his early movies, *The Big Broadcast of 1938*, he sang 'Thanks for the Memory', which thereafter became his signature song. Then in 1940 Hope made *Road to Singapore*, the first of six successful *Road* films with Bing Crosby, and during the Second World War formed a troupe of entertainers, who toured relentlessly, entertaining allied troops wherever they were, including combat zones. Hope continued to do this subsequently in Korea and Vietnam and became a sort of male forces' sweetheart. He received five 'special' Oscars, and in 1998 was given an honorary knighthood from the country of his birth.

Husband, Tony *(1950-)*

Busy cartoonist and illustrator of greetings cards, whose previous jobs included window-dressing and jewellery repair. His work has appeared in many publications, including *Punch*, *The Times* and *Reader's Digest*, and he has contributed 'The Yobs' strip cartoon to *Private Eye* since 1985.

Jerome, Jerome K(lapka) *(1859-1927)*

Clerk, schoolmaster, actor and journalist who became editor of *The Idler* in 1892 and started a two-penny weekly, *Today*. His account of a trip up the Thames from Kingston to Oxford, *Three Men in a Boat* (1889), is a classic of late Victorian whimsy. He wrote several other books, including, in a similar but less enduring vein, *The Idle Thoughts of an Idle Fellow* and *Three Men on the Bummel*, describing a tour of Germany.

Jones, Terry *(1942-)*

The Python best known for playing the piano naked and dressing up as women, Jones, born Terence Graham Parry in Colwyn Bay, met fellow *Monty Python* founder Michael Palin (qv) at Oxford, where they began a writing partnership. Jones' post-Python career has included children's books such as *Eric the Viking* and *The Curse of the Vampire's Socks*, and forays into his favourite subject of medieval history.

Kington, Miles *(1941-)*

Witty raconteur, after-dinner speaker, writer and double bass player with the Instant Sunshine group, whose first job was jazz critic for *The Times*. Kingston worked at *Punch* from 1967, wrote the 'Moreover' column for *The Times* and has been a daily columnist for *The Independent* since 1986. He is perhaps best known for the invention of Franglais, the entertaining pidgin French that he has turned into four books.

Larry (Terry Parkes) *(1927-2003)*

Cartoonist who acquired his 'Larry' alias as a school teacher in Peterborough when pupils saw *The Jolson Story* starring Larry Parkes. He created the 'Man in Apron' series for *Punch*, followed by 'Man at Office', 'Man at Work', 'Man and Wife' and 'Man's Best Friend', and was also the longstanding illustrator of *Private Eye*'s Colemanballs feature.

Laurie, Hugh *(1959-)*

Schooled at Eton and began his career at Cambridge University, where he was not only President of Footlights but also a rowing blue. Laurie enjoyed a longstanding collaboration with Stephen Fry (qv) on TV in *A Bit of Fry and Laurie* as well as *Jeeves and Wooster* and *Blackadder*. He has found new fame on both sides of the Atlantic as a curmudgeonly but brilliant doctor in the American TV series *House*.

Lear, Edward *(1812-88)*
Artist and writer who was sent to the Mediterranean by the Earl of Derby and exhibited the resulting pictures at the Royal Academy between 1850 and 1873, as well as publishing several illustrated travel books such as *Sketches of Rome*. Lear was a great lover of Italy, and he spent his later years there in St Remo. He is best remembered for his 'nonsense' verse, originally written for the grandchildren of his patron, Derby, and first collected in book form in 1845 as *A Book of Nonsense*. Several further volumes ensued, including perenially popular poems such as 'The Owl and the Pussycat' and 'The Jumblies'.

Lebowitz, Fran *(1951-)*
Ace American wisecracker who has been hailed as a modern Dorothy Parker (qv) and claims that 'my favourite animal is steak'. Her best-known book is *Metropolitan Life* and she has appeared regularly as Judge Janice Goldberg in TV's *Law and Order*.

McGill, Donald *(1875-1962)*
Master of the saucy seaside postcard, who sold more than a million cards in a single Blackpool shop in 1939. Three years later, McGill was the subject of an essay by George Orwell, and in 1954 was successfully prosecuted for obscenity at Lincoln Magistrates Court. One of McGill's favourite characters was the silly vicar. For example – Silly vicar: 'And what's the baby's Christian name?' Woman pushing pram: 'I haven't had time to think of

one. I've spent six months trying to think of a surname.'

McLachlan, Edward *(1940-)*
Cartoonist and regular contributor for more than 40 years to many papers and magazines, including *Punch*, *Private Eye* and *The Sunday Telegraph*. He also delves into the world of children's illustration and advertising.

Marquis, Don *(1878-1937)*
Writer who tried verse as a teenager and then moved to various papers in Washington DC and Atlanta before joining *Uncle Remus' Magazine* and, in 1909, the *New York Evening Sun*, where he contributed a daily column called 'The Sun Dial' from 1913 to 1922. This, featuring such inventions as Archy the cockroach and Mehitabel, the alley cat, established Marquis' reputation and were followed by three 'Archy and Mehitabel' books in the late 1920s and early 30s. He also wrote numerous books, poems and plays, of which the best-known was the Broadway hit *The Old Soak*. Never healthy, Marquis died relatively young, leaving an unfinished autobiography called *Sons of the Puritans*, published posthumously in 1939.

Martin, Dean *(1917-95)*
Singer, actor and gag-teller who boxed as a teenager as Kid Crochet (he was born Dino Paul Crocetti). Martin formed a successful partnership with the comedian Jerry Lewis before graduating to movies and becoming a key member of the Frank Sinatra-led Rat Pack. He was a smooth schmoozer and crooner who sent himself

up in 1960s' spoof spy movies as Matt Helm – a kind of sozzled James Bond.

Marx, Groucho *(1890-1977)*
Groucho began his stage career in vaudeville as part of the Six Musical Mascots, including his three brothers Chico, Harpo, and Zeppo, an aunt and his mother, Minnie, who was a yodelling harpist. Later the four brothers became the Four Nightingales and finally the
▼

Marx Brothers. In the early 1930s they made several movies, including *Animal Crackers* and *Duck Soup* before Zeppo retired from film in 1935. The remaining three continued with more cinema successes such as *A Night at the Opera*, *The Big Store* and *Love Happy* before they split up in 1948 to follow separate career paths. Groucho with his trademark Balkan-dictator moustache, cigar, tail-coat, outrageous eyebrows and lubriciously suggestive leer is remembered best as a specialist in one-line wisecracks, such as 'I never forget a face, but in your case I'll make an exception' and 'You're only as young as the woman you feel'.

Mason, Jackie *(1931-)*
Outspoken American stand-up comic and ordained rabbi who first came to prominence on TV in the *Ed Sullivan Show* in the early 1960s. Mason famously called New York Mayor David Dinkins 'a fancy schvartze with a moustache'.

Matt (Matthew Pritchett) *(1964-)*
Resident pocket cartoonist on *The Daily Telegraph* since 1988. 'Matt' is the grandson of master short story writer V.S. Pritchett and son of *Daily Telegraph* columnist, Oliver.

Mencken, H(enry) L(ouis) *(1880-1956)*
A son of Baltimore through and through, Mencken began his career as a police reporter on the *Baltimore Morning Herald* in 1899. After a spell as city editor he switched to the *Baltimore Sun* in 1906 and was associated with this paper for the rest of his life. In 1908 he began reviewing for a witty magazine, *The Smart Set*, assuming the joint-editorship in 1914. Ten years later he left to found the *American*

Mercury. In these various capacities Mencken dominated American criticism, vigorously attacking every sacred cow into which he could sink his teeth. Many reviews and essays were collected in a six-volume set of *Prejudices*. 'Journalism,' he maintained 'is the art of afflicting the comfortable and comforting the afflicted.'

Merton, Paul *(1957-)*
Cut his comic teeth at London's Comedy Store club in the 1980s before his big break on the topical game-show *Have I Got News for You* in 1990. Merton, born Paul Martin, is one of the great ad-libbers, a skill he uses to great affect on radio, particularly in the fast-talking show *Just a Minute*.

Miller, Jonathan *(1934-)*
Angular stork-like brainbox who first came to prominence as a member of the *Beyond the Fringe* team, with Alan Bennett, Dudley Moore (qv) and Peter Cook (qv). Miller, the most cerebral of the four, carved out an independent reputation as a theatre and opera producer, TV presenter and pundit, polymath, qualified doctor and authority on almost everything.

Milligan, Spike *(1918-2002)*
Comic improviser of genius and original Goon in the seminal 1950s radio series, *The Goon Show*, Milligan suffered from a bipolar disorder that precipitated many nervous breakdowns. He wrote and starred in stage productions of *Oblomov* and *Son of Oblomov*, composed poetry and wrote numerous books, including *Puckoon* and *Adolf Hitler, My Part in his Downfall* – one of a series based on his service in the Second World War. When his friend and fellow-Goon Harry Secombe died Milligan said, 'I'm glad he died before me because I didn't want him

to sing at my funeral.' At Milligan's funeral a Secombe recording was played.

Monkhouse, Bob
(1928-2003) ▼

Comic and TV quiz-master whose photographic memory made him a formidable gag-teller. After school at Dulwich College, the young Monkhouse spurned a career in the family custard business for stand-up and gag writing for the likes of Bob Hope (qv), Frank Sinatra and Dean Martin (qv). His later fame in the 1970s and 80s came largely from quiz shows such as *The Golden Shot*, *Celebrity Squares* and *Family Fortunes*, where his slick American-style presentation set a new pattern in British TV. In Monkhouse's last years, he returned to stand-up and found a new audience with his quick-fire delivery.

Moore, Dudley *(1935-2002)*
The musical member of the original *Beyond the Fringe* team (he held an Oxford organ scholarship) who accompanied himself on brilliant piano spoof

sketches and led the jazz-playing Dudley Moore Trio. He played fall-guy for Peter Cook (qv) in improvised Pete and Dud TV sketches in the *Not Only, But Also* series of the 1960s. In mid-life Hollywood beckoned, and Moore became an improbable pint-sized sex symbol in films such as *10* (1979) with Bo Derek and *Arthur* (1981) with Liza Minnelli. His last years were marred by brain disease.

Morecambe, Eric *(1926-84)*
Known and loved as the taller (and funnier) half of the Morecambe and Wise team. In other words the one without the 'short fat hairy legs' but with trademark spectacles, pipe and infectious laugh. Morecambe was born John Eric Bartholomew but took the stage name of his hometown, first teaming up with **Ernie Wise** (1925-99) in 1941. They became Britain's favourite comedy team and hold the record for the most viewers for a single TV show – around 28 million for the 1977 Christmas Special. Eric's great passions included birds, Long John Silver and Luton Town Football Club.

Nash, Ogden *(1902-71)*
One of the greatest comic verisfiers, Nash became a through-and-through New Yorker, although his family had given their name to the city of Nashville, Tennessee. He began as a teacher in Newport, Rhode Island, where he was effectively hounded out by his unruly pupils and so moved to New York where he worked as a bond salesman, advertising copywriter and manuscript reader as well as contributing distinctive verses to a number of magazines, including *The New Yorker*, whose editorial staff he later joined. Nash's sharp, quirky rhyming reflections on such subjects as women's hats, salads, parsley,

diets, bankers, debts and everything else under the sun were collected in such volumes as *Hard Lines*, *Parents Keep Out* and *You Can't Get There From Here*. He also wrote librettos with S.J. Perelman (qv), including the Broadway musical *One Touch of Venus*.

Norden, Denis *(1922-)*
One half of a scriptwriting and radio and TV performing duo with **Frank Muir** (1920-98), Norden was the mildly saturnine one with the deep laconic voice. Together they wrote many scripts for Jimmy Edwards, especially his radio show *Take it From Here*, which in the 1950s introduced the characters Ron and Eth, two members of the Glum Family, who resurfaced in TV form in 1978. Norden performed with Muir in the radio show *My Word* and in 1977 introduced Britain to *It'll Be Alright on the Night*, the pioneer TV out-take programme.

Palin, Michael *(1943-)*
Began cabaret and comic career at Oxford University, wrote for 1960s satire shows and was an original member of the Monty Python team. He followed this with his own TV comedy series *Ripping Yarns* (1976) and appearances in films such as *The Missionary* (1982) and *A Private Function* (1984). Palin has become a professional Mr Nice Guy – to his often-expressed annoyance – partly on the back of his TV-screened voyages round the world, the Pacific and the Himalayas.

Parker, Dorothy ▼
(1893-1967) New York convent girl (born a Rothschild) who joined *Vogue* magazine in 1916 and moved to *Vanity Fair* the following year. After her marriage to Edwin Parker was dissolved in 1927 she kept her married name but was known, curiously, as 'Miss Parker'. She turned freelance in 1920 and published her first volume of verse, the best-selling *Enough Rope*, in 1926. A year later she became a book reviewer for *The New Yorker*, the magazine she was linked with for much of her professional life. In the early 20s she was, with such witty *New Yorker* luminaries as Robert Benchley and James Thurber (qqv), a founder of the Algonquin Round Table. Here she quickly established a reputation as one of the cruellest and cleverest of the cruel, clever conversationalists. Parker wrote a bittersweet volume of later poems *Not So Deep as a Well* and one of short stories – *Here Lies*. After her marriage to the writer Alan Campbell she decamped to California, returning to her spiritual home in New York after he died in 1963.

Peattie, Charles *(1958-)* and **Taylor, Russell** *(1960-)*
Creators of the 'Alex' strip cartoon about the venal City of London bankers Alex and Clive, which began in the short-lived *London Daily News* in 1986, perfectly capturing the 'greed is good' mood of that decade. The cartoon resurfaced in *The Independent* in 1987, and is now a feature of the *Daily Telegraph*.

Perelman, S.J. *(1904-79)*
One of America's most original humorists, Perelman began to contribute to *The New Yorker* in 1931. The same year he was enlisted by the Marx Brothers to assist on screenplays of *Monkey Business* and, in 1932, *Horsefeathers*. He was happy with both of these but less so with subsequent films and gave vent to his hatred of Hollywood in an hour-long TV show in 1959 called *Malice in Wonderland*. In 1956, however, he did win an Oscar for the screenplay for *Around the World in Eighty Days*. His disenchantment with America led to a brief exile in London but he gave that up after less than two years and returned home to be wittily rude about it. He published many books and a Broadway play, *The Beauty Part*, about American cultural affectation.

Perry, Jimmy *(1923-)* and **Croft, David** *(1922-)*
Writers of the enduringly popular TV sitcom *Dad's Army* (1968-77) – said to be based on Perry's experiences in the Home Guard in the Second World War. The two also wrote the successful sitcoms *Hi-de-Hi!*, set in a Butlin's-type holiday resort, and *It Ain't Half Hot, Mum*, another wartime comedy, this time following the fortunes of an army theatrical troupe in India.

Pont (Gavin Graham Laidler) *(1908-40)*
Named after a family joke on the name Pontifex Maximus – the Roman term for 'high priest'. After tuberculosis robbed him of a future in architecture, Pont moved into cartoons, and drew his celebrated series 'The British Character' for *Punch* in the

1930s. Pont's life was short but his influence great, pushing modern pictorial humour on from the wordy, fussy style of the Victorians and Edwardians to simple, often single-figure, drawings with one punchline. Strangely for such a talented humorist, he said, 'I do not try to draw funny people. I have no sense of humour. I try very hard to draw people exactly as they are'.

Pratchett, Terry *(1948-)*
Prolific novelist, regarded by some as one of the best English-language satirists. After writing his first story at 13, he never stopped. Among many others, he has produced more than 30 books in the hugely popular fantasy Discworld series, including *Wyrd Sisters*, *Soul Music* and *Reaper Man*. These have contributed to a phenomenal 27 million books sold in 27 langues.

Read, Al *(1909-87)* ▼
Lancastrian sausagemaker turned stand-up comic, mainly on radio, although with a penchant for on-stage cross-dressing with po-faced catch-phrases such as 'You'll be lucky, I say you'll be lucky' and 'Right monkey!'. He transferred to TV in 1963 with the show *Life And Al Read*.

Rivers, Joan *(1933-)*
Remorselessly and acknowl-edgedly face-lifted American comedienne (born Joan Alexandra Molinsky) who got her big break in the mid 1960s on *The Ed Sullivan Show* and Johnny Carson's *The Tonight Show*, and had a cameo part opposite Burt Lancaster in the 1969 movie *The Swimmer*. She has worked ever since on radio, TV and film, bouncing back from numerous setbacks, including the suicide of her producer husband in 1987.

Rudner, Rita *(1956-)*
American talk show queen and comedienne who, after starting life as a dancer, broke through on *The Tonight Show*. She has also written two comic novels, *Naked Beneath My Clothes* and *Tickled Pink*, and co-wrote the UK film *Peter's Friends* (1992).

Runyon, Damon
(1884-1946)

At 14 Runyon ran away from his Kansas home to fight in the Spanish-American War, and took up journalism on his return. From 1900 to 1911 he specialised in heavyweight boxing but also covered war in Mexico and Europe. His syndicated sports column, 'Both Barrels', ran from 1918 to 1937 when it was replaced by the more general column, 'The Brighter Side'. In the 1930s Runyon began to write stories of New York low life which made his reputation to such an extent that the adjective 'Runyonesque' was coined to describe the dialect his characters spoke. These magazine stories were first collected in a 1931 volume called *Guys and Dolls*. Several others followed, but after his death his name began to sink into oblivion. The production in 1950 of Frank Loesser's musical based on *Guys and Dolls* ensured that his work and reputation would endure.

Rushton, Willie *(1937-96)*

Burly cartoonist who was at Shrewsbury School with the writers Christopher Booker, Richard Ingrams and Paul Foot. With them Rushton helped found the satirical magazine *Private Eye* in 1961 and drew the logo of 'Gnitty', a parody of the *Daily Express*'s 'Crusader' figurehead, which has appeared on the cover of every *Eye* since. Rushton came to wider notice as a performer on 1963 TV series *That Was the Week That Was* where he specialised in imitations of the languid Prime Minister, Harold Macmillan. His publications included *Day of the Grocer* (Grocer was the *Eye*'s nickname for Prime Minister Edward Heath), *Pigsticking – A Joy for Life* and *Alternative Gardener*: a compost of quips for the green-fingered.

Saunders, Jennifer *(1958-)*

One half, with Dawn French (qv), of the comedy duo French and Saunders. They met at The Central School of Speech and Drama in London and cut their comedy teeth at the Comic Strip club in the late 1970s – although advised initially to stick to teaching. Their *French And Saunders* show, a TV constant since 1987, has included brilliant spoofs of films such as *Misery* and *Silence of the Lambs*. Saunders went on to have global success with the *Absolutely Fabulous* series in the 1990s which she co-wrote and starred in. She is married to fellow-comedian Adrian Edmondson.

Searle, Ronald *(1920-)*

English cartoonist and illustrator long domiciled in France. Searle was captured by the Japanese at fall of Singapore in 1942 and spent the rest of war on the dreaded Burma Railway, where he managed to compile a collection of harrowing drawings, concealing them from his captors under the mattresses of comrades suffering from cholera. After the war he achieved fame as the creator of the ghastly St Trinian's girls and the equally appalling schoolboy Molesworth in *How to Be Topp* with words by Geoffrey Willans. Although continuing with cartoons, notably with a series of studies of cats, Searle has spent more time on serious painting and exhibited widely throughout Europe.

Seinfeld, Jerry *(1954-)*

American comic who, after the common proving ground for New York stand-ups of Catskill Mountain resorts, broke through on Johnny Carson's *The Tonight Show* in 1981, followed by success on similar shows hosted by David Letterman and Merv Griffin. In 1990 he created with fellow former stand-up Larry David the TV show *Seinfeld*, one of the most popular and influential sitcoms ever. ▼

Sellar, W(alter) C(arruthers) *(1898-1951)* and Yeatman, R(obert) J(ulian) *(1898-1968)*

The two first met as undergraduates at Oriel College, Oxford, Sellar going on to become a schoolteacher, and Yeatman an advertising manager at Kodak. Together they wrote the classic spoof textbook *1066 and All That* (1930), subtitled 'A memorable history of England comprising all the parts you can remember including 103 Good Things, 5 Bad Kings and 2 Genuine Dates'. The facts, if not actually wrong, were over-simplified in much the same way as would have happened in the history lessons of Sellar's and Yeatman's youth. The book first appeared in *Punch* and was followed by a less successful sequel, *And Now All This*, as well as an equine and a horticultural equivalent, *Horse Nonsense* and *Garden Rubbish*.

Sellers, Peter *(1925-80)* ▼
Actor and comedian, one of The Goons and a master of funny voices and characters. Sellers was christened Richard, but his parents, both theatre entertainers, called him Peter after a still-born elder brother. By the time *The Goon Show* ended in 1960, he was already an established actor in British films such as *The Ladykillers* (1955) and *I'm All Right Jack* (1959). His genius for playing myriad comedy characters attracted American filmmakers and Sellers went on to appear in dozens of movies, including *Dr Strangelove* (1964), *What's New Pussycat?* (1965) and the Pink Panther series, in which he played the unforgettably bumbling Inspector Clouseau. By contrast, Sellers' private life was messy – he married four times, each wife subjected to his tantrums and self-obsession. His final joke was to insist on having 'In the Mood', a tune he hated, played at his funeral.

Simmonds, Posy *(1945-)*
Cartoonist associated with *The Guardian* since she arrived from the *Sun* in 1972, first as an illustrator and then, in 1977, with a strip cartoon series called 'The Silent Three of St Botolph's'. This recognisably *Guardian*ish trio, Wendy Weber (plus husband George), Jo Heep and Trish Wright, teetered on the brink of middle age and middle class, and epitomised all the concomitant phobias and foibles about work, family, sex, holidays and much else. Simmonds has also created the cartoon series 'Literary Life' for *The Guardian*, the graphic novel *Gemma Bovery* and children's books such as *Fred* and *Lulu and the Flying Babies*.

Smythe, Reg *(1917-98)*
Butcher's boy who served in the Northumberland Fusiliers then took to cartooning and created the character of Andy Capp for the *Daily Mirror* in 1957. The name is a word play on the idea that Andy is a 'handicap' to his wife Flo. In early years Capp, whose eponymous headgear was always pulled down over his eyes, was forever fighting with Flo – she armed with a rolling pin and he with a cigarette always attached to his lower lip. When the tobacco and domestic violence became too much for a modern audience, Andy gave up smoking and took to marriage guidance. After his death, Smythe left enough material for more than a year's worth of strips but the character (permanently based in the northeast of England, like his Hartlepool-born creator) has now been taken on by Roger Mahony and Roger Kettle. Capp is popular in more than 50 countries – in Ghana he is An'Dicap, in France André Chapeau and in Germany Willi Wakker.

Taylor, J(ohn) W(hitfield) *(1908-85)*
Cartoonist whose early interest in cartoons was not dimmed by a career as a schoolteacher. Taylor contributed to a number of magazines, including, from 1935, *Punch*. Taylor's spare, uncluttered drawing style, often relying on an uncaptioned, purely visual joke, inspired contemporary and later cartoonists.

Thelwell, Norman *(1923-2004)*
Cartoonist and mainstay of *Punch* (for which he drew more than 1500 cartoons) from the early 1950s, Thelwell specialised in such traditional middle-class pursuits as motoring, golf and pony-clubbing. The image of stout shaggy ponies being vainly kicked towards fences in a gymkhana by the jodhpured and hard-hatted children of the Volvo-owning classes became almost more real than the reality. His 32 books have sold more than 2 million copies in Britain.

Thompson, Robert *(1960-)*
Prolific cartoonist hailing from Yorkshire, where the *Hull Star* first published his work while he was still a student. Thompson contributes to *The Times*, *Spectator*, *The Observer*, *The Guardian*, *Private Eye* and *Reader's Digest* among many others.

Thurber, James *(1894-1961)*

American humorist and cartoonist who lost the sight in one eye, aged six, while playing with his brother. The accident caused him to be rejected for military service in the First World War and led him to joke that if he ever wrote an autobiography he would call it 'Long Time No See'. After a chequered and only moderately successful career in his hometown of Columbus, Ohio, as well as in Paris, France, he moved to New York. After having 20 stories rejected by the newly founded *New Yorker* magazine, he became a leading contributor. He served briefly as Managing Editor, but spent most of his time collaborating with E.B. White on the chatty 'Talk of the Town'. In 1933 he left for a life of self-employment, completing numerous short stories, plays, novels and collections of cartoons. His most famous work is the short story 'The Secret Life of Walter Mitty', about the ultimate sad, hen-pecked fantasist. This was filmed in 1947, with Danny Kaye in the title role.

Tidy, Bill *(1933-)*

Took up cartooning in 1957 after military national service and time in a Liverpool advertising agency. Tidy is the quintessential northcountry-man, beer-drinker and Preston North End fan who specialises in blousy barmaids and pigeon-fancying, cloth-capped, salt-of-the-earth, working men as exemplified in his *Private Eye* strip cartoon 'The Cloggies – an everyday story of clog-dancing folk'.

Tomlin, Lily *(1939-)*

Versatile actress who first emerged in the late 1960s on the American TV show *Rowan and Martin's Laugh-In*, where she created several characters,

including Ernestine the hoity-toity telephonist who used to say, 'A gracious good morning to you … have I reached the party to whom I am speaking'. Tomlin has acted in numerous films, including *Nashville* (1975), *Nine to Five* (1980) and *I Heart Huckabees* (2004). ▼

Took, Barry *(1928-2002)*

Longstanding writing partner of Marty Feldman (qv), most memorably on the surreal 1960s radio series *Round the Horne*, which introduced the world to such outrageous characters as Rambling Sid Rumpo and Dame Celia Molestrangler. Took was best known to the public, however, as the presenter of the TV feedback programme *Points of View*. He also hosted the BBC Radio 4 current affairs gameshow *The News Quiz*, and was credited with bringing the Monty Python team together at the BBC.

Townsend, Sue *(1946-)*

Creator of Adrian Mole, one of the great comic child fictions, although allegedly based on her son's character while at a Leicester comprehensive school. The first Mole story was entitled *The Secret Diary of*

Adrian Mole aged 13¾ and was turned into a TV series in 1985. It has been followed by four sequels, the most recent being *Adrian Mole and the Weapons of Mass Destruction*, where the anti-hero is now an angst-ridden 38-year-old single parent. Townsend has also written *The Queen and I*, an affectionate fantasy of the Royal Family as they would be had they been ordinary and lived on a council estate.

Twain, Mark *(1835-1910)*

Author, wit and raconteur who was born Samuel Langhorne Clemens in Missouri but adopted the name 'Mark Twain' from a call used on Mississippi river boats when sounding water depths. His best-known books were *The Adventures of Tom Sawyer* (1876) and *The Adventures of Huckleberry Finn* (1884). After unsuccessful years as a prospector and miner Twain took to journalism and had his first breakthrough with 'The Celebrated Jumping Frog of Calaveras County' in the *New York Saturday Press*. He went bankrupt in the 1890s but clawed his way back to relative affluence with a world lecture tour. Born in the year of Halley's Comet, Twain vowed to die on its next appearance – a prediction he successfully fulfilled.

Ustinov, Peter *(1921-2004)*

Raconteur, wit, playwright, actor, UNICEF ambassador and all-round funny Renaissance man, who was London-born but of mixed Russian, German, French and Italian descent. He played a memorable Emperor Nero in the film *Quo Vadis?* (1951) and won two Oscars for his roles in *Spartacus* (1960) and *Topkapi* (1964), although he is perhaps best remembered as Hercule Poirot, a part he first played in *Death on the*

Nile (1978). Ustinov's writings included the film *Romanoff and Juliet* and a humorous autobiography, *Dear Me*. His later life was notable for tour-de-force one-man theatricals. When asked what he would like on his tombstone, Ustinov replied, 'Keep off the grass'.

Waugh, Evelyn *(1903-66)*
Comic novelist of genius, beginning with the 1928 dissection of life in a dim boarding school, *Decline and Fall*, and reaching a humorous climax with *Scoop* (1938), a novel about journalism based on his own experiences of war in Abyssinia. Waugh became more serious (and personally depressed) in later life with a series of Second World War novels – the *Sword of Honour* trilogy – and *Brideshead Revisited* (1945), his celebration of British stately home Roman Catholicism. Waugh was often drunk and nearly always grumpy, once remarking, typically, that surgeons, having removed a cancerous growth from his friend Randolph Churchill, should be congratulated for removing 'the one part of Randolph that was not malignant'.

West, Mae *(1893-1980)*
Legendary sex goddess (born Mary Jane West) and determinedly bad girl of Hollywood whose famously pneumatic figure caused American aircrew of the Second World War to christen their inflateable life-jackets, Mae Wests. She began acting in amateur theatricals aged seven and turned pro at eight. In 1906 she went into vaudeville as part of a song-and-dance team and then on to Broadway revues. The big breakthrough came in 1926 when she starred in her own play, *Sex*, which earned her ten days in prison on obscenity charges. She consolidated her

outrageous reputation with a quintessentially Mae West performance in the title role of the play *Diamond Lil*, which was later made into the film *She Done Him Wrong* (1933), where she delivered one of her most memorable lines when she said to Cary Grant, 'Come up and see me some time'. Despite stage work and nightclub work she was absent from the cinema from 1943 until 1970 when she produced a tour de force performance in the film version of Gore Vidal's novel, *Myra Breckinridge*. ▼

Whitehouse, Paul *(1959-)*
Welsh-born comedian who was a plasterer in Hackney when he first met his early writing partner Harry Enfield (qv). His big break came in 1994 with the huge success of the rapid-fire TV sketch series *The Fast Show*, where he also began to display considerable talent as a character actor. Whitehouse has now turned to comedy-drama, writing and appearing in the TV series *Happiness* and, in 2005, playing all 25 patients of a psychotherapist in *Help*.

Wilde, Oscar *(1854-1900)*
Irish poet, playwright and wit of genius combined with fatal flaws leading to his early self-destruction. Wilde was educated in Dublin then at

Magdalen College, Oxford, where he won the coveted Newdigate poetry prize in 1878 and earned a reputation for flamboyance and spontaneous epigrams. His most brilliant work nearly all appeared in the 1890s. This included a novel, *A Picture of Dorian Gray*, and the plays, *Lady Windermere's Fan*, *A Woman of No Importance*, *An Ideal Husband* and *The Importance of Being Earnest*. In his not-so-private life Wilde was an ostentatious, mannered bi-sexual who conducted a scandalous affair with Lord Alfred Douglas, son of the notoriously hard-line Marquis of Queensberry. As a result of his abortive libel action against Queensberry, Wilde was sentenced to two years hard labour and subsequently went into exile in France where he died under the assumed name of Sebastian Melmoth.

Williams, Kenneth ▶
(1926-88)
Wittily camp son of a Euston hairdresser whom he hated, while adoring his mother. Williams initially wanted to be a serious actor but found little success until spotted playing the Dauphin in George Bernard Shaw's *Saint Joan* by the producer Denis Main Wilson, who signed him up for the radio show *Hancock's Half Hour*. For just over ten years from 1958 he achieved great acclaim in the radio shows *Beyond Our Ken* and *Round the Horne*, written by Barry Took and Marty Feldman (qqv), where he played such over-the-top characters as the folk-singer Rambling Syd Rumpo and the ludicrously camp Sandy. His spontaneous wit made him a popular guest on talk shows and he was a longstanding mainstay of radio's *Just a Minute*, as well as one of the key players in the Carry On films. Williams'

much enlivened by a monstrous regiment of formidable aunts, bevies of benign baronets, priceless peers, swooning debutantes and chinless Charlies. Sadly Wodehouse, who could be hopelessly naïve, blotted his copybook by making a series of harmless but misconstrued broadcasts after being captured by the Nazis while living in France during the Second World War. Some people never forgave him.

Wood, Victoria (1953-)

Comedienne from Ramsbottom in Lancashire not afraid to make a joke of her northern roots – in one of her shows a snooty BBC announcer says, 'We'd like to apologise to our viewers in the North. It must be so awful for you up there'. Wood appeared on the TV talent show *New Faces* aged 20, joined Esther Ranzen's consumer show *That's Life*, where she sang her trademark comic songs, and then moved into stand-up and TV sketch shows. Wood has also made a successful stab at sitcom with *The Dinnerladies* (1998-2000) and in 2005 brought one of her most popular sketches, the hilarious spoof on creaky soap operas, 'Acorn Antiques', to the London stage as a musical.

Youngman, Henny (1906-98)

American newspaper and radio commentator Walter Winchell called Youngman 'The King of the One-Liners'. Sometimes he interspersed these wisecracks with bursts of not very good violin playing, but his act was usually a volley of gags. He once managed to tell fifty jokes in eight minutes. When New York launched a dial-a-joke service in the 1970s three million people in a month phoned to hear thirty seconds-of Henny. His best-known line was 'Take my wife – please'.

private life was unhappy, his homosexuality a trial and when his diaries were posthumously published it was revealed that the final entry before his death (which may or may not have been accidental) was 'Oh, what's the bloody point?'

Williams, Robin (1951-)

Hyper-active American comedian and actor who made his breakthrough in 1978 as the alien Mork in the TV series *Mork and Mindy*. He flopped in films of *Popeye* (1980) and *The World According to Garp* (1982) but received wider acclaim playing a father-pretending-to-be-a-Scottish-nanny in *Mrs Doubtfire* (1993) and the voice of the Genie in Disney's *Aladdin* (1992). Williams has since moved into more serious film roles, but can still be exhaustingly hilarious if caught on his own.

Wodehouse, P(elham) G(renville) (1881-1975) ▶

Quintessentially English novelist who studied under the same Dulwich College English teacher as the thriller-writer Raymond Chandler and ended his days as an American citizen living on Long Island, New York. Wodehouse began his career as a novelist with a series of more or less facetious school stories, the most successful of which featured a slightly chinless character called Psmith. In 1923 he wrote *The Inimitable Jeeves* and introduced the eponymous butler or 'Gentleman's Gentleman' who shimmered about on behalf of the hopeless Bertie Wooster, attempting to bring order and sanity where there was otherwise precious little. It was characteristic that Jeeves was actually named after a Warwickshire cricketer whom Wodehouse much admired. His fictional world might have been rooted in reality but it quickly assumed preposterous proportions, sustained and

Index

'... and it's good night from him.'

RONNIE BARKER

TALLULAH
BANKHEAD

'Don't mention the war!'

JOHN CLEESE

D

Dudley: How do you manage to breathe?
Sir Arthur Streeb-Greebling: Through the mouth
and the nose – the usual method, in fact.

PETER COOK AND
DUDLEY MOORE,
'RAVENS'

'Who stole the cork from my breakfast?'

W.C. FIELDS

'A pint? Why, that's very nearly an armful!'

TONY HANCOCK, THE BLOOD DONOR

Will the real Sherlock Holmes
please stand up 260-1
Knoxville 31

L

la Frenais, Ian 208-9, 385
Laidler, Gavin Graham
    see Pont
lamb 357
lamppost 241
landmines 185
Land of Hide and Seek, The 108
Lane, George Martin 67
la Nougerede, Alande 363
Larry 33, 35, 103, 392
Last Supper, The 236-7
last words 29, 268
laughing cavalier 233
Laurie, Hugh 320-2, 392-3
Law, Denis 214
law and order 190-209
lawn tennis 229
lawyers 197, 202-3, 205
Lay of the Lone Fish-Ball, The 67
Lear, Edward 37, 122-3, 393
Lebowitz, Fran 57, 393
Leigh, H.S. 283
Leighton, Robert 307
leprechaun 220
Levin, Arnie 307
Lewis, Joe E. 74
Lewis, Mark 23
library as murder scene 194-5
life assurance 137
lifeboats 113
light-bulb changing
    lawyers 205
    Members of Parliament 264
    programmers 305
limbs 34
limericks 122-3, 359
liners 149
lion and lamb 357
lions 14-15, 112, 163, 228, 251,
    332-3
lions and Christians 228, 332
liquor quicker 76
literature 254-61
litigation 197
lobsters 117
London 119, 120
London Underground 109, 152
Longden, Deric 350-1
Lorenz, Lee 371
Los Angeles 104, 307

love 82-101
    actors 88
    fortunes 136
    milkman 93
    oneself 88
Lowry, Ray 269
Luck of the Bodkins, The 113
Lumberjack Song, The 105

M

Macaulay, Thomas 263
Macinnes, Colin 163
Mad Dogs and Englishmen
    110-11
Mahood, Kenneth 267
man's best friend 338-9
Manchester 119
Mancroft, Lord 216
Marber, Patrick 204-5, 226-7,
    260-1
Marquis, Don 255, 393
marriage 284-91
    angelic wife 370
    aphorisms 291
    army 185
    guidance 291
    happiness and otherwise 90-1
    know-alls 289
    local politicians 270
    magician 284
    old age 23
    sister-in-law 287
    stepchildren 278
    three wishes 284
    tunnel of married love 82
    see also love and sex
Martham 31
Martin, Charles E. 239
Martin, Dean 220, 393
Marx, Groucho 10, 49, 81, 83, 84,
    162, 177, 255, 278, 291, 303,
    335, 393-4
Maslin, Michael 314
Mason, Jackie 141, 394
Mastermind 248-9
matches 147
Matt 81, 137, 216, 394
Matthau, Walter 44
McCoshan, Duncan 220
McGill, Donald 117, 258, 393
McLachlan, Edward 50, 62, 64, 71,
    76, 81, 141, 151, 154, 159,
    167, 184, 191, 192, 198, 211,
    217, 235, 251, 265, 351,
    352, 393

McMurty, Stan 74
medical examinations 167
medicine 41
mediums 375
meetings, work 304, 314-15, 323,
    326
Members of Parliament 264
memoranda 318
memory loss 17, 23, 293
memory man 212
men and love 82-101
Mencken, H.L. 271, 394
Merchant, Stephen 18, 75,
    168-9, 328-9
Merton, Paul 33, 394
Metcalf, Fred 46, 65, 199, 281,
    289, 333, 339
Mexico 103, 106
Michelangelo 236-7
middle age 8, 19
military history 170
military intelligence 177
Miller, Jonathan 364, 394
Milligan, Spike 48, 83, 103, 140,
    175, 182, 193, 233, 308-9,
    352, 394
Mirachi, Joseph 353
missiles 167
Mizner, Wilson 88
model cars 311
models (artists) 234, 235
moderation, voice of 271
modernism 233
Monet 238
money 130-47

'I have the body of an eighteen-year-old.
I keep it in the fridge.'

SPIKE
MILLIGAN

'People of Jewusalem! Wome is your Fwend!'

Ernie: Tell me, do you serve anyone, sir.
Eric: We serve crabs?

MORECAMBE AND WISE

MICHAEL PALIN, THE LIFE OF BRIAN

'I wish I had a twin, so I could know what I'd look like without plastic surgery.'

JOAN RIVERS

PETER
SELLERS AS
INSPECTOR
CLOUSEAU

'We had gay burglars the other night. They broke in and rearranged the furniture.'

ROBIN WILLIAMS

U

V

W

X, Y, Z

'I thought coq au vin was love in a lorry.'

VICTORIA WOOD

Acknowledgments

Every effort has been made to trace and contact copyright holders prior to publication. If notified, the publisher undertakes to rectify any errors or omissions at the earliest opportunity.

Text Credits

DOUGLAS ADAMS: extracts from *The Hitchhiker's Guide to the Galaxy: The Original Radio Scripts* (Pan, 1985), and from *The Salmon of Doubt: Hitchhiking the Galaxy One Last Time*, reprinted by permission of Macmillan, London, UK; 'Kamikaze' (with Chris Keightley) for *A Kick in the Stalls*, Cambridge Footlight Review 1976, reprinted by permission of Ed Victor Ltd for the author.

JAMES AGATE: extract from *Ego 6*, copyright © The Estate of James Agate 1944, reprinted by permission of PFD, www.pfd.co.uk on behalf of the Estate of James Agate.

CAROLINE AHERNE, CRAIG CASH and **HENRY NORMAL**: extracts from *The Royle Family My Arse* (Granada Media, 2001), reprinted by permission of the publishers, Carlton Publishing Group.

NANCY ASTOR: reprinted by permission of Sir Edward Ford.

PAM AYRES: 'The Wonderbra Song' from *With These Hands* (Weidenfeld & Nicolson, 1997), copyright © Pam Ayres 1997, reprinted by permission of Sheil Land Associates Ltd.

MAURICE BARING: reprinted by permission of A.P. Watt Ltd on behalf of The Trustees of the Maurice Baring Will Trust.

RONNIE BARKER: extracts from *It's Goodnight from Him – The Best of the Two Ronnies* (Hodder & Stoughton Ltd, 1976), reprinted by permission of the publishers.

PATRICK BARRINGTON: 'The Diplomatic Platypus' first published in *Punch*, reprinted by permission of Punch Limited.

BEACHCOMBER: (see J.B. Morton)

HILAIRE BELLOC: 'Henry King' and 'Jim' from *Cautionary Tales for Children*, copyright © Estate of Hilaire Belloc 1907, 'Lord High-Bo' from *More Peers*, copyright © Estate of Hilaire Belloc 1911, 'The Game of Cricket' from *Letters from Hilaire Belloc* edited and selected by Robert Speaight (Hollis and Carter, 1958), copyright © Estate of Hilaire Belloc 1958, reprinted by permission of PFD, www.pfd.co.uk on behalf of the Estate of Hilaire Belloc.

ROBERT BENCHLEY: reprinted by permission of Nathaniel R. Benchley.

ALAN BENNETT: (see Peter Cook)

JOHN BETJEMAN: 'Executive', 'A Subaltern's Love-song', 'Hunter Trials' and 'In a Bath Teashop' from *Collected Poems* (John Murray, 1978), reprinted by permission of the Publishers.

THOMAS BLACKBURN: extract from *Selected Poems* edited by Julia Blackburn (Carcanet, 2001), reprinted by permission of Carcanet Press Ltd.

CONNIE BOOTH: (see John Cleese)

TIM BROOKE-TAYLOR: (see John Cleese)

CRAIG BROWN: extract from *This is Craig Brown* (Ebury Press, 2003), reprinted by permission of The Random House Group Ltd.

CRAIG CASH: (see Caroline Aherne)

GRAHAM CHAPMAN: (see John Cleese and Monty Python)

ERIC CHAPPELL: extracts from *Rising Damp: The Complete Scripts* edited by Richard

Webber (Granada Media, 2002), reprinted by permission of the publishers, Carlton Publishing Group.

G.K. CHESTERTON: reprinted by permission of A.P. Watt Ltd on behalf of The Royal Literary Fund.

WINSTON CHURCHILL: copyright © Winston S. Churchill, reprinted by permission of Curtis Brown Ltd, London, on behalf of the Estate of Sir Winston S. Churchill.

JOHN CLEESE: 'Butterling', 'The Last Supper', first performed by John Cleese and Jonathan Lynn in *A Poke in the Eye with a Sharp Stick* for Amnesty International, 1976; 'BBC BC' (with Bill Oddie); 'The Good Old Days' (with Marty Feldman, Graham Chapman and Tim Brooke-Taylor), first performed in *At Last the 1948 Show*, and extracts from 'The Builders', 'Gourmet Night', 'Communication Problems' and 'The Germans' (with Connie Booth) from *The Complete Fawlty Towers* (Methuen, 1988), reprinted by permission of David Wilkinson Associates. (See also Monty Python.)

DICK CLEMENT and **IAN LA FRENAIS**: extracts from *Porridge: The Scripts* edited by Richard Webber (Headline, 2002), reprinted by permission of and Richard Fletcher for the authors.

BERYL COOK: extract from *The Works* (Penguin, 1978), copyright © Beryl Cook 1978, reprinted by permission of the author c/o Rogers, Coleridge & White Ltd, 20 Powis Mews, London W11 1JN.

PETER COOK: extracts from *Tragically I was an Only Twin: The Complete Peter Cook* edited by William Cook (Century, 2002), reprinted by permission of David Higham Associates; 'Hand Up Your Sticks!' from *Pieces of Eight*, reprinted by permission of David Higham Associates, 'Take a Pew' (with Alan Bennett, Jonathan Miller and Dudley Moore) and 'The Great Train Robbery' (with Alan Bennett) from *The Complete Beyond the Fringe* (Methuen 1987, 2003), reprinted by permission of Methuen Publishing Ltd.

STEVE COOGAN, PETER BAYNHAM, ARMANDO IANNUCCI and **PATRICK MARBER**: extracts from 'Knowing Me, Knowing You' from *Alan Partridge: Every Ruddy Word. All the Scripts from Radio to TV. And Back* (Michael Joseph, 2003), Radio Show scripts copyright © Armando Iannuchi, Steve Coogan & Patrick Marber 1992, TV Show scripts copyright © Armando Iannuchi, Steve Coogan & Patrick Marber 1994.

TOMMY COOPER: extracts from *Just Like That!* (Virgin, 1994), copyright © Tommy Cooper 1994, reprinted by permission of Virgin Books Ltd.

WENDY COPE: 'Loss' and 'Two Cures for Love' from *Serious Concerns* (1992), reprinted by permission of the publishers, Faber & Faber Ltd.

BILL COSBY: 'Noah and the Neighbors', words by Bill Cosby, copyright © Manger Music Inc, USA, reprinted by permission of B. Feldman & Co Ltd, London WC2H 0QY c/o EMI Music Publishing Ltd (UK) and of Kristen Glasgow for Roy Silver, Manger Music, Inc.

NOËL COWARD: 'The Order of the Day' from *Collected Revue Sketches and Parodies* edited by Barry Day (Methuen Drama, 1999), and 'Mad Dogs and Englishmen' from *The Complete Lyrics* edited by Barry Day (Methuen, 1998),

reprinted by permission of Methuen Publishing Ltd; one-liner reprinted by permission of NC Aventales AG, Successor in Title to The Estate of Noël Coward via Alan Brodie Representation Ltd.

QUENTIN CREWE: reprinted by permission of Candida Crewe.

DAVID CROFT: (see Jimmy Perry)

RICHMAL CROMPTON: extract from *William—The Good* (George Newnes, 1928), reprinted by permission of A.P. Watt Ltd on behalf of Richmal Ashbee.

RICHARD CURTIS and **BEN ELTON**: 'Potato' from 'Blackadder II' (1985), 'Ink and Incapability' from 'Blackadder the Third' (1987), 'Goodbyeee' from 'Blackadder Goes Forth' (1989), all extracts from *Blackadder: The Whole Damn Dynasty* by Richard Curtis and Ben Elton (Michael Joseph, 1998), collection copyright © Richard Curtis, Ben Elton, John Lloyd and Rowan Atkinson, reprinted by permission of Penguin Books Ltd.

PIERRE DANINOS: extract from *Major Thompson & I*, translated by W. Marmaduke Thompson (Jonathan Cape, 1957), reprinted by permission of The Random House Group Ltd.

BEN ELTON: (see Richard Curtis)

HARRY ENFIELD: 'Smashie and Nicey' from *Harry Enfield and His Humorous Chums* (Penguin, 1997), copyright © Harry Enfield 1977, reprinted by permission of Penguin Books Ltd.

BARRY FANTONI (Ed): *Private Eye's Colemanballs* (Andre Deutsch/Private Eye 1982) and *Private Eye's Colemanballs 12* (Private Eye 2004), copyright © Pressdram Ltd 2005, reprinted by permission of Private Eye/Pressdram.

MARTY FELDMAN: extract TM/© 2005 Marty Feldman, reprinted by permission of CMG Worldwide, www.CMGWorldwide.com for the Estate of Marty Feldman. (See also John Cleese.)

MICHAEL FLANDERS: words (with music by Donald Swann) of 'Design for Living', copyright © 1959 The Estates of Michael Flanders and Donald Swann from *The Songs of Michael Flanders and Donald Swann* (Hamish Hamilton, 1977), reprinted by permission of International Music Publications Ltd. All Rights Reserved.

W.D.H FOUGASSE (Cyril Kenneth Bird) and **McCULLOUGH**: *You Have Been Warned – A Complete Guide to the Road* (Methuen, 1935); copyright holders not traced.

JOHN FOWLES: reprinted by permission of Anthony Sheil, Gillon Aitken Associates on behalf of the author.

DAWN FRENCH: (see Jennifer Saunders)

CLEMENT FREUD: reprinted by permission of the author.

STEPHEN FRY and **HUGH LAURIE**: 'Troubleshooters' from *A Bit of Fry and Laurie* (Mandarin, 1990), reprinted by permission of David Higham Associates.

RAY GALTON and **ALAN SIMPSON**: extracts from *Hancock's Half Hour* and *Steptoe and Son*, reprinted by permission of Tessa Le Bars Management for the authors.

RICKY GERVAIS and **STEPHEN MERCHANT**: extracts from *The Office* (BBC, 2002), reprinted by permission of PFD, www.pfd.co.uk on behalf of the authors.

TERRY GILLIAM: (see Monty Python)

HARRY GRAHAM: 'Quiet Fun' from *Ruthless Rhymes* (Edward Arnold, 1984), reprinted by permission of Laura Dance.

MICHAEL GREEN: extracts from *Tonight Josephine and Other Undiscovered Letters* illustrated by John Jensen (Martin Secker & Warburg, 1981), text copyright © Michael Green 1981, from *The Art of Coarse Acting* (Hutchinson, 1964, revised and rewritten 1994), copyright © Michael Green 1994, and 'The Rime of the Ancient Cricketer' from *The Art of Coarse Sport* (Hutchinson, 1965), copyright © Michael Green 1965, reprinted by permission of Sheil Land Associates Ltd.

JOYCE GRENFELL: 'Ethel' from *Stately as a Galleon*, copyright © Joyce Grenfell 1978 (to be published by Hodder as *George Don't Do That and Stately as a Galleon*), reprinted by permission of Sheil Land Associates Ltd.

ANDY HAMILTON: 'A Bit of Diabolism', reprinted by permission of Berlin Associates, for the author.

JOHN HEGLEY: 'Why I didn't get you a Valentine', 'Poem about Losing My Glasses', and 'My Mum's Dog' from *Glad to Wear Glasses* (Deutsch, 1990), copyright © John Hegley 1990, reprinted by permission of PFD on behalf of the author.

A.P. HERBERT: extract from *Uncommon Law* reprinted by permission of A.P. Watt Ltd on behalf of The Estate of Jocelyn Herbert and the Executors of the Estate of Teresa E. Perkins.

ERIC IDLE: (see Monty Python)

BRIAN JOHNSTON: reprinted by permission of Barry Johnston.

TERRY JONES: 'Hendon' (with Michael Palin) from *Frost Over Christmas*, reprinted by permission of Fegg Features Ltd c/o Casarotto Ramsay (see also Monty Python).

CHRIS KEIGHTLEY: (see Douglas Adams)

MILES KINGTON: reprinted by permission of Rogers, Coleridge & White Literary Agency, for the author.

IAN LA FRENAIS: (see Dick Clement)

HUGH LAURIE: (see Stephen Fry)

FRAN LEBOWITZ: one-liner, copyright © Fran Lebowitz, reprinted by permission of International Creative Management, Inc.

DERIC LONGDEN: extract from *The Cat Who Came in from the Cold* (Bantam, 1991), reprinted by permission of The Random House Group Ltd, and PFD on behalf of the author.

COLIN MACINNES: reprinted by permission of The Royal Literary Fund.

GROUCHO MARX: extract from *The Essential Groucho* edited by Stefan Kanfer (Penguin Books, 2000) and one-line quotes reprinted by permission of Groucho Marx Productions, Inc.

JACKIE MASON: reprinted by permission of the author.

WALTER MATTHAU: extract TM/© Walter Matthau, reprinted by permission of CMG Worldwide, www.CMGWorldwide.com, for The Matthau Company.

HENRY LOUIS MENCKEN: reprinted by permission of the Enoch Pratt Free Library, Baltimore, in accordance with the terms of the bequest of H.L. Mencken.

STEPHEN MERCHANT: (see Ricky Gervais)

FRED METCALF: sketches from *The Morecambe and Wise Show*, copyright © Fred Metcalf 1979, reprinted by permission of Sheil Land Associates Ltd on behalf of Fred Metcalf.

JONATHAN MILLER: (see Peter Cook)

SPIKE MILLIGAN: 'Soldier Freddie' from *A Dustbin of Milligan* (Dobson Books, 1961), extracts from *Puckoon: A Novel* (Blond, 1963), 'The Eden Project' from *Spike Milligan's Transports of Delight* (Sidgwick and Jackson, 1974), 'Expel Elephants' and 'Van Gogh' from *Mad Medley of Milligan* (Virgin, 1999), 'A Family Man' from *The Essential Spike Milligan* compiled by Alexander Games (Fourth Estate, 2002), and extracts from *The Goon Show Scripts* (Woburn Press, 1972), reprinted by permission of Spike Milligan Productions Ltd.

MONTY PYTHON (Graham Chapman, John Cleese, Terry Gilliam, Eric Idle, Terry Jones, and Michael Palin): extracts from *Monty Python and The Holy Grail: Screenplay* (Methuen, 2002), *Monty Python's The Life of Brian (of Nazareth)* (Methuen, 2001), *Monty Python's Flying Circus: Just the Words, Volume 1* (Methuen, 1989), *Monty Python's Flying Circus: Just the Words, Volume 2* (Methuen, 1999) and *The Brand New Monty Python Bok* edited by Eric Idle (Methuen, 1973), reprinted by permission of Methuen Publishing Ltd.

DUDLEY MOORE: (see Peter Cook)

ERIC MORECAMBE and **ERNIE WISE:** extracts from *The Morecambe and Wise Show* written for them by Fred Metcalf used by permission of Billy Marsh Associates for the Estates of Eric Morecambe and Ernie Wise.

J.B. MORTON: extracts from *Beachcomber* (Heinemann, 1963), copyright © Estate of J.B. Morton 1963, reprinted by permission of PFD on behalf of the The Estate of J.B. Morton.

OGDEN NASH: lines from 'Let's Not Climb the Washington Monument Tonight', lines from 'England Expects', 'Reflections on Ice-breaking', 'The Kipper', 'A Word to Husbands', and 'The Dog' from *Candy is Dandy: The Best of Ogden Nash* (Andre Deutsch, 1994), reprinted by permission of Andre Deutsch Ltd, Carlton Publishing Group and Curtis Brown Ltd, New York; 'Carlotta' and 'The Sweetbread' reprinted by permission of Curtis Brown Ltd, New York.

HENRY NORMAL: (see Caroline Aherne)

BILL ODDIE: (see John Cleese)

MICHAEL PALIN: 'Christmas Oath' from *The Frost Report* and 'Hendon' (with Terry Jones) from *Frost over Christmas* reprinted by permission of The Gumby Corporation Ltd (see also Monty Python).

CLIFF PARKER: 'The Angler's Prayer' from *Hook, Line and Stinker* (Peter Wolfe 1975, Sphere Books 1983), copyright © Cliff Parker 1975, reprinted by permission of Michael Motley Ltd for the author.

DOROTHY PARKER: 'General Review of the Sex Situation', 'Unfortunate Coincidence' and 'Social Note', all copyright 1926, renewed © 1954 by Dorothy Parker, from *The Portable Dorothy Parker* edited by Brendan Gill, copyright 1928, renewed © 1956 by Dorothy Parker, reprinted by permission of the publishers Viking Penguin, a division of Penguin Group (USA) Inc., and from *The Best of Dorothy Parker* (Duckworth, 1979, 1996), copyright © The Estate of Dorothy Parker, reprinted by permission of the publishers, Gerald Duckworth & Co. Ltd.

SYDNEY JOSEPH PERELMAN: reprinted by permission of PFD for the author's Estate.

JIMMY PERRY and **DAVID CROFT:** extracts from *Dad's Army: The Complete Scripts* edited by Richard Webber (Orion, 2003), reprinted by permission of The Orion Publishing Group Ltd.

STEPHEN POTTER: extract from *The Theory and Practice of Gamesmanship* (Rupert Hart-Davis, 1947), reprinted by permission of Julian Potter for the Stephen Potter Estate.

TERRY PRATCHETT: extract from *Mort* (Victor Gollancz, 1987), reprinted by permission of Victor Gollancz, a division of The Orion Publishing Group Ltd.

AL READ: (see Ronnie Taylor)

DAVID RENWICK: 'Mastermind' written for *The Two Ronnies*, reprinted by permission of Tim Hancock at Roger Hancock.

PAUL RODRIGUEZ: reprinted by permission of the author.

DAMON RUNYON: reprinted by permission of American Rights Management Co.

JENNIFER SAUNDERS: 'Health Expert' (with **DAWN FRENCH**) from *A Feast of French and Saunders* (Heinemann, 1991), reprinted by permission of The Random House Group Ltd and PFD on behalf of the author; extracts from *Absolutely Fabulous* (Penguin, 1995) reprinted by permission of PFD on behalf of the author.

W.C. SELLAR and **R.J. YEATMAN:** extracts from *1066 and All That* (Methuen & Co, 1930), reprinted by permission of Methuen Publishing Ltd.

ALAN SIMPSON: (see Ray Galton)

LOGAN PEARSALL SMITH: reprinted by permission of the London Library.

GERTRUDE STEIN: reprinted by permission of David Higham Associates.

WILLIAM SUTCLIFFE: extract from *Are You Experienced?* (Hamish Hamilton, 1997), copyright © William Sutcliffe 1997, reprinted by permission of Penguin Books Ltd and Lutyens & Rubinstein Literary Agency.

RONNIE TAYLOR: 'Try it the Other Way Round' written for *The Al Read Show* and performed by Al Read, reprinted by permission of Mrs Irene Taylor, Taylor-Vision Ltd.

DYLAN THOMAS: reprinted by permission of David Higham Associates.

JAMES THURBER: extracts from *The Thurber Carnival*, text and illustrations by James Thurber, copyright © 1973 Rosemary A. Thurber, reprinted by permission of the Barbara Hogenson Agency, Inc.

BARRY TOOK (with Mat Coward): extracts from *The Best of Round the Horne* (Boxtree, 2000), reprinted by permission of Macmillan, London, UK.

SUE TOWNSEND: extracts from *The Secret Diary of Adrian Mole aged 13¾* (Methuen, 1982), copyright © Sue Townsend 1982, reprinted by permission of The Random House Group Ltd and Curtis Brown Group Ltd, London.

PETER USTINOV: reprinted by permission of The Ustinov Foundation.

R.J. YEATMAN: (see W.C. Sellars)

EVELYN WAUGH: extracts from *Scoop* (first published Chapman and Hall 1938, first published Penguin Books 1943, Penguin Modern Classics 2003), copyright © Evelyn Waugh 1928, and from *Decline and Fall* (first published 1928, Penguin Modern Classics 2003), copyright © Evelyn Waugh 1938, reprinted by permission of Penguin Books Ltd and Little, Brown & Co., Inc.

KATHERINE WHITEHORN: reprinted by permission of *Saga Magazine*.

ERNIE WISE: (see Eric Morecambe)

P.G. WODEHOUSE: 'Franglais' from *The Luck of the Bodkins* (Herbert Jenkins, 1935), extracts from 'Rodney Fails to Qualify' and 'The Magic Plus Fours' in *The Heart of Goof* (Herbert Jenkins, 1926), and 'The Spot of Art' in *Very Good, Jeeves!* (Herbert Jenkins, 1930), reprinted by permission of The Random House Group Ltd and A.P. Watt Ltd on behalf of The Trustees of the Wodehouse Estate. One-liner reprinted by permission of the Random House Group Ltd.

VICTORIA WOOD: 'Service Wash' from *Up To You, Porky: The Victoria Wood Sketch Book* (Methuen, 1985), reprinted by permission of Methuen Publishing Ltd; Jokes reprinted by permission of the author c/o McIntyre Entertainments.

Picture Credits

The following abbreviations are used in the picture credits: **T** top; **B** bottom; **C** centre; **L** left; **R** right.

UK Front & Back Cover Drawing by Mel Calman © S & C Calman **6 & 7** Topham Picture Library/Arena Pal/John Timbers **8** Simon Drew **9** Daddy cartoons from *The Best of Daddy* by Rupert Fawcett. Published by Boxtree **10** © Punch, Ltd/Martin Honeysett **11 T** © Punch, Ltd/Michael Heath **B** Daddy cartoons from *The Best of Daddy* by Rupert Fawcett. Published by Boxtree **12 T** Reproduced by kind permission of PRIVATE EYE.© Pressdram Ltd (2005)/Hector Breeze **B** Reproduced by kind permission of PRIVATE EYE.© Pressdram Ltd (2005)/Martin Honeysett **16** © Charles Peattie and Russell Taylor. Alex cartoon appears in *The Daily Telegraph* **17 T** Daddy cartoons from *The Best of Daddy* by Rupert Fawcett. Published by Boxtree **B** Daddy cartoons from *The Best of Daddy* by Rupert Fawcett. Published by Boxtree **18** BBC Photo Library **19** © Punch, Ltd/Nick Baker **21** The Kobal Collection/Films of Record **22** © The Spectator **23 T** © The Spectator **BL** © The Spectator **BR** © The Spectator **25** BBC Photo Library **26** © Punch, Ltd/Pont **27** © Posy Simmonds *Peaceful Twilight Years* (1981) permission granted by PFD on behalf of Posy Simmonds **28** BBC Photo Library **29 T** Reproduced by kind permission of PRIVATE EYE.© Pressdram Ltd (2005)/Heath **B** © Punch, Ltd/Tony Husband **30** BBC Photo Library **32** www.CartoonStock.com/Tom Prisk **33 T** © Punch, Ltd/Larry **B** Born Loser cartoons © 2002 United Feature Syndicate, Inc. Distributed by Knight Features. Reproduced with permission **34 T** © The Spectator **B** © The Spectator **35 T** © The Spectator **B** Reproduced by kind permission of PRIVATE EYE.© Pressdram Ltd (2005)/Larry **37 TL** Glen Baxter **TR** Glen Baxter **40** BBC Photo Library **41** By permission of Adrian Raeside and Creators Syndicate, Inc **42** BBC Photo Library **43 T** © The Spectator **B** www.CartoonStock.com/Mike Baldwin **44** © The Spectator **45** © The New Yorker Collection 1992 Leo Cullum from cartoonbank.com. All Rights Reserved **46** Rex Features Ltd **47** © The Spectator **48 T** © The New Yorker Collection 1997 Chon Day from cartoonbank.com. All Rights Reserved **B** © 2005 Tim Haggerty from cartoonbank.com. All rights reserved **50** *McLachlan* by Ed McLachlan 2001 by permission of Methuen Publishing Ltd **51** BBC Photo Library **52** BBC Photo Library **54** © The New Yorker Collection 1986 Bernard Schoenbaum from cartoonbank.com. All rights reserved **55 T** Glen Baxter **B** Steve Best **56** BBC Photo Library **59** BBC Photo Library **61** BBC Photo Library **62** Reproduced by kind permission of PRIVATE EYE.© Pressdram Ltd (2005)/Edward McLachlan **63 T** © S & C Calman **B** © 2005 Charles Barsotti from cartoonbank.com. All rights reserved **64 T** © Punch, Ltd/Holte **B** *McLachlan* by Ed McLachlan 2001 by permission of Methuen Publishing Ltd **65 T** © Punch, Ltd/Andy McKay **B** Rex Features Ltd/ITV **67** Topham Picture Library **68** © Punch, Ltd/Chic Jacob **69 L & R** © 1954 Ronald Searle by kind permission of the artist and the Sayle Literary Agency **70** By permission of Peter Waldner and Creators Syndicate, Inc. **71 T** *McLachlan* by Ed McLachlan 2001 by permission of Methuen Publishing Ltd **B** © The Spectator **72 T** Mirrorpix **CL** © The New Yorker Collection 1949 Peter Arno from cartoonbank.com. All rights reserved **72-73** Mirrorpix **73 T** © 2005 Jack Ziegler from cartoonbank.com. All rights reserved **CR** Reproduced by kind permission of PRIVATE EYE.© Pressdram Ltd (2005)/John Glashan **74 T** © The New Yorker Collection 1964 Peter Arno from cartoonbank.com. All rights Reserved **B** © Punch, Ltd/Stan McMurtry **75** BBC Photo Library **76 T** © Punch, Ltd/Michael ffolkes **B** McLachlan by Ed McLachlan 2001 by permission of Methuen Publishing Ltd **77** © Posy Simmonds *Perpetuum Immobile* (1979) permission granted by PFD on behalf of Posy Simmonds **80 T** www.CartoonStock.com/Fist **B** © 1948 Ronald Searle by kind permission of the artist and the Sayle Literary Agency **81 T** © Punch, Ltd/Ed McLachlan **CR** © Punch, Ltd/Matt **B** © Punch, Ltd/Riana Duncan **82** © The Spectator **83** Steve Best **84 T** © The New Yorker Collection 1973 Dean Vietor from cartoonbank.com. All rights reserved **B** © Punch, Ltd/J.W.Taylor **86** By permission of Peter Waldner and Creators Syndicate, Inc. **87 T** © The New Yorker Collection 1938 Carl Rose from cartoonbank.com. All rights reserved **B** © The New Yorker Collection 2004 Danny Shanahan from cartoonbank.com. All rights reserved **88** © Punch, Ltd/Pont **89** © Punch, Ltd/David Haldane **90** © Punch, Ltd/Ed Fisher **91 T** Eileen Brockbank **B** © Charles Peattie and Russell Taylor. Alex cartoon appears in *The Daily Telegraph* **93** Daddy cartoons from *The Best of Daddy* by Rupert Fawcett. Published by Boxtree **94** By permission of Benita Epstein and Creators Syndicate, Inc. **95 T** © The Spectator **B** Steve Best **96** The Kobal Collection/Columbia **98** © The Spectator **99** Express Syndication/Carl Giles **101** Rex Features Ltd/Everett Collection **102** © Punch, Ltd/Pete Dredge **103** Reproduced by kind permission of PRIVATE EYE.© Pressdram Ltd (2005)/T Parkes **105** The Ronald Grant Archive/Python Pictures **106 T** © The New Yorker Collection 1976 Ed Arno from cartoonbank.com. All rights reserved **B** © The New Yorker Collection 1931 Richard Decker from cartoonbank.com. All rights reserved **107** © Punch, Ltd/Frank R.Gray **109 T** © Punch, Ltd/Ken Pyne **B** © Punch, Ltd/Robert Thompson **110** Hulton Getty Images **112** © The Spectator **113** © Punch, Ltd/David Myers **114** BBC Photo Library **117 L & R** Donald McGill @ Pharos International Ltd **118** The Ronald Grant Archive/Python Pictures **121** BBC Photo Library **125** BBC Photo Library **127** BBC Photo Library **130** © S & C Calman **131 T** © The New Yorker Collection 1991 Bernard Schoenbaum from cartoonbank.com. All rights reserved **B** © Charles Peattie and Russell Taylor. Alex cartoon appears in *The Daily Telegraph* **132** Popperfoto **133 T** © The New Yorker Collection 1993 Sam Gross from cartoonbank.com. All rights reserved **B** © Punch, Ltd/Andy McKay **135** Yorkshire Television **136** Steve Best **137 T** © Charles Peattie and Russell Taylor. Alex cartoon appears in *The Daily Telegraph* **B** © Punch, Ltd/Matt **140** © 2005 Leo Cullum from cartoonbank.com. All rights reserved **141 T** © Punch, Ltd/Edward McLachlan **B** Mirrorpix **144** © 2005 Charles Barsotti from cartoonbank.com. All rights reserved **145 T** © 2005 Leo Cullum from cartoonbank.com. All rights reserved **B** © The Spectator **146** The Ronald Grant Archive/Columbia Pictures **148** © Punch, Ltd/David Haldane **149 T** www.CartoonStock.com/Richard Jolley **B** www.CartoonStock.com/Stan Eales **150 T** © The Spectator **CL** © The New Yorker Collection 2000 Leo Cullum from cartoonbank.com. All rights reserved **B** © Punch, Ltd/Nick **151** *McLachlan* by Ed McLachlan 2001 by permission of Methuen Publishing Ltd **152 T** © Punch, Ltd/Pont **B** © H.M. Bateman Designs Ltd **153 T** Express Syndication/Carl Giles **B** © Peter Brookes as published in The Times **154** © Punch, Ltd/Edward McLachlan **155** © Punch, Ltd/Kenneth Beauchamp **158** © The Spectator **159** McLachlan by Ed McLachlan 2001 by permission of Methuen Publishing Ltd **160 T** © The Spectator **B** www.CartoonStock.com/Mike Baldwin **161** © Punch, Ltd/Estate of Russell Brockbank **162** The Kobal Collection **163** © Punch, Ltd/Estate of Russell Brockbank **164** Steve Best **165 T** Belt Up © 1974 The Estate of Norman Thelwell by permission of Methuen Publishing Ltd **B** © Punch, Ltd/Andy McKay **166** www.CartoonStock.com/Robert Thompson **167** © Punch, Ltd/Ed McLachlan **168** BBC Photo Library **169** BBC Photo Library **170 T** Glen Baxter **B** © Punch, Ltd/Bill Tidy **171 T** © The New Yorker Collection 1958 Richard Decker from cartoonbank.com. All rights reserved **B** Reproduced by kind permission of PRIVATE EYE.© Pressdram Ltd (2005)/Nick Newman **174** © H.M. Bateman Designs Ltd **176** Rex Features Ltd/Michael Fresco **178** Reproduced by kind permission of PRIVATE EYE.© Pressdram Ltd (2005)/Neil Bennett **179** © H.M. Bateman Designs Ltd **181** BBC Photo Library **183** Yorkshire Television **184** Reproduced by kind permission of PRIVATE EYE.© Pressdram Ltd (2005)/Edward McLachlan **185 T** © Punch, Ltd/Fougasse **B** Glen Baxter **187** BBC Photo Library **190** Reproduced by kind permission of PRIVATE EYE.© Pressdram Ltd (2005)/Tony Husband **191 T** McLachlan by Ed McLachlan 2001 by permission of Methuen Publishing Ltd **B** Steve Best **192 T** Reproduced by kind permission of PRIVATE EYE.© Pressdram Ltd (2005)/Edward McLachlan **B** © H.M. Bateman Designs Ltd **193** Hulton Getty Images **194** © Peter Brookes as published in *The Times* **195 T** © Punch, Ltd/H.M.Brock **B** © The New Yorker Collection 1991 James Stevenson from cartoonbank.com. All rights reserved **197** Herman cartoons © 2002 United Features Syndicate, Inc. Distributed by Knight Features. Reproduced with permission **198 T** *McLachlan* by Ed McLachlan 2001 by permission of Methuen Publishing Ltd **198-199 B** Express Syndication/Carl Giles **199** Topham Picture Library/Arena Pal/John Timbers **200-201** Hulton Getty Images **201** www.CartoonStock.com/Rob Baines **202** Reality Check © 2002 United Feature Syndicate, Inc. Distributed by Knight Features. Reproduced with permission **203 T** Reproduced by kind permission of PRIVATE EYE.© Pressdram Ltd (2005)/Ken Pyne **B** Reproduced by kind permission of PRIVATE EYE.© Pressdram Ltd (2005)/David Austin **204** BBC Photo Library **205** © Punch, Ltd/Bud Grace **206** © The New Yorker Collection 1948 Chon Day from cartoonbank.com. All rights reserved **207 T** © The New Yorker Collection 1953 Claude Smith from cartoonbank.com. All rights reserved **B** Reproduced by kind permission of PRIVATE EYE.© Pressdram Ltd (2005)/J. Banks **209** BBC Photo Library **210** Steve Best **211 T** © The Spectator **B** McLachlan by Ed McLachlan 2001 by permission of Methuen Publishing Ltd **212** Mirrorpix **213 T** Steve Best **B** © Punch, Ltd/Peter King **214** Steve Best **215** The Ronald Grant Archive/British Lion **216** © Punch, Ltd/Matt **217** *McLachlan* by Ed McLachlan 2001 by permission of Methuen Publishing Ltd **218** BBC Photo Library **220** www.CartoonStock.com/Knife **221** Steve Best **222 T** © The New Yorker Collection 1988 Jack Ziegler from cartoonbank.com. All rights reserved **BL & BR** The Compleat Tangler © 1967 The Estate of Norman Thelwell by permission of Methuen Publishing Ltd **223** Reproduced by kind permission of PRIVATE EYE.© Pressdram Ltd (2005)/Nick Newman **224** Express Syndication **225 T & B** Thelwell Country © 1959 The Estate of Norman Thelwell by permission of Methuen Publishing Ltd **226** BBC Photo Library **227** © The Spectator **228 T** © Punch, Ltd/Harley Schwadron **B** Beryl Cook © 2000 taken from The Bumper Edition, Victor Gollancz, London. Reproduced by permission of Rogers, Coleridge & White, London **229** © H.M.Bateman Designs Ltd **231** Glen Baxter **232** Reproduced by kind permission of PRIVATE EYE.© Pressdram Ltd (2005)/Philip Thompson **233 TR** Steve Best **CL** © The Spectator **BR** Glen Baxter **234 T** Reality Check © 2002 United Feature Syndicate,Inc.Distributed by Knight Features. Reproduced with permission **B** © The Spectator **235 T** *McLachlan* by Ed McLachlan 2001by permission of Methuen Publishing Ltd **236** Rex Features Ltd/The Everett Collection **238** Steve Best **B** © Punch, Ltd/Bud Grace **239 T** © The New Yorker Collection 1933 Rea Irvin from cartoonbank.com. All rights reserved **B** © The New Yorker Collection 1947 Charles E.Martin from cartoonbank.com. All rights reserved **240** Yorkshire Television **241** © The New Yorker Collection 2002 Alex Gregory from cartoonbank.com. All rights reserved

READER'S DIGEST PROJECT TEAM

Editor
John Andrews

Art Editor
Louise Turpin

Editorial Assistant
Gail Paten

Picture Research
Liz Heasman
Rosie Taylor

Text Rights
Paulette Dooler
Connie Robertson

Proofreader
Lynne Davies

Indexer
Ian D. Crane

READER'S DIGEST GENERAL BOOKS

Editorial Director
Julian Browne
Art Director
Nick Clark
Head of Book Development
Sarah Bloxham
Managing Editor
Alastair Holmes
Picture Resource Manager
Martin Smith
Pre-press Account Manager
Penny Grose
Product Production Manager
Claudette Bramble
Senior Production Controller
Deborah Trott
Origination
Colour Systems Limited, London
Printing and binding
Partenaires-Livres, France

CONCEPT CODE UK1631/L
BOOK CODE 400-144-01
ISBN 0 276 42958 3
ORACLE CODE 250001969H.00.24

CONTRIBUTORS AND CONSULTANTS

Simon Brett

As a Light Entertainment producer for BBC Radio, Simon initiated such programmes as *Weekending* and *The Hitchhiker's Guide to the Galaxy*. After two years producing comedy for London Weekend Television, he became a full-time writer in 1979. As well as many humorous crime novels, he wrote the best-selling *How To Be A Little Sod* series of books, and edited *The Faber Book of Parodies*. Simon has continued to write radio comedy, including the series *No Commitments*, *Smelling of Roses* and *After Henry*, which was also turned into a successful TV series, starring Prunella Scales and Joan Sanderson.

Tim Heald

Tim had his first article published in *Punch* in 1961, while still a schoolboy. He went on to work on Fleet Street, where he was a features writer on the *Daily Express* and a contributor to the 'Atticus' column in *The Sunday Times* and the humorous political column 'Pendennis' in *The Observer*. Tim has also written crime and comic novels, and acclaimed biographies of Prince Philip, Barbara Cartland and Brian Johnston.

THANKS ALSO TO THE FOLLOWING FOR THEIR HELP IN PREPARING THIS BOOK:

Colin Goody, Design; Bobbie Mitchell, Copyright Clearance; Austin Taylor, Design; Rachel Weaver, Editorial.

LAUGHTER IS THE BEST MEDICINE was designed and edited by The Reader's Digest Association Limited, London.

First edition copyright © 2005
The Reader's Digest Association Limited,
11 Westferry Circus, Canary Wharf, London E14 4HE

Copyright © details for individual entries, see Acknowledgments. For copyright reasons, the book is not for sale in the USA or Canada.

We are committed to both the quality of our products and the service we provide to our customers. We value your comments, so please feel free to contact us on 08705 113366 or via our website at: **www.readersdigest.co.uk**
If you have any comments or suggestions about the content of our books, email us at **gbeditorial@readersdigest.co.uk**